WOMEN
OF
ANCIENT
ROME

WOMEN OF ANCIENT ROME

TO SURVIVE UNDER THE PATRIARCHY

LYNDA TELFORD

AMBERLEY

First published 2023

Amberley Publishing
The Hill, Stroud
Gloucestershire, GL5 4EP

www.amberley-books.com

British Library Cataloguing in Publication Data.
A catalogue record for this book is available from the British Library.

ISBN 978 1 3981 0699 4 (hardback)
ISBN 978 1 3981 0700 7 (ebook)

1 2 3 4 5 6 7 8 9 10

Typesetting by SJmagic DESIGN SERVICES, India.
Printed in the UK.

Contents

1 Background to Traditions 7

2 The Family and Daily Life 40

3 Marriage and Motherhood 71

4 Religion – Priests and Priestesses 105

5 Wealth and Poverty 143

6 The Outcasts 175

7 Slaves and Prostitutes 212

8 Age, Disease and Death 249

Endnotes 283

Bibliography 305

Index 311

1

Background to Traditions

In February 2020, a small, forgotten underground chamber in the Forum in Rome was opened to reveal some items that are approximately 2,600 years old. One of these was a part of a cylindrical stone block, apparently part of an ancient altar. The other was a small stone sarcophagus. These dusty and seemingly insignificant items are actually of great importance. Archaeologist Dr Patrizia Fortini, said of the finds: 'the excavated area represents a place which, in the history of the Roman imagination, speaks to us about the cult of Romulus.'

Romulus and Remus were reputedly born of the God Mars and the daughter of the King of Alba Longa. The mother's uncle, Amulius, who usurped the throne, put the twins into a basket and set them adrift on the Tiber. They were washed up beneath a fig tree and found by a she-wolf, who suckled them, saving their lives.

It seems a pity to spoil the legend of the wolf, but it must be remembered that 'lupa' the she-wolf was also a term used to describe a prostitute. The idea that some woman, even one of easy virtue, had pitied the infants and fed them, sits with us rather better than that of a real wolf, who would very likely have fed them to her cubs. The godlike father of the twins, supposedly Mars himself, may be accepted more easily, for many important people claimed descent from the Gods, the famous family of Gaius Julius Caesar being an example, as they claimed their descent from the Goddess Venus.

After the 'lupa' saved their lives, the twins were brought up by a shepherd named Faustulus and his wife Acca Laurentia, until they reached adulthood. They later deposed Amulius from the throne of Alba Longa and restored the rule to their grandfather. When this was done, they decided to found a settlement of their own on the Palatine Hill. Due to a quarrel between them over boundaries, Romulus was eventually to kill his brother Remus.

Romulus became the first king of Rome in 753 BC and some believe that he was buried in the area where the new finds were discovered, although the small stone 'sarcophagus' (likely an ossuary) which was unearthed there appears to date from around two hundred years later than the dates given for the twins. It was, in fact, the second time that this sarcophagus had been found, along with the remains of the stone altar, although it was the first time that their significance has been recognised.

Between 1899 and 1905 the archaeologist Giacomo Boni excavated the area beneath the Capitoline Hill, where the most important temple in ancient Rome once stood. On this high point above the Forum was the temple dedicated to Jupiter Optimus Maximus (Jupiter Best and Greatest). There were also temples there serving others, including Fortuna Primigenia (Fortune of the Firstborn), Honus et Virtus (a cult of military commanders) and Ops (the deity of plenty). On first finding this sarcophagus, Giacomo Boni described it as 'a rectangular tub-shaped crate, made of tufa', which is the rock that forms Capitoline Hill itself.

In the 1930s, during the era of Mussolini, a monumental staircase leading to the Senate House was built over the site, which is very close to the Lapis Niger (black stone), believed to be one of the oldest relics in Rome. With the associated Vulcanal, or sanctuary of Vulcan, it constitutes the only surviving part of the original Comitium, or assembly area. This precedes the Forum in date and is believed to have derived from an archaic cult site, dating from the seventh or eighth century BC. The origins of this area were obscure and mysterious even to the Romans, but it was always considered to be a very sacred place.

Since the 1950s the area has been covered in concrete, to protect the site of the Vulcanal. Below this was a slab of black marble, probably installed by Lucius Cornelius Sulla (138-78 BC) to protect the holy site. This marble slab was edged with a low, white parapet, intended to mark out the space, as the location was venerated by Romans as being the tomb of Romulus himself. Inscriptions found there refer to ritual law, including a warning that anyone who damaged, defiled or in any way violated the area would be cursed. Also found there were dedicatory statues and evidence of sacrifices. These date to between the fifth and seventh centuries BC.

The antiquarian Verrius Flaccus, a contemporary of Augustus, whose work now only survives in the Epitome of Pompeius Festus, described a statue of a resting lion, placed on each of two bases, on either side of the original 'U' shaped altar, '... just as they may be today seen, guarding graves.'

The Lapis Niger itself had the speaker's platform of the Comitia, which later became the Republican Rostra, built right up against it, adding further prominence to the site. Excavations are ongoing, although the Lapis Niger is not visible, being several feet below the present ground level.

Dr Fortini has stated her belief that the area probably represents an early shrine to Romulus. However, it is my suggestion that owing to its location, it may well represent something even more exciting. The Temple of Jupiter Optimus Maximus was built close to it, almost towering over it, on the hill itself. This is a placement similar to that of the later Basilica of St Peter, built as closely as possible to the presumed tomb of its patron saint, also straddling the area of the Circus in which he reputedly died. Similarly, it is logical to assume that the tomb of Rome's founder, Romulus, should lie beneath the shadow of its most powerful protector, Jupiter, and that this knowledge of its location did indeed pass down to Sulla, who further ensured its protection with a black marble cover. It is possible that the 'legend' of the tomb was in fact a reality, with the bones or ashes of Rome's founder buried there – even in a replacement ossuary at a slightly later date. The traditions of Rome's earliest beliefs are indeed centred on this most sacred area, and in ancient Rome these same traditions would become a fundamental part of both political and domestic life.

Surprising though it may seem, women were important in ancient Rome. Not that they were given any political authority in the proudly militaristic society that Rome became, but they were important precisely because of its very masculine code. They were required to replace the losses suffered by the armies in their campaigns of conquest and expansion and they needed to ensure the continuance of the great families, whose expertise, courage and determination helped to push forward the Roman military machine, providing not only the next generation of soldiers and statesmen, but also the next generation of mothers of the right type. These needed to be 'proper' Roman women, well brought up, educated and dutiful, disciplined and capable of training their own daughters in their turn.

Both sexes were well versed in the need to sacrifice themselves for the greater good of Rome and maintain the 'mos maiorum' which was the established order of things. Mos was established custom and, in this context, maiorum referred to the ancestors and forebears, in short, the way things should always be done.

The Romans had to deal not only with the prospect of losses in battle, but also the problem of a falling fertility rate. Many historians like to blame this on the lead pipe-work which fed water to the city, although similar lead pipes did not noticeably affect the high birthrate of the Victorian era. Therefore, from the Rape of the Sabine Women, to the later Empresses, women did have an important role to fulfil. However, control was also considered necessary. The Romans had a horror of the idea of women running wild, being allowed too much freedom, which would inevitably lead to licence.

Rome could never have had a female absolute ruler, such as Egypt's Cleopatra, as no woman could openly rule in Rome. Some of the later Empresses were a source of scandals, but they paid for their excesses when they went too far. On the contrary, far from allowing laxity, in the earliest state a version of salic law existed[1]. The fanciful film images of Cleopatra entering Rome in her glory, did not and could not happen. Once the Republic was formed, no King or Queen could enter Rome's centre at all. The boundary, or pomerium, was marked by white stones called 'cippi' to mark of the heart of Rome, beyond which all else was considered merely Roman territory. It kept the city's centre sacrosanct, although it did expand over time, as when Lucius Cornelius Sulla enlarged the boundary in 80 BC. Visiting royalty were obliged to stay outside of it, viewing Rome only from the then outskirts, in line with its determination never again to allow a king within its centre.

Even Rome's own generals, fresh from military triumphs, could not enter the city itself while they still held 'imperium', or the authority of office, which was denoted by the red ribbon they wore around the breastplate. Those who were awaiting celebration of their formal Triumph after a successful campaign sometimes had to camp with their legions on the Field of Mars for months, until the Senate allowed them a set date for their formal entry. Then they would parade with their troops, display prisoners and booty, and briefly wear the terracotta-coloured face of the God Jupiter Optimus Maximus.[2]

The Lex Curiata would be passed by a special assembly of the thirty Curiae, to endow a curule magistrate with Imperium. Occasionally, a man would be rewarded with 'imperium maius' which gave the holder superiority over all men except a Dictator. This was awarded to a number of men towards the end of the Republic but became much rarer over time owing to the Republican desire to prevent any one man from gaining absolute power.

In Rome's earliest days there had been kings, starting with the Romulus who killed his twin brother over a boundary dispute. These brothers were the very essence of Rome's history. However, Romulus, who reigned from 753 BC to 716 BC, had no son to succeed him, so senators decided who would be the next king. This set two important precedents, one being that the title was not necessarily hereditary and the other that the chosen man could be an 'outsider' – as the man chosen to succeed Romulus was Numa Pompilius (715-672 BC). He was of Sabine blood and had never been to Rome. It was also decided at the time that a new king could not be elected from the ranks of the senate, or the senators might fight among themselves for the honour. Numa Pompilius was a good choice, with a long and peaceful reign, but not so the third king of Rome.

Tullius Hostilius (672-642 BC) was far more warlike, although by destroying Rome's rivals he made Rome into the chief city of Latin-speaking people. He built the assembly hall in the Forum, the Curia, where the senate met.

Next was Ancus Marcius (642-616 BC) who was Numa's grandson. He built the first bridge across the Tiber and founded the city of Ostia at the mouth of the river, to become Rome's seaport.

Fifth was Lucius Tarquinius Priscus (616-579 BC) who was of Greek blood but hailed from the Etruscan city of Tarquinia. He was a great warrior and builder and constructed the Cloaca Maxima, the huge sewer that follows the ancient course of the Spinon canal, fed by streams from the neighbouring hills and which drained the Forum area. He laid out the horseracing track, the Circus Maximus, and also drew up the plans for the great temple of Jupiter Optimus Maximus on the Capitoline. (The Capitoline was originally known as Asylum Hill but changed its name due to a skull being found there in the reign of the first Tarquinius.) Priscus was assassinated by the sons of Ancus Marcius.

Then came Servius Tullius (579-534 BC) who had been a slave in the royal household but rose to prominence. When Tarquinius Priscus was killed, his sons were too young to succeed, so the widow put forward

Servius Tullius. He extended the city and gave it fortifications. He also excavated the underground cell at the foot of the Capitoline, which became the Tullianum, where enemies of the state were strangled.

He was followed by another Lucius Tarquinius (534-509 BC) who was a son, or grandson, of the first. He was to acquire the Sibyllene Books of prophecies. He was known as Tarquinius Superbus, or Tarquin the Proud. He had seized the kingship on the assassination of Servius Tullius, which he had helped to arrange. He dedicated the temple of Jupiter, but his reign was full of intrigues and scandals, so he was eventually deposed by a group of Patricians led by Lucius Junius Brutus, and the Republic was then established.

It was believed that Romulus himself had devised the original and almost indissoluble marriage rite, the confarreatio (meaning a sharing of spelt), which put a wife entirely in the power of her husband. She could not divorce him, but he could, in certain circumstances, divorce her: for adultery for instance, or for drunkenness, which was believed to lead to unchastity. This extreme form of permanent marriage would later be eased and by the end of the Republic the more binding confarreatio had largely been replaced by a civil ceremony for the majority, which made divorces more common. The confarreatio was then used only by the more traditional Patrician families, or where a religious position demanded it.

The original Romans, a settlement of warlike young men from Alba, south-east of Rome, inaugurated the earliest of the city's traditions. They do not seem to have taken women with them when they moved to Rome, and their neighbours were unwilling to oblige by offering their daughters, as the young men were considered to be little more than barbarians. In order to counteract this, the young men held a 'festa', which would later become known as the Consualia. During this gathering, they seized all the attractive females they could reach and ran off with them. These women were mainly Sabines, and the act would be commemorated by the tradition of carrying a (presumably unwilling) bride over the threshold, re-enacting the forcible seizure of a wife.

The idea that a woman might be of value in a personal sense did not arise. Only a woman of exemplary character and obedience was considered worthy. Any woman who lapsed from the required level of 'spectacular virtue' could quickly find herself punished.[3] Women's failings would come to be placed at the centre of Rome's legends. One example was the battle between the Horatii in Rome and the Curiatii in Alba, in the seventh century BC. They were enemies due to an argument whether Rome should join Alba, or Alba join Rome. One of the Alban Curiatii was betrothed to a girl of the Roman Horatii and she had made him a cloak to wear at their wedding. She next saw the cloak when one of her brothers carried it back to Rome in triumph, soaked in her lover's blood. Her brother saw her grief at the death of her beloved, and ran her through with his sword, saying that he was sending her to join the man, since she grieved for him and not for her brothers or for Rome, '... so shall perish every Roman woman who sheds tears over Rome's enemies!'[4] This then was the power of the Paterfamilias, or head of the family, particularly with regard to the females. Whether this was actually the father, or a brother, or an uncle, he was in total control and held the power of life and death.[5]

Under the early Roman state, women were named for their family only. A member of the Julia gens, (all tribal names were feminine), from which Gaius Julius Caesar sprang, would be named Julia, as would her sisters also. A member of the Cornelia clan would be a Cornelia, and the various different females in a family would be distinguished either by nicknames, or simply numerically, as Prima (first), Secunda (second) or Tertia (third) etc.

Large families of girls would not be hoped for, and unwanted girl children sometimes suffered exposure to the elements.

A girl would keep her family name on marriage, such as Sulla's third wife, Caecilia Metella Dalmatica, whose names not only commemorated her distinguished father, the Pontifex Maximus (chief priest) Lucius Metellus Dalmaticus, but were also a reminder of her father's power over her, a man who, like her future husband, would always be aware of his and the family's honour.

Dalmatica was married at the age of around nineteen to the far older Marcus Aemilius Scaurus, who was the Princeps Senatus, an ally of her family and a politician of great power. She bore him a son and a daughter but also fell in love with Sulla, a Patrician without money who had his way to make. After her first husband's death and Sulla's divorce of his second wife, they were able to marry, but in the meantime Scaurus had kept her locked up, so that she could not shame him by her obvious preference for Sulla.[6]

Roman history is littered with stories of the dire results of the frailty of women. At the end of the reign of Tarquinius Superbus, one of his sons, Sextus Tarquinius, had a wager with his cousin Lucius Tarquinius

Collatinus regarding the chastity of their wives while they were away from home. Collatinus won the bet, as they found his wife innocently weaving with her slaves when they returned, but Sextus Tarquinius was annoyed, both at losing the bet (his own wife had been out at a party) but because he then lusted after Collatinus's wife Lucrezia. He visited her and forced her to sleep with him by threatening to kill a slave and leave the man's naked body in her room, telling the world that he had executed the slave after having found him alone with her. However, she told her husband and father what had happened, then her honour demanded that she killed herself with a dagger. Her body was exhibited in Rome's Forum and the scandal brought the downfall of King Tarquinius.

Later, in 449 BC, the fifteen-year-old Verginia caught the eye of Appius Claudius, then chairman of the commission of ten (the Decemviri), which was set up to publish laws. One of his clients, Marcus Claudius, claimed her with a fictional story about her having been a child of his household, stolen from some of his slaves. Appius Claudius, disregarding all evidence to the contrary, granted Verginia to the slave, being '… spoiled by the greatness of his position, his soul turgid, and his bowels inflamed by love of the girl'.[7] Verginius could see only one way to save his daughter's honour, so stabbed her to death. Her body, like Lucrezia's, was exhibited with lamentations. The Decemvirs were deposed and Appius Claudius was arrested and subsequently committed suicide. Despite the innocence of such women having been proved, their lives were still demanded as a sacrifice to family honour, and the results were used as a warning to other females to avoid any temptation to stray.

There are also many stories of women being horribly punished for using poison to rid themselves of aged husbands or oppressive fathers. Of course, in all countries there are many 'poisoning' tales, as gastric disorders were imperfectly understood and it is easy to blame someone with whom the victim had had a disagreement.

The first recorded poisoning trial in Rome is from 331 BC, when many citizens had died mysteriously. There were so many in fact, that a slave gave evidence (whether voluntarily or otherwise) and the authorities decided to take action. A number of married women were found to be brewing concoctions, which they claimed were tonics. On being required to prove the innocence of the potions by drinking them personally, they promptly died. The authorities were then said to have arrested one hundred and seventy other women who were executed. Livy says of this particular scandal 'this story is not in all the history books, only in some, so I hope it may not be true...'[8]

However, not all women were resentful victims of harsh men, many Roman women were proud of their city and its achievements, despite the demands and pressures of living a second-class life in it. There is a charming story of the dedication of a temple to Venus Calva (Venus the Bald) in commemoration of loyal Roman women who had given their hair to make bowstrings when the Gauls besieged the capital in 390 BC. At around the same time women made the state gifts of their jewellery, when Brennus the Gaul sacked the city and demanded a ransom of a thousand pounds of gold before he would leave. During the Second Punic War, in 215 BC, the year after Rome's disastrous defeat at Cannae when Hannibal was victorious, the Tribune Oppius passed a law allowing women only half an ounce of gold, forbidding them to wear dyed fabrics, or use carriages in the city (except for priestesses). There is no record of the women objecting to these measures, which they may have considered reasonable in an emergency situation.

There were evidently successful marriages, where the parties were in sync with each other and with Rome's aims. Some wives understood the pressures that Rome's men had to bear, the demand that they be always strong, always firm and in control. Affection did help, but it would still be a long time before traditional ideas changed regarding the need of a young woman to be able to feel something for the man she married and whose children she was expected to bear. Men in unhappy marriages were always able to find consolation elsewhere, but for the woman the consequences of committing adultery were dire, although a loveless marriage was a bleak prospect for life.

In a time such as the Second Punic War, with very high casualty figures, women could do little but be silent sufferers, supporting Rome without complaint. It was a time when the Sibyllene Books were frequently consulted.[9] These were the books of prophecies of the Sibylla, or Oracle. The most famous of these oracular Priestesses lived in a cave at Cumae, on the Campanian coast. The Sibyllene Books themselves, originally written on palm leaves and later transferred to paper, were reputed to have been acquired by King Tarquinius Priscus. He had been offered a dozen of them, for a certain price, which the King refused to pay. The Sibyl went away, taking the books with her, but returned a short while later, this time carrying only nine. For these she demanded the full original price. The King contemptuously refused and again she left, but not before making it clear that the books would be destroyed and the King would never know what they had contained.

Later still, she reappeared, but this time with only half a dozen books. The King, who had not only had time to reflect but had been pressured by his advisors, gladly paid the full price for only half of the original books. The Sibyl was never seen again, and the books were put into the safekeeping of priests. By the time of Gaius Marius (157-86 BC) they were so revered that they were in the care of a special college of ten minor priests (the decemviri sacris faciundis) and were avidly read during any crisis in the hope that a prophecy could help the situation. Even much later, when Octavianus, the adopted son and heir of Gaius Julius Caesar, wished to marry Livia Drusilla, who was already married and pregnant with her second child, the prophecies were consulted (and possibly 'adjusted') in order to make her divorce and remarriage appear to be 'a right act'.

When the Sibyllene Books were consulted in 205 BC, with the fortunes of war quickly changing, they announced that Hannibal would be forced to leave Italy if the 'Great Mother' Goddess was brought from Pessinus in Phrygia and on 4 April 204 BC (a day always celebrated afterwards by the games called the Megalensia) the Goddess arrived, and turned out to be a huge black stone. Livy recorded that the holy stone was carried into Rome by a series of respectable matrons, who took it to the Temple of Victory on the Palatine, where it became known as the Magna Mater, or Great Mother.[10]

As might be expected, there is a more supernatural version of the story, which was stressed by the Claudii family as one of their number was traditionally involved. In this version, when the ship carrying a statue of the goddess was at the mouth of the river, it ran aground. All efforts to dislodge it failed. Eventually, a married woman stepped forward, one Claudia Quinta, whose reputation was rather unsavoury. She prayed aloud to the goddess that the ship would be freed and could follow her into Rome, *if* her morals were beyond question. This happened, and the ship moved slowly along, landing safely in Rome, thereby confirming that Claudia Quinta was innocent of wrongdoing. When the temple to the goddess was dedicated in 191 BC, a statue of the lady was included and although the temple was twice burned down, the statues within it were never damaged.

Sir James Frazer wrote that 'popular tradition naturally favoured the miraculous version of the story...but we may assume that Livy's is truer to history.'[11]

From 200 BC the history of Rome was recorded by many men whose works have not survived, but they were available to Livy and other writers, so we are able to connect to these distant times. Among them was the most austere and moralistic of men, the elder Cato (Marcus Porcius Cato 234-149 BC), also known as Cato the Censor. He was not only a Patrician but a writer of note, particularly conservative and anti-Hellenistic, also much opposed to the Scipio family and all they stood for. These were all traits which he passed down to his great-grandson Marcus Porcius Cato Uticenses, born in 95 BC.

Cato the Elder was particularly harsh on the subject of moral decline and the subsequent weakening of men:

> If every married man had been concerned to ensure that his wife looked up to him and respected his rightful position as her husband, we should not have had half the trouble we do with women ... instead they have become so powerful that our independence has been lost ... we have failed to restrain them as individuals. Woman is a violent and uncontrolled animal, you must keep the reins firmly in your own hands ... consider the regulations of the past, designed to control their licence, and even with these you can hardly control them ... once they achieve complete equality they will be your masters.

There was a great deal more in the same style, and he went on to say that a greed for gold creates female rivalry and anger. He mentioned the Latin allies, whose women were allowed far more of it than Roman women and blamed it for their extravagance and free living, pitying their husbands who had to try to deal with them.[12] It was an attitude shared by many other Roman men, and while such ideas were fashionable many women would have found their home life restrictive and unhappy.

Cato was related to the Scipios but detested their love of Greek culture, with its un-Roman connections. He was far from being the only Roman male who regarded the Eastern cults with something like horror, expecting every kind of debauch from them, although at the same time it was always considered that any Roman man who could not speak Greek was uneducated. It was acknowledged that much of Rome's religious system and culture originated in Greece, although the Romans considered that they had refined them. They also looked down on the Greeks because they could not achieve military eminence, unlike Rome, as the Greek system allowed for too many rival factions who fought each other, never creating the cohesion that the Roman system did. This was particularly clear after the Social War (91-87 BC) when 'being a Roman' was something to be especially proud of.

Cato was voluble in his dislike of the Cybele cult, along with the castrated priests who went with it.[13] The public celebration, the Megalensia, had to be altered to fit in with Roman conventions, but other cults would also gradually make their way to Rome and in time become accepted. Even the interest of some women in political matters would become acceptable, so long as the women concerned were of good birth and education, although even then they were allowed no active participation in political affairs.

In 63 BC a woman named Fulvia (daughter of Marcus Fulvius Bambalio), of good birth and education but morally apparently rather loose, contacted Marcus Tullius Cicero to give him information regarding the Catiline conspiracy. She was the wife of Publius Clodius Pulcher, a Patrician of great wealth and standing, but a young man who had a streak of mischief that led him and his two sisters into scandal and notoriety. They liked to pretend that they had committed incest together, in order to shock respectable society, although when the accusations became widespread one of his sisters found herself divorced and disgraced on the strength of it. The Claudii had always been known for their arrogance and were a law unto themselves. More sensible Roman women avoided that kind of fame, so their names do not appear in the histories, but even then there were some who delighted in pushing the boundaries of accepted decency.

Appius Claudius Pulcher, the Consul for 143 BC and father-in-law of Tiberius Gracchus the Tribune, provoked a war with the Salassi in the area of the Val d'Aosta. After losing thousands of Roman troops, he forced a second engagement during which, he claimed, he had killed five thousand enemy troops. He asserted his right to celebrate a Triumph on the strength of this rather meagre success. The Senate was unimpressed and refused permission for the show he wanted. Undaunted by official opposition, he declared that he intended to have it anyway, even if it meant paying for it himself, although that would rather defeat the object. With typical Claudian stubbornness, he went ahead.

The Senate was not prepared to accept having its position gainsaid on the matter and decided to send a Tribune to veto the proceedings and prevent him holding the celebration. However, his second daughter, another Claudia of course, was a Vestal Virgin and on hearing that her father's Triumph would be stopped she threw herself into her father's arms at the start of the procession and, holding onto him, was carried through Rome with him in the Triumphal chariot. Because of her sacred presence, the Tribune did not dare to intervene, and her father achieved his Triumph without interruption. It was unique in having a woman at the front of the parade, and perhaps also unique in its demonstration of Claudian determination.[14] However, she only got away with it because of her standing as a priestess, and such behaviour was not generally to be admired in a woman.

One of the genuinely most admired of Roman women was Cornelia, known as the Mother of the Gracchi. Her ill fated family suffered terribly in their pursuit of what they considered to be right, and any ordinary woman would have been bowed down by grief, though not Cornelia. Her courage and resilience was held up as an example to all women, and showed the correct spirit and fortitude. Cornelia was born in the 190s BC the second daughter of Publius Cornelius Scipio Africanus, the great hero of the Second Punic War. Her mother was the noblewoman Aemilia Paulla. Cornelia's full name was Cornelia Scipionis Africana. The Punic Wars were a series of three wars between Rome and Carthage, fought from 264 BC to 146 BC. (Punic is from the word Punicus meaning Carthaginian and refers to their Phoenician ancestry).[15] These conflicts eventually resulted in the destruction of Carthage and the enslavement of its people, once Rome took control of the Mediterranean. The proud, heroic Roman spirit was encapsulated in Scipio Africanus.

The young and highly educated Cornelia was to marry Tiberius Sempronius Gracchus in 172 BC. He was many years her senior but she bore him twelve children (unusual for a Roman family), although only three of them survived to adulthood, Gaius, Tiberius and Sempronia.[16]

Throughout the marriage Cornelia was active in political circles, having been surrounded by politicians all her life. She was widely read and highly cultured, exactly the sort of Roman matron to be a fine example to and teacher of her children. She was also a writer and quickly became famous for her common sense as well as for her solid virtues.

Cornelia's husband died in 154 BC after a successful career, during which he was awarded two Triumphs for military prowess, and served twice as Consul, in 177 and 163 BC. Cornelia had no intention of retiring from political life after his death; in fact, such was her fame that a proposal of marriage was sent by no less a person than King Ptolemy VIII of Egypt, but this was correctly refused. Cornelia would concentrate on raising her sons to follow in the footsteps of their illustrious ancestors.

To explain the tragedy of the Gracchi, it is necessary to recount a little of the economic changes which had taken place in Rome itself and in Italia at that time, and the land problems which these created. Some of the changes were due to the Punic Wars, but there was also an influx of wealth from the provinces, upsetting the traditional rural economy based on the peasant farmers, who also made up the bulk of the Roman army. Devastation had resulted from Hannibal reaching Italy and many farms were neglected or even abandoned. It would take far more than hard graft to restore them, as working against the prosperity of the small farmers was the importation of corn from Sicily and Sardinia. The army was able to use much of this excess grain, but the pinch could still be felt by farmers by the time of the Gracchi brothers.

A second problem was that army conscription meant that the small farmer could be away from home for long periods, and often returned to find a ruined property or even one taken over by another.[17] Unfortunately, an even more damaging problem was in the increased amounts of land (the 'ager publicus') which was held by the state for lease or sale, allied to the increasing numbers of available slaves to work it, due to the late wars. Many administrators had become very rich, and land was always the best way to invest surplus cash.

New landholders were far less likely to actually live on the land and a new system of large estates (the 'latifundia') came into being, which could be easily worked by slaves. These mixed estates pushed out the small farmers who did not have the funds to compete. Free men began to abandon the land, increasing the problem of landholders snapping up and amalgamating the smaller farms, while dispossessed farming families headed for the cities. There were no new industries in the cities, even in Rome, to accommodate and absorb the influx of new labourers, who became a huge mass of unemployed and unemployable, leading to general unrest.[18]

There was just one proviso, in that the amount of the ager publicus that any one individual was supposed to hold was 500 iugera (approximately 300 acres).[19] Unfortunately, the state had a habit of turning a blind eye to the official limit, particularly when the landholders were senators. It was undeniable that it was better for the land to be worked than left neglected, even if it meant that the strict letter of the law was ignored.

The development of the latifundia was accelerated by the way the state had disposed of the 'ager publica populus Romani' in the past. This was land acquired during Rome's Italian expansion. When Rome was victorious it usually confiscated around a third of enemy territory, leaving the losers with the rest. This ager publicus land could found colonies, be allotted to Roman citizens, or be sold. The best districts, such as the 'ager Campanus' in Campania brought in a good revenue, but much of the land was in less fertile areas. There was also inadequate administration in Rome to deal properly with all the land available. Roman citizens, and sometimes allies too, could occupy it as squatters, known as 'possessors' by paying a rent, known as 'vectigal'. However, it would have been unjustifiable financially to create government departments specifically to oversee the collection of such small rental payments, so in reality the squatters simply took the land over as their own.[20]

There was obviously a need to check the acquisitions of greedy landowners and restore the peasant farmers to their land, to recreate a better balance. During the Consulship of Laelius in 140 BC, the question of the reform of public land was raised but without a result.

Cornelia's elder son, Tiberius Sempronius Gracchus, one of the Tribunes for the year 133 BC proposed a 'lex agraria' (land law) to make the land available by allotment. Everyone holding more than the 500 iugera limit should give up their surplus, although to recompense the holders, some of whom had held the land for years and considered it to be their own property, a concession was made. This would allow 500 iugera for the landholder, plus 250 for his sons, up to a total limit of 1,000 iugera.[21] This was then intended to become the actual property of the holders in perpetuity, and not subject to any form of rent.

The reclaimed land was to be distributed to Roman citizens in small amounts, usually around 30 iugera (15 acres), and this would be subject to a small rent. Unfortunately, the majority of the landowners most likely to lose out by the redistribution were, of course, senators. They had put money into the land, in some cases building on it, mortgaging it, or even using it as dowry for a daughter. They had acquired vast tracts of it, easily managed by the slave gangs, who were often housed in barrack-like buildings. These gangs were easily bought and just as easily replaced, and it was more financially viable to get all possible work out of them and then simply buy more. This intensive farming was highly lucrative, and as senators were not supposed to engage in trade, owning such land was often their main source of income, if they were not fortunate enough to inherit money. The proposed changes naturally created strong opposition.[22]

However, Tiberius Gracchus had gone about pushing through his reforms by using an old precedent of taking it to the People's Assembly, thereby excluding the senate. Perhaps he had hoped merely to avoid futile argument with those who could not be expected to agree, but he must also have been aware that his Tribunate was limited and his time in office likely to run out if things did not happen quickly enough. It was an unpopular move and his Bill was vetoed. He pressed on, adjusting the Bill slightly to pacify the opposition, and he urged his fellow Tribune Marcus Octavius to withdraw the veto. He then attempted to depose Marcus Octavius, which the Assembly approved, and another Tribune was elected in his stead, ensuring that the agrarian bill was passed.[23]

Passed, but it was something else to try to make it work. It needed an agrarian commission, to be agreed by the Assembly, including Tiberius, his younger brother Gaius (who was then on duty in Spain) and his father-in-law Appius Claudius Pulcher. Opposition had not ceased, and much of it came from his cousin Scipio Nasica, the Consul for 138 BC, who had recently succeeded his father as Pontifex Maximus.

Nasica was one of the largest holders of public land and resented having to lose any of it. He obstructed the work of the commission in several petty ways, but also began a campaign of virulent personal abuse of Tiberius in the Senate. Tiberius also promoted another law that the commissioners would have the power to decide what constituted public land and what was private. These reforms were inevitably held back by financial problems as the Senate still controlled the purse strings.[24]

There came news that the King of Pergamum had died and made the Roman people his heirs. Tiberius had been quickly informed of this as his family had connections with the King, so he immediately tried to introduce a bill to authorise the use of the wealth for settlers. For the Senate, this was going far too far. It not only assumed that Rome intended to accept the bequest (Rome was then reluctant to make further overseas acquisitions except when absolutely necessary), and indicated that Tiberius had anticipated an affirmative response, but it was also dangerously close to meddling in foreign policy, which was above his authority as a Tribune.

His own role in the bequest was questioned, links with Pergamum examined and there was even a suggestion that he intended to make himself a king! This was anathema.[25] The attacks showed how widely based the opposition had become. He was losing friends, as the generally selfish land reform opposition had turned into something far more serious, creating great anxiety about his long-term intentions. He was surprised to realise that his deposition of the Tribune Marcus Octavius had 'trampled on the holy office of the Tribunes'[26] but it was the accusation that he might be aiming for regal powers that horrified the most, though it was almost certainly untrue. The citizens of Rome had grown up with stories of the evils of kingship, so the mere suggestion of it became a rallying cry for all those who resented the problems he had created, and it was decided that he must be stopped.

The day of the election arrived with its threats of violence and riot accentuated by the fact that Tiberius Gracchus was standing again, hoping to achieve another year as a Tribune. This was not unheard of, but in his case he could certainly expect opposition. People were out in force and the other Tribunes had been affected by the atmosphere. Tiberius worked hard to convince the people that without him they would be merely slaves to the rich, and that he feared for his own and his family's lives, due to the anger of his opponents. He must have been convincing, because a crowd of supporters were said to have accompanied him home and stayed on guard all night to give him protection. His eloquence had achieved an adjournment until the following day, but tempers did not die down.

The next day he and his friends and supporters walked to the Capitol. When the tribes[27] were summoned to vote, disorder broke out.

Hostile Tribunes tried to prevent the vote and Tiberius's opponents tried to get into the voting area, while his supporters tried to keep them out. In the nearby temple of Fides (public faith), the Senate was meeting, debating whether anything could be done to prevent him from being re-elected. Some Senators even indignantly declared that they would kill him themselves, and this was reported to Tiberius. It is not now certain whether he had a majority, but he had arranged with his supporters that he would give a signal if he felt that his life was threatened ... and he gave it. His bodyguard closed around him and drove the opponents out of the Assembly with such fury that people fled in terror and the doors of the temple of Jupiter Optimus Maximus were shut. Wild stories abounded that Tiberius had declared himself a Tribune, without election, but it was clear that his signal had caused the riot.

The Pontifex Maximus, Scipio Nasica, took the opportunity for revenge on the cousin he hated, and on the whole popular movement which offended his ideals.[28] Nasica was a member of the conservative nobility, a keen moralist and descended from five successive Consuls from his father's family, and from Scipio Africanus on his mother's side (as was Tiberius Gracchus). He was a man of courage and sagacity, but on that day his abilities as an orator worked against the need for good order. Despite the suggestion that he may have only intended to break up what the Senators saw as an illegal assembly, his appearance, wearing his full ceremonial regalia, unfortunately appeared to sanction the violence.[29]

The supporters of Tiberius ran off at the sight of the Pontifex and Senators with their own gang of thugs, all carrying weapons. One Tribune, Satureius, becoming over-excited and out of control, broke the leg from a bench while Tiberius was calling for the people to remain calm. Someone in the crowd cried out a warning, but Tiberius was struck on the head with the bench leg, and when he fell to the ground another man hit him with a cudgel. Two to three hundred of his supporters were also killed on the Capitoline Hill. Later, it was regarded as a mark of honour that none of them had been killed with an iron weapon, which would have been taboo in the sacred area, but the wooden weapons had been enough. Gaius Gracchus pleaded to be able to have his brother's body for burial, but all the victims were flung into the Tiber without distinction.

What of Cornelia, the mother, and Claudia, the wife of Tiberius Sempronius Gracchus? What of his sister Sempronia, bound to

Scipio Aemilianus in a loveless marriage? How did these women feel at the murder of their protector, the man who had become their Paterfamilias?

The shock of that day of rioting would never be forgotten in Rome, so how much more appalling for Cornelia, a politically minded woman who had doubtless discussed her son's policies with him and offered him advice? Perhaps even worse for Sempronia, the victim of an arranged marriage to a cousin who disapproved of her brother's opinions, to hear that her husband, then serving in Spain, had triumphantly declared his feelings on hearing of his brother-in-law's death by quoting Homer, 'So perish anyone else who tries to do the same!'[30]

Cicero was to speak of Nasica as a man 'who though a private citizen restored the state of freedom from the tyranny of Tiberius Gracchus' and Plutarch was to record that 'Since the Kings were driven out, this was the first civil unrest to be settled by the blood and murder of its citizens.'[31]

Over time, feelings remained strong regarding the murder of Tiberius. Plutarch considered that 'the rich' had been far more motivated by anger and greed than by the arguments they claimed against him, yet Cicero referred to the murderers as 'men who filled the whole world with the glory of their names'. Opinions would remain poles apart, but there was a general sadness among ordinary people that Tiberius had attempted to help. There was a belief that a good man had died: 'easily the first in birth, in good looks and in eloquence, he far surpassed his contemporaries in wisdom, in speaking and in ability, indeed in every accomplishment.'[32]

But it was not over. For some time, his brother Gaius held back. He must have been gratified to see that his brother's policies did not entirely die with him. Valeriuis Maximus commented that the Senate showed wisdom by punishing the Tribune, yet preserving his law. Another land commissioner replaced Tiberius (Publius Licinius Crassus, the father-in-law of Gaius Gracchus) and the work continued. But if the land reform was to go ahead, Nasica would have to go.

By 131 BC Gaius Papirius Carbo was on the scene; a talented man, the same age as Tiberius Gracchus, who had been one of his supporters. He introduced a Bill allowing a man to stand for re-election as Tribune as often as he wished, which brought in debates about the rights and wrongs of the fate of Tiberius. Carbo's main purpose was to stir up feelings again, and Scipio Nasica was unwise enough to be dragged into the arguments. He stood up in open assembly and declared that Tiberius had been justly killed, adding the proviso '...if he had been planning to take over the state'. He was no match for Carbo, and from then on, his popularity fell away. After his death the Gracchan opposition was led by Scipio Aemilianus, the husband of Sempronia, creating a very difficult position for her.

Gaius Gracchus had kept in the background, serving twelve years in the army rather than the required ten. He only then sought election. He was also one of the land commissioners (some of the boundary stones are carved with his name) and he was far from idle, but a Gracchus could not expect to live his life in obscurity. He was a great orator and over a couple of years there were rumours that opposing leaders were becoming alarmed at his appearance on the political scene, and that they would have to prevent him from becoming a Tribune, too.

When Scipio Aemilianus died suddenly in 129 BC suspicion fell upon not only Gaius, but also on his mother Cornelia and his sister Sempronia, Scipio's widow. Slaves were questioned, as usual under torture[33] and there were rumours that the victim had been smothered with a pillow. Other rumours were of poison, but it may possibly have been a natural death. There was reputedly no mark on the body, except in Plutarch's version of events. Whatever the truth, there was no judicial enquiry into Scipio's death and many were relieved that he had gone. Others simply did not wish to see Gaius Gracchus implicated in the matter.

Scipio's death had a symbolic importance rather than a real one. He was the last of the old-style leaders, although a man of only modest military achievement. His influence was due far more to the stature of his distinguished family than to his own abilities.[34]

After 129 BC Gaius Gracchus prepared to make his move, with four main bodies to persuade. The first were the knights (the Equestrian Order) and their flourishing businesses. The second were the Italians who were resentful about their inferior status to Romans. Third were the poor citizens, hungry for land and with a great, though unreliable, vote. Fourthly were the provinces, at the outskirts of a rather neglected and under-exploited empire. Gaius was contemplating an even more profound realignment of Roman politics than his late brother, which only became clear when he had power. Behind his peaceful exterior he burned with determination to avenge his brother's murder: 'nobody comes and speaks before you for nothing, but what I ask of you is not money, but that you should think well of me and hold me in honour.'[35]

He gave the impression that although resentful of his brother's death, he still proceeded with caution, intending to consolidate a firm power base before he made a move, with the intention of going much further than his brother had ever attempted.

The eighteen centuries of the Roman 'knights' were by that time businessmen and bankers. These were the very groups that Lucius Cornelius Sulla would one day subdue, because of their greed and reluctance to help the impoverished state in its times of need.[36] These men had much in common with all but the greatest Patrician families. In 129 BC, a proposal was made for men who entered the Senate to hand back their Public Horses, and therefore cease officially to be knights. It seems a small point, but the cost of the animals was negligible in comparison to the honour of possessing one.[37] The dominant voice had passed from the Patricians to these men who were financiers and in reality controlled Rome's wealth, very few of whom had anything to do with military matters.

There was to be a real attempt to pacify the genuine resentments of Rome's Italian allies, as the land reform had exposed the inferiority of the Italians to a disastrous degree. There was, in 126 BC an attempt made to expel all 'foreign'-born residents from Rome itself. It was very likely intended as an anti-Gracchan measure, trying to keep the Italian allies away from the consular elections, but it was countered by Fulvius Flaccus who proposed, in 125, to extend full Roman citizenship to any Italians who wanted it, which would have proved an immensely popular move.

The hungry poor looked like becoming hungrier still when a plague of locusts destroyed the crops in East Africa, followed by a widespread pestilence. Supplies and prices were badly affected, even though an African king, Micipsa, sent Rome some of his own grain to help out 'in honour of Gaius Gracchus'. This received a chilly reception in Rome because of the Gracchan connection.[38]

It may have been a sign of this Gracchan influence that the consuls of 124 BC founded a new colony, Fabrateria Nova, to replace the destroyed Fregellae. This had been a 'Latin rights' community, situated on the Via Latina, just over the border into Samnium. It was loyal to Rome until 125 BC, then revolted and was crushed.[39] Gaius Gracchus cleared himself of charges that he had encouraged Fregellae to revolt, and then declared himself as a candidate in the next elections, to stand as a Tribune in 123 BC.

He was already by then more controversial than his brother and more dangerous, due to his widespread interests and growing popularity. The elections were held on the Campus Martius to allow more space and although many Patricians opposed him, that did not matter. Due to the organisation of the Plebeian Assembly, their approval was not required.

He came fourth in the elections and on 10 December 124 BC he took office as a Tribune of the Plebs, intent not only on reform, but also on revenge.[40]

In the nine years since the death of Tiberius Gracchus, Rome had been dominated by that family's politics. As soon as Gaius was a Tribune he spoke with great grief and anger of the death of his brother. He was also extremely defensive over the reputation of his mother, Cornelia, who had long been the power behind her sons. When someone spoke slightingly of her, Gaius responded with fury, saying 'How dare you insult Cornelia, who bore Tiberius? How can you compare yourself with her? Have you borne such children as she did? You are a man, but the Romans know that she has kept away from men for longer than you have!'[41] This rapid and bitter defence of Cornelia made clear her power within the family, although outside of it she had to play the part of the modest and retiring Roman matron.

Once Gaius had power, he moved swiftly, with the help of Fulvius Flaccus. One of his first targets was Marcus Octavius, and he proposed a law that any magistrate once deprived of office could not hold office again [42] However, at the request of his mother he withdrew the law, sparing Octavius. This was not altruistic, as Gaius's hatred stayed the same, but his apparent mercy raised his personal popularity still further, it appearing to be an act of charity on his part. It raised Cornelia's public profile also. Certainly, no Tribune would dare to attempt to veto Gaius's proposals during that year.

Gaius did punish the man who had instigated the killing of his brother, but by exile, not murder. He concentrated on preparing new and better laws, including a grain law, always popular with the people who needed to buy their grain cheaply. It was far less popular with their superiors, who badly wanted to be able to sell it dear! Though some of those more privileged people could always be seen queueing for their cheap supply along with the poorer citizens.

The Mediterranean had for centuries been a centre of small traders and manufacturers, but Rome's business interests would develop into large-scale proto-capitalism, needing organisers who could handle public contracts. These were the 'Publicans', supplying army or building contracts and also dealing in tax-farming, by which they paid a specified advance sum to the state for the right to collect defined taxes, keeping the surplus. They had grown vastly rich during the Punic Wars but still needed social contacts at the highest level, which is where the knights came in, being businessmen with connections to the best families.[43]

While the knights who ran companies were interested in business rather than politics, with the Senators the opposite was true, although Gaius Gracchus intended to alter the Senate's power monopoly – after which the knights would become vital, to provide a firm foundation for his proposed laws. He was also keen to mobilise the wealth of Roman provinces and was willing to spend money, but unlike most politicians he wanted solid revenue to pay for it all.

Asia was the key. It was hugely wealthy and even in Cicero's time a dozen provinces brought in fifty million denarii annually.[44] But Gaius protested that the revenues sent to Rome were often less than they should be and he attacked the Senatorial Commission organisers, making an impassioned speech to the people on the matter.

In 123 BC he made his own law to secure Asia's taxes of one tenth of annual produce, which allowed Rome's treasury to cope with its military expenditure and other commitments.[45] The Publicans would still benefit from tax-farming, but that was unavoidable, as the Roman State then had no direct civil service in control of all the complicated assessment and collection work. Gaius's law had the effect of transferring political control and the knights began to abuse their new powers. They put a halt to prosecutions involving bribes and suborned false accusers against the rich. Corruption ceased to be investigated and conflicts were generated that would last long into the future.[46]

Cicero considered that 'taxes are the sinews of the Republic, and the men who bring them in are rightly regarded as the mainstay of other classes.'[47] However, others claimed that the Senators were becoming slaves of the knights, and that by sacrificing the provinces to Publican greed, Gaius had incited them to hate Roman rule. It could be said that he had laid the foundations of empire, but not all men possessed his insight and vision, and he would be required to pay the price.

While Gaius was busy empire-building, the hostility towards his policies was growing. There are over thirty sites referred to in the Book of Colonies, and although founding these was not unprecedented, he was acting on a larger scale. He continued for a second year in office and his power was growing, but he proposed to lead the first colony ever to be established with full Roman rights – at Carthage of all places.

The horrors of the three devastating wars had not been forgotten, and the fact that Hannibal had reached the very gates of Rome was still a nightmare. Gaius, still only 31, dealt well with all the problems, but an even more revolutionary bill was then proposed, to extend the Roman franchise to all the Italian allies. He was still working with Fulvius Flaccus and he was friendly with the Consul Gaius Fannius, who would soon take up office, but he was still skating dangerously close to an accusation of beginning a 'reign', something that had ended his brother's life.

The freeborn Italians were in three main groups. Just over a third of them were full Roman citizens. Then there were Latins, and Latin citizenship had been extended beyond the area of old Latium, and many colonies had been given 'Latin' rather than Roman status. This meant they had certain marriage and property rights and also the right to vote. If they migrated to Rome they could attain Roman citizenship, although they were still considered second-class.

The other half of the population, the Italians or merely 'allies', were distinct from the Latin speakers. They were bound to Rome by various treaties but did not participate in the Roman state itself. They had trading opportunities, but although they fought for Rome, they received no direct benefits and were considered to be distinctly third-class.[48] Gaius's new bill was complicated but generally the Latins would receive Roman citizenship and the Italians/allies would move up one stage to receive Latin rights. There was a precedent of sorts, when Latin rights had been granted to the offspring of Roman soldiers serving in Spain. What was radical in Gaius's proposal was its scale. It would greatly affect the voting rolls, but it also gave the impression that receiving Latin rights was a kind of 'halfway house' on the way to full Roman rights. Fulvius Flaccus played a large role in this; he had attempted something similar in 125 BC. It had evoked great hostility towards him from fellow Senators, much of which now also fell on Gaius, and he was blamed for 'trouble-making'.

Early in the new year of 122 BC, the Bill to enfranchise the allies went before the Assembly. The Tribune Marcus Livius Drusus promptly vetoed it.[49]

Marcus Livius Drusus was from a distinguished family. His father Gaius Livius Drusus had been Consul in 147 BC along with Publius Cornelius Scipio. They were both grandsons of the Aemilius Paullus who had fallen at Cannae.[50] Drusus's action against the Franchise Bill amazed Gaius, and Drusus gave no explanation for it. He did not have to by the terms of his Tribunate, and he was more formidable an opponent than Octavius had been to Tiberius. Gaius needed to be away from Rome to establish his new colony at Carthage, and he had hoped to have his bill passed quickly. He decided to go to Carthage first, later returning to deal with getting the bill through, leaving Fulvius Flaccus to hold the position in Rome. During this time Drusus, also in Rome, concentrated on drafting various 'crowd-pleasing' Bills. He emphasised that these were all approved by the Senate and were concerned only with the welfare of the people. He proposed the establishment of twelve colonies, each of approximately three thousand settlers, but formed of destitute citizens. Drusus then removed even the small rents that had been proposed, thus generating huge popularity, although the Senators may have shuddered at the proposals, even though they had to recognise that they would result in generally better relations between the Senate and the people.

Gaius, meanwhile, was facing more difficulties in Carthage, due to the scale of his plans. However, despite destruction from war and the locusts, the land was still fertile and could not be abandoned, some of the allotments being large ones of two hundred acres apiece. The main problem he faced was superstition. After Carthage had been destroyed, the area was soundly cursed, with the intention that nobody would live there again. Mysterious happenings began to frighten the people, and although these were likely caused by human hostility rather than that of spirits, the Romans were a very superstitious people and were always concerned if religious matters did not seem to be in order. Despite this, Gaius pressed ahead and on his return to Rome he found that Flaccus had lost ground. Gaius saw the Consular elections approach knowing that the most likely candidates were already hostile towards him, the worst of them being Lucius Opimius, whom Gaius had previously defeated.[51]

Opimius greatly resented Gaius for having denied him the honour of a Triumph, and by then he had supporters and was ready for a Consulship. It began to seem as if Gaius's moment had already passed. To his credit, he realised this, and moved house to a poorer area to be surrounded by his own supporters. He and Flaccus tried to open up Carthage to all colonists, enfranchised or not, and openly criticised the lifestyles and behaviour of the rich and arrogant nobles. His opponents countered with their own accusations, and Drusus offered a bill to prevent any Latin being beaten while on military service, which was a valuable concession, as even Roman citizen soldiers had only had the privilege for a generation. [52]

Although crowds poured into the city, and many of them were Gracchan supporters, the Senatorial leaders had another card to play. A proclamation was issued saying that nobody who did not possess voting rights should stay in the city, or nearer than five miles to the city, while the bills were being voted on. Gaius then issued his own counter-edict denouncing the Consuls and promising to protect his own supporters, but he no longer had the power to do it and helplessly watched on while his Bills were rejected by the Assembly. He was desperate to regain effective support and when a gladiatorial fight was due to be staged in the Forum[53] seats were constructed for the magistrates to sell at a profit. Gaius had these seats torn down to allow the poor people to watch the show free of charge, but the action cost him the election.

It was then too late for him to withdraw from public life. His opponents wanted a showdown and were determined to force him into a corner. The heaviest attack concerned Carthage, with claims that even the Gods opposed it, citing wolf attacks, storms, split boundary posts and other phenomena as evidence of their wrath. The anti-Gracchan feeling in the Senate had spread, and its intransigence was formidable. The great noble families, many related to his personally, were implacably hostile to him, led by Opimius.

At this point Cornelia appeared openly, although she must have participated from behind the scenes throughout. One story claims that at this point she emerged from the shadows and issued instructions from her retreat at Misenum. She is said to have hired a bodyguard composed of Italians and sent them into the city in disguise.[54] The day arrived when the vote regarding the fate of Carthage was to be taken, presided over by Opimius. The usual sacrifice preceded it, and it was recorded that Gaius Gracchus appeared to be agitated. He may well have been, as violence was expected, even by the absent Cornelia.

An attendant, carrying the sacrificial victim's entrails, stopped and spoke to Gaius, some people claiming that the words included an insulting gesture. The man was pushed away, then seized and stabbed to death with the specially sharpened pens used for voting. Gaius protested that they were playing into the hands of their enemies by indulging in any violence, but it was already too late to avoid a general brawl. Fortunately, this was stopped by a sudden rainstorm, although the damage was done. The Senators, by that time over-excited and pretending to be in fear for their lives and led by Opimius, then passed the 'Senatus Consultum de Res Publica Defendenda' or Ultimate Decree, for the first time. This permitted the Consuls to take whatever measures they thought fit to protect the state from harm. Defence of the state was always their prime duty, although at that point in 121 BC there was no real enemy, merely a little civil unrest which was already calmed. However, Opimius ordered the call to arms for the following day, summoning Senators, knights and their armed retainers. There was also a band of mercenaries, Cretan archers, and the fact that they were there at all proves beyond reasonable doubt that Opimius had planned his move well in advance.[55]

It was said that the Gracchans gathered in the Forum that evening, with Gaius walking over to the Sempronian Hall and the statue of his father who built it. His thoughts may have been bitter, knowing what the following day was likely to bring. Away in Misenum, Cornelia, his mother, must have been anguished, being aware of the forces then ranged against her son, on whom all the family's hopes then rested. Plutarch reported that Gaius then wept, before returning to his lodgings.[56] Many people had seen Gaius Gracchus shedding tears in the Forum. They walked him home, spending the following night guarding him.

The Forum began to fill from dawn, and Opimius put an armed force on Capitoline Hill overlooking the Forum area. He took up his own station at the Temple of Castor.[57] In the morning, Opimius summoned the Senate and demanded that Gaius Gracchus and Fulvius Flaccus attend to account for their behaviour. Fulvius armed his followers and stationed himself on the Aventine Hill, a good distance from the Forum. Gaius set off as if heading for the Forum, wearing a formal toga and carrying only a small dagger. His wife, Licinia, with her son beside her, said farewell to him. Plutarch claimed that she wept and then fainted, fearing the worst. She was then carried to the house of her relative, Lucius Licinius Crassus.

Gaius joined Flaccus on the Aventine and Flaccus's son, Quintus, was sent to Castor's to try to negotiate a compromise, but he returned with the demand that they should submit and beg for mercy. When he tried again, he was arrested and Opimius gave the signal for a general attack. Flaccus and his remaining son fought, but Gaius would not. As Opimius and Brutus advanced up the slope, Gaius fell back to the Temple of Diana, determined to do the honourable thing and meet death by his own hand. However, his friends prevented him, taking away his weapon.

Opimius had by that time offered to spare anyone who changed sides, and many people did. Gaius and his friends, Pomponius and Laetorius, ran for their lives.[58] By the time they reached the Sublican Bridge, the oldest bridge in Rome, Gaius had suffered a sprained ankle, so they stopped to face their pursuers, intending to give Gaius a chance to escape. With only his servant, Philocrates, Gaius reached a grove sacred to the Goddess Furina. When his enemies caught and killed Laetorius and Pomponius, he knew he could go no further. Determined not to be taken alive, he asked his loyal servant to kill him, which he did. Philocrates then killed himself.[59]

Opimius had promised that whoever brought him the head of Gaius Gracchus could have its weight in gold, so there was a scuffle over it. This was eventually won by a man named Septimuleius, who carried it on the end of a spear. When weighed it was an extraordinary eighteen pounds, because Septimuleius had removed Gaius's brain and filled the cavity with lead. That part of the story may, of course, be apocryphal, but it is recorded by Plutarch.

On the Aventine Hill, two hundred and fifty Gracchan supporters had died and their bodies were denied burial, being flung into the Tiber, as those of Tiberius Gracchus and his friends had been twelve years earlier. Even then Opimius was not satisfied and ordered the deaths of up to three thousand friends, clients and supporters of the Gracchan movement. The houses of the leaders were looted and their wives and families were forbidden to wear mourning for them. Gaius's widow Licinia could not recover her marriage portion until her uncle, the Pontifex Maximus Scaevola, spoke up for her. Even then he was obliged to abase himself by admitting that Gaius had been entirely responsible for the riots, and for his own death.

It was also reported that Gaius's headless corpse had been sent to his mother, Cornelia, in Misenum.[60] This is unlikely, as the whole point of throwing bodies into the Tiber was to prevent them having any kind of formal funeral, a last blow landed on the family.

The brothers were gone but would always be remembered. The importance of the story of the Gracchi cannot be overemphasised and it is supremely important to our understanding of how the Republic worked and the Roman mindset within it. These men and their followers were killed because they had challenged the 'mos maiorum', yet they were still honoured for their courage. Statues were erected to them and shrines sprang up where they had died, making them places of offerings almost as if they were gods. They embodied all that was best in the Roman spirit, in memory, if not while alive, although they had failed in their objectives.

They had to fail, because they had gone too far for Republican feeling, too close to that spectre of kingship of one man and one absolute rule that was too appalling to contemplate. Only Caesar would go further, making himself Dictator in Perpetuity, but he would also die for it. Yet in the long term the aims of the Gracchi were not destroyed, merely postponed. The reverence with which they were granted an honoured place in Republican history shows the essential ambivalence of Roman attitudes to authority.

It was Opimius who was vilified; the Consul who had engineered the death of Gaius Gracchus was, in the end, considered to be the lesser man. Cicero said of him 'you had no right to put to death even the most criminal citizen without a trial,' yet Cicero would find himself doing the same when he had the power in his hands and was facing social unrest. It was accepted that, despite its obvious dangers, public life was greater and more important for a man to engage in than intellectual pursuits, and that any Roman's best training was in experiencing politics.[61] Cicero remarked that ' a republic is the common property of all the people, and this is not a haphazard collection of people, but an organised group associated by assent to a common code of justice and a common advantage.'

What of the women? The wives of the Gracchi brothers disappear into history, picking up the threads of their lives as women have always had to do. Yet the mother of the Gracchi came to be a symbol, representative of all that was great and venerable in Roman women. She had educated and advised her sons, devoting her life to their careers. She was no shrinking violet, always in the background and afraid to speak. She certainly supported their political reforms and may have instigated some of them, working in the background but in such a way that she was remembered as their guiding force, not their wives. Though she lived in retirement at Misenum, she was never forgotten, even after her sons were dead. She led an active social life, was often visited and her letters were published. It was recorded that she always showed great pride in her illustrious father Scipio Africanus and spoke of her sons with equal pride and with no weak show of grief. Cornelia was a politically minded woman and became the examplar of Roman Stoicism, understanding suffering yet maintaining dignity and wisdom; she was the ideal Patrician.[62]

But was she all that she seemed? Was she frustrated by feminine restrictions, wanting to live her own life but having always to work through her sons? It seems certain that the lives of highly educated and intelligent women such as Cornelia's were wasted in the purely domestic sphere that shackled them, particularly if they had no sons of ability and ambition to work through. Did she push them, perhaps a little too much? We know that Gaius wept publicly outside the Sempronian Hall on the evening before he died: but was he grieving for the failure of his plans, or for the loss of the ordinary family life that he would never know? There was obviously affection between him and his wife, but he left her to pursue a very dangerous path, knowing that disaster was always a step away.

Cornelia's Stoicism towards the end of her life was much admired. But did it cover natural grief, or was resentment also present? If she had been born a man could she have done better and succeeded in her aims? We will never know her thoughts on the deaths of her brilliant sons, but we may be able to catch a glimpse of the smouldering fires of the 'real' woman underneath the façade by looking again at the death of her daughter Sempronia's husband.

Cornelia's daughter was married to Publius Cornelius Scipio (known as Aemilianus Africanus). He was actually the son of Lucius Aemilius Paullus but was adopted by Publius Cornelius Scipio at his mother's death. He had fought with distinction in Spain and Africa, even winning the prestigious Corona Graminia (known as the Grass Crown).[63] Unfortunately, though closely related, the Scipio family and the family of the Gracchi had often been opposed. Perhaps the marriage between him and Sempronia had been intended to heal the breach, but it proved to be loveless and unhappy. After Tiberius Gracchus was killed in the riots, Publius made his approval clear. Three years later, in 129 BC, he proposed a measure transferring the powers of the Gracchan land commission to the Senate. Shortly after that, he died.

It was widely reported that not only was his wife Sempronia suspected of having had a hand in his death, but her revered mother Cornelia also. Rumours were often wild when a man of stature died without clear cause, but to suspect Cornelia of wrongdoing was almost unbelievable. What was the truth of it? Did she harbour such resentment against her son-in-law that she had actually ordered something done to promote his death? Her status and wealth, plus the Gracchan cause, were all high-profile enough to allow her to hire someone to do the work for her, knowing that accusations against her would be quashed.

There was, of course, no prosecution, nor were any formal charges ever made, for who could openly accuse Cornelia, the daughter of the great Scipio Africanus, that example of Roman fortitude, who had already suffered so much? Her almost saintly reputation would never allow it. However, it is very tempting to think that under Cornelia's cool exterior, great fires burned. It would have been simple enough for her and her remaining son Gaius to have arranged something, knowing that her immense standing would protect her from censure.

Her reputation remained undamaged by it, and by her obvious connection to her son Gaius's policies which were to follow it. Publius Cornelius Scipio was a high-profile man, but his death and the suspicions which surrounded it were never investigated. After Cornelia's death a bronze statue was erected in her honour, with the inscription on it 'Cornelia, daughter of Africanus, mother of the Gracchi'. This statue was later restored by the Emperor Augustus.[64]

Her daughter Sempronia made one more appearance in the pages of history many years later, in the time of Gaius Marius and Sulla, when a young man claimed to be the illegitimate son of Tiberius Gracchus. His name was Lucius Equitius and he had served in the legions, owned property and land, and had enough money to qualify for admittance into the Ordo Equestor.

He was said to have looked very much like Tiberius Gracchus, and he also had opposition, quite possibly from the same sort of people who had feared and opposed his supposed father. It was decided to ask Sempronia whether Lucius Equitius was likely to be her brother's son. When she appeared before him and the official witnesses, she looked him up and down and rejected the idea completely, refusing to countenance that her idolised brother could have fathered him and that he was her nephew. Her total repudiation put an end to his career hopes, and Sempronia also faded again into the background. This incident – whether apocryphal or not – reveals the desire of the people, even the need, for the romance and tragedy of the Gracchi story, the need to preserve the memory of heroes, as well as their pivotal role in the making of the history of the Republic.

There could likewise be no greater embodiment of the Republican spirit than the sacrifice of Marcus Porcius Cato (Cato the Younger 95-46 BC), the Stoic and opponent of Gaius Julius Caesar. When Caesar had taken over the Republic, he defeated Pompeius Magnus and Sextus Pompeius and killed 10,000 surrendering Romans after the Battle of Thapsus because they had fought for Pompeius. Caesar destroyed the Republican cause by declaring himself Dictator for Life and Cato quickly realised that the Republic he had served was gone for good, and he had no intention of living in the Rome Caesar was making. He made a suicide attempt, which initially failed. He was in agony, with a stomach wound stitched and bandaged, but there was still hope he could recover. Cato, determined not to live with the 'one-man-rule' that Caesar was forcing upon Rome, tore off his bandages and ripped his wound open, dying with a last contemptuous gesture towards the man he knew would have pardoned him. He hated Caesar and all he represented, knowing him to be an opportunist, a betrayer of all that Patricians stood for and contemptuous of the Republican ideals, believing himself to be the material of kingship, although he dared not use the title.

Cicero was asked to write a short piece of work to commemorate Cato's terrible end and although he was aware that he, too, was under surveillance by the supporters of Caesar the Dictator; he wrote enough to keep Cato's brave sacrifice and his reasons for it alive in Roman minds.

> Sinewy in thought and in person, indifferent to what men said of him, scornful of glory, of titles and decorations, and even more of those who sought them, defender of laws and freedoms, vigilant in

> the public interest, contemptuous of tyrants, of their vulgarities and presumptions, stubborn, infuriating, harsh, dogmatic, a dreamer, a fanatic, a mystic, a soldier, willing at the last to tear the very organs from his stomach rather than submit to a conqueror – only the Roman Republic could have bred such a man as Cato, and only in the Roman Republic did such a man as Cato desire to live.[65]

Such was the ideal Republican spirit, still to be respected even after its dilution by the exigencies of empire – determined, principled, even unbending, but indisputably honourable.

2

The Family and Daily Life

It is sometimes claimed that all prominent Romans had three names, which is not quite true. Some Romans, of the Patrician class particularly, proudly carried three names, and sometimes even more as further family honours were added. Some of the wealthy and prominent Plebeian nobles had three names, but the vast majority of ordinary Romans only had two. The five 'classes' of Ancient Rome were Patricians, Equites (or Knights), Plebeians, Freedmen and slaves. There could be a certain amount of movement between these groups as time went on. A slave could become a freedman or a freedwoman, and some of the noble Plebeian families were as wealthy as the old Patrician families by the later years of the Republic.

The family name showed the 'gens' to which a person belonged and in women of rank it became their general name. For example, the family name, or nomen, of Julius Caesar was Julius, being of the gens 'Julia'. The prenomen, or given name, was Gaius, while the last name, by which he later became known, was neither his given name nor his family name, nor until later was it even a title. It was the family's cognomen of 'Caesar'. This was given to distinguish different branches of a family, or as a mark of honour, or merely as a nickname which stuck. It could even be a near-insult. Some of the less complimentary ones were either extremely witty or heavily sarcastic and the bearer would be obliged to carry it regardless.

One example of a man who changed his cognomen was Gnaeus Pompeius Magnus. He came from a famous military family – his father was Gnaeus Pompeius Strabo – and he was involved in the Social War between Rome and the Italians. Although he was awarded a Triumph for his work for Rome, his methods could be brutal, and he was always unpopular with the people. The cognomen 'Strabo' actually meant 'cross-eyed' and although it did not necessarily mean that its holder suffered from strabismus, one of his ancestors may have done. However, his son, whether out of dislike of the name or as a way of dissociating himself from his rather notorious father, chose to call himself 'Magnus' instead, meaning 'Great'. His confidence in himself was not misplaced and he became not only great but highly popular, making good on his change of name.

The famous name of Caesar, pronounced Kaiser, actually meant 'a good head of hair' which was unfortunate in the case of Gaius Julius as he began to lose his fair hair quite early. He then wore his civic crown (of oak leaves) on every possible occasion, partly to cover the fact that his hair was thinning, and partly to hold his remaining hair in place. We know this fact about the Dictator, as his devoted soldiers made up marching songs about him, not only referring to him as a hero, but calling him 'the bald adulterer' as a further tribute to his successes at seducing the wives of his colleagues.

Some of the origins of these cognomen are now, unfortunately, lost to us but we are aware of the meanings of several of them. Some of them are self-explanatory, such as Publius Cornelius Scipio Africanus, the greatest general of the Second Punic War, whose fourth name was given to commemorate his great victory.

In order to differentiate further, it became necessary for some families to add extra explanatory names, resulting in names such as Quintus Caecilius Metellus Pius Scipio Nasica. This extraordinary name resulted from Quintus Caecilius Metellus being the son of Publius Cornelius Scipio Nasica. He was eventually adopted (possibly by will) by Quintus Caecilius Metellus Pius, and the two names were put together. The women of a distinguished family could also carry the family cognomen, as in the case of Sulla's wife Caecilia Metella Dalmatica, whose cognomen was awarded to her father Lucius Caecilius Metella after he conquered Dalmatia in 118 BC. Another example of this type is Balearicus, assumed by a Quintus Caecilus Metellus after he conquered the Balearic Islands in 123-122 BC.

Some of these additional names could also be very complimentary, as with the family of Publius Clodius Pulcher. The family name was actually Claudius, although they preferred to call themselves Clodius, an affectation which became accepted, so the 'gens' was Claudius, while 'Pulcher' meant beautiful. It was fortunate that this family were reputed to be unusually attractive.

Other cognomina were obvious descriptions, as with 'Postumius' meaning born after the father's death. 'Rufus' meant red-haired, while 'Lentulus' referred to being tardy or slow. 'Scaevola' meant being left-handed. Less flattering was 'Galba' which meant pot-belly. It seems a pity that famous men with great achievements are now known primarily by their cognomina, as in their own time they would have been referred to by nomen and prenomen, for example as Gaius Julius or Gnaeus Pompeius.

Families also tended to re-use the same first names, or prenomen, to such an extent that in some cases the first name gives a clue to the family, in favouring Gaius, Lucius, Publius or Marcus. The Romans also abbreviated almost everything, so that written or carved names would be shortened, making Appius into Ap, Aulus into A, Gaius usually appears as a C (because this name was originally Caius), while Gnaeus is Cn. When the name was Marcus, an M is sufficient identification, with M' for Manius. Therefore, Marcus Antonius is shown as M.Ant.

A woman of the family carried the 'gens' name, such as Julia, Metella or Clodia, but so also would any sisters she had. To avoid complete confusion, many female names of younger daughters became either diminutives, such as Drusilla or Julilla or sometimes a pet name would be used. Charming perhaps, but they indicated a distinctly inferior position, as they had no personal name of their own. Their role was very definitely to support their families, rather than making a name for themselves. They were expected to uphold the respected name of their family, respect won by the efforts of a male ancestor, rather than any personal achievement.

In any Roman family of standing, the Paterfamilias was the head of the family, the maker of decisions, and certainly in the early Republic had absolute authority over his wife and children. That authority could not be taken lightly. In those early days his power of life and death was very real and it could be used. He was allowed to kill, without any retribution, if he thought that wife or child had badly overstepped the boundaries. Even during the later Republic, when the actual killing of family members became rare, it was still not unusual for an aggrieved father to cast out a son who was considered to have failed him. He could 'adopt out' a son, usually to a family connection of equal standing, and that son would take the name of his 'new' family for life. He could 'adopt in' a son, if he did not have one of his own, to carry on his own family line. He could also divorce his wife quickly and easily if he chose to do so, once the marriage rules had eased. Usually in the case of divorce, the dowry of the wife would be repaid, but not always, particularly if she had committed adultery. He could in certain cases force a daughter to divorce her own husband if the son-in-law did not match expectations, or even if he merely found a better match for his daughter, one of greater benefit to the family. His power over his household was total, and even in a marriage where the parties were fond of each other, he would still expect to be obeyed and respected.[1] These rights over his family were protected by law.

The weakness and intellectual limitations of women in general were given as the reason for this control. It was the underlying principle of Roman legal theory and mandated all women to be under the custody of a man. If the Paterfamilias was the father, and he died, then the authority would pass to the nearest male relative, unless another guardian had been designated by his will. A guardian was required when any woman performed an important transaction. Even Julia Felix, a landowner in Pompeii, who was rich, well-educated and well-known, had to work through agents in the absence of a male authority figure. Cornelia, mother of the Gracchi, had been obliged to work through her sons. If a woman's guardian withheld approval of something she needed to do, she might apply to the magistrates, and if the matter was serious enough the guardian could be made to change his mind, or occasionally another guardian might be appointed. However, these were rather rare cases, where the wealth and standing of the woman concerned and of her family would have to be considered.

For a woman less wealthy, and therefore less important, being a pawn in her husband's hands was simply the way things were. Very few women were really 'sui iuris' meaning 'in own hand.' If a wealthy widow without sons to guide her was in control of her own property, she could quickly become a target for fortune hunters. If she married foolishly, she would find herself without independence again, and probably far worse off under the control of a new husband who would use her fortune as his own.

The only young and single women in Rome who could be considered to be in sui iuris were the Vestal Virgins, who had a very particular role to play – and their apparent privilege was not complete, of course. They and their chastity were vitally important for the well-being of Rome itself. They did not live with their birth families from an early age, they came under the absolute authority of the Pontifex Maximus. There were only ever six of these special women, who were chosen from the highest families at the age of seven or eight. They would serve Vesta for thirty years, during which time their dowry was invested for them, securing their future. If, at the end of their thirty-year term of service, they wished to leave, they were then free to do so and were then even allowed to marry, although few ever did, as marrying a Vestal was considered unlucky.

The laws of guardianship dictated that in some cases the powers of the Paterfamilias could exceed even those of the woman's husband, as in the admittedly rather uncommon instances of a father forcing a daughter to divorce her husband. Though the stringent old marriage laws had certainly eased over time, even during the reign of the Emperor Augustus Livy wrote: 'Married women were obliged to conform themselves to their husbands, having no other refuge, while husbands rule over their wives as possessions.'[2]

Shortly after the Battle of the Colline Gate in 82 BC, when Lucius Cornelius Sulla was triumphant, he wished to draw his ally Gnaeus Pompeius Magnus closer. He persuaded Magnus to divorce his wife Antistia, in order to marry the daughter of Sulla's wife.

She, Caecilia Metella Dalmatica, had been previously married to Marcus Aemilius Scaurus, the deceased Princeps Senatus, who had been many years her senior. She had, however, produced two children during her marriage with him. The boy eventually became a Governor of Sardinia, in 55 BC, and the girl, Aemilia Scaura, was married to Manius Acilius Glabrio, (who would become a Consul in 67 BC). She was already pregnant by her husband Glabrio, when her stepfather Sulla decided that he wanted her to marry Pompeius Magnus. The proposed alliance was far more important than her current marriage, so Sulla arranged her divorce from Glabrio and remarried her to Pompeius Magnus. This was despite her protests and those of his wife, Dalmatica. However, Magnus had the ability to charm, and by treating them well he made his wives content, including Aemilia Scaura, despite her initial reluctance. Unfortunately, she was to die giving birth to the child of her previous husband within the year, and her surviving baby, which was a boy, was handed back to its natural father in accordance with custom.[3] Sulla's action may have seemed harsh, but as her stepfather he was her Paterfamilias and had control over her and her future, always with the family's ultimate benefit in mind.

Betrothals, marriages and even divorces among the upper classes were arranged between the men for the political and financial profit they could provide. Sentimental reasons were not considered. Although large families were unusual in Republican Rome, it was also true that any man would need to produce not only a son and heir, but 'spare' children whose marriages would allow him to connect in the future to other important families.[4]

In the late Republic, large numbers of connubial alliances are reported, and the shifts and contrivances can seem very complicated. For example, when Caesar tried to gain the favour of Pompeius Magnus, he betrothed his only daughter Julia to him. She had already been betrothed to the immensely rich Servilius Caepio, who was the son of another Servilia, Caesar's long-standing mistress. To compensate the young man for the broken betrothal, Magnus then offered his own daughter to Servilius Caepio, although she was already betrothed to Faustus Sulla, the son of Caecilia Metella Dalmatica and the then-deceased Sulla. In the end, Pompeia did marry Faustus Sulla and Julia Caesaris married Magnus. Caesar himself decided to marry the young Calpurnia and arranged for her father, Lucius Calpurnius Piso, to be made a Consul.[5] Cato had protested against this use of women to cement political alliances, but he had divorced his own wife Marcia to further his friendship with Hortensius, then when Hortensius died he took her back and remarried her.

Even the Emperor Augustus, who was famously devoted to his sister Octavia, was not above using her as a political tool. He married her to Marcus Antonius to seal an alliance which he knew would not last. When Marc Antony abandoned Octavia for Cleopatra, which Augustus had expected, he thereby spoiled Marc Antony's reputation as Octavia was widely revered in Rome. The Porticus of Octavia, between the Theatre of Pompeius and the Circus Flaminius, was built around 27 BC by Augustus in honour of his sister. This remaining gateway originally led to a large piazza containing temples and shops and was decorated with every luxury, including several bronze equestrian statues by the Greek master sculptor Lysippos.

Relatives have always been used to gain advantage and some women are ambitious on their own account, using their charms to attract distinguished men. The aristocrat Valeria Messala, who was to become Sulla's fourth and final wife after the death of Caecilia Metella Dalmatica, met him at the games. As the story goes, she passed behind Sulla, seated in honour at the front, and leaned on his shoulder to take a small piece of lint or wool from the back of his clothing. As he turned around in surprise, she simpered that it was 'nothing' and that she had picked off the tiny piece of fluff because she 'wanted to share in the Dictator's good luck'. Sulla was immediately interested, but not without taking the precaution of investigating her family's status and background, even though it was said that he repeatedly turned around to look at her during the performances as the day progressed. He was obviously reassured as to her lineage and a marriage offer was made and accepted. Sulla did not have long to live, (he died when he was sixty) and we have no information of the girl's own age at that time, but she bore his final child after his death, a daughter named Postumia.[6]

We have been dealing so far with privileged, high-status women, and unfortunately, as with all periods of history, these are the people whose life stories are more likely to have been recorded. At the other end of the scale, the underprivileged led much the same lives as they always have, and these people usually go unrecorded. These are the women who serve in one capacity or another, the people who tend to become collateral damage during wars, or the peasantry during peacetime, the faceless masses at all times. An attempt will be made to describe their lives in Chapter Five, but for the moment we will deal with the middle sort. These are women who were neither from famous families, nor destitute, but those who lived in ordinary, perhaps averagely prosperous families, mothers of children, helpers of their husbands, the women who lived normal lives.

These women, as at most times in history, were recognisable by their clothing. The Romans were no strangers to sumptuary laws, restricting certain luxury goods to the elite. However, as in all other periods, the Romans found that such laws of one kind or another were not only difficult to enforce, but also most unpopular. They did, from time to time, introduce Bills to prevent too much money being spent on weddings, feasts, funerals and so on. Likewise, the richest fabrics and jewels were supposedly only for those of the highest families. However, if a man was making good money from his business, why should he and his family deny themselves? Men liked good food and wine and the company of their friends, so considered that what was spent on feast and entertainment should be limited only by the available cash-flow. Women liked nice clothes and whatever jewellery they could afford, and again, why should they not enjoy the fruits of their labours? Naturally the finest fabrics and the most glamorous jewels were impractical for the wife of a butcher or shopkeeper, but there was nothing preventing such a woman from buying what she could and wearing it on special occasions, except the law.

Women throughout the Roman period wore similar clothing, which was loose and comfortable for their climate, and although the fabrics themselves could vary enormously depending on wealth and status, the style of the clothing actually changed very little for a long period, with any fasionable alterations being only minor.

A woman's clothing was based on a light shift, or sleeveless under-tunic, called the 'intusium' with a bra-like 'fascia' or 'strophium' beneath it. The garments the world would see were the tunic, which from the first century BC was called a 'stola', covered by a 'palla' or long rectangular shawl, which could be raised to cover the head. The lower edge of the palla reached the knees, and this garment survived without great change until the third century AD, after which its size was reduced.[7]

Although Roman women's fashions may seem to us to have remained the same throughout those centuries, we are not able to see from pictures or statues the small changes. Women love novelty, most particularly in their clothing, so fashions did doubtless move on, from season to season, with heavier or lighter fabrics and colours.

It is in the region of colours that most people mistake what ancient Rome and its people looked like. The Romans loved colour, so the largely white world which we often imagine as a background for them was not the world they knew. Statues and temples, shops, houses, streets and even political slogans painted on walls, all blazed with colour and we must accept that clothing did, too. The 'togate' male, proudly attending the Senate in his official garments did wear a kind of uniform, with his woollen toga carefully bleached and chalked to make the off-white wool appear as white as possible. However, for normal daily life this heavy garment was discarded in favour of the tunic, which could be as brightly coloured as one wished. Similarly for the women, only the priestesses would wear white regularly, while all others wore brightly coloured tunics and shawls, even if the usual daily wear of the working woman necessitated 'sensible' or practical colours. The Romans were skilled with dyes, even for the hair, so white was certainly not the only, or even the preferred, choice in their world.

Silk was mentioned by Aristotle in the fourth century BC, but it was rare. Silkworm culture did not reach Europe until the sixth century AD, so that all silk used before then had to be imported. It came from China (Serica) and was horrifyingly expensive, with a pound's weight of silk worth a pound's weight of gold by the third century AD. Not only was it extremely expensive, but its thinness and transparency made it a little 'indelicate' and un-Roman for modest Roman matrons, but that was probably its attraction for those who could afford it. Later, the silk was blended with cheaper yarns, which reduced the price. There were a wide range of dyes for clothing, with sea-green, saffron, myrtle, rose, acorn, Thracian crane, almond and varying shades of all these, darker and more glowing colours being very popular. Ovid recommended white for dark-haired ladies and black for those who were fair. There were also various shades of flame, brilliant scarlet, deep blues and amethyst. Amethyst, for the wealthy, could reach true Tyrian purple, which was blackish at first sight, but gleaming when catching the light. Not for everyone, of course, but the shellfish dyes, first put to good use at Tyre in the Eastern Mediterranean, were well known.[8]

Certain colours came to be preferred wear for brides, or associated with prostitutes, and a few of the more daring shades would be considered rather too bright for respectable wear but were no doubt still very tempting. Worn with items of jewellery glittering in the sunshine, even a decoration of plain glass beads could look charming and attractive, while the real thing, if it could be afforded, would be stunning and much envied. That, of course, has always been the point of elaborate personal adornment.

Women who used colour on their hair probably didn't like to admit it. Republican hairstyles were simple, while the later Empire ones went from the sublime to the truly ridiculous. Certain 'German herbs' helped colour enrichment or even made possible a total change. Fair hair has always been considered attractive and if one's own hair was too dark to take bleaching agents without turning orange, there was always false hair available. This was also very useful for the older ladies, whose hair would naturally thin with age, or if a woman wanted a total colour change without the risk of permanent damage to her own hair. Blonde hair cut from the heads of German women might be the answer and was in great demand. Ovid observed that 'She has a mass of hair, but all bought! She puts her money down and some other woman's hair is hers, and she buys it without a blush.'[9]

For those people unwilling to wear someone else's hair it was back to the colourings. Certain experiments have been made with materials such as rock alum, quicklime, crude soda and wood ash, sometimes combined with old wine, which served as a 'lightener' for the hair. It was found that if the preparation was left on the hair overnight, or preferably even for several days, it gave a reddish-gold colour to the hair. So their treatments could certainly work, although being obliged to wear the concoction on one's head for several days must have been difficult, if not embarrassing.[10] Not only that, but many men did not like the idea of their wives colouring their hair, or even wearing make-up, which they certainly also did. Cruel jokes were very often made about the whole process of a woman preparing herself for the day, and the products she would need to use to make her appear presentable. Ovid was always prepared to poke fun:

> You perpetrate unbelievable extravagances to make a kind of tapestry of your hair, sometimes to be worn as a sort of sheath to your head, with a lid to the top of you, like a helmet on a stick. Sometimes for it to be an elevated platform built up at the back of your neck.[11]

With all the effort and the preparations used, it is no wonder that many women lost their hair due to unskilful dyeing or the over-enthusiastic use of hot tongs in an attempt to produce flowing waves. It was perhaps an even greater pity to go to all that trouble then have the efforts unappreciated by one's husband, who might be quite unimpressed and much prefer his wife to look as nature intended.

Regarding the use of make-up, one writer rather ungallantly opined that:

> If you saw women getting out of bed on a morning, you would find them more repulsive than monkeys. That is why they shut themselves up and refuse to be seen by a man ... a troupe of serving maids, as ugly as their mistress, surround her. Plastering her unhappy face with a variety of medicaments ... innumerable concoctions in the way of

> salves are used to brighten her unpleasing complexion ... a mirror, a jug, a multitude of boxes, enough to stock a chemist's shop, jars full of mischief, tooth powders or stuff for blackening the eyelids.[12]

Such masculine distrust of woman's wiles is not confined to the Ancient Rome of course: 'I have heard of your paintings too, well enough. God has given you one face and you make yourselves another. You jig and amble, and you lisp...' (*Hamlet*, 3.1.)

Museums are full of the many mirrors, combs, little jars, tweezers, hairpins, glass bottles and other little necessaries which, far from being objects of ridicule, tend to bring these women back to life for us, and allow us a glimpse of the things that they considered to be important.

Bright colour wasn't just for hair, clothes and lips. In ancient Rome it was everywhere. The Roman world, far from being dull, was glowing with colours. Excavations have proved this by giving us their beautiful floors, including the famous 'unswept floor' design, which has scattered in the mosaic nutshells, orange peel, and other detritus of a meal, giving the impression that a feast had just ended. There were painted walls and ceilings, stories of legends and deities, pictures of gardens or shady groves, flowers, birds, trees and fountains, glorious painted ornamentation to brighten the surroundings. One might assume that we are back with the wealthy again, but it is not necessarily the case.

Walk down a Roman street in Pompeii and one is surrounded by colour. Bright terracotta roof tiles, brilliantly painted slogans on walls, gardens with their flowering trees, all set off by blazing sunshine and an azure sky. The markets were also full of life and colour, the Romans loved flowers and they were regularly bought, not merely for the home but for festivals, sacrifices, and Triumphs. The Campo di Fiori is now, as it has been for centuries, full of rich scents and vibrant life.

Statues were not left plain, whether they were stone, marble or even bronze. They were painted brilliantly, but also as naturally as possible, to represent in colour the person or creature portrayed. There is the head of a divinity, crowned with vine leaves, from the site of the Temple of Victory made at the beginning of the third century BC. Its face and hair are painted realistically, with tanned skin tones topped off by dark, curling hair.[13]

The original equestrian statue of Marcus Aurelius, now in the Capitoline Museum, still has some of its gold covering visible on the horse the Emperor is riding, which must have been blinding in the sunlight. It is a revelation to realise that the stark white statues we now see were once brightly coloured and these things were for the enjoyment of everyone, on public display. The Romans lived in a vibrant world, which was crowded, noisy, often smelly, but also alive, scented, and full of sunshine and activity. Fortunately, due to the climate, it was always possible to spend a large part of one's time out of doors, which meant that the less fortunate who could not afford to live in a beautiful house surrounded by gardens could still enjoy the weather, watch public displays and ceremonies, and feel that they were a part of the things.

Not all the people living or working in Rome were wealthy, nor were they even citizens, but the Roman way of living was destined to spread throughout what would become a vast empire, and it had an effect on every place it came in contact with. Roman opinions, religions, and way of life became accepted in many other countries and people would soak them like sponges; everything from legal matters to the way the Roman calendar worked.

The Romans had a twenty-four-hour day and night, but the hours were not equal in length. Daylight and darkness each had their twelve hours, but these would have only represented equal time periods at the Equinox. Hours of light and darkness could both stretch and shrink, depending on the seasons. There were public sundials from the third century BC and from the second century BC there were also public water-clocks, which could be adjusted to fit the season.[14] Numerous public sundials have been found at Pompeii and Herculaneum and inscriptions record gifts of public clocks. In wealthy private houses, a slave would call out the hours, but of course the system was not accurate. A common complaint was that 'philosophers will agree sooner than clocks will.'[15]

As a rough guide, the 'first' hour of the day was considered to be around six or seven in the morning, and the twelfth about five or six in the evening. A daylight 'hour' at the winter solstice in Rome would actually only be about forty-five minutes in duration, but in summer would stretch to around an hour and a quarter.[16] Confusingly, the Latin word 'hora' did not mean just the hour itself but could also mean the beginning, the duration, or the conclusion of it. It is not surprising that unpunctuality was endemic and often a great nuisance. Summer days, stretching from 4.30 a.m. to 7.30 p.m. contrasted with winter ones lasting from around 7.30 a.m. to 4.30 p.m. For people whose homes or businesses lacked adequate light, there must have been vast differences between the lives they led in winter and their way of life in summer, when much of Rome's social life was moved outside. Many avoided the tedious dark by sleeping longer, but people whose work had to be done at night, such as bakers who needed to be ready for early customers in the mornings, must have been irked by the difference. Incidentally, bakeries were popular only from the second century BC, as before that all baking was done at home.

We still carry the Roman days of the week into our own times, with the days named for the planetary gods, once the seven-day week became accepted. These days were Moon, Mars, Mercury, Jupiter, Venus, Saturn and Sun. These come to life easily in modern Italian, with Monday as lunedi, Tuesday as martedi, Wednesday as mercoledi, Thursday as giovedi and Friday as venerdi. The day itself, divided into its twelve hours, began at sunrise with hora prima, the last, hora duodecima, ended at sunset. The night hours were divided into eight 'watches' for convenience, as might be expected of a military society, named vespera, prima fax, concubia, and intempesta. While media noctis inclination was midnight itself, it was followed by gallicinum, conticinum, and diluculum, which were between midnight and sunrise.

The way the year was worked out could be even more complicated. To 153 BC it had two beginnings, 1 January, shortly after the winter solstice, and the civil year began on 1 March (in earlier times this had been on the 15 March). This is commemorated in the names of the months and by this method July was the fifth month, named reasonably enough Quinctilis, until being later renamed July in honour of Julius Caesar. This would also happen to August, named for the Emperor Augustus, which was originally named Sextilis, or sixth month. The months of October, November and December still carry their numerical names of eight, nine and ten.

In 45 BC Julius Caesar changed the calendar. March, May, July and October had thirty-one days each. February had twenty-eight days, and the remaining months had twenty-nine each. The normal year was 355 days long, but during eight lunar years of 354 days the year slips 90 days ahead of the sun. The ancient Greeks dealt with this by adding on an extra month, three times in each eight-year period.

The Romans, unsurprisingly, dealt with it differently. Sometimes they simply ignored it, although the College of Pontiffs was supposed to deal with it by putting in an extra month in alternate years. Unfortunately, this sequence was never automatic and if the College of Pontiffs did not give specific instructions for it to be done, it wouldn't be. Although this was one of their responsibilities, not everyone saw the need to have the dates of the months fitting the actual seasons. However, if no attempt to correct it was made, the calendar would gradually work its way out of step with the seasons, by as much as two and a half months. This happened at the end of the Punic War, and their equivalent of harvest festival was held before the grapes could even be harvested.[17]

This 'slippage' was not always down to sheer carelessness. Sometimes a 'long' year was preferred for tax purposes, or at other times pressure might be brought to bear by a politician who, for his own reasons, preferred a 'short' year. This happened when Marcus Tullius Cicero had to leave Rome in order to take up his Governorship of Cilicia, in the year 51 BC. Cicero did not want to have to leave Rome at all, so needed a 'short' year so that he could return sooner. So unwilling was he to fulfil his duty that he wrote that his appointment 'was contrary to my wishes and quite unexpected'.[18]

These irregularities were brought to an end by Gaius Julius Caesar during his Dictatorship. The 'last year of confusion' was 46 BC, which was extended, not merely by one, but by three intercalary months, making it an impressive 445 days long, in order for the dates to catch up with the seasons. The Julian calendar was then introduced on 1 January 45 BC and from then onwards February was a twenty-eight-day month, but instead of having a 29th of February, the Romans inserted a day between the 23rd and 24th days instead.

The days of the week were reckoned by their distance from the following Nones, Ides or Kalends, so they went backwards rather than forwards. The Kalends was the first day of each month, so far so good; the Nones was the fifth day of the short months and the seventh day of the long ones. It was named Nones because it was always the ninth day before the Ides. But the Ides was itself a moveable day, being the thirteenth day of the short months and the fifteenth day of the long ones. Confused? You should be. Especially those of us who still need to recite 'Thirty days hath September…' even to know where we are with our own simpler calendar.[19] So, for instance, the date of 16 March would be referred to as 'the seventeenth day before the Kalends of April'. To add to the confusion, the Romans added to their reckonings of days, the days at both ends as well as the ones in between.

Every eighth day was a market day, known as a Nundinae or ninth day, because of the calculation including the day at both ends. However, by the late Republic, the idea of a seven-day week was taking hold, which was partly due to the spread of astrology and also to the amount of business done with Jewish businessmen, who always maintained a week of six days of work and one day of rest. The first public record of the seven-day week is from a calendar from the Sabine area, dated between 19 BC and 14 AD.

In Pompeii, a wall painting was found showing the correct weekly order of the seven days, along with the planets 'controlling' them, Sun, Moon, Mars, Mercury, Jupiter and Venus, with Saturn for Saturdays. But their weekly order was reached by starting with Saturn due to his importance.

From the second century BC Romans were accustomed to doing business with Jewish families and became familiar with their habit of closing on their Sabbath day. However, the idea of a working week which culminated in some kind of a Sabbath, devoted either to prayer or merely relaxation, did not appeal to the Romans. Some Roman writers went so far as to criticise the idea, calling the day off a form of idleness. The Roman Nundinae was never intended to be a day of rest, on the contrary, traders were busier than ever on that day, and there was certainly no concept of a day for stopping all work.

The actual markets were held on different days in neighbouring towns, although with a planetary week of seven days, by the end of the Republican era, and a market interval of eight days, the markets had to become flexible. Therefore, if one were held on a certain day in one town, then the following week it would need to be on the following day, to allow for the one-day difference.[20]

Again, to prevent general confusion, there were inscriptions showing the names of towns, along with the days of the week. Holes were made against the town names and the appropriate day, so that a marker could be inserted to make it clear on which day the market would be held in each place. There have been at least five of these found, from the Latium and Campania areas.[21] No doubt the routine of the market days, being familiar, worked perfectly well and no differently from modern people consulting a calendar.

A time naturally came when the old eight-day cycle of Nundinae was given up, making one particular day of the week the market day, and sometimes the markets were held fortnightly. One inscription showed that when senatorial permission was given for a citizen to hold a market on his estate, it was stipulated that the market should be held twice monthly, being four days before the Nones and twelve days before the Kalends, so even in that year, 138 AD, the old method of dating by the Kalends, Nones and Ides was still used.[22]

One thing about this routine, which greatly affected regular family life, was the necessity of avoiding ill-omened days when starting any new venture or arranging any kind of celebration. Unfortunately, there were several kinds, including the three days in the year when the 'Mundus' was opened, to allow the spirits of the dead to wander freely on the earth. The Mundus was a beehive-shaped pit, usually kept covered, which was believed to be an entrance to the Underworld. Its origin is a mystery, but there is evidence of a mundus-pit on the Palatine.[23] The days of its annual opening were 24 August, 5 October, and 8 November. Other days when the spirits of the dead might be expected to wander freely were at the 'Parentalia' which ran from the 13th to the 21st of February, and the days of the 'Lemuria', which fell on the 9th, 11th and 13th of May.

These were days of reverence for one's ancestors when families would particularly remember their dead. It was common on these days to visit tombs, taking offerings and doing them honour. This often took the form of having a meal or some refreshment there, to share not only with the living family but also with the deceased. They were considered to still be important within the family group. Some tombs were large enough to accommodate full family gatherings, where the refreshments on offer could be shared with the deceased in the form of a libation, which showed respect.

More than eighty days in each year carried an unlucky taint, so that it was very unlucky to marry in the month of May, possibly due to the Lemuria, a superstition which still endures, although most people who avoid that month for their nuptials will not remember why it is out of favour. The first half of June was also unlucky for the Romans, and a marriage should certainly not be celebrated on the Kalends, the Nones or the Ides of any month. For a truly superstitious people, life was already fraught with dangers and risks of offending the gods, so tempting fate on the bad days was asking for trouble and not to be contemplated.

Other 'dies religiosi' were days when it was unlucky to do anything non-essential, such as making a journey, recruiting soldiers, or even holding a meeting in the Comitia. These were not quite as dangerous as the days following the monthly Kalends, Nones or Ides, (which were considered so very unlucky that they were referred to as 'dies atri' or dark days) but they were certainly bad enough to cause people to consult with astrologers, or in political life consult the auspices, before making any important decisions. All this must have had a very stultifying effect on daily life.

Cassius Dio[24] said he believed that it was inauspicious for public life if the first day of the first month of the year (originally March, but later January) was to coincide with the Nundinae. The public disasters of 78 BC and 52 BC were attributed, by him to that unfortunate coincidence.[25] In 40 BC a day was inserted into the calendar, to be compensated for by the withdrawal of another day later on, to attempt to prevent it happening again. In reality, the additional day in 40 BC was likely to have been inserted due to a misplaced leap year in the new Julian calendar. There must have been many occasions when the Nundinae coincided with unlucky days.

Unfortunately, the introduction of the Julian calendar produced yet another 'unlucky' day, which was the extra day (24 February in leap years). It is interesting to note that even Cicero, sceptic though he generally was, in concert with the majority of educated people, hesitated to negotiate his daughter's betrothal in 56 BC during the two inauspicious days following the Latin Festival. [26] It is not possible at this distance in time to understand fully just how superstitious the average Roman actually was. It is like trying to compare the beliefs of a modern European regarding the 'sanctity' of holy days with the attitude of that person's medieval ancestors.

In the days of the Republic there were forty-five regular festivals, occurring on a fixed day each year, and shown on the public calendars as being 'dies festus' or 'feriatus'. The expenses were met by the public treasury of the state. They were, in most cases, anniversaries of dedication of altars or temples.

Apart from the Kalends of March, and the Poplifugia (for Jupiter) on the fifth day of July, no festivals were held earlier than the Nones in any month, the fifth or seventh days, and public notice was always given when festivals were due. A great many other days were given to public games, 'the ludi', which were separate from the dies feriati and probably a great deal more popular.

Games were themselves generously spread out, having eighteen days given to them in April, eight in July and a further fifteen in September, after the death of Julius Caesar another was added in his honour for September, making it sixteen. There were another fourteen days of games in November. Towards the end of the Republic, seven more days of games were added in honour of Sulla to commemorate his victory at the Battle of the Colline Gate in 82 BC. These were held from 26 October to 1 November annually.[27] Later, a further eleven days were added in honour of Caesar. The Romans obviously enjoyed sufficient leisure without needing to arrange a Sabbath day of rest in each week.

Rome's security and that of all Roman families depended on her fighting men, and campaigning also had its season. The levies of conscripts would generally be called up in March, and it was at this time that the sacred Shields of Mars, the ancilia, were brought out by the Priests of Mars, known as the Salii. Mars was honoured by a series of festivals as each campaigning season came round, when the young men would be kitted out by their devoted mothers and sisters, with home-made tunics, cloaks and the usual pairs of socks, packed to travel with them, as the women had always provided.

The moveable feasts were in addition to all these, and the dates would be announced each year by the Consul or a Praetor, by one of the priestly colleges or by a secular dignitary.[28] These festivals were known as the Feriae Conceptivae. The Latin Festival was the most important of them and lasted three or four days. It was always held early in the year as, in Republican times, when Consuls actually commanded the armies in battle, the festival had to be held before they left Rome.

There were also Feriae Imperativae, which were special occasions when the Senate voted and the Consuls chose days of offerings to the Gods. These could consist of prayers for intercession in times of trouble, or thanksgiving for a victory, perhaps days when a successful general was permitted to celebrate a Triumph on his return to Rome, although there were rarely more than two Triumphs in one year, and quite often none.[29]

Probably people actually attended only the most exciting or important days, and certainly the old 'agricultural' festivals came to have less significance to city dwellers. Cicero's correspondence shows how much attention was actually shown by an educated man during the Republic. There are between nine hundred and one thousand letters of his which survive, yet there is no suggestion that he observed the religious festivals at all.[30] On several occasions Cicero dated his letters by using the name of the current festival day, with references being made to the Quirinalia, Terminalia, Liberalia, Saturnalia and the Compitalia, but these were apparently used merely as dates in the calendar, and it seems that they held no particular religious significance for him. He did propose to confer the 'toga virilis' the sign of manhood, on his nephew Quintus Cicero on the Festival of Liberalia, but it seems that it was only because it was the traditional day to do so. He also mentions the Saturnalia (2 January in 49 BC) only because it was a general holiday for the servants. On the whole, prominent people tended to regard the festivals largely as an excuse to retire to their country villas if they had them, away from all the fuss.

Again, it should be borne in mind that the ordinary person did not actually cease work on most of these days, except perhaps during the games, which was a passion shared by all. The only actual requirement on religious days was that workers should down their tools and stand aside respectfully for a few minutes as a religious procession passed by. This was because it was considered that a religious day would be profaned or polluted if the priests saw men at work. Warning of the approach of such a procession was usually given by a crier, who walked on ahead of the formal proceedings.[31]

A small number of festivals did mean a general holiday. The Festival of Anna Perenna, on the 15 March, originally New Year's Day, was one when people tended to get very drunk by attempting to drink one cup of wine for every further year of life they hoped to enjoy. Four days later, the Quinquatrus was a holiday for those people who followed the Goddess Minerva, but especially for schoolchildren and their teachers. The only evidence available regarding the full-day holidays taken by workmen comes from Roman Egypt, where some contracts for apprenticeships or work-sheets have survived on papyrus. These concern the days off allowed to jewellers and weavers. In one case eighteen days per year were allowed, and another allowed twenty days, provided that they were taken on festival days. In a third case, thirty-six days per year were allowed, without any stipulation being given about them being on festival days only. Lucian's 'Parasite' says that every craftsman had at least one or two days off per month, so we may assume that the working man generally had days off to spend with his family.[32]

Some families had enough money to own a small villa in the country in order to escape the stifling summer heat of the city, a great blessing. If other family members, or even friends, had somewhere outside the city, then visits could be made, otherwise there was the spa. Records of more than a hundred spas have been found, where people could go for the 'cure' intended to improve gout, rheumatism, or various intestinal ailments, whether real or imaginary. Sulphur has for centuries been used for skin ailments and the sulphur baths at Albulae, within easy reach of Rome, were very popular.[33]

Bathing was always popular, even necessary. If one was wealthy enough there were private baths, but the public ones were always well attended. It was not, however, considered to be a 'family' activity as women did not generally bathe with men, particularly in the more austere Republic. In Pompeii at the time of Nero, the baths had different times of day for men and women to attend. Where the baths were large enough there were separate facilities entirely, with women entering through a different door. While always perfectly adequate, the female side was not on a par with the male side. This was presumably due to the men tending to meet there in the afternoons socially. They could do business there, eat or drink, have a massage, and while away several hours with friends. Women were expected to bathe then go home, so although they could, and did, meet friends there, there was no really appealing area to encourage them to linger too long. They were expected to have other things to do than loiter away the afternoon, as the men did.

There was a small fee involved for being allowed to bathe, and sometimes a politician, hoping for votes, would donate a 'free' day as a way of appearing magnanimous. As the Romans did not use soaps as much as oils, it was customary to coat the body, then scrape the oil, dirt and sweat back off with a curved instrument called a strigil, before actually entering the water. Oils could be bought at the baths, or people might take their own, often carried by a slave who would also do the scraping.

There is a story about the Emperor Hadrian visiting the baths. One day he noticed that, instead of using a strigil to scrape oil from his back, one man was rubbing his back against the wall. On being asked why he was doing this, the man replied that he was far too poor to afford to buy a slave to do it for him. The Emperor was sympathetic and ordered that the man be given enough money to buy a slave. On a later visit, Hadrian saw several men lined up and all vigorously rubbing themselves against the walls, hoping to attract the Emperor's attention. Unimpressed by their antics and their claims of poverty, he merely ordered that each man be provided with a strigil and be told that they should then scrape each other! This story indicates two things about the Emperor. One was that he wasn't stupid, and the other was that, despite having bath-houses of his own always at his disposal, he still considered it sensible occasionally to be seen to bathe with his subjects, to display the common touch. This was very important, even for the Imperial family. Even Julius Caesar was assassinated, so the later emperors, if they were wise enough, made some show of understanding the common people and sharing their way of life. Occasional displays of generosity also did no harm in the popularity stakes.

The facilities at the baths increased in elegance as time went on and, like the Emperor, wealthy people found it convenient to use the public baths even though country villas usually had their own, certainly by the second century BC. Even quite small villages also had some form of public bathing. Pliny's Laurentine villa had its own bath-house, but the village nearby had three public baths. Pliny said that he found it was 'a great convenience, if you arrive at the villa unexpectedly, or with the intention of staying only a short time, so that you are not inclined to have the fires lit in your own bath-house'.[34]

Some people bathed more than once a day, but even if it was personally more like once a week, it was the general habit for men to go to the baths after the midday meal or late in the afternoon. Sometimes a later bathe was desired as a means of sobering up after drinking too much at dinner. Women tended to bathe in the mornings, if they were obliged to use the same facilities as the men. Under the Republic, the baths in Rome closed once it was dark, although outside the city lamps were used so that bathing could continue after nightfall. Rome did not catch up with this innovation until the days of the early Empire.

Whether women were using their own baths or sharing those of the men at different times of the day, it is clear that the heating controls were turned down for the women. The Stabian baths at Pompeii, whose facilities were up-to-date and kept separate, were definitely kept cooler on the women's side than they were for the men, nor did the women have access to the outside space of the Palaestra for exercising or relaxing after bathing, as the men did.[35] There were, however, the equivalent of cafes close by, where women could see their friends if they did not intend to go straight home.

A notice outside the men's baths at Trastavere in Rome stated 'MEN'S BATHS. NO WOMEN ADMITTED. BY ORDER.' But at Praeneste a notice suggests that on 1 April, for the Festival of Fortuna Virilis, women were allowed to sacrifice and perhaps even bathed at the men's baths. Women tended to wear a pair of panties in the baths, but men usually bathed naked. This gave rise to the convention that a man should not attend the baths with his own sons once they reached puberty. Whether this was to save their modesty, or his own, or because they might lose respect for their Paterfamilias if they saw him naked, is not clear. Again, women slightly lost out on the charges, as the men paid around half an 'as', while the women were usually charged double that.

It would appear that, as new public baths were built, the older ones were given over to the women. Even after two new public baths were built at Pompeii it is clear that the old one was kept in use, which is shown by the up-to-date Flavian styles of decoration within it. There is similar evidence available at the baths at Ostia.

There were also, at one point, 170 completely free warm-bathing establishments in Rome we know of, and these had increased in number by Pliny the Elder's time. These were very useful indeed for poorer people, but it also seems likely that some of them offered other services than merely bathing, and sometimes even allowed men and women to bathe together. They would not, therefore, be the type of places that respectable women would want to frequent, nor would their husbands allow it.[36]

Any respectable middle-class female would spend most of her time at home, although any woman married to a tradesman or shopkeeper found life far busier, and perhaps more interesting, as she would be expected to help her husband with his work. She also naturally exchanged visits with family and friends, but she would have duties to perform other than the social niceties. She would not only have to run her household but attend to the upbringing and early education of any smaller children she might have. The older children might have private tutors, or, if this was too expensive, they could attend schools in Rome which often taught in the streets, where a teacher would set up in a quiet corner and charge each pupil a small fee.

One of the most important duties of any woman who spent most of her time in the home was weaving. From the earliest days it had been essential for her to provide the family's clothing by weaving the cloth herself. It continued to be considered a properly ladylike tradition, and even as late as the reign of the Emperor Augustus, the Emperor wore home-made cloth inside the house. It is said that he insisted that the women of the Imperial family kept up the tradition of home-weaving, in the tradition of the earlier Roman women who not only produced cloth for tunics, but also linens, blankets, towels and all other fabrics used by the family.[37] This work alone would have kept them almost continually busy, even with slaves to deal with other domestic work. As time went on and labour generally became more specialised, the need for women to weave at home became less essential, along with such daily tasks as the family's bread being produced within the household, which was handed over to professional bakeries. However, traditionally minded men still liked to see their women weaving, and some, like Augustus, still proudly wore the results of their wife's labours, even if only privately within the home.

In any such situation, the expressed wishes of the husband and father should be obeyed. It was the duty of the woman to run the house as efficiently as possible, and to rear the children to be respectful and obedient. Even the Empress Livia Drusilla, the wife of Augustus, played her part in creating the ideal Roman family, though a woman with firm opinions of her own might be quite likely to share those opinions with her husband when they were alone. Fortunately, her marriage with Augustus was a love match, so she was far more fortunate than many women of the time and was more likely to enjoy certain freedoms within marriage and a greater likelihood of harmony at home.

The Empress Livia Drusilla (born 59/58 BC) who would later be renamed Julia Augusta after her formal adoption into the Julian family in 14 AD, was the daughter of Marcus Livius Drusus Claudianus and his wife Aufidia. Livia had been married first to Tiberius Claudius Nero, a cousin of Patrician status. Livia's father committed suicide after the Battle of Philippi, but her husband had continued to oppose Octavianus/Augustus. Her first child, the future Emperor Tiberius, was born in 42 BC and two years later the family had to flee the country to avoid the persecutions of Marcus Antonius, Marcus Aemilius Lepidus and Octavianus.

They joined with Sextus Pompeius who opposed the new Triumvirate, in Sicily. After peace was finally established and an amnesty announced, Livia returned to Rome and was introduced to Octavianus in 39 BC. She was then pregnant with her second son (Nero Claudius Drusus). Octavianus divorced his wife Scribonia in order to marry Livia very shortly after Scribonia gave birth to their daughter, Julia the Elder. Tiberius Claudius Nero had already been persuaded, or forced, to divorce Livia to free her to marry Octavianus. Her ex-husband actually gave her away at her second wedding, in his position as her Paterfamilias. Livia Drusilla and Octavianus were happily married for fifty-one years, after becoming the Emperor Augustus and the Empress Julia Augusta. She outlived him by fifteen years, dying at the age of eighty-six or eighty-seven. She was deified thirteen years after her death.

Unfortunately, for most women the family home was not a spacious house with gardens, nor in a salubrious area of the city. Nor was it a villa in the country. The majority of Romans lived in 'insulae' or apartments (insula means island). These blocks of apartments could rise several floors above the busy streets and were often rented out by slum landlords. They were equally often poorly built and very small, becoming more shoddy in structure the higher they rose, both to save weight and to save building costs. There are still some of these apartment blocks remaining in Rome, and it is surprising how small and dark they are, probably one of the reasons why their residents spent so much of their time out of doors. They also quite often caught fire, although many of them had no cooking facilities and were little more than a basic shelter. Not for these people wall paintings and mosaic floors, or the inlaid furniture bought by the husband.[38]

In these properties there was no money for slaves, and no space in which to house them. In the days of the Republic, it had been considered that the inability to own even one slave meant that an individual was of the poorest level. Even rather higher up the social scale, unless one belonged to a wealthy family, the rooms within any house would be small, especially the sleeping chambers, which were also usually quite dark and airless.

Except in the most expensive houses, the private rooms were fairly basic, with all the available money being spent 'for show' and lavished on the rooms that other people were likely to see and admire and hopefully envy. Tables, often of beautiful and valuable citrus wood, were very popular. Ornamented couches and chairs were also an extravagance of those who had money to spend, while others concentrated on collecting expensive ornamental fish to live in pools in their gardens. These fish could sometimes find themselves the pets of Emperors, and wore jewelled rings attached to their fins to display their owner's wealth.

Women who had money to spend often preferred jewellery. A woman's jewellery was likely to remain her own even if she divorced, whereas everything in the home belonged to the husband. Pearls were a great Roman favourite and many pairs of pearl earrings have been discovered. In Republican times the Porticus Margaritaria at the end of the Forum beyond the Domus Publicus of the Pontefex Maximus was the centre of this luxury trade, with shops selling perfumes, jewels, and especially pearls (margaritae). Pliny the Elder remarked that 'If a husband complained about his wife's expenditure on jewellery, she was quite likely to retort "what about your tables?" in reply.'[39]

One item that any family of status would want to display in their atrium was their collection of wax ancestor masks, the 'imagines', which were shown off either in small temple-like boxes or hung on the walls of the entrance to the house. They confirmed the illustrious descent of the family, as they could only be displayed when one member of the family had done something worthy, such as becoming Consul. A collection of such masks would prove that a family had been active in affairs over generations.

The beautifully painted and bewigged wax images, made to look as lifelike as possible, were items of enormous reverence, and once a man was considered worthy his mask would be made and added proudly to the collection, or perhaps hopefully began a new collection. This honour was very occasionally extended to a man who was not consular but had performed some other extraordinary service for Rome. When a man of family died, actors would be employed to wear the masks and impersonate the ancestors, as if the honoured dead had attended his funeral in person.

There were many things on which people who had, or were able to acquire, money could squander their resources. A woman named Ummidia Quadratilla kept a private company of dancers, who performed both publicly and privately at her house. When she died in 107 AD, at the advanced age of just over eighty, they were inherited, along with two-thirds of her property, by her grandson. The grandson along with his wife and family had lived in the house for many years, and he had ostentatiously refused ever to watch his grandmother's dancers perform. After her death, they gave just one more public performance and were then dismissed.[40]

Most women did live 'normal' lives, going out of their houses to shop, to go to the baths, to make visits, worship at temples, or be entertained by some public spectacle. Women sometimes went with their husbands to dinner parties, and they would certainly be permitted a social circle of their own among women of their own class, so long as the husband did not suspect his wife of adultery or any other wrongdoing.

In Rome a woman was not allowed to drive around the city. The privilege of travelling in a 'carpentum', a small covered wagon pulled by two horses, was reserved for Vestal Virgins and other priestesses; but women did normally travel in a type of sedan chair (a sella) or in a litter (a lectica). A litter was rather grander and far more comfortable, but for a short distance a chair could be hired, if the woman did not possess one of her own, and this would be cheaper than a litter. For any longer journey, a litter carried by bearers was by far the smartest way to travel. It was covered and curtained and the finest may even have had windows.[41]

A variety of legal restrictions were placed on the use of these litters in the city. Caesar would only allow them at certain hours and even then, only for use by ladies of a certain age. Generally, it appears that for women to travel around the city they needed to be of a certain rank also, which would give them the status to have pedestrians pushed out of the way to let their litter through.

There were, of course, always the usual complaints about women gallivanting about, enjoying freedoms which some men viewed with suspicion. Ovid complained that there were so many places for them to go to, that they could not easily be kept an eye on.[42] It does seem, however, that he was fretting more about the activities of a favourite mistress than a wife, when it might be reasonable that his suspicions and jealousy should be aroused. A mistress would also have far more opportunities for enjoyment than would a wife; chances to meet other men and make her lover wonder what she got up to when he could not see her, having more freedom than would be allowed to a wife. This is the real reason for Ovid's railing against women having too much freedom.

In the preface to his *History of Rome*, Livy, though then writing about the reign of Augustus, bewailed the loss of the good old standards of true Republican days:

> I hope everyone will pay keen attention to the moral life of earlier times. To the personalities and the principles of the men, responsible both at home and in the field, for the foundation and the growth of empire, and will appreciate the subsequent decline in discipline and in moral standards, the collapse and disintegration of morality down to the present day. For we have now reached a point where our degeneracy is intolerable, and so are the measures by which alone it can be reformed.[43]

He had a point if Augustus's own daughter Julia was used as an example of loose living. Despite her many affairs, it was remarked on that her children closely resembled her then husband, Marcus Agrippa. She replied to enquiries by saying 'I never take on a passenger unless the ship's hold is already full,' thereby using her legitimate pregnancies as a cover for her affairs.

It has always been easy to look back and consider that previous generations were better, braver, more competitive, more successful, more moral and well behaved. The Republic with all its problems could hardly be described as a perfect time, but Livy would have been dismayed if he could have seen to what levels the newly formed empire could fall. At least in the rule of Augustus and Livia there was a role model of sorts, as both parties to that marriage were sensible and concerned for Rome's welfare.

Cato, during the Republic, had been just such another backward-looker, being an admirer of the old Roman austerity, who modelled himself on his great-grandfather Marcus Porcius Cato the Censor (234-149 BC). He had been a statesman, a writer and a soldier who served in the Second Punic War, and had always emphasised the true Roman virtues, particularly those of simple country living.

His great-grandson, another Marcus Porcius Cato[44] shared the Roman stage with such men as Cicero, Caesar, Pompeius Magnus and others of the final great years of the Republic. He was never an easy man, nor was he a happy one. He studied rhetoric and Stoic philosophy, which were powerful influences on his life and career. He divorced his first wife for adultery, but his relationship with his second, Marcia, was highly unusual. His good friend Hortensius wanted to marry again as he had no children. Cato stoically divorced his wife so that Hortensius could marry her. Some said that this unusual act was because Cato feared that his love for her was too great, and against his belief that he should keep a distance between himself and others, and not indulge in close relationships which could only bring pain. His sacrifice of his marriage to his friend's need would be, in his opinion, a correct act. However, Hortensius and Marcia had no children and when Hortensius died Cato remarried Marcia.[45]

Cato's stern, unbending character was even out of sync with the Republican values he professed, as he practised a level of austerity that was fast losing favour. He was passionately attached to an ideal that was dying, and while times were changing, he was being left behind. Gaius Julius Caesar had already ridden roughshod over the principles of the few men like Cato, pressing on with his belief in his destiny to be Rome's sole ruler (although he would never dare to use the title of king). For Cato, the distance from Rome's moral and political ideal that Caesar had already travelled was uncomfortable enough and he chose suicide, not only to end his life but as a political protest, when he believed that the old Republic was dead.[46] Cato's character probably made him very difficult to live with and he believed that resistance could prevent times from moving on, even though such resistance made life more unpleasant for his family than it needed to be. In common with other people who stood outside of what was normal, he was considered comical by young people, who were eager to embrace the delights of modern life. Yet, later, when those same people looked back, Cato could be viewed differently – as a man who refused to be seduced by new and often tawdry distractions, one who had upheld all that was most noble in the standards of the virtuous man, who opposed the very idea of a Dictatorship in Perpetuity, or kingship by another name.

A Dictator was intended to be a Roman magistrate appointed by the Consuls on instructions from the Senate, to deal with an extraordinary crisis in government. His duties were primarily military, his other title being Magister Populi or Master of the Infantry. He then appointed a Master of Horse, or Magister Equitum. These functions were intended to leave one Consul free to carry on with the civilian government while the crisis was dealt with. The post was for six months only, or the length of one campaign season. Alone among magistrates, the

Dictator was fully indemnified against all of his actions while in office and could not be brought to trial for them when he stepped down.

Sulla used his period of office (from 81 BC) to enact new laws and frame a new constitution, but he did eventually step down (in 79 BC) and went into retirement as he had promised to do. When Caesar became Dictator he had no intention of ever stepping down, carrying his dictatorial powers much further than Sulla ever had, to the despair of those people who regretted the loss of the Republic.

It was certainly true that Republican women were less emancipated, lived simpler lives and perhaps did behave with more circumspection than women during the Empire. However, the male versus female struggle had gone on for centuries and family life has always been a series of advances and retreats. Even in societies where women have been firmly controlled there has been a place for the woman of decency and common sense who manages to have her say without being strident – and a sensible man will entrust his household and the upbringing of his children to her. Only an extremist such as Cato would wish to tear the heart out of his household by giving his wife to another man, not because their marriage had failed, but because he feared that his strength of feeling would give her undue influence over him. Such Stoicism was the old face of Rome and things would certainly change. However, not all women were decadent and the best of them would retain the old values without strict supervision from a father or a husband.

One of the few ways in which a Roman woman could acquire some independence was, surprisingly enough, through the practice of medicine. Not just as midwives and nurses, or through the use of folk medicine or charms as wise women, but as respected female doctors, known as Medicae. They were skilled in female ailments and although they most likely dealt largely with women and their particular problems, there is no evidence that they practised this branch of medicine exclusively. Some of these women were probably slaves or freedwomen, but many came from families already connected to the medical profession. These women were not drawn from only one class but were from many levels of society. While later women, in medieval Europe, were restricted to the practice of the 'magic arts' and their attempts at cures openly criticised as being 'only prayers and charms'[47] by more fortunate males who had had the privilege of some sort of medical training, these Roman medical women were treated respectfully and were indeed respectable, responsible and capable people, as is shown by the memorial to one such Medicae, Julia Saturnina of Merida, whose epitaph was written by her husband. It describes her as 'an incomparable wife, the best physician, and a most virtuous woman'.[48] It would seem that this woman, and others like her, led industrious and very useful lives, and could be greatly missed.

Unfortunately, such Medicae were generally fewer in number than their male counterparts, the Medici, although in the field of women's problems these 'obstetrics' often served in place of male doctors. There were many women (and husbands) who did not like the idea of being intimately examined by a man, and who found it far easier to discuss symptoms with another woman, who might be expected to more fully understand the feelings of the sufferer. Soranus said 'the public is wont to call in midwives in cases of sickness or when the women suffer something peculiar, which they do not have in common with men.'[49]

This emphasis on midwifery should not detract from the more varied work that these women did. There were many women, of all classes, who did not wish to confide in a male doctor, or who might not be permitted to do so, such as the Vestals, who were always attended by professional women doctors, highly trained in all forms of medicine. Even Martial, a writer who was usually quite sarcastic regarding the achievements of women, spoke very highly of the Medicae.[50] They had a position of vastly higher status than the 'herb women' of later centuries and were better trained and more widely accepted than their medieval descendants, earning their position of respect. One of them, a lady named Victoria, was so highly thought of that the Imperial Physician Theodorus Priscianus, during the fourth century AD, dedicated his book on gynaecology to her, with the words 'artis meae duice ministerium', meaning 'the sweet teacher of my art'.

The famous physician Claudius Galenus (Galen)[51] often referred in his writings to the use of female doctors for women's diseases. One of his more famous quotes refers to a patient's reliance on a good doctor, saying that 'Confidence and hope do far more good than physic.'

It is reassuring to know that Roman women were not neglected in medical matters and were able to rely with confidence on other women, at every level, to whom they could confide their symptoms with reasonable expectation of receiving a cure, or at least help. They could be sure of the sympathy of another woman, who could share their concerns and help to ease their problems, a woman who had 'seen it all before' and understood the pressures of women trying to hold their place in a male society. It is very important to realise that women could, and did, manage to live fulfilled and useful lives, albeit usually within the family structure.

Within that structure they could also engage in trade, as women certainly did work as merchants and in the markets. They could be active as scribes and entertainers of various kinds, and an intelligent and capable woman was invaluable in any family with a shop or business, helping her husband by dealing not only with customers but also keeping the books.

In up-market areas they could help to provide and sell luxuries for the wealthy and were known to design clothing and jewellery to be made and sold. All Romans were expected to work hard, and the women working within the family would also bear and raise the next generation, who made all the effort worthwhile. These women, occupying a place between the richest and the poorest, found freedoms not necessarily available to either, and in the bustling, noisy, colourful and exciting world of Rome, who is to say that they did not actually have the best of it?

3

Marriage and Motherhood

Although a Roman woman was subject to her father, and then after marriage to her husband, she was not expected to live in seclusion as Greek women generally did. Along with her husband she had definite responsibilities to her family, especially to her new family after marriage, where she would be expected to take an active role and run the indoor household. She was responsible not only for the smooth running of that household, the control and direction of servants and the upbringing of children, but also for the religious cult of the family she would help to create.

Towards the end of the Republican period a definite sense of emancipation began to take place. This was by no means a full allowance of freedom, but it did mark a change from the absolute and sometimes stifling domesticity previously expected of many women. This change was largely due to the form of marriage itself. By then there were three forms of marriage, in every case requiring that the woman submit herself to some male, either a husband, or in some cases, remaining under the control of the father.

The first of these was known as 'coemptio' and was a primitive form of bride-purchase. In fact, the groom made a fictitious 'purchase' of the bride in the presence of witnesses. He paid a small sum, 'nummus unus', to the woman's father or legal guardian, and received her in exchange.

The second was basically a union based on cohabitation, as with a common-law relationship, which is supposed to be exclusive, yet is not a legal form of marriage. There must, in Roman times, have been some form of declaration between the parties that they intended to participate in this form of semi-marriage union, or there would have been nothing to distinguish it from a man merely living with his mistress. Perhaps for this reason, in this form of union the man did not acquire full authority over his 'wife' until they had lived continuously together for over a year. This simpler form was commonly known as 'usus' marriage. Some men (and women) got around the year's cohabitation rule which made the arrangement more permanent by separating themselves from their partner for three days in each year, thus breaking the necessary continuity.

The third form of marriage, 'confarreatio' was by far the most binding, as mentioned earlier, dating back to the earliest days of Roman marriages. Even then, and even under the Empire, it was considered to be the only fully legitimate form of marriage for members of the nobility and certainly for the most important of the priesthoods, which were the Pontifex Maximus, the Rex Sacrorum (the second ranking Pontifex), the Flamen Dialis, the Flamen Martialis, and the Flamen Quirinalis. After the performance of a confarreatio marriage, divorce became enormously difficult and complicated. So much so, that it made the marriage effectively indissoluble.[1]

By the end of the third century BC a 'free' form of marriage had become far more usual and acceptable, except among those whose social or religious standing demanded more. In this form the wife was even able to retain her personal property outside of the marriage and away from the control of the husband. It also made the prospect of divorce, or 'diffareatio', far more attainable.

By the time of the early Empire, during the reign of Augustus, new legislation provided a way for women to free themselves from the formal supervision of male guardians. According to the 'jus liberorum', any freeborn woman who bore three children for Rome, and any freedwoman who bore four, became exempt from formal guardianship.[2] This not only contradicted the doctrine that a woman could not be sensible enough to rule herself, without the advice of a man, but then rather unfortunately suggested instead that her common sense descended upon a woman through her womb, rather than her brain. However, the new rule didn't make very much difference to how business was actually conducted, and even after a law of Claudius in the first century AD had abolished automatic guardianship of agnates over women, many illiterate women were forced to continue to have documents signed for them by a male relative.[3]

In all of these methods of contracting a family relationship, the most obvious feature of the woman's change from maiden to matron was in her change of habitation. Less obvious was whether her father or guardian had decided that she should remain under his own authority, or whether he had transferred that authority, along with the woman, to the power or 'manus' of the new husband. This was entirely the decision of the Paterfamilias. If the marriage was conducted with 'manus' then the bride became a part of her husband's family, so far as any property rights were concerned, and she would be treated almost as though she were his daughter and under his full authority. However, even in a 'manus' marriage, the bride's blood relatives could continue their involvement with her and continued to be a part of her future guidance and with concern for her welfare.

In early Rome Cato the Censor (234-149 BC) had claimed that husbands had unlimited rights to judge the behaviour of wives and could inflict the death penalty for adultery or for drinking wine. This horror of a drinking woman was so prevalent that even in 153 AD a woman donor to a male collegium made a point of excluding herself from the drinking, towards which she had also donated.[4]

By the time of the late Republic, a marriage without manus became the more common form. This is thought to have been due to the fact that a full 'manus' marriage would take the bride fully into the family of the husband, thereby giving her some rights to her husband's property. The family of the bridegroom preferred to avoid this, if possible, often stipulating that the marriage be without manus. Similarly, if the woman was a member of a wealthy family, they would prefer a marriage to be non-manus, so that in the case of a divorce the woman's property could be reclaimed by her birth family.

Unfortunately, the rise of marriages without manus tended to lead to a general instability of marriages, making many unions during the late Republic rather fragile things, and few of them particularly long-lasting. Any wife who was able to return to her birth family, with her fortune intact, was naturally less likely to be amenable to any husband's control.[5]

It gave the woman far more freedom since the father or legal guardian, whose authority she was still officially under, actually lived in a different house, therefore could not see how she normally behaved, and the husband with whom she lived did not have full legal control over her. Unfortunately, this worked both ways, and the wife could just as easily find herself quickly replaced. The greater number of children a man had, the more he could arrange good marriages for them, with families whose relationship could be beneficial to him. Therefore, very many upper-class marriages were made merely for the sake of shifting alliances, and then they could easily be dissolved if those allegiances changed. The only blessing with this system was that there was no stigma attached to having been divorced, as it was realised that personal affection often had little place in these marriages, so that feelings were not hurt and the parties were assumed to marry again elsewhere without rancour.

Gaius Julius Caesar was married three times, not counting his relationship with the Egyptian Queen Cleopatra VII, which was legal under Egyptian law, but not by Roman law. Lucius Cornelius Sulla married four times and Gnaeus Pompeius Magnus married five times, actually marrying his second wife, Aemilia Scaura, while she was pregnant with the child of her first husband, as we have seen.[6] The women concerned in these political matches were not necessarily consulted. Such matches were intended to begin or continue a political agreement and were easily dissolved to suit expediency.

Octavianus broke a betrothal to Servilia in order to become betrothed to Marc Antony's stepdaughter Clodia. He then broke that arrangement too, in order to marry Scribonia, who bore him his only daughter Julia (he was her third husband), then he divorced Scribonia in order to marry Livia Drusilla. She, in turn, had had to be divorced from her then husband Tiberius Claudius Nero, in order to marry Octavianus, even though she was pregnant by him with their second child. After divorce all children became the property of the father, which was the only fly in the ointment in this rapidly shifting marital game of musical beds, as the women lost their children.

Augustus was later to dictate the marriages of his sister Octavia the Younger (69-11 BC), who was married first to Gaius Claudius Marcellus Minor, then to Marc Antony for political purposes. This making and remaking of alliances must have made the marriage bond a very fragile and temporary thing, and it must have seemed sensible to avoid investing any great emotional commitment into these unions, when they were likely to be dissolved and remade with someone else. It must, however, have made life very unstable for the women, knowing as they did that they would lose husband, home and children if circumstances changed.

Every woman hoped for children with her current husband, greatly fearing to be infertile, even allowing for the possibility of losing them if a divorce loomed. Though they would, in such cases, no longer be a part of her life, she might hope to meet with them again years later and hopefully know that they did not attribute any blame to her for having to leave them. Yet she would still have missed their years of development and they would appear later in her life as virtual strangers.

At one point, during the reign of Augustus, many women could have found themselves affected by his law regarding the remarriage of childless women between the ages of twenty and fifty. Any woman considered still young enough to bear a child was to remarry a year after the death of a husband, or within six months from the date of any divorce. Only if she had been divorced by her husband for adultery would she be forbidden to remarry.

During the Republic, a widow was expected to show respect towards her deceased husband by not marrying again within ten months, in the Empire that period later became twelve months. Any woman who breached these rules risked having to relinquish any inheritance from her late husband, and was barred from intestate succession, except from her closest relatives.[7]

Despite all the potential problems, any girl's first marriage was a time of joy and hope. Marriage was allowed from the age of twelve for a girl and fourteen for a boy, although they did not usually take place at such a young age. With the lower classes there was always delay due to the problem of providing a dowry, and although this was not a problem with wealthy families, the young couple would still very likely be in their late teens before they married. Deference to the wishes of the parent or guardian would be expected, although the girl's mother might hope to have some input in the choice of a husband for her daughter.

There was a story from the second century BC that the great Scipio Africanus, having just arranged the marriage of his daughter Cornelia at a male-only banquet, was berated by his wife on his return home. She was angry, saying that she had a right to be consulted as the girl was 'her daughter as much as his' and she went on to say that 'even if he intended to marry Cornelia to Tiberius Gracchus himself, she ought to have been consulted!' Fortunately, that was the very man he had just agreed the marriage with, so the mother was mollified at the best possible match for her daughter, but the sentiments she had expressed were still considered to be viable.[8] Only in the household of a man such as Cato the Younger, at the end of the Republic, where the women were expected to submit to old-fashioned notions of discipline, and were obliged to accept his decisions with subservience, would there have been no argument at all.

Families frequently asked the opinions of friends, when looking for suitable marriage partners for their children. Once the children approached puberty recommendations would be asked for and the future partners discussed. Any marriage conducted between young persons who had not achieved puberty was illegal, as was the marriage of close relatives, known as 'incestum'. This had originally been punishable by death, later by deportation, but the definition of how close a relative could be, and marriage remain legal, changed over time. Once the marriage of second cousins was banned, but by the second century BC even first cousin marriages were allowed. The Emperor Marcus Aurelius and his wife Faustina the Younger were first cousins. Public opinion had been shocked in the year 49 AD when Messalina was chosen to be the wife of the Emperor Claudius, as he was her uncle. By the fourth century AD marriages between uncle and niece were again forbidden.[9]

There were also the unions which were forbidden by custom, such as marriages between Romans and foreigners, which accounted for the illegality of the relationship between Caesar and Cleopatra, and later Marc Antony and Cleopatra, although they were both legal by Egyptian law. A Roman woman might not marry a slave, before 445 BC a Plebeian could not marry a Patrician. A senator could not marry a freedwoman, nor could even the descendant of a senator. This meant that after the Lex Julia of 18 BC, any female descendant of a senator through male descent, could not marry a freedman, which may have proved awkward when a man who could rise to the consulship might have the children of a freedman as nephews or nieces, and they could be from an otherwise wealthy and eligible family.[10]

A woman who lived in the provinces could not marry any official in the Roman administrative service of that province, nor, sensibly, could she marry her guardian if she was a ward, nor could her guardian marry her to his own son or grandson.[11] If any of these conditions were transgressed, then the marriage would be invalid and any children born of it would be illegitimate.

Legal status could be a problem. When a fully Roman woman married a fully Roman man, then their children were Roman. If a Roman woman married a man who was not a Roman citizen but possessed 'conubium', which was the right of intermarriage, then their children would not be Roman citizens. If, however, the man did not have the right of intermarriage, their children would follow the mother's rights and they would then have Roman citizenship. This practice was to change with the passing of the Lex Minicia (date unknown), after which a marriage between a Roman woman and a husband who did not have 'conubium' would mean that the children inherited the inferior state of their father. The Emperor Hadrian later altered this law to allow these children of a Roman mother and a Latin father to automatically be full Roman citizens.[12]

A girl or woman could not marry without the consent of her guardian, though theoretically she could appeal at court against any unreasonable refusal. Even as a young widow (under the age of twenty-five) her relatives could bring pressure to bear if she wished to marry someone they considered unsuitable. They could even appeal to a magistrate in order to prevent such a marriage.

Betrothal in infancy did take place, although later in the Empire it became law that a child must be able to understand what was said, therefore it must be no younger than seven years old. Augustus legislated that an engagement was not to be recognised in law if the girl was under the age of ten, although that didn't prevent Octavia, daughter of the Emperor Claudius, from being betrothed to Lucius Junius Silanus when she was a year old and he was about fifteen.[13] Any informal agreement to marry, even made before witnesses and in writing, could later be renounced by either party with the phrase 'condicione tua non utor'.

Betrothal gifts could be exchanged, but were usually fairly simple, although a man could make a substantial gift to the bride before the wedding, known as the 'donato ante nuptias' which would be given back to him by the bride's family, along with her dowry, at the marriage itself. This increased the amount she would receive if she were widowed. This had to be agreed before the marriage, as Roman law forbade the exchange of substantial gifts between husband and wife. The engaged couple, then known as 'sponsus' and 'sponsa' would seal the agreement with a kiss, and the man placed an iron ring on the third finger of the woman's left hand, believed to be directly connected to the heart, a superstition which has stood the test of time.

Fixing the marriage day was not, of course, merely a matter of personal choice. There were so many unlucky days which were not considered suitable for marriages, whose prohibitions and superstitions had to be abided by, particularly for a first marriage. Nobody could afford to invite bad luck to the wedding by marrying on a day considered inauspicious.[14]

It was impossible to conduct any marriage when the spirits of the dead were at large, as they were mischievous, and if the wandering spirit happened to be the bride's deceased husband, he could be potentially vindictive. For this reason, the Parentalia had to be avoided, which took place in the third week in February. The days when the Mundus was opened were particularly bad, allowing the spirits to rise up from the Underworld to interfere with the lives of the still living. There was also the month of May, when families usually made sacrifice to the spirits of their dead – this superstition has also stayed with us, with the saying 'Marry in May, rue the day!'

The first half of June, now so popular, was for Romans when the Temple of Vesta was cleaned, with the sweeping away of all the bad old things from the previous year, so that was also inauspicious, presenting another limitation. Early in March, when the Priests of Mars, the Salii who danced, moved the Sacred Shields was yet another. These shields, it was believed, numbered among them just one which had come down from Mars himself, but nobody knew which was the actual gift of the god. This prohibition was due to the idea that 'arms meant fighting, and fighting should be alien to the spirit of marriage.'[15]

Festival days were also bad for a first marriage, but acceptable for subsequent marriages. The reason for this was that a first marriage should be attended by a large and joyful wedding party, but on a day of festival it was unlikely to attract a sufficient turnout due to other distractions. A smaller wedding, with fewer guests, was appropriate for a remarriage, so that problem did not arise.[16] The Kalends, Nones and Ides were generally 'black' days so again were not suitable days for a bride to begin her religious duties in her new home.[17]

The best days for weddings, especially the all-important first wedding, were considered to be the second half of June, as it was considered the season of growth and fruitfulness. This is another superstition we tend to keep, although in the case of brides in northern countries the hope for good weather has to be a factor. The deities of marriage luck, Ceres, Tellus, Picumnus and Pilumnus, were all gods and goddesses connected to the land and agriculture, which was a survival from the time when Romans were primarily farmers.

Once all of these obstacles had been negotiated and the arrangements were made, the wedding itself could finally take place. There was a succession of ceremonies at the bride's parents' house, including one where she surrendered her childhood toys before embarking on adult life. Similar ceremonies would have been taking place at the groom's home before the couple were dressed in their formal robes.

The bride's hair was traditionally parted into six sections, 'sex crines', which were fastened with wooden fillets, 'vittae' at the top of her head, in a cone shape known as a 'tutulus'. This was a style reserved only for brides on their wedding day, and for priestesses. The parting of the bride's hair was meant to be with an iron spearhead, in the early days it was considered particularly lucky if this could be done with one that had killed a gladiator! This traditional requirement was sometimes mocked by the poets, who remarked on brides having their hair parted with 'spears dripping blood', though it is hardly likely that the family went quite that far.

The bride's veil was a fine transparent oblong, more like a wide scarf, in a vibrant flame-orange colour that matched her shoes. A wreath of marjoram was placed on top of the veil. The wedding gown was a 'tunica recta', which meant it was a tunic woven on an old-fashioned upright loom. This was usually a fine muslin-like fabric, often white or cream in colour. From the wedding day the bride would wear a matron's stola, so it was the final time she would wear the young woman's tunic. It was knotted at the waist with a woollen girdle tied in the 'knot of Hercules' for good luck.[18]

The bride was then taken in procession to the groom's parents' house. In Republican times this was preceded by the taking of the auguries to make absolutely sure of good fortune for the day ahead. During the ceremony the bride would declare herself the groom's wife with the words, 'Ubi tu Gaius, ego Gaia' meaning 'If you are Gaius, I am Gaia' thus declaring herself the female half of a partnership, although the bride's name did not actually change and she did not take her new husband's family names. She was then led by the 'pronuba' or bridesmaid, who had to be a woman who had only been married once, and the bride joined hands with her husband. A sacrifice took place, usually of a pig, and if the marriage was the most binding one of confarreatio the couple would sit on chairs covered by sheep's fleeces and share spelt-cakes.

The marriage contract itself, the 'tabulae nuptiales' would be read out by the auspex, although in earlier times, and certainly during the Republic, this duty was taken by a full priest. The contract would be then signed by as many as ten of the guests. A contract survives from a marriage that took place in the first century AD in Roman Egypt. It shows that the bride's clothing and jewellery was itemised, with the value of each article recorded.[19] After the contract was signed, the guests wished the couple good luck, 'feliciter', and the wedding feast followed. This was generally limited to a certain amount of expenditure, due to the Lex Licinia Sumptuaria, or luxury law, which forbade excesses.

In the evening the bride was taken to her new home, after being formally removed from the arms of her mother. It showed a becoming modesty if the bride showed some reluctance at that point. She was then accompanied by friends and family, with a good deal of shouting and many vulgar comments, one of the catcalls on such occasions being 'talasio' which had largely lost its original meaning but is believed to have dated from the original capture of the Sabine women, when the most attractive of the captives was reserved for a powerful Roman named Talasius.

People threw walnuts for children to pick up, while three young boys, who must be sons of still-living parents, played a part in the procession to the couple's new home. One of the boys walked in front of the bride carrying a torch which had been lit in her former home, while the two others held her hands. Again, it appears that this represents leading the bride gently into her new life. When the procession reached the house, the torch was thrown away and there was a scramble to catch it, as it represented good luck. This torch is today replaced by the bride's wedding bouquet.

The bride was required to rub oil and fat on the doorposts, and wreath them with wool. She was then lifted over the threshold by the bridegroom.[20]

Once inside the house, of which the bride was then the mistress, she passed her hand over bowls of fire and water, to signify that she would from then onwards be the controller of the necessities to provision the household. In the entrance hall, or atrium, a small marriage bed would have been set up, but this was not for the use of the newly married couple. It was for their spirits, the bridegroom's 'genius' and the bride's 'juno'. One of the young boys would finally escort the bride to her new bedchamber, where she was prepared for bed by women who had only been married once, and after she was ready and the women retired, the bridegroom was admitted. The following morning, the new mistress of the household would make offerings to the family's household lares, and for the first time take part in the religious observances of her new family.

In Rome, a woman who had been married only once had a certain standing, she was known as 'univarae' and the relative importance of that was shown by only such women being considered suitable to prepare the bride for her marriage bed. Subsequent marriages, though perfectly usual, did not have the same importance as the first one. They would be performed with far less ceremonial, certain parts would be missed out altogether, and the whole wedding would be conducted in a quieter manner. However, a bride who was marrying for the first time was entitled to the full ceremonial, even if the man she was marrying had been married before.

The full performance was not always carried out even with first marriages. Many families would not have been able to afford the expense, but the main parts, the flame-coloured bridal veil, the signing of the contract, the sacrifice and some sort of wedding feast followed by a procession to the new home, would generally be attempted.

The amount of the bride's dowry would, likewise, be determined by the wealth and standing of the families concerned. By the time of the early Empire, one million sesterces was a recognised sum in high-status marriages, although at the end of the Republic, when Gaius Julius Caesar gave that sum to Gnaeus Pompeius Magnus along with his only daughter Julia, he was obliged to borrow it from Marcus Licinius Crassus (known as 'Dives' or the rich.)[21] Before his death, the elder Scipio had settled a dowry of fifty talents on each of his two daughters. One silver talent was approximately 25kg in weight, (or 50/55 lbs) and the fifty-talent dowry was the substantial sum of a million and a quarter sesterces, a great deal of money.

The dowry, whether large or small, was usually paid in three equal instalments, each part paid annually, and for many families it sometimes proved difficult to find such a sum. When the daughter of Cicero, Tullia, was making her third marriage to Dolabella[22] in 50 BC, the three usual instalments of the dowry were due for payment on the first day of July, of the years 49, 48 and 47 BC. When each date came round, Cicero would write frantically to his banker Atticus, asking him to tell him where he could find the money! By 47 BC he had even begun to wonder whether it might be better for him to arrange a divorce for his daughter, as he was becoming so desperate about the money still owing, even though if she was divorced, it would mean him losing the two-thirds of the dowry already paid over.[23]

The pursuit of money through marriage was an age-old problem, and in Plautus's play *Mostellaria*, the audience was addressed from the stage with the words: 'You husbands, with a lot of old women for wives, to whom you have sold yourselves for a dowry...' The remark probably caused discomfort to a fair number of the audience.[24]

The dowry was actually intended to represent the bride's contribution to the expenses of setting up and running the new home. In the older form of marriage, it had become the absolute property of the husband, as did the wife. But even by the third century BC there were certain cases of recovery. Later on, when the freer forms of marriage became more common, it could always be recovered, eventually, even if the wife was the guilty party in a divorce.

This ability of the widow or divorced wife to be able to claim back her dowry was essential for her upkeep and perhaps even to attract another husband. The keeping back of part of the dowry by the ex-husband in cases of divorce had two reasons. One was that any children of the marriage would automatically stay with him and would be an expense to rear. The other reason was punitive, and if the wife was the guilty party in the divorce, the husband could claim one-sixth of the money if she were an adultress, one-eighth of it if her fault was less, and one-sixth for each child, up to a maximum of three children, so in an extreme case a wronged husband could actually retain as much as two-thirds of the entire amount due to the wife. It would be a powerful reason for good behaviour as the loss of it could leave the woman seriously short of money for her future.[25]

Good behaviour in other spheres was also expected. A wife was supposed to support her husband, to treat him always with respect, to show him affection, and to bear his children and raise them. She was to make proper Romans of them, in accordance with their social standing, and ensure that they were educated correctly. She was to be the upholder of religion within the home, the fount of respectability and tradition in her household. Although many wives did not live up to this ideal, the desire for it always remained.

Even when the Emperor Augustus wanted his women to produce the cloth for the family on their own looms, which was going out of fashion, it was a nod towards the old traditions, a desire for the women to behave in the way Roman women had always done.[26] Spending time at the loom had always been considered a particularly laudable domestic activity for the respectable woman, although many of the younger and more fashionable wives were leaving their looms to gather dust.

The first and most important work for a woman was the creation of a family, the birth of children. The Roman marriage contract stated explicitly that it existed for this reason. In a society as expansive and territorial as that of Rome, which did not generally rely on paid mercenaries, a continuous supply of recruits for the ranks was absolutely vital. Romans believed that country people made the best soldiers, and also that those people who lived on the land were able to produce the largest and healthiest families.

However, persuading young men to marry was not always as simple as it seemed. For any young man, spending time with a mistress of his own choice rather than a woman of his father's choice, was far preferable. The casual relationship was free of the heavy responsibilities of a marriage, and if affection faded it was easy to move on. The Lex Julia de Maritandis Ordinibus of Augustus recognised this reluctance and outlined incentives and penalties to increase families. Some men, also, preferred men to women, although in Rome this was not entirely a problem, as homosexuality was only considered reprehensible for the passive partner. Men who preferred men were still expected to produce a family, so their private attractions were not expected to affect their obligation to become fathers. Whether this preference was vastly important to them or rather less so, they were still expected to do their duty, and usually did. It was every man's responsibility to marry a woman of suitable standing and produce children for Rome.

During the five-year census, if a man did not have children, though married and of a suitable age, he was likely to be asked the reason. He might be encouraged to divorce a barren wife and try again with another marriage, so important was that need for a supply of children. Some relationships obviously survived this, but the temptation to make a fresh start given sanction by the pressure of the state must have meant the end of many marriages, even if they were contented enough in other ways.

The great Republican general Lucius Cornelius Sulla divorced his second wife because she had produced no children, though he later freely admitted that the love of his life was the actor Metrobius, with whom he had a long-standing relationship. This homosexual relationship did not prevent Sulla marrying four times and producing five healthy children.[27]

This 'secret' side to the life of many men was ignored by their wives, though many of them cannot have remained unaware that their husbands' emotional life was centred elsewhere, just as it would have been if he spent his leisure hours with a favourite mistress. It was something that could not be allowed to interfere with the 'mos maiorum' or the way things ought to be – literally translated as 'custom of the ancestors'.

As we have seen, few men could have been so eager to abide by the letter of the law than Cato the Younger, a man immune to wrongdoing and incapable of corruption. His second wife Marcia, the daughter of Lucius Marcius Philippus, was a correct Roman wife, although his rigid sense of duty considered personal affection to be of no importance. Few men could be so stern and have such strength regarding intimate family relationships.[28]

It is interesting to note that the ancient writers recounting the story of his divorce of his wife (and they are many), never give any indication whether Marcia was consulted or not about his decision. Was she hurt or angry at the idea of being cast off? Did she have any real affection for him? Or did she manage to share his uncomfortable views regarding duty, and stoically accept the change? It is difficult to imagine that she had no feelings either way, particularly as she would be required to leave her children behind. Could she really just accept the fact of changing husbands because she was told to? There is also the question of whether Cato's self-sacrificing way of life had become tedious to live with. They had had three children together, but in her marriage to Quintus Hortensius there were none. Perhaps he was indeed too old, but he was very wealthy, and she may have had an easier time while she was with him than she had with Cato, for whom austerity was a virtue. Her own father had agreed to the divorce, and also to her later remarriage, while Cato was reputed to have given her away at her wedding to Hortensius. Self-sacrifice could apparently go no further, although the number of times this story was recounted shows that it was highly unusual, even in those mercenary times.[29]

Perhaps the clue lies there. Marcia lived with Hortensius for several years, and when he died she was left a very wealthy widow. At this point Cato offered to re-marry her and she accepted him. Was this merely to have her children back? She did go back to her original family eventually, and the story certainly gave the cynics plenty of amusement, which Cato ignored with his usual indifference. Did Cato really 'lend' her to his friend for a few years because he feared he cared for her too much? She was a proper Roman matron who had already produced three children for the family, so was it that it was hoped she could produce a child for Hortensius, or was there something more mercenary involved? She certainly returned to Cato far wealthier than when she left him, and perhaps his sense of what was fitting did not prevent him from increasing his wife's fortune, which would eventually benefit his children by her. His full motives cannot now be known, but the situation certainly shows him to have been far deeper and more complicated than the rather one-dimensional character he is usually painted as. It might have been expected that Cato would have taken another wife during those years that Marcia lived with Hortensius, but he stayed alone, just waiting for her to become available again. When she did he immediately offered remarriage, which makes one suspect a long-term plan rather than merely a friend's need.

Not all relationships went so smoothly. For a mistress, the prospect of having children would be far less welcome. The mistress is always in a very insecure position, dependent on the man's love and affection, which can be a fleeting and unreliable thing. Even in a longer-lasting relationship of several years standing, the woman still risks being cast aside when novelty wears off, or when a suitable marriage is offered. For her, another relationship is certainly less likely if she has another man's children in tow.

Many concubines in the late Republic and early Empire were freedwomen, and often educated, elegant and very attractive. They could provide the charm and vitality that a dull and properly 'Roman' wife might feel was beyond her, or even believe unnecessary. Roman poetry is full of the delights of these beautiful and tempting women, with whom a marriage was out of the question, even if love, for a time, was not. Such a delicate relationship could quickly and easily become available, and for the already-married man there were problems of censure, possibly jealousy at home and divided loyalties, particularly if a child or children resulted from the liaison. The children of a mistress, even if they were loved and cared for, could never be legitimate, and did not become so even if it were ever possible for their parents to marry, so they could never be his heirs, merely an encumbrance that most men could readily do without. This, of course, meant the use of contraception, useful for mistresses, if not for wives.

Contraception, if it worked, was far less dangerous for the woman than risking an attempted abortion. Amulets and magic potions could be tried, and men had plenty of suggestions. Pliny suggested cutting open the head of a hairy spider and removing the two worms believed to live inside it. They were then to be worn on the body tied in deerskin. Aetius recommended the liver of a cat, to be worn on the left foot, or better still part of the womb of a lioness – first catch your lion? Perhaps the smell of rotting animal parts would put off any suitor...

The rhythm method was used, but the writers believed that the most fertile time was just as monthly menstruation ended, so that couldn't be said to be reliable. Some people recommended that the woman hold her breath at the moment the man ejaculated, after which she should squat, sneeze and drink something cold. Lucretius joined in with his theory that whores should wriggle their hips during intercourse, to divert the seed. He did not, however, recommend this sort of behaviour for wives. Perhaps it might suggest an embarrassing amount of experience to the husband?

The most effective methods, and those most likely to succeed, were of course those methods which blocked the uterus. Soft wool covered with either oil or honey has been used for centuries to catch the seed, and later, vinegar was substituted for the sweeter options. Coitus interruptus is not mentioned in the Roman suggestions, although whether because this was not used, or whether it was so obvious that everyone did it anyway, so that it did not require a mention, is not clear.

Abortion was practised, and it often proved fatal. Public opinion was very much against the idea of a woman losing her life in such a way. The Emperor Domitian was reputed to have seduced his own niece Julia, the daughter of Titus, and then when she proved to be with child he demanded that she have an abortion. Unfortunately, the attempt did prove fatal for her.[30] Juvenal, writing in the second century AD, said of abortionists '...so great is the skill and so powerful are the drugs of the abortionist, who is paid to murder mankind in the womb.' During the rule of the Emperor Septimius Severus at the end of the second century AD, attempting an abortion was made a criminal act.[31]

The Elder Pliny, who suggested that even the smell of a lamp being extinguished was likely to produce a miscarriage, refers to abortion as if it were quite common. He also said that there were two periods during a pregnancy, in the fourth and eighth months, when risk of miscarriage was particularly likely.[32]

An unwanted illegitimate child was more easily disposed of if the mother carried it full term. Exposure on a hillside was not uncommon and was the conventional way of disposing of unwanted children, whether illegitimate or not. Some children born of liaisons outside of marriage were allowed to live, and although a child born of a concubine could not claim Roman citizenship, it could be recognised as a 'natural' child of its father, and some fathers actually provided for their children born in this way.

There was also a use for the unfortunate unwanted ones left outside to die. Not all of them did. Poor families quite often exposed a child that they could not afford to feed, and sometimes wealthier families exposed if they considered they already had enough to provide for, or if for some reason the Paterfamilias did not wish to acknowledge the child, which alone made it a part of the family. But many of these children were rescued, sometimes by humble families seeking children, or by people seeking future workers. The law made clear that an exposed child, after being rescued, could be brought up either as free or slave, depending on the whim of the rescuer, probably also because it was acknowledged that not all of these children were low-born. It was certainly a good way for poorer people to acquire unpaid help, for no more than the expense of raising the child.

Of course, the law also led to abuses, with young people once grown and useful being sold as slaves or into brothels as prostitutes. There were, however, some happy endings. Some North African funerary inscriptions record deep gratitude towards rescuers who had brought up a child and cared deeply for it. There were examples of kindness received and gratitude for a start in life, 'Patrono Benignissimo' and 'patronae benignissimae' being the usual terms used. Sometimes the foster parents recorded their fostered children in affectionate terms.[33]

Adoption of children did happen officially but was generally concerned with boys just below the age of puberty being transferred into another branch of the same family, or to another family to which they were connected. The adoption of girls was not usual, nor in these circumstances, was the adoption of babies. Prominent Roman families, while quite willing to adopt an heir, wanted to know what they were getting and taking on very small children was far too much of an unknown quantity when the outcome was important. The greater the family, the more necessary it was for them to have a male heir, so it was not uncommon to adopt a boy of suitable birth and breeding, and also hopefully adequate intelligence, to make up the lack.

The two elder sons of Aemilius Paullus were adopted into the Cornelii Scipiones and the Fabii Maximi respectively, in the second century BC. Likewise, when Galba adopted Calpurnius Piso in AD 69 it was to save a family from extinction. When Hadrian adopted Aurelius Antoninus he said, 'There were none of the hazards and uncertainties which must exist with a man's own children.' For this reason, it was also possible to adopt a young adult as a suitable family heir.[34]

Roman families of wealthier parents were not usually large – after all children must be provided for, not only in their upbringing, but in the provision of a career or a suitable union. Boys must be helped up the ladder of military and political attainment, and girls needed to be married off to a suitable man, who would be interested not only in the girl herself but what dowry she would bring with her.

Starting a youth on the 'cursus honorum' brought with it a daunting amount of expenditure. For the more important families, with consular aspirations, there were many steps to climb. The first was being admitted to the senate, either by seeking election as a quaestor or by co-optation of the censors. Even if he already was a senator, a man must serve as a quaestor, after which he then had to be elected as praetor, and only after that could he try for a consulship. For military families the upward ladder, and the expense, would be similar. For a girl, her dowry expectations would rise along with the wealth and importance of her family, along with their possible connections, another matter for the prospective bridegroom to consider, as connections could open many doors. Because of this, many families tried to limit their children sensibly, in order to give those children they did have a better start in life, and enough family money to draw on to establish themselves.

There were, of course, some large families in Rome, and we have already considered the twelve children borne by Cornelia, mother of the Gracchi, although only three of those children survived. The children of Germanicus only seemed noteworthy to Romans due to them being born of alternate sexes, boy, girl, boy and girl.[35] Pliny gives us an example of a man who left a large number of descendants, one Quintus Metellus Macedonius, the Censor of 131 BC. He had four sons, two daughters, and at his death left eleven grandchildren.

Another, Gaius Crispinius Hilarius of Fiesole, was credited with six sons, two daughters, twenty-seven grandsons, eight granddaughters and eighteen great-grandsons. Unfortunately, his years of endeavour to satisfy the duty of providing ample progeny were all wasted. It was said that he sacrificed his entire family on Capitoline Hill.[36] As human sacrifice, except death in battle, was unacceptable at that time we can only assume that the story is apocryphal, as least as far as the deaths were concerned.

However, despite the polite distaste at the idea of a large family, the habit of easy divorce and regular remarriage did produce substantial families of half-siblings and stepchildren. Marcus Antonius had children by three different wives, and his wife Fulvia had already had several children by her previous husbands Publius Clodius Pulcher and Gaius Scribonius Curio. Vistilia, the mother of General Corbulo and the future mother-in-law of the Emperor Gaius Caligula, produced children with six different husbands, which doubtless created a tangled interconnection of relationships.

Other marriages foundered due to having no children at all, such as that of Sempronia, the sister of the Gracchi brothers, and her husband the famous Publius Cornelius Aemilianus. This is the man who died in rather suspicious circumstances with his wife's family being widely suspected of having had a hand in his demise. Perhaps the relationship between the pair was so poor that they spent very little time together, and it was a marriage in name only. Pliny said of their relationship: 'She had lost her looks and there were no children, so they had begun to hate each other.' [37] Perhaps their animosity was more personal than political.

In any society a rich heiress finds herself desirable as a marriage partner, but unfortunately the very thing that makes her wealthy, usually that there are few children in the family, can be inherited in the same way as her fortune. The man who is tempted by the heiress might be less happy to find that his own family turns out to be small, or even non-existent.

Certainly, miscarriage was a frequent mishap for Roman women. The beloved daughter of Gaius Julius Caesar, Julia, had a miscarriage in the early years of her marriage to Pompeius Magnus. A year further on, she was to die in childbirth. This was far more than just a personal tragedy for the men involved, as her loss broke up the political Triumvirate of her father, her husband and Marcus Licinius Crassus.

The third wife of Pliny the Younger[38] suffered a miscarriage, which he recorded in his letters to her grandfather and her aunt: 'You will be sorry to hear that your granddaughter has suffered a miscarriage. Silly girl, through failure to recognise that she was pregnant, she neglected to take certain precautions and did things that should have been avoided. She has learned her lesson and indeed she might have died.'[39]

Pliny's cheerful acceptance suggests that he fully expected his wife to be more successful another time, but unfortunately his confidence was misplaced and despite having three wives, he remained childless.

For women who did conceive and carry their child to term there were other worries to face. Not only was infant mortality high but the loss of women in childbirth, or shortly afterwards, was especially high throughout the social classes, in part as a result of simple ignorance. Aulus Gellius was of the opinion that a child could be born at any time after seven, nine or ten months of gestation, but not after eight months. Plato prescribed physical exercise for women during pregnancy and also suggested that a female should not become a mother before the age of twenty, lest she produce weak or sickly children.[40] Malnutrition could also account for some of the large infant mortality rate, particularly amongst the poor, whose diet was generally limited. Soranus suggested that 'Women who digest their food easily, and do not continually have loose bowels, and are of a steady and cheerful mind' were the most likely to be able to produce children successfully.[41] He also concerned himself with treatments for morning sickness and the problem of unnatural cravings, which he described as '...things not customary, like the eating of earth, charcoal, tendrils of the vine, or unripe and acid fruits.' While he agreed with Plato about gentle exercise, he declared that 'sexual intercourse is always harmful to a pregnant woman.'

The services of a good midwife would be booked early, for those people who could afford such help. For poorer people many rural matrons combined the preparation of herbal medicines with midwifery and sometimes a little attempted magic. Soranus said that a midwife should have short fingernails but long fingers. She also required strength of mind and body. Some midwives were slaves, but the majority were freedwomen, and there are several of Italian or Gallic origins whose names are recorded. The most superior of these were well-read women who trained in the many branches of female medicine and could treat various conditions in addition to dealing competently as was possible with pregnancy and the perils of childbirth.[42]

Home deliveries were usual and a male physician would only rarely be sent for, only if there was some difficulty which caused concern. Soranus advised that the prospective mother should rest on a bed during the early stages of the labour, but she could then be moved to a birthing stool or birthing chair before the child was about to emerge. There is a famous tombstone at Ostia, in the Isola Sacra Necropolis, showing the birth of a child. The mother is sitting up in a birthing chair, which had an opening in the front of the seat. She is being supported from behind by another woman, who clasps her arms around the mother's upper body. Sitting in front of the mother, on a lower stool, is the midwife, named as Scribonia Attica. The tombstone was erected in her honour by her husband, Marcus Ulpius Amerimnus, who was also a physician and surgeon. The midwife is shown turning her face slightly away from the mother, to avoid giving her embarrassment by appearing to stare fixedly at her genitals. The mother's hair is hanging loose, as it was believed (up until medieval times) that to loosen the mother's hair and also any belts, girdles or other knotted fastenings in her clothing would help to draw down the child and prevent any constriction. As always, the level of personal hygiene of the midwife or doctor, along with that of any assistants, could mean the difference between life and death for the mother and the child.

The spread of the female Medicae, well trained in women's complaints, and particularly in dealing with childbirth, must have been a great advance. Even though Soranus of Ephesus was the most famous gynaecological and obstetrical writer of antiquity (he was born in 98 AD), it was still recognised that gynaecology was a province in which specialists were required, and that properly trained women had a great advantage in this field. While Medicae might well have taken the advice of a consultant physician, these women were far more than mere intermediaries. Many of them gained enormously wide experience and were perfectly capable of dealing with all female conditions. Galen dedicated an early work of his, the book 'On the anatomy of the Uterus' to a midwife,[43] so it is clear that these Medicae were expected to be able to read and fully understand a medical treatise, as well as being experienced in the practical side of the business.

In Roman medicine, the life of the mother was paramount and in cases of extreme difficulty the child might have to be dismembered in order to save the mother's life. While some treatments might seem 'rough-and-ready' (or even terrifying) today, by the time of the early Empire great medical minds were attempting to deal sensibly with all kinds of conditions. In fact, Soranus's book, *Gynaecology*, was so advanced that some of its drawings of the womb and foetus in utero were still being copied in medieval times.

Both Soranus and Galen broke with a tradition that believed the womb was mobile and could travel across the abdomen. Even in Galen's day, Aretaeus of Cappadocia maintained the false Hippocratic doctrine of the 'wandering womb' and despite the common-sense teachings of Soranus and Galen, this belief was unfortunately also prevalent in medieval Europe.[44] Superstition and false information have always been the enemies of good health and sensible hygiene. Many doctors believed that the womb and its accompanying menstruation played a general part in purging the whole of the female body, and therefore helped to promote its general health. Soranus, on the contrary, devoted a chapter to this in his book in which he firmly refuted the idea and confirmed that 'It does not generally contribute to their health, but is useful for childbearing only. Conception cannot take place without menstruation.' He regarded virginity, rather than menstruation, as the secret of women's better health: '... for pregnancy and parturition exhaust the female body and make it waste greatly away, whereas virginity, safeguarding women from such injuries, may suitably be called healthful.'[45]

In view of what Soranus believed to be a threat to the lives of very young women, he also gave advice on the appropriate time for first sexual intercourse:

> Since the male merely discharges seed, he does not run any risk from the first intercourse. The female, on the other hand, receives the seed, and conceives it into the substance of a living being. In this respect, she is endangered if defloration is earlier than necessary ... it is good to preserve the state of virginity until menstruation begins by itself. This will be a definite sign that the uterus is then able to fulfil its proper function ... the first menstruation usually takes place around the fourteenth year, and this age is then the natural one, indicating that this is the earliest time for defloration.[46]

Soranus went on to give instructions on the cutting of the child's umbilical cord and the delivery of the afterbirth. He discussed swaddling techniques, with concerns about how to prevent ulceration of the baby's skin while it was wrapped. He even discussed the best types of bedding for a child. He criticised the women who went to great lengths to quiet crying babies, and preferred mothers to breast-feed, though he was firm that this should not begin until three weeks after the birth, in the meantime advocating the use of a wet-nurse where possible, in order to give the mother's body time to recover. He said that wet-nurses should not be younger than twenty or older than forty, and they should be healthy with clean habits, of large frame and preferably with a good colour. The woman used should have medium-sized breasts, 'lax and soft, but not wrinkled', and not 'discharging milk over-abundantly'. She should also be self-controlled, sympathetic, good tempered, abstain from sex, drinking and all other pleasures or any kind of incontinence, as he believed that sexual pleasure 'spoils or diminishes the milk'.

All Romans believed that the character of the wet nurse could be passed onto the baby she fed, through her milk. A bad character could possibly 'stain' a child's character for life, whereas a placid and easy-going woman would help to rear a more even-tempered child. The wet nurse could also exert some influence over the family she worked for, as she could expect to be a part of it for some considerable time, and very closely involved with it. She needed to be able to act with discretion regarding what she might see or hear while employed within the house. Weaning did not take place until well after the first year, often between the ages of sixteen months and two years old. This was a sensible precaution in a world with no sterile conditions and was by far the safest diet for the child. The child whose mother had little or no breast milk, and whose family could not afford to employ a wet-nurse, was in a grim position. Aristotle remarked on the habit of not naming any child during its first week of life, as so many infants were expected to die during those first crucial days.[47]

If the child survived, then it became a time of joy and ceremonial. When the father took the child in his arms for the first time and raised it aloft, it was his acknowledgment that it was his own child, and a member of the family. On the eighth day for a girl, or the ninth day for a boy, was the 'dies lustricus', or the day of purification. On that day the child could receive its name.

After the legislation of Augustus (the Lex Aelia Sentia and the Lex Papia Poppaea) it was necessary to register a child's birth within thirty days. This 'professio' could be performed by the father, the paternal grandfather, or by the mother, either directly or through an agent. In Rome itself, this took place at the Aerarium Saturni, or Treasury, which was situated in the basement of the Temple of Saturn in the Forum.[48]

If the birth had taken place in the provinces, it would be registered at the provincial record office, or Tabularium Publicum. Records of births were posted publicly and preserved officially, and a birth certificate was given to the family. After Marcus Aurelius, the births of illegitimate children were also required to be properly registered. One of the details required was the hour of the birth, which was considered necessary for any future astrological calculations, and many of the surviving tombstones actually give a list of the deceased's age by years, days and hours.

One of the main developments in the education and general upbringing of children was during the change from the Republic to the early Empire. Mothers surrendered their duties more and more to slave-women. History records with pride the mothers who undertook the early education of their children themselves, such as the women of the Gracchi, the family of Julius Caesar and Octavianus. A boy usually received his education at home until he was around six years old, then passed into the hands of his father. He might tutor the boy himself or find a suitable slave or freedman to do it. Often a suitably well-educated slave would be bought, this was the 'grammaticus' who often tutored his master's children alongside the children of the family's relatives and friends. Some of these highly educated men were worth an astonishing amount of money, for their skills and also their trustworthiness. The Grammaticus who was freed by Quintus Catulus, the Consul of 102 BC, was named Lutatius Daphnis, and he had been sold twice, each time for the fantastic sum of seven hundred thousand sesterces.[49]

There were also schools away from home to which a boy could be sent, although often only for the later stages of his education. In the Empire of Vespasian there were 'public' schools, which were the schools of public professors. Quintilian, the first of Vespasian's professors of Latin rhetoric in Rome, had such a school and was a 'teacher by Imperial appointment' and therefore highly prestigious.

The boy – or indeed the girl – who was taught outside the household would go at the age of six or seven years to a primary school, where they would be taught for four or five years. There they would learn to read and write and also to understand elementary arithmetic. St Augustine, when grown, is reported to remember with horror this period of his education and had memories of being thrashed for idleness. Much of this elementary teaching would take place in rooms at the edge of the Fora, or even under the colonnades, screened only by a curtain. Children at these types of schools would have a holiday every eighth day, on the Nundinae, because the sounds from the nearby markets beyond the curtain would have drowned out the voice of the teacher or else caused other distractions.[50]

Secondary education was in grammar, syntax and literature, with either the same Grammaticus or a different specialist teacher. Higher education, from the years of around thirteen or fourteen, would be in the hands of a 'rhetor' and this consisted of rhetoric, history, and arithmetic, along with geometry, music and astronomy as subjects considered useful for relaxation in the life ahead. In Imperial Rome these schools were in rooms attached to the libraries of the Forum of Trajan (the 'schola Traiani') or in the Athenaeum of Hadrian.[51]

The basis of any young man's future in administration would be the theory and practice of law. This was studied after the end of formal education, and the young women would be excluded. This was partly because women were not officially allowed to plead at court, and partly also because by then they would be back in the hands of their mothers, or other female relatives, being trained in the necessary women's things to prepare them for marriage and their own future responsibilities as wives and mothers.

The ultimate goal of each woman's life was not always so clear cut as it might appear. Apart from a good husband and the hoped-for children, who would justify the marriage, the actual living together could often prove to be a very different thing to learn. The prevalence of divorce and remarriage rather took the shine off the hopes and dreams, and although it is not fair to suggest that all marriages were difficult, a great many were obviously unsatisfactory in one way or another.

While it is known that Augustus and Livia had a famous love match, they had at least had the opportunity to choose each other. It is to be hoped that many other Roman families managed to achieve an affectionate respect for each other and were able to provide an emotionally secure home for their children, despite in many cases having their partners chosen for them.

Normally, by the end of the Republic, it would be a 'free' marriage, in that the woman remained under the final authority of her Paterfamilias, being her father or chief male relative. Until the second century AD a father could 'recall' his daughter and divorce her from her husband against her will, but it was rare.[52] Also in Republican times, the young wife married in this way would not be referred to as the 'Materfamilias' of the family. For this she would need to have been married by the old-fashioned and more permanent method of confarreatio.

Whether technically the Materfamilias of the family or not, the wife still had responsibilities and social duties to perform. She did not live in a form of purdah, as the Grecian women still did. Of course, her crowning achievement would be in producing a male heir for the husband, but she would also be judged on her attitude towards any stepchildren she might have acquired as a result of his previous marriages.

Octavia, sister of the Emperor Augustus, was famous for her kindness towards her various stepchildren, even the ones that her husband Marcus Antonius produced in adultery with Queen Cleopatra VII. Of those three children, orphaned by the suicides of their parents, the girl Cleopatra Selene was to later marry King Juba II of Mauretania. The two boys, Alexander Helios and Ptolemy Philadelphus, unfortunately disappear from history, as did Cleopatra's son by Caesar, known as Caesarion. The removal of these boys was a political decision, and nothing to do with any care they received from Octavia, who was known to love children.[53] As well as her own daughters by Marcus Antonius, Octavia was known to have cared for his two sons by his marriage to Fulvia, the granddaughter of Gaius Gracchus.

After the legislation of Augustus, the Lex Julia de Maritandis Ordinibus of 18 BC, the birth of a third child to any woman would have been a particular reason for rejoicing. These third children were considered the mark of the successful and properly productive family. The parents, having done their duty, were then entitled to several material rewards. There would, for instance, be no restrictions on the amount of any legacies they could receive (for women's inheritance was otherwise limited). The mother, if not already independent, officially received her full legal independence. The father would receive taxation benefits, and usually increased prospects of promotion. Unfortunately, many worthy parents failed to achieve the 'Right of Three Children' or 'honoris causa' even within the Imperial family. Plutarch remarked sourly about the attempts to gain these benefits 'People are marrying and breeding, not in order to produce heirs, but to qualify for inheritances.'[54]

In the later Republican and in the early Empire it became more common for women to share the interests of their husbands, and many marriages benefited from the loyalty and support of their wives. If the husband was in business, or dealt with the administration of property, his wife could not only help him but would be more capable of dealing with her own matters if she were widowed. She would be in a far better position to deal with the livelihood that the husband had built up for the family.

Many ladies of higher status were deeply involved in political matters. Certainly, Marcus Antonius's wife Fulvia had always – owing to her position as a member of one of the highest and most respected families and also because of her immense wealth – considered herself well able to advise her husbands, pressing forward her opinions. Marcus Antonius finally divorced her for what he considered to be her political interference in his military concerns, although she saw it as assistance. However, he was at that time already deeply involved with Cleopatra, so his easy irritation with his wife, whom he had married for precisely that status and wealth and her ability to promote his career, was probably not entirely Fulvia's fault.

Many marriages were, or became, affectionate and long-lasting. Not everyone changed partners at the first sign of a disagreement. Pliny the Younger was to write that when apart from his beloved wife, he missed her every moment of the day.[55]

Julius Classicianus, the Procurator of Britain (a financial secretary) died in London and his wife Julia Pacata erected a monument to his memory, describing herself as 'infelix uxor' or unhappy widow. One woman, named Annia, when asked why she would not marry again, despite still being young and attractive, said 'If I find a good husband I will be in constant fear of losing him. If I pick a bad one, then why, after already having had the best, should I have to put up with the worst?' Sensible sentiments indeed. Sometimes such sentiments lasted a lifetime and after the death of her husband, Servius, Valeria Messala refused to remarry. Despite still being considered young and having had offers, she had denied them all. When asked why, she replied 'As far as I am concerned, Servius is still alive. He always will be.'[56]

Women such as these, the 'univarae,' were deeply respected because of being faithful to the memory of deceased husbands and by holding them in esteem they were themselves esteemed. Their own reputations grew and they were honoured in their own right, as being good examples of what a Roman marriage should be.

Other women were not so fortunate in having that requited love. Some husbands still kept their women at home as if they were prisoners, fearing adultery. If a wife was innocent of any wrongdoing, then such treatment could lead only to rebellion and resentment. At the end of the Republic, in one of his satires, Varro wrote 'A husband must either put a stop to his wife's faults, or learn to put up with them. In the first case, he makes her into a better woman, and in the second he makes himself into a better man.'[57] Sensible advice, although many men found it difficult to ignore the faults of their wives; likewise the lack of children still fractured many relationships and not every family wished to adopt.

Plutarch tells a story in his life of Aemilius Paullus regarding Aemilius divorcing his wife Papira, which surprised his friends and they criticised him for it. He replied:

> This shoe of mine is new, but it pinches, just where you cannot tell. It is a mistake for a woman to rely on her wealth, her breeding, or her good looks. She should think more of the qualities which affect her husband's life ... those traits of character which make for harmony or otherwise in the domestic relationship.

One famous marriage where such harmony was in short supply was that of Cicero. Marcus Tullius Cicero was married to Tarentia, a strong-willed and ambitious woman, whose half-sister was the Chief Vestal, Fabia. Tarentia had brought a large dowry into the marriage, which amounted to some four hundred thousand sesterces and included two tenement blocks in Rome, woods in the suburbs, and a large and productive farm in the country. The pair were married 'sine manu' (without hand) meaning that Tarentia kept control of her money. They had two children, a daughter Tullia, born in 76 BC, and a son Marcus, born in 65 BC. Cicero was not without his own funds, but his expensive hobby of buying villas and furnishing them with beautiful things, together with his inability to maintain any position of political leadership, brought a great deal of friction into the marriage.

Tarentia was hungry for political power and tried to push her husband forward, never believing that he was trying hard enough to gain prestige. She was constantly frustrated by the lack of that steady progress upwards that she thought him capable of, if he would apply himself properly. The annoyance of this brought out all that was sharp and domineering in Tarentia's character. The friction between them depressed Cicero and made him even less able to be the man she expected him to be. Their relationship suffered badly, and all of Cicero's emotional life centred on his beloved daughter Tullia. This girl was married three times, but it was her third husband who was the greatest disaster.[58]

As Tullia's second marriage was coming to an end, Cicero set his sights on the distinguished Patrician, Tiberius Claudius Nero, becoming Tullia's third husband. He believed that with this reasonable man his daughter could be safe and happy. However, at the time when Tullia became free of her second husband, Cicero was absent in Greece. While he was away, Tarentia gave her permission for Tullia to marry Publius Cornelius Dolabella (80-43 BC). This man had already been married and had a son. Born a Patrician, he had had himself adopted as a Plebeian in 47 BC purely for political gain. He wanted to be elected Tribune of the Plebs, which would give him the opportunity to try to force through a law cancelling all debts. He was deeply in debt at that time. This idea of cancellation of debts was a populist move, but never succeeded, as it would naturally destroy the financial stability of the state. Dolabella was a dissolute and promiscuous man and once married to Tullia he treated her very badly. His behaviour brought great unhappiness to both Tullia and her father and caused the final rift in the marriage between Cicero and Tarentia, as Cicero naturally blamed her for the disastrous marriage of their daughter.[59] Their thirty-year marriage came to an end and Cicero remarried, to a young woman named Publilia. A divorce was also arranged for Tullia to free her from the dreadful Dolabella, but by that time Tullia was already pregnant with her second child by him, the first infant having died.

She bore her second son in January of 45 BC just after her divorce from Dolabella, but she died a month later and the infant also died.

It was a loss from which Cicero never recovered. His new wife, Publilia, had never had any real place in his heart, so they also divorced later that same year.

Cicero seems to have been a lonely and unfulfilled man, with his closest friendships being with his brother Quintus and his banker Atticus, with whom he exchanged much correspondence. He lived in a crowd, yet apart from his devotion to Tullia had always been isolated, and this solitariness had spilled into his public life, making him often uncomfortably outspoken and losing him friends, despite his many gifts and his increasing fame as an orator.

Another story of mercenary marriage, from the time of Gaius Marius in the first century BC, concerns one Gaius Titinius from Miturnae, who attempted to divorce his wife yet still retain her substantial dowry, on the grounds of her immoral character. Gaius Marius quickly realised that the husband had been fully aware of the woman's defects of character before he had married her. He had simply done so with the idea of using her faults as a way of getting his hands on her money. Marius solved the problem by giving the woman a trivial sum as a fine for her unsuitable behaviour, but he fined Titinius the whole amount of the dowry that he would be able to retain from the divorce.[60]

The main concern of the Emperor Augustus was the creation of children, perhaps because of having only one unsatisfactory child of his own. (His daughter Julia was eventually banished to an island for immorality.) His legislation of 18 BC, the Lex Julia de Adulteriis Coercendis, addressed the question of sexual continency in wives, and represented the first time in Roman history that the adultery of married women was criminalised. Likewise, the already mentioned Lex Julia de Maritandis Ordinibus of the same year was to encourage larger families, though it has to be admitted that both these laws were aimed primarily at the upper classes.

The loyal grieving widow or the single divorced woman had no claim on Augustus, what mattered was that the women of Rome should bear and rear as many children as possible. For this they were encouraged to marry and remarry, although later Emperors were to regard too many marriages as an impropriety, and Constantine was to abolish the rules by which Augustus had penalised celibacy.

Some unhappy marriages might eventually produce the happy ending of freedom or even wealth. Unfettered responsibility to enjoy one's later life was described as an 'orbus' or 'orba', which might even include enjoying the futile attentions of fortune hunters. Solon told Croesus: 'Call no man happy, until he is dead.' But Martial went one step further: 'Call no man happy unless his wife is dead – particularly is she is rich!'[61] But then Martial was famous for his cynicism.

For others, the ideal, faithful, pleasant and fruitful marriage was the aim of any sensible person. Good health had to play a part in this, and with the family still being of prime importance, the health and well-being of the family was the basis of the success of the Roman state.

The midwife, Scribonia Attica, whose tomb at Isola Sacra at Ostia has already been mentioned, was a good example of the upwardly mobile woman who could be an inspiration to others. Her mother, Scribonia Callityche, was of Greek origin and could possibly have been a slave. Scribonia the Younger, in her marriage to the successful surgeon Marcus Ulpius Amerimnus, had certainly done very well for herself, particularly in achieving success in her own profession. She was exactly the sort of woman Soranus of Ephesus most praised when writing about the world of childbearing: 'She should be literate, with her wits about her. She should be possessed of a good memory, loving her work, not unduly handicapped with regard to her senses.' It also went without saying that she should be eminently respectable.[62]

Though literacy was certainly an advantage in the preparation and prescription of medicines, some tricks of the female medic's trade, certainly concerning the aspects of contraception and abortificants, tended to be 'female secrets', which were passed on by word of mouth only, rather than being written down.

Respectability, though required, might not always be quite what it seemed. The author Eurapius, in the fourth century AD, described a hostess in a Roman wine shop who was busy serving a customer called for by a neighbour requesting that she attend immediately at a difficult childbirth. She did so, leaving her customers waiting, and when the birth was over she returned. She washed her hands and went on serving her customers their wine. Midwifery could be a part-time job, with many women merely helping out locally as required. Women such as Scribonia Atticus, who specialised in it, and took the title of 'Obstetrix' as her due, may well have been the exception for ordinary women.[63]

With uncomplicated births, the assistance of women of the mother's family was probably enough, with one massaging with warm olive oil, and another perhaps helping to encourage breathing to manage the pain. Soranus refers to women 'pressing their breath' at such times, so this method of pain relief seems to have been well known. If things became more difficult or a child was badly positioned, midwives and doctors could turn it, although the ancient texts do not make any mention of the use of episiotomies, or the cutting of the perineum to facilitate the child's birth. There are also no references to forceps or any similar instruments.

If the worst should happen, the life of the mother took precedence, even if it meant loss of a much-desired child. The baby might be cut up and removed with hooks. Latin texts have various recipes for remedies to aid the expulsion of the placenta, as doctors and midwives were fully aware that its retention was very dangerous for the mother.

The preference for extended breast-feeding has already been referred to, but the great powers attributed to breast milk did not stop at feeding infants. It was used in cases of phthisis – a respiratory illness – or as an antidote to certain poisons, and it was even expected to help with certain eye complaints. Instructions for the preparation of eye medicines often recommended that the ingredients be diluted in human breast milk, which seems to have been used as a very versatile substance.

Should a woman die in childbirth, the law required that the infant, if still alive, should be cut from her body to attempt to give the child a chance of life. This was the truth of the Caesarean operation, not that Caesar was delivered in that way, as no woman was expected to survive such invasive and dangerous abdominal surgery, although there have been a few reports of the procedure being successful over the centuries, with the mother and her child managing to live through it. However, before the use of effective anaesthesia and without any suitable antiseptic methods, the attempt would be difficult in the extreme, with an appallingly high risk of infection afterwards.[64]

Partial anaesthesia could be managed with wine, and with poppy juice. However, the incision would cause any patient to sober up very quickly, and the pain would have been excruciating. Even in relatively modern times the procedure was only attempted in the most extreme cases, as a last resort. Other problems often experienced in antiquity were injuries sustained during the birth, such as tears or perforations.

Egyptian women faced the same problems as their Roman cousins, and the Kahun Papyrus of 1850 BC records the period pains, labour pains, miscarriages and birth injuries of women before the Roman period. The Greek word 'hustera' for womb gives us 'hysteria', which was believed to be due to female problems. Unfortunately, the Kahun Papyrus also give credence to the idea of the 'wandering womb' in which the womb was not fixed but capable of erratic movements around the abdomen, causing equally erratic behaviour in women.[65] It would appear that whether the prospective mother gave birth to her child squatting on the birthing bricks in Egypt, or sitting upright in a Roman birthing chair, the help she would receive was very much the same, and that giving birth was always a hazardous business with a random outcome.

As we have seen, the Roman women were acutely aware that the earliest days or even years of a child's life were a fragile time, when infant and child mortality rates could easily bring tragedy to any family. The divorce laws which gave the father custody of all his children in the event of the break-up of a marriage, seem to suggest that women were fairly casual regarding young children, being quite blasé about the possibility of losing them. However, while these women were certainly encouraged to look to the future rather than dwell on the past, there is much evidence which is quite contrary to the idea that Roman women could face the loss of a child with equanimity. Acceptance of the will of the gods was certainly considered a virtue, but that did not mean that the anguish of loss was not keenly felt, or that young children were not loved and valued by their parents.

The proliferation of small headstones, or even the creation of beautiful and valuable sarcophagi dedicated to deceased children, may come as a surprise, but they clearly show that their loss was deeply and genuinely mourned. The Capitoline Museum in Rome has a very fine collection dedicated to children, one of which comes from the Jewish area in Rome and shows two young boys, with a charming small image of pet dogs playing, carved above it. Another headstone, from Pompeii, also shows a small boy playing with his pet dog, and a rather splendid sarcophagus shows a reclining female, quite young, with a small dog lying beside her.

The Capitoline Museum is also the home of the most impressive and moving of the child burials. Found in the Trastevere area of Rome, the remains are those of a small female child of around four years old. She was buried with great reverence between 10,000 and 8,000 BC and the wealth of her grave goods show us that she must have been of high status. The child's skeleton lies on a bed of broken pottery sherds and is surrounded by blocks of tufa, which as well as surrounding her remains, apparently supported a low roof over her. She was buried with bronze jewellery and pottery, and by her side is a bowl containing grain. Alongside her left leg is the jawbone of a lamb, a meat offering.

The great care taken with the burial of this little girl, with such love and respect, is amazing, considering that her death took place at a time when such a small female child might have been considered expendable. This was obviously not the case and her death and burial were carefully dealt with and equally carefully marked.

More than many monuments, this burial shows a love of children for their own sake, even at a very early period of Rome's history. This is very reassuring and it serves to remind us that this unknown child, buried so very long ago, represented someone's lost hopes.[66]

4

Religion – Priests and Priestesses

There is little doubt that some Romans were cheerfully cynical about the gods, and that they only paid lip-service to the state religion. However, public opinion was such that the majority, usually brought up by devout mothers, preferred to comply with the normal rituals and routines.

There was also a strong superstitious sense, leading to the concern that offending any god could provoke some dreadful punishment, over and above the usual difficulties of life. Performance of religious duties continued, with for many people a deep desire not to bring the wrath of the Gods down upon the heads of themselves or their families – or indeed onto the Roman state, which everyone had a duty to support.

As we have already seen, the first action of any bride on the morning after her marriage was to make the offering to the household Gods, which had become hers also. The duty and responsibility of respect towards these deities was a fundamental part of ensuring the welfare of the family. These offerings were usually only of grain, or small cakes made of spelt flour, or perhaps flour mixed with salt, 'mola salsa'. Horace mentions a domestic scene where a small amount of food was 'burned in the flame' for the offering to the household Gods. Other regular offerings could include flowers, honey, milk, cheese, fruit or wine.

The Lares[1] were among the oldest of all the Roman Gods. They were faceless, without sex, shape or any mythology. They protected the family as the Lars Familiaris, or the voyagers on the seas as the Lars Permarini. The Lares Praestites, also known as the public Lares, looked after the workings of the state.

There was one particular oath which was very special, and when made it could not be broken. This was dedicated 'By Sol Indiges, Tellus and Liber Pater as witnesses'.

These early 'numinous' Gods could bring terrible vengeance on anyone who swore in their names and then broke the most sacred of oaths. Sol Indiges was a sun deity, Tellus represented the earth, and Liber Pater was a fertility God, associated with the wine and the harvest. Another ancient deity was Salus (of good health) who was later rather superseded by Aesculapius, a god of medicine, whose temple still stands next to that of the goddess Isis/Aset in Pompeii.

These protected and directed everyone and everything, from the weather to the correct functioning of a doorway, or a public crossroads. Crossroads were very important, being a place where people met, so the contradictory forces could also meet there and would need to be appeased. It was common to site small shrines at a crossroads to invoke the protection of friendly deities, and there was often also a bar, where people could refresh themselves. The bar could serve another function, as its owner would pay for its prime position by maintaining the local shrine. There was frequently also a fountain or small watercourse at such a crossing point, quite often with a Silanus head pouring fresh water from its open mouth.[2]

By the time of the Republic, these Lares could be represented as youths, usually two, often running with a small dog. This did not mean that the Romans believed that there were only two of them, or that they had a dog, but it was a way of attempting to represent an elemental force, something young, swift and attractive, and which could assist people if approached properly.

It is a mistake to imagine that the Romans simply copied all their gods from the Greeks. As time went on, some of the major gods and goddesses acquired names and physical forms, but the ancient Numina, still faceless and formless, had their important place. The Pantheon itself,[3] which now contains altars to Christian saints, was originally built to display statues of the most important gods of the Romans, by then familiar as to faces and attributes. However, the temples to the old gods were still vitally important, perhaps more so, and they were still clung to, with a temple to a deity such as Ops (plenty), which was in a prominent position on the Capitol. This temple had an emergency fund of silver bullion stored inside its podium.[4] When even these original deities began to acquire familiar faces, they were given 'families', so it was then said that Ops was the wife of Saturn, and that their children were Jupiter, Neptune, Pluto, Juno, Ceres and Vesta. Saturn's own temple was very large and important,[5] its podium a warren of corridors and 'cells' which contained the Roman treasury.

Another such was Fides, or faith, also given a temple on Capitoline Hill, which was dominated by the immense temple of Jupiter Optimus Maximus, or Jupiter Best and Greatest, who was the chief of the gods. Also on that hill, sharing the most sacred space, were Jupiter Feretrius, (of treaties and armaments), and Fortuna Primigenia (Fortune of the First-born). There was a slightly smaller temple for Honus et Virtus, a cult of military commanders. Close to the present-day Antoninus and Faustina was originally a temple dedicated to the Lares Prestites, or the public Lares.

Until the end of the Republic and long before the state religion began to lose its hold, even the most brilliant and independently minded men, such as Sulla, Gaius Marius, Caesar and Pompeius Magnus, all duly paid their respects to the appropriate Gods, particularly when about to begin a new venture or start a new campaign.

In the Largo Argentina in Rome, known as the Area Sacra in the Campus Martius, stand the four oldest temples. These were saved from destruction by Mussolini when they were discovered in 1922. They were rescued from casual demolition (along with the beautiful Ara Pacis and the Tomb of Augustus), at a time when Rome's greatness was again beginning to be celebrated and appreciated.[6] Even if they were intended to be used as a prop to aggrandise his own regime, the Dictator Mussolini deserves some credit for insisting that they be preserved.

The area of the Campus Martius (literally the Field of Mars) is where the legions camped before and after campaigns. The four ancient temples are now below ground level but are clearly visible from the surrounding roads. Three of them are rectangular and one is round. The round one, known as Temple B, is from the second century BC, and was dedicated to Fortuna Huiusce Dei, the Fortuna of This Day, the only temple known to have been so dedicated. A large and beautiful head and limbs of the goddess in white marble was found at the site and are now in the Centrale Montemartini Museum. At this temple prayers were said and offerings made prior to generals leading their troops out of this side of Rome.[7]

The dedications of the other three temples are not so certain, but they are presumably dedicated to Juturna (Temple A), Feronia

(Temple C), and the Lares Permarini (Temple D). This Area Sacra was always an important place, and eventually the Theatre of Pompeius Magnus would be built, literally backing up to the Temple of Fortuna. This huge edifice, which stretched from the Area Sacra to the Campo dei Fiori, held meeting places, shops, and fine statuary, as well as one hundred columns around its open square. Two of the statues which decorated it are now in the Capitoline Museum, huge half- human half-goat figures, supporting baskets of fruit and flowers. Also within the immense Theatre complex was a curia, or meeting place, with a temple high above it, dedicated to Venus Victrix. It was within this curia, with only a wall separating it from the Temple of Fortune of the Present Day, that Julius Caesar's phenomenal personal luck finally ran out. He was assassinated there, reputedly falling in death at the foot of the larger-than-life-sized statue of Pompeius Magnus.

As might be expected, Fortuna, in one of her many guises, was a very popular goddess. Sulla was always said to carry with him a small image of Apollo,[8] but he became devoted to Fortuna after she showed him favour in battle. He later took the additional name of 'Felix' (Lucky), due to her support of him, and always made offerings at her temples. Apart from Huiusce Dei, Fortuna could be represented in her different aspects as Primigenia (of firstborn children), Fortuna Brevis (of fickle luck), Fortuna Dubia (of doubtful fortune), Fortuna Mala (of bad luck), or Fortuna Faitrix (of life). Also particularly popular was Fortuna Muliebris (of women), so that she had something to offer most people who might feel in need of her help. Her varied incarnations show that the Romans had Gods who were able to cover every eventuality, and many of the more important ones had different 'faces' for different needs.

Venus also had many different aspects – from Venus Libitina at the Registry of Roman Citizen Deaths, through Venus Obsequens (protectress of adulterers), and Venus Erucina (protectress of prostitutes). She could also be Venus Victrix (Victorious), whose temple crowned the auditorium of Pompeius's Theatre.

Juno was another who could do more than one job. She was Juno Regina (Queen of the Gods), Juno Lucina (of the Registry of Roman Citizen Births), and Juno Moneta (the giver of timely warnings). The temple of Juno Moneta, once adorning the Arx and where the church of Santa Maria in Aracoeli now stands, was another with a secret held within its podium: it was the site of the Roman mint.

More unusual gods and goddesses were Mens (proper Roman thinking), and Janus (whose name gives us January). He controlled both looking back into the past and also forward into the future with his double-facing images. He also looked after the opening and closing of doors, which was far more important than it first appears, for a door represents the security of a building, and in a wider sense that of the State itself. It also represents what might be on the other side of a door, either in the past, to be turned away from as something possibly ended, or in the future as something which either had to be dealt with, or which would give opportunities. He could control whether a person accepted, rejected, or embraced events, so his help was very useful in making important decisions.

Mars was God of War, but also Bellona, on the Campus Martius, was the Goddess of War with Foreign Powers. Her temple, next to that of Apollo Sosianus the God of Medicine and Healing, was on the other side of the Vicus Triumphalis from the Capitoline Hill.[9] The close relationship with war and healing had been long established, with gods of war and destruction always having their counterpart of healing and medicine. The ancient Egyptian goddess Sekhmet combined the two forces within herself, as Sekhmet the Destroyer and also Sekhmet the Healer. She is also Goddess of Truth and Justice so that the double-sided aspect is present again, with one of her incarnations being powerful enough to be the Judge of Rightness, the dispenser of the necessary punishments, and then finally the Healer, able and willing to repair the wounds inflicted in the cause of that justice. The tripartite aspect of this deity was later translated into the Christian religion as the Holy Trinity, which unfortunately also disallowed the enormous power that ancient religions had always assigned to female deities, without feeling that masculinity was affronted. This emphasis on Egyptian religion is important, as many other religions were derived from the gods and goddesses of their pantheon, including the Virgin Mary and the Christ Child, being related to the Goddess Aset/Isis and her son Horus. Romans were able to accept and assimilate the beliefs of others alongside their own, even making 'Roman' versions of the Egyptian Gods, whereby human figures dressed in Roman military uniform can be seen with animal heads.

The Temple of Bellona differed from others in that, beyond its steps and votive altar, was an area of open ground designated 'Foreign Territory'. When a war was imminent, a flagstone would be lifted to expose the ground beneath, into which a spear was thrown from the temple steps, to declare war on the foreign power concerned. The landing of this spear in the ground would officially declare the start of hostilities.[10]

The centre of Rome itself was crowded with temple buildings, and although such a proliferation of religious buildings may seem excessive, different deities would tempt different people, or would be prayed to for different reasons, as with Christianity, where a follower might prefer a particular saint whose attributes could be needed. As with the medieval Christian religion, when it was regarded as an act of faith for people to contribute towards the cost of a new church, likewise a wealthy Roman might make a vow to erect a temple to a particular favourite, in exchange for certain benefits.

From its eminent position overlooking the Forum, the huge and vitally important temple of Jupiter Optimus Maximus watched over the temples below it, where the large temple of Saturn rubbed shoulders with Concord (amiable co-existence). Slightly further down, the temple of Castor and Pollux (the Dioscuri), was quite close to Vesta (the sacred flame) and the Well of Juturna, from which the priestesses of Vesta drew their water. Also in the area were Venus Cloacina, (Purification of the waters), Vediovis (young Jupiter the God of Disappointments), and Janus.[11]

The small round temple of Vesta, which stood just beyond Castor and Pollux was very special. The continuous burning of the sacred flame embodied Rome's luck and security. The original temple was made of wood, as were many of the earliest ones. Over-enthusiastic tending of the sacred fire had on more than one occasion resulted in the temple being burned down and having to be rebuilt. The remains presently on the site, though very attractive, are from a reconstruction done in 1933, and are merely intended to suggest the form the actual temple took, when it was finally built in stone. Some fragments of the original have been incorporated into this present form, as they were rebuilt by Julia Domna, the wife of Septimius Severus, in 200 AD.[12]

Next to Vesta's temple the Well of Juturna is another reconstruction from 1953-55. It is said to be the site where Castor and Pollux watered their horses, after the Battle of Lake Regillus at Frascati just outside the city, in 496 BC.[13] This battle was decisive in preventing the last king of Rome from regaining his throne, and so might be seen as the beginning of the real Republic. Even in later centuries, when their own residence was supplied with running water, the Vestals still ritually drew a jug of water daily from Juturna's spring. Their own dwelling, the Domus Vestae, was behind the Vesta temple, and was where the six Vestal Virgins lived and from where they tended the sacred flame that should never be allowed to go out.

Slightly further down was another temple cluster, with the Public Penates near to Jupitor Stator, the stayer of army retreats, positioned at either side of the Via Sacra and close to the public Lares, or Lares Prestites. Later, during the Imperial period, the immense double temple of Venus and Rome would also be built in this area in front of the Ampiteatro, or Colosseum.

Above the Forum itself, on the Palatine Hill, overlooking the Forum on one side and the area of the Circus Maximus on the other, was the temple of the Asian Great Goddess, the Magna Mater. In this area the Patrician families originally lived, enjoying cooler air and a slight separation from the crowded Forum below. Excavations show the foundations of some of their houses situated where the Imperial households would later live, showing the area's importance and exclusivity.[14]

Not far away, on the Forum Holitorium nearer to the river, which was the area of the fruit and vegetable markets, stood the temple of Mater Matuta, the Goddess of mothers and childbearing, along with another temple to Fortuna, this time dedicated to the protection of virgins and pre-pubescent girls.

For a Roman, religion was not merely a matter of offering sacrifice and prayer to whichever deity was preferred, in the hope of favour. It was far more a form of contract between the human and the deity. The supplicant, in return for the prayers, sacrifices and loyalty, actually expected something in return. It was never a matter of blind faith, although the Romans could be devoted enough, for them it had to be a two-way thing, with the god or goddess giving something in return for the faith and trust offered. Many Romans believed that they did get something in return, as when Lucius Cornelius Sulla attributed his military successes to Fortuna, not the Apollo whose image he had previously carried with him. It was to Fortuna that he had prayed when things were difficult for him, and it was Fortuna who showed him the way clear to gain success. To her then, he directed his prayers and his thanks.[15]

Other people doubtless did the same, with belief that their chosen deity could, if he or she chose, listen to their requests and act to help them. This was always done, however, with typical Roman commonsense, that also told them that if their chosen deity failed to live up to expectations in upholding their part of the bargain, then the contract between them was broken and no future offerings could be expected. There was no shame in turning one's attention to another deity, in the hope of a better result.[16]

There were surprisingly few female priests involved in Roman religion, considering the number of goddesses whose temples were strung across Rome. Even when these temples were considered places of great power and were popular with the public, they were more often than not served by priests.

The Pontifex Maximus was the high priest, the highest rank of all, and his was a position elected for life, as is the present Pope who holds the ancient title of Pontiff. Jupiter Optimus Maximus was believed to have taken up residence in his temple on the Capitol and for this reason, at every new year, the new Consuls who were about to begin their year of office went in procession to perform sacrifice to the Best and Greatest. The first senate meeting of the year was also held within this temple, showing his pre-eminent position among the gods of Rome.

The original Pontifex, unlike the present Pope, was expected to be married, as were the priests of all the 'Roman' religions, except for the Vestals themselves. Only later, when Eastern religions such as Isis and Magna Mater arrived in Rome bringing with them their celibate and tonsured priests, did habits change to accommodate them. Even then, the strangely dressed and celibate priesthoods were at first looked on as oddities and considered to be 'un-Roman'. For a time, the worship of Isis was forbidden, as being altogether exotically too different and clashing too much with Roman sensibilities, as well as having unfortunate Egyptian connections, which at that time created suspicion.

Below the Pontifex Maximus were the Flamen priests – the Flamen Dialis, Martialis, and Quirinalis. Of these, the holder of the office of Flamen Dialis was probably the most oppressed by his position. He was the subject of many regulations and proscriptions which affected his daily life. He was the most senior of the Flamines, and his wife had to also be rather special as unlike the wives of the other priests she became a priestess on marriage to him, becoming the Flaminica Dialis.

These two had to be married according to the old rite of confarreatio, they must both be Patrician by birth, and they must have both sets of parents living at the time of their appointment. Their position was also for life. Their lives were loaded down with taboos – the Flamen Dialis could not be allowed to see, or touch, a dead body. He could not touch iron, nor could he use iron to cut his hair or to shave. He could not wear leather taken from any animal killed for that purpose, nor could he touch a horse, eat beans, or any form of leavened bread. He could not have any kind of knot about his person, so being shod was a problem, with neither buckles or laces allowed. On official occasions he had to wear an ivory helmet with a spike on its top, held in place by a woollen ring. It must have been a desperately uncomfortable position to hold, despite its grandeur. The Flaminica Dialis was bound by almost as many taboos as her husband, and if she should die before he did he was obliged to resign, as this particular priesthood was a joint position.[17]

As Flamen Dialis, a man could obviously not become a soldier, which is why the elderly Gaius Marius, when he realised that the young Gaius Julius Caesar was likely to become a great general, appointed him as Flamen Dialis. This honour effectively prevented Caesar from taking up the normal life of an ambitious and capable young man, which Marius had probably feared would lead Caesar to gain the sort of fame that would eclipse his own achievements. In time, Caesar was excused the position and was able to take up his career and earn his place in history, but not before he had to perform the office for some time.

One of the few goddesses served exclusively by women was Vesta. She was important in a domestic setting, as one of the oldest deities, representing the home and the hearth. Even when some of the older Roman gods began to take on human forms, Vesta remained faceless and formless, being represented only by the sacred flame itself.

It cannot be over-emphasised how important to Rome this sacred flame was, being vital for cooking and warmth, for sacrifice and cremation, yet also dangerous. It was the centre of the family hearth, the basis of daily life, but within the temple of Vesta it became far more. The fire tended by the Vestal Virgins became the very symbol of the city's peace and security, and the promise of its continuity. The Vestals who tended the flame were aware that their continued virginity was also of vital importance to Rome's luck and future prosperity. For them, the loss of chastity was punishable by death.

Initially, the Vestals had shared a large residence with the family of the Pontifex Maximus, although with entirely separate quarters. This residence was situated just behind Vesta's small temple, with the part where the Vestals lived being known as the Atrium Vestae. The other half, where the Pontifex and his family lived, was the Domus Publicus. The Via Nova ran along the back of this double property, at the foot of the Palatine Hill, and had shops and houses along its length. The priestly property faced the Regia, and the temple of the Lares Prestites, the Regia being a small building, rather oddly shaped, and so old that it was on a different axis to the other buildings around it. It served as the office of the Pontifex Maximus but was also an inaugurated temple which contained shrines and altars to Rome's oldest gods, Opsconsiva, Vesta, Mars of the Sacred Shields, and it also housed the archives of the Pontifex.

The present remains of the House of the Vestals, still to be seen in the Forum, were completed in 113 AD, replacing earlier buildings on the same site. The courtyard and garden were flanked by two-storey colonnades, with columns of Carystian green marble below and red and white limestone above. Their spacious and comfortable quarters reflected the enormous importance of these young women.[18]

There were only six Vestals at any one time, and it was an incredible honour to have a young daughter chosen to be sent to the Domus Vestae for training. These girls were chosen every five years, from the highest-born families. It was a very solemn occasion when twenty girls between the ages of six and ten (both of whose parents must be still living), were selected by the Pontifex Maximus. From these candidates, one girl would be chosen by lot.[19] When the lucky girl was decided upon, she was taken from her family by the Pontifex who then addressed her as 'Amata' and repeated the traditional words of acceptance into the temple.

She was immediately taken from her birth family and, more importantly, out of the control of her father. From that moment on, she would inherit nothing from her birth family, nor could she leave anything to any of them in her will. She had become quite separate from them, her new family became the other Vestals, and her new Paterfamilias was the Pontifex Maximus. However, she could still be in touch with members of her original family, as we know from the reports of the Vestals having close relations with the ladies of Patrician families when they were adults, which would include her own. They would share festivals and celebrations with other ladies, particularly important 'female-only' occasions, such as the Bona Dea (Good Goddess) ceremonies, which took place twice a year. Despite the authority of the Pontifex Maximus over these holy women, they were legally independent, as is shown by their ability to eventually make wills of their own.

She was given a sum of money as her dowry, which would be invested carefully on her behalf to ensure her security when she retired, after her thirty years of service to the goddess. By the time of the early Empire, this 'retirement fund' could amount to as much as two million sesterces, which was roughly twice the amount of a wedding dowry for a girl of a wealthy family. If the girl's original family was unable to provide a suitable dowry for her on her admission to the Domus Vestae, then the state would provide it, being aware that many of the best 'old' families, from whose ranks these girls were chosen, had become short of ready cash over the years.

It was customary for a Vestal to retire after her thirty years' service, but it was not essential. If she preferred, she could continue as a Vestal for her lifetime. Any woman who preferred to leave at the end of her term of service could do so, and claim the money invested on her behalf; she was even free to marry once she was no longer officially a Vestal, though very few did. As previously mentioned, it was considered rather unlucky for a man to marry a woman who had been dedicated to the goddess. At the end of her term at the Domus Vestae, the average Vestal would still only be in her late thirties, young enough to have an interesting and enjoyable life, and with sufficient money to provide for her comfort.[20] However, for a lady who had risen through the ranks to achieve the position of Chief Vestal, it may have been considered something of a reduction in status for her to become just another unmarried lady. Many preferred to continue, not only with the single, slightly nun-like existence, but also the position of immense power, respect and influence which being a Vestal gave them, and with the almost sacred eminence it also gave. One lady named Occia, who had become a novice in 38 BC, died after having given fifty-seven years to service in the temple, in 19 AD. Another long-serving Vestal was Junia Torquata, who had been a Vestal for sixty-four years at her death.[21]

When the young girl first joined the Vestals, her colleagues might all be far older than her and she would immediately realise that the 'three

Seniors' had special privileges. Most important of all was the Chief Vestal, whose correct title was 'Virgo Vestalis Maxima' and who had great power and prestige. The new child entrant would be trained by the others, not only regarding the great responsibility of keeping alight the Sacred Flame, but the other important duties performed by them.

Their virginity was vitally important for Rome's continuing good fortune and something that had to be protected at all costs. If a Vestal became ill and had to be nursed outside of the official residence, the Pontiffs would decide the suitability of whichever household was chosen to receive her. It would confer honour on that household, but it would have to be one which was firmly under the control of a respectable matron of high birth. If ever charges were brought against the Vestals, they would be considered and judged by the Pontiffs, under the authority of the Pontifex Maximus himself.[22]

Apart from protecting the flame and themselves, they had other duties which were performed on behalf of the state. There was a succession of religious festivals, taking place at intervals throughout the year, at which their participation was essential. Two of the most important of these happened in the spring and the autumn.

Throughout Rome there were twenty-seven small shrines, known as the 'Sacra Argeorum' and on 17 March small rush puppets, similar to corn dollies, were deposited in these shrines. They were meant to represent human figures, which had been bound hand and foot. On 15 May a great procession was held, in which the Consuls and magistrates took part along with the Pontifices, the Vestals and the wife of the Pontifex Maximus. The women all wore mourning garments for this, instead of their usual light-coloured clothing. They collected the small straw dolls from all the shrines and took them to the River Tiber, where they were thrown into the water from the Pons Sublicius, the oldest bridge in Rome.

Both Ovid and Dionysus of Helicarnassus were eyewitnesses to this ceremony, and were impressed by it. Its interpretation is disputed, but one explanation is that the dolls represented the sacrifice of old men, who were once thrown into the Tiber in a time of famine, and there is a record of this kind of human sacrifice having been performed in 440 BC. That old custom gave rise to a saying still in use in Cicero's time: 'Off the bridge with the sixty-year-olds.'[23]

Another possible, and rather less grim, explanation for the 'deaths' of sixty-year-old men, is supposed to refer to the 'Saepta' or voting area on the Campus Martius. Originally an open area, it was accessed by a walkway, which men over the age of sixty were no longer expected to use to cast a vote, as their age disenfranchised them. Hence the call to throw 'older men off the bridge' could also refer to their voting rights ending.

Gaius Julius Caesar later built the Saepta Julia, to replace the ancient 'Ovile' voting area. This new voting area can clearly be seen on the Forma Urbis Romae, which is the map of the city, as it was in the early third century AD. Parts of this building can still be seen close up against the western wall of the Pantheon, and its remains are now unfortunately few, although it was originally 310 metres long and 120 metres wide. It was faced with Traventine marble and possibly had a second floor. This Porticus Argonauturum was also supplied with water from the Aqua Virgo, which supplied the majority of the buildings on the Campus Martius.

Despite the possible nod to ancient and unpleasant ceremonies, this festival does not appear to have been a solemn one. All the attendant dignitaries wore their best clothes, people carried the usual garlands of flowers which were a part of most Roman festivals, and they would have followed the Vestals as they collected and eventually disposed of the little dolls. There was probably also the usual feast afterwards.

Another 'dark' occasion, which did unfortunately live up to its grim connections, took place in the middle of October. It was joined to one which had already been performed on 15 April, the Festival of Fordicidia. Thirty-one cows in calf were slaughtered and the calves were pulled from their mother's bodies to be cremated. Their ashes were kept in the storehouse of the Vestals until later in the year.[24] On the Ides of October, the best war horses of that year were chosen to race on the Campus Martius. The nearside horse of the winning team was then sacrificed to Mars, on an altar placed close to the racetrack, killing the champion horse with a spear. Its head was then cut off and covered over with small cakes, while its tail and genitals were cut off and taken to the Regia in the Forum, where the horse's blood was dripped onto the altar of Mars of the Sacred Shields. Some of the blood was also mixed with the ashes of the calves which had been slaughtered in the April ceremony.

In the earliest years, the horse's head would be fought over by two teams, if the Via Sacra crowd won the head, it was nailed to the outside wall of the Regia. If the Subura team won, it was nailed to the wall of the Turris Mamilia, which was the Subura area's largest building. The tail and genitals which had been taken to the altar of Mars were also eventually burned by the Vestals, and also mixed with the ashes of the calves, then stored until the following 21 April, which was the Feast of Parilia, when bonfires were lit and a little of the mixed blood and ashes was distributed to each fire as a purifying agent for the sheep and sheepfolds, in order to avert diseases from the flocks.[25]

Another vitally important task of the Vestals was the recording and storage of all Roman citizen's wills, which went into their vast storeroom for safekeeping. This was an important service to the city. All the wills were registered carefully, then retrieved and read after a death took place.[26]

However, not all the life of any Vestal was taken over by tedious religious or dutiful ceremonial. They had any possibility of a normal family life removed from them as young girls, and in this they would grow up to be similar to nuns, but they were not isolated. They were able to enjoy many freedoms, including visiting friends, attending dinner parties; there is a record of a banquet which took place on 24 August 69 BC at which four of the Vestals were present. The dinner was given to celebrate the installation of a new Flamen Martialis by an Augur. The attendant Pontiffs occupied two tables, and the Vestals, along with the wife of the new Flamen and his mother-in-law, sat at a third. Even the menu for that official occasion is known, with the thirty dishes on offer including asparagus, oysters and several different sorts of pâté.[27]

All the Vestals were highly respected. When they travelled through the streets of Rome on official occasions, they were always attended by a lictor. This was the man who attended curule magistrates, who bore a bundle of rods which denoted his office. He was both a bodyguard and an indication of one's importance. A Vestal was entitled to have one lictor attend her during the Empire, when a woman of the Imperial family was allowed two. A Praetor or a Provincial Governor was allowed six, with twelve assigned to a Consul. During the Republic, a Dictator was entitled to have twenty-four. Any Vestal also had the authority to annul the sentence of any felon she met while she was on a journey, and she even had the power to stop an execution from taking place, if she wished to use it.

Vestals were allowed friendships and contacts outside the Domus Vestae and regularly met with other women of status. As long as they performed their religious duties correctly, and behaved correctly, they lived lives of comfort and security. One of the minor privileges of being a Vestal was being given seating right at the front at the games. Women were generally allowed to sit with men during the games, although not usually at the theatres, where the content of the plays was likely to be bawdy and considered unsuitable for them.

The purity of the Vestals should never be in doubt – however, these were young and attractive women, and temptations could be experienced. Men were actually allowed to visit the Atrium Vestae during the daytime to see their relatives, although this was not allowed after nightfall. It did allow them to meet with young men, the friends of brothers and cousins, and there were times when moral laxity was not only suspected, but 'corruption' could be proved.

The life of privilege and respect which the Vestals were afforded also had its downside. After the disaster of the Battle of Cannae in 216 BC, the Romans were so devastated that they looked for someone to blame. The responsibility for the appalling defeat was laid at the door of the Vestals, as only some laxity within their House could account for what had happened. Two Vestals were singled out and accused of lack of chastity. It is unlikely that these two women were actually guilty of any wrongdoing, but they became the scapegoats for the Roman people who could not believe that so profound a defeat could have been visited on them, unless the goddess had been insulted. The women were found guilty and sentenced to death.[28] These women had to suffer the punishment of being buried alive, as laid down by the law, sacrifices on behalf of a people who had suffered a defeat they weren't expecting and could not comprehend.

Corruption within the whole college of Vestals was alleged at the end of the second century BC and in 114 BC the Pontiffs held an enquiry and decided to condemn one Vestal to death. The following year, on the motion of the Tribune Peducaeus, who had accused the Pontiffs of partiality, a court was set up to re-try the matter and this time two of the Vestals, who had earlier been acquitted, were also condemned.

Immorality among the College of Vestals was sometimes suspected for no better reason than that a young woman had rebelled slightly against the heavy and rather drab clothing she was expected to wear for life.[29] A trial in 420 BC was described by Livy, when a Vestal named Postumia had aroused suspicion regarding her purity, simply for her sense of humour and liking for pretty clothes. The poor girl must have been terrified, knowing that her life was at stake; she was certainly innocent of any real crime. She was, in fact, found not guilty but the Pontifex Maximus ordered her to 'stop making jokes and, in her manner of dress, to aim at looking holy, rather than trying to look smart'.[30]

There are also one or two rather unlikely stories regarding miracles which proved the innocence of an accused Vestal. One Aemilia, whose morality was questioned because she had let the Sacred Flame go out, prayed publicly to Vesta to exonerate her, then threw onto the cold embers a piece of linen. The sudden blaze which followed placed the girl's innocence beyond doubt. On another occasion, a Vestal named Tuccia, in another incident of the same sort, was said to have proved her innocence by carrying water from the Tiber in a sieve which did not leak.[31]

In 73 BC, Fabia, the half-sister of Cicero's wife Tarentia, was alleged to have been seduced by Catalina, though it is likely to have been a political accusation intended to damage his reputation. Fabia was at that time the Chief Vestal, and her brother-in-law Cicero already had issues with Catalina, which suggests that the accusation was indeed fraudulent. However, any accusation of this kind was always dangerous for a Vestal. Another Vestal, Licinia, was accused of having had improper relations with Crassus, who was her cousin. Crassus freely admitted that he had visited her and spent a fair amount of time with her, but typically for the man who was known as 'Dives' or 'the Rich' he said he had been trying to buy land from Licinia at rather less than the full market price, therefore he was far more interested in making money than in her body. He was well known for his cupidity and he was acquitted.[32]

Although the Vestals were not really expected to marry once they retired, Fabia (Tarentia's half-sister), on her retirement at the age of thirty-seven, was not only still attractive but perhaps more importantly was very wealthy. She became one of the few retired Vestals to acquire a husband. Unfortunately, the man she married was Publius Cornelius Dolabella, always charming to the ladies, always in debt, and very much after her dowry. The marriage was a disaster, confirming the idea that the Vestals did better to avoid close relationships with men after they retired as well as before. When Fabia and Dolabella finally divorced, he later went on to marry Fabia's niece Tullia, the daughter of Cicero, another unhappy marriage centred on the acquisition of money.

When the Pontiffs did take seriously a charge against a Vestal, which was usually due information being gathered from a slave, whether given willingly or not, the woman at the centre of the investigation would be suspended from duty. She was forbidden to then part with any of her slaves, in case they were needed for evidence. These charges against her (which were technically described as 'incest') or an accusation of high treason, were the only times when the evidence of a slave could be taken against his or her employer, and this was usually taken under torture.[33] If the evidence was considered serious enough against a Vestal, she would then be tried officially by the Pontiffs.

If a Vestal Virgin had simply let the Sacred Fire go out, she could expect to be thrashed by the Pontifex Maximus. However, if she should be found guilty of sexual misbehaviour her partner was to be flogged to death in the Comitium. The Vestal herself faced a rather more delicate but far more lingering death. Due to the prohibition against anyone killing a Vestal, she would be sentenced to be buried alive in a small underground chamber under the Campus Sceleratus, out by the Colline Gate.

There is a full description from Plutarch of the way in which such a sentence was carried out.

> A small underground chamber is constructed with access from above by a ladder. It contains a bed, a lighted lamp and small portions of the bare necessities of existence, such as bread, water, milk and oil. This is so that the Romans may feel easy in their consciences and nobody can say that by starvation they have murdered a woman consecrated by the most sacred rituals. Inside a litter enclosed by curtains, bound and gagged, so that her cries may not be heard, they carry the victim through the Forum. People make way for the procession in utter silence, and deep dejection. There is no spectacle in the world more terrifying and in Rome no comparable horror. When the cortege nears the end of its journey, the attendants undo the bonds, and, after he has prayed in silence, stretching out his hands to the Gods to explain the necessity of his act, the Pontifex Maximus takes her by the hand, a thick cloak hiding her face, and sets her on the ladder. He and the rest of the Pontiffs then turn away, while she descends the ladder. Then the ladder is pulled up, and the entry to the chamber closed and covered with deep earth, level with the surrounding ground.[34]

Fortunately, this ghastly drama was not an everyday event; there are fewer than ten occasions in the whole history of Rome when this punishment is known to have been exacted.[35] It is unlikely that it was performed at all in the last hundred and fifty years of the Republic, so it is extraordinary that the Emperor Domitian should revive it. In 83 AD he decided to reform the morals of the state.[36] Three of the Vestals, half of the Sacred College, were invited to commit suicide after accusations of sexual corruption, while the men accused with the women were banished. Later, the Pontiffs were summoned again and the Chief Vestal, Cornelia, who had been absolved at the end of the earlier examinations, was then condemned, unheard and in her absence, to be entombed, while her supposed seducer was beaten to death.[37]

Pliny the Younger records Cornelia's fate:

> The Pontiffs were at once dismissed to see to the death and burial. Cornelia stretched out her hands to Vesta, and to the other Gods, and among other protestations cried out more than once, 'How can Caesar think me corrupt, when my sacred ministrations brought him to victory and triumphs?' Whether she said this in hope of mercy, or in mockery, from confidence in her own integrity, or from contempt for the Emperor, who can say? Whether innocent or not, she certainly gave the impression of clear innocence, as she was conducted to her doom. When she descended the ladder to the tomb, her dress caught up, and she turned and freed it. The executioner offered her his hand, but she turned away from it and shrank back, as if, by a final display of her integrity, she was guarding her pure and chaste body from contact with something foul.[38]

The vicious injustice of the emperors continued. In 215 AD the Emperor Caracalla seduced a Vestal Virgin, then condemned her and two others to be buried alive. Slightly later, in 220-221 AD the Emperor Elegabalus married the Vestal Aquilia Severa. He had divorced his wife for the purpose and personally absolved Aquilia from her vows. They had no children, but he had assured the senate that, as he was the High Priest, and his wife had been a Priestess, any children that they might have would certainly not have been born ordinary mortals.[39] Such excesses may have made Romans wish themselves back in the days of the Republic, when the friction between various consuls would have seemed like a breath of fresh air in comparison.

The Pontifex Maximus was free to choose his own wife, within the normal social expectations of a Patrician holding high office. The Flamines, priests of Mars and Quirinus and the Flamen Dialis had to marry a woman who still had both parents living, and they had to marry by the old and complicated ritual of the confarreatio, women who must also abide by the same conditions. The wives of the Flamen Quirinalis and the Flamen Martialis, who would hold no official position personally, would also need to live their lives in accordance with the expectations of the rank of their husbands. However, the wife of the Rex Sacrorum, who became the Regina Sacrorum, and the wife of the Flamen Dialis, who became the Flaminia Dialis, became officially priestesses, with the Flaminia Dialis being a priestess of Juno. They were obliged to observe rigorous formality with regard to dress and were subject to restrictions. The office of Rex Sacrorum was a remnant of the time of the old kings, the holder of it was 'king of the sacred rights' who oversaw the religious observances traditionally performed by the king. During the Republic he was the second-ranking pontifex in the hierarchy and his life was hedged around with almost as many taboos as that of the Flamen Dialis, as was the life of his wife.

The Flaminia could not climb more than three rungs of any ladder, she could not bathe during the month of May, or comb her hair in the first half of June, or on those days in March when the Priests of Mars danced. She was also forbidden from cutting her fingernails in the first half of June. This may have been to obey the rules of purification, as the Vestals were clearing out their storehouse on 15 June, after which they carried all the rubbish to be thrown into the river. This ended a period of inauspicious days, after which life returned to normal.[40]

Under the Empire, the spread of emperor-worship brought into existence a number of new positions for priestesses in the provinces, who were charged with the worship of the women of the Imperial family. These were the royal women who had been consecrated as goddesses, and occasionally the priestesses would include a number of unmarried girls or even married women who were required in exceptional circumstances to perform propitiatory acts for Juno or one of the new goddesses. However, these women could not be considered to be priestesses in the full sense of the title.[41]

For all the religious rituals from which women were excluded as being purely 'men's concerns' such as Hercules and Mithras, there was one vitally important religious festival which took place twice yearly, concerned with the worship of the Goddess which no man could approach, this was the worship of the Bona Dea.

Roman men tended to make salacious jokes about this purely female cult, with much speculation about what the women got up to while they were alone, centred around drunkenness and ceremonial whipping, when all men, including male slaves and male animals, were banned from the house while the festival went on. The Bona Dea, a faceless and formless goddess with a penchant for snakes, who liked to be fed with eggs and milk, was also known as the Good Goddess. Her rituals included feasting and dancing and the drinking of a good deal of wine, normally forbidden to women, so it was on these occasions referred to as 'milk'.

The gathering which took place during May at the Temple of the Bona Dea on the Aventine was known as the 'Waking up of the Goddess'. There was another in December, unsurprisingly known as 'Putting the Goddess to sleep', which took place at the home of one of the senior curule magistrates. The lady of that house was the hostess, with other ladies of high status and what Vestals could be spared from tending the Flame as guests. This ceremony took place at night, so all the males of the host family had to stay elsewhere until the following morning, and all statues and pictures of males which could not easily be removed had to be covered up.[42] It has been suggested that the paintings on the walls of the Villa of the Mysteries in Pompeii showed an initiation into the cult of Bacchus, though some of the imagery seems to show a depiction of part of the Bona Dea ceremony, although this cannot be confirmed.

Whatever the truth of what transpired at these ceremonies, they were certainly aimed at a very private and female-only congregation, probably all the more so as the women knew that, despite all the jokes, the men would go along with its secrecy because the Bona Dea was considered an important Goddess, whose goodwill was essential for Rome's safety and prosperity. Like all Rome's religious observances, the rituals had to be performed without a hitch, or they would have to be started all over again. Should the rituals be interrupted, it was considered most unlucky, with the aborted ritual being described as 'nefas', or sacrilege. The men, who arranged to stay out of the women's way on these occasions, accepted that the deeply religious aspect of these gatherings could not be compromised by any selfish or foolish action on their part. This was respected until 62 BC, when the winter Bona Dea festival was indeed compromised by a very stupid piece of foolishness which had far-reaching consequences.

That year the 'Putting the Goddess to sleep' ceremony was held at the house of the Pontifex Maximus, Gaius Julius Caesar. This was not due to his priestly standing but because he was the Praetor for that year. His mother, the formidable Aurelia Cotta, was the official hostess, despite Caesar's then wife Pompeia Sulla being present. She was considered something of a nonentity despite her high birth, and Aurelia, who also lived at the Domus Publicae, still ruled the household.

During the early part of the proceedings, when a party atmosphere reigned, a slave named Habra gave Aurelia the appalling news that she suspected one of the hired musicians, who had arrived to play for the ladies, was actually a man![43] Aurelia was horrified at the idea of such sacrilege taking place. She immediately had the musician in question apprehended, and all the guests were required to leave, except the senior ladies and the Vestals. Once unveiled, the intruder proved to be Publius Clodius Pulcher, heir of an important family, but a man who had already made a name for himself as a risk-taker, debaucher, and performer of unconsidered jokes and general foolishness. He and his wife, the heiress Fulvia, along with his sister Clodia (who was then married to Quintus Caecilius Metellus), were typical bored, rich, do-nothings who were accused of every vice, from un-Roman thinking to incest. They were childish in their desire to shock and cause mischief.

Publius Clodius was a Quaestor-elect who had already several times discredited his noble family, but despite his well-known desire for excitement and notoriety, one still wonders why he would choose to do so ridiculous and potentially dangerous a thing, knowing the importance of the ceremony. Was it really only due to a delight in wrongdoing, or did it conceal something even worse?

There were later rumours that he had entered the house of the Pontifex Maximus Caesar to conduct a sexual intrigue with Caesar's beautiful but rather dim wife, Pompeia. This she firmly and tearfully denied, but on hearing of the intrusion Caesar felt he had no alternative but to divorce her, with the famous words: 'Caesar's wife must be above suspicion.'[44]

Caesar's mother Aurelia became one of the chief witnesses against Clodius at his subsequent trial, which took place in May of 61 BC, making it clear that she had unveiled and recognised Clodius within the house at that time. Aurelia was devout, eminently respectable and greatly admired, but was the redoubtable noblewoman also secretly glad to be able to rid her son of a barren wife, whom she may have considered not quite good enough? Certainly, given Aurelia's impeccable status and her reputation for absolute probity, her testimony was guaranteed a sympathetic hearing.

The general horror felt at the intrusion of the sacred ceremony, which would certainly have to be performed again on another date, cannot be overestimated. Despite the habit of speculation and smutty jokes about what the women were doing when they had drunk too much of their 'milk' and relaxed a little, it still was a vitally important religious occasion, and its defilement could have serious repercussions for Rome as a whole. The trial of Publius Clodius had been widely demanded and it was expected he would be punished severely, despite the fact that no existing law actually covered what he had done.[45]

Cicero, probably pressured by his own formidable wife Tarentia, who was not only a friend of Aurelia's but half-sister to that Fabia who was at the time still the Chief Vestal, rather unwisely became involved in the general outcry about the trial, and the Pontiffs and Vestals were all asked for their opinions. The Vestals did, in any event, have to make the arrangements for the ceremonies to be performed again, to ensure that the sacrilege was wiped out, and that the Bona Dea would continue to give Rome her sacred protection.

In his own defence, Clodius rather foolishly claimed that he had not been present at the house on the night in question. He said he was a good ninety miles away from Rome at the time, at a place named Interamna. However, several witnesses swore that they had seen him in Rome that morning, and Cicero himself gave evidence that Clodius had called on him at his own house in Rome earlier that day, which would have prevented him from reaching Interamna by nightfall. Despite all this, the jury found Clodius 'not guilty', although Cicero and the others concerned clearly believed otherwise.[46] Unfortunately, the evidence which Cicero had given against Clodius became the basis for a strong enmity, which was to cause trouble in the future.

There is another, possibly apocryphal explanation of why the guilty Clodius was so surprisingly acquitted at a trial for such a serious matter and with evidence stacked against him. This is that the Vestalis Maxima Fabia and Aurelia Cotta, Caesar's mother, requested the jury that they let the Goddess deal with Clodius, rather than having men impose a sentence. It is said that they had asked for the matter to be left in the hands of the Goddess, who would deal with Clodius in her own way and in her own time, and in view of the religious nature of the offence, this was agreed.

For some time afterwards, Clodius appeared to settle down and concentrate on his career, but privately he had already laid plans to become a Tribune of the Plebs, a position which would give him the power to work against his enemies, including Cicero. Being a Patrician, this position was not open to him, so he determined to find a well-born Plebeian who would be willing to adopt him. Clodius settled on one Publius Fonteius, who in 59 BC agreed to adopt Clodius as his son. As the 'adoption' was then against the regulations of the adoption process, and Fonteius was actually younger than the man he proposed to adopt, it was clear that it was merely a ploy to allow Clodius to stand for the political position he wanted, turning a serious matter into a farce.

When Clodius did achieve his aims, he became exhilarated by his increased power and authority and employed a gang of thugs and ex-gladiators to control the streets of Rome on his behalf. He lost the favour of Pompeius Magnus due to his behaviour and then in 56 BC he dared to impeach Titus Annius Milo, accusing him of public violence, even though the incident stemmed from Milo trying to defend his house against a gang of thugs marshalled by Clodius.

Milo and Clodius both stood for public office in 52 BC. Milo was hoping for the Consulship (for which he had put on games costing one million sesterces). However, no election could take place at all, due to disturbances in Rome. On 18 January 52 BC, Clodius was returning to Rome when he met Milo, who was travelling to Bovillae. Both had armed followers with them, and there was a scuffle. Clodius had ridden past the carpentum in which was seated Milo's wife, Fausta Sulla, then turned back to rejoin the fracas in defence of some of his men who had become separated from him. Clodius was then wounded by a lance thrown by one of the men defending Milo's party and was taken to a nearby tavern. Milo then gave the order for the matter to be settled once and for all by the killing of Clodius Pulcher. He was dragged from the tavern and killed, his body left lying in the road.[47]

Cicero would later defend Milo at his trial, pointing out that the situation had not been planned, which was shown by the presence of

Milo's wife and her servants at the time. Despite his excellent defence, he could not prevent Milo from being exiled for the death of Clodius. However, there was widespread belief at the time, particularly among the followers of the Goddess Bona Dea, that Clodius had died close by a little wayside shrine dedicated to that Goddess, and that she had finally exacted her own retribution.

There would be other less Roman goddesses who would also make a place for themselves in the pantheon of deities, and the most important of these was certainly Isis. Also known as Aset, Iset, Ast or Usef, she is the Goddess of limitless attributes, ranging from magic and fertility, motherhood with virginity, death, re-birth and healing. Her names refer to her queenship, and the throne that was her symbol, as the Queen of Heaven.

The God Geb (earth) and his wife Nut (sky) had four children – Osiris, Aset, Nepthys and Set. Osiris was killed by Set, but his sister-wife Aset/Isis searched for his remains, collected them and breathed new life into them for long enough to conceive their son Horus. She possessed absolute power, and even as part of the Memphis Triad, or Trinity, always took the dominant place. When initially introduced into Rome, she became very popular with women and also with slaves and the lower classes, due to her teaching of re-birth and reincarnation, which promised the opportunity of a better life next time.

The Romans were always very adept at incorporating other people's deities into their own circle of gods, and they associated Osiris with Serapis and Aset with Demeter or Aphrodite. Isis was a universal deity, not confined to one gender of worshippers or to one area. She would eventually be worshipped as far afield as Britain and Afghanistan, honoured by both the eastern and western empires, and she appealed to all kinds of people as her religion spread.

However, in Rome, Isis worship faced some difficulties at first. Augustus, in particular, had issues with Egypt itself and the troubles he had had with Marcus Antonius and Cleopatra, so he chose to pretend that the Egyptian religion was pornographic. Tiberius was also against it, but Rome both wanted and needed Egypt, which was immensely rich in gold, gems and particularly in the grain that the hungry and expanding Rome always needed. Egypt's fertile Nile valley was capable of producing two harvests per year, fed by the silt-rich soils of the inundation – which was controlled by the God, Hapi. When the Romans tried to clamp down on the growing new interest in the Egyptian religion, as from time to time they did, executing its priests and destroying its temples, it was because of its immense popularity with the people. It was beginning to take attention, and the all-important revenues, away from the Roman deities. Caligula finally legitimised the Isis religion to ensure its safety, and he employed an Egyptian chamberlain. Both Hadrian and Marcus Aurelius tolerated it.

The Iseum, which was not open to the street and the eyes of any passers-by as Roman temples were, had an inner sanctuary. There was also a small building usually within its enclosure, which contained a small pool of Nile water. The Festival of Isis took place on 5 March, when Isis sailed the seas to find the body of her husband Osiris. The enactment of Passion Plays was on 28 October, telling the story of the killing and resurrection of Osiris, along with the devotion of the Virgin Goddess, who was also the mother of their son Horus. The similarities between this ancient religion and the Christian one, which eventually took its place, are obvious.[48]

Isis worship was persistent, with Roman emperors shown as Pharoahs worshipping the Goddess at Philae, where Hadrian added a new gate to the temple complex there during his reign (117-138 AD). Worship of Isis was very difficult to eradicate and it flourished until the reign of Justinian (527-565 AD). For the preceding centuries it had continued to give the relatively new Christian religion a very serious amount of competition, in fact at one point almost obliterating it in favour of Isis, whose rites were still being fiercely defended in the sixth century AD.

Temples were spread over the eastern and western empires, although unfortunately the vast one which once stood in Rome no longer exists. It was a very large complex, close to where the present Pantheon stands, with part of its compound under the church of Santa Maria sopra Minerva. 'Minerva' refers to a smaller temple of Minerva which once stood on the site. The Isis temple shared space with Serapis, a hybrid deity from the reign of the first Ptolemy, who was a general of the army of Alexander the Great. Serapis was a Hellenised version of the Egyptian bull god Apis, which included Osiris and even elements of Zeus. The buildings of this large double temple compound included a processional way along which was a channel of water, representing the Nile. In the area where this channel of water once ran was a pink granite crocodile, representing Egypt. This charming reptile is now in the Egyptian Department of the Vatican Museum. Also on display are many representations of the gods and goddesses of Egypt, many found at the site, along with some of the granite columns which lined the processional way, with their carved priests performing the sacred rituals. The Bernini elephant, which now stands in the Piazza in front of the church, carries on its back one of the obelisks from the Isis temple, another is in front of the Pantheon, and yet another in the Piazza del Popolo.[49] Another large Isis temple stood beyond the Via Labicana, where the Piazza Iside still has the remnants of its brick-built base. There were also several other shrines to the goddess within Rome.

Although Rome has lost its Isis temples, others still exist, particularly the charming small one at Pompeii, the original of which was built in the second century BC. Its precinct can still be seen, along with its small 'cella' and the hall behind where the worshippers could meet, with the houses of the priests only a short distance away.[50] It is widely believed that, during the period between Pompeii's earthquake in 63 AD and the eruption of Vesuvius in 79 AD the worship of Isis had become even more popular than the traditional Roman gods, as it offered something more, beyond death itself, which the Roman gods did not. They were primarily concerned with life, and what came after was believed to be nothing more than a long sleep, unless one was an emperor who could become a god.

The Isis temple in Pompeii appears to have been one of the first public buildings to be rebuilt after the earthquake of 63 AD. In fact, the temple of Venus, on the other side of the Forum, was not rebuilt at all by the time of the eruption sixteen years later. This has to mean that the Isis religion was considered more important and had its supporters among Pompeii's elite. There were certainly Isis followers who were involved in the town's political life, as several electoral posters had been added to the temple's external walls.[51] 'All the followers of Isis call for Gnaeus Helvius Sabinus as aedile.' And also, 'His client Popidius Natalis and all the followers of Isis call for Cuspius Pansa as aedile.'[52] These slogans show that the Isis religion had crossed the social boundaries and was no longer a cult confined to women or the poor.

It is known that when the eruption finally destroyed Pompeii in 79 AD, ending the worship of Isis which had begun in that town in the second century BC along with everything else, some of the priests of Isis fell victim to the general destruction. They had faithfully performed their twice-daily ceremonies – at sunrise and around 2pm – and their processions, along with their worshippers, many of whom were women. Unlike so many Roman religions, women were not forbidden from taking an active part in the rituals and could hold high positions within the religion. When the temple was discovered in 1765, ashes and small pieces of burned bone were found on its main altar. Two burial holes in the courtyard held the burned remains of figs, pine-kernels, nuts and dates, and large numbers of coins and vessels, and there was also a male skeleton, apparently crushed beneath the columns of the collapsed portico, who may have been a priest.[53]

Another foreign import to Rome was the goddess Magna Mater, from Phrygia. She was also known as Cybele. A statue of this goddess was dated to approximately six thousand years old. She is usually depicted as a seated woman flanked by leopards and was a symbol of very powerful female forces. She was believed to have been exposed to die as a child but was raised by panthers. This of course has echoes of the supposed origins of Romulus and Remus. Her religious cult had connections with Ishtar and the Romans tended to identify her with Rhea and called her the Great Mother. She was attended by priests who were obliged to castrate themselves before her image, sacrificing their manhood before they could serve the goddess. No man who was still entire could attend her ceremonies. Female priestesses were allowed, and the castrated male priests were responsible for dances, divination, and the healing aspects of the cult.

Midwives were generally connected to the Great Mother because of her association with motherhood and children, but the cult always held an aura of eastern mystery and sexuality, and the idea of priests castrating themselves never sat comfortably with Roman males, who could barely get used to the idea of the celibate Isis priests. The Magna Mater religion remained very popular with women, but its eastern and erotic aspects never allowed it to gain full popularity, nor did it ever become totally acceptable, as did the Bona Dea and even the Egyptian Isis.[54]

It was believed that divine will could be read and understood from signs sent by various gods, and this was an important aspect of Roman religions. There were signs which had been asked for, and those which occurred spontaneously.

Before any major state decision could be made, the will of heaven needed to be ascertained. When two or three ranks of magistrates were present, for example a consul, a praetor and an aedile, only the most senior of those magistrates could make the request. The standard sign came from the observation of the flights of birds, and the magistrate empowered to ask for a sign was said to 'take the auspices', which came from the word 'auspicia' or bird-watching. He would sit in the open and designate an area of the sky to which he would give his attention, watching for any movements. In Rome itself, a special site, the 'Auguraculum' on the Capitol, was reserved for this purpose. The magistrate would be attended by one of the fifteen members of the College of Augers, who recited the ceremonial prayer and would interpret (while blind-folded) anything that the magistrate reported as having been seen in the sky. This practice was so important to decision-making that in 99 BC, when one Tiberius Claudius Centumalus built a house which obstructed the view from the Auguraculum, he was made to demolish it.[55]

Outside of Rome this ceremony might have to take place without an Auger being present, although the correct interpretation of the flight patterns, songs, pitch, intonation and frequency of the activities of the birds was complicated, and much also depended upon the time and the season of the year.

Another method was to watch for lightning rather than the movements of birds. Lightning was the prerogative of Jupiter, and so this could be the most important sign of all. It would eventually be almost automatic for a magistrate, when he took the Auspices on entering office, to 'see lightning' or some flash of light on his left, which was considered a lucky omen. A copy of a calendar giving the significance of sounds of thunder for each day of the year has survived. For example, if it thundered on 3 December, 'a shortage of fish would make people eat meat' or if it thundered on 19 August, 'women and slaves will commit murder.'[56]

If lightning appeared to a magistrate who was taking the Auspices before a public assembly, it meant that the meeting could not take place that day. It is far easier for a man to claim that he has seen a flash of light than the movements of birds unseen by others, so it was sometimes open to abuse. The Consul Bibulus (59 BC) merely needed to say that he intended to withdraw to 'watch the sky' (servare de caelo) for all public business to be immediately suspended indefinitely. He at one point left his post for so long that he was able to prevent Caesar passing legislation that Bibulus opposed.[57] It was said of him that if he looked for lightning hard enough, he would certainly find it.

Marcus Calpurnius Bibulus was not Caesar's only powerful opponent. In the early days when Gaius Marius had impeded the young Caesar's military aspirations by making him Flamen Dialis, which prevented him from becoming a soldier, he was only released from the post by Lucius Cornelius Sulla, then holding the position of Dictator. However, Sulla, who also saw what Caesar might become, only gave him that release after warning the people who had pleaded Caesar's cause that 'In him I see many Mariuses!'

The documentary sources for early Roman history were the records kept by the Augers, who recorded religious occurrences interpreted as divine interventions. These were the 'unasked for' omens. Livy filled his *Ab Urbe Condita* with signs and portents and he considered that by his time the people had grown too neglectful of the gods. He recorded all such events as genuine signs that the Gods had sent, although he did not try to interpret them. For 169 BC he recorded:

> At Anagria a torch was seen in the sky, and a cow talked. At Menturnae the sky appeared to be on fire. At Reate it rained stones. At Cumae the statue of Apollo wept for three days and three nights. In Rome a crested snake was seen in the temple of Fortuna Primigenia. A palm tree grew in the forecourt of the temple of Fortuna and it rained with blood. A further omen, not officially recognised, occurred at Fregellae, when a spear blazed for two hours without being consumed by the fire.[58]

Lucan[59] wrote of the signs shown to the army of Pompeius Magnus before the Battle of Pharsalus:

> ... the whole sky set itself against this march, the troops were bombarded with thunderbolts, fireballs, and meteors. The standards could not be pulled from the earth, and were made so heavy by swarms of bees that settled on them, that the standard bearers could not lift them. They seemed to weep at the prospect before them. The bull that was to be sacrificed kicked over the altar and ran away and no replacement for it could be found in time.

No wonder the soldiers became afraid when all those signs of terrible luck appeared at the same time. They had good reason to be. Despite having the larger army, Gnaeus Pompeius Magnus was defeated at Pharsalus by Gaius Julius Caesar on the 9 August 48 BC. Pompeius survived the battle and fled to Egypt, where he was then killed on arrival on the order of Pharoah, who mistakenly believed that Caesar would be pleased at the murder of his enemy, who had been his one-time close friend and son-in-law.[60]

One form of omen to which Romans paid great heed was the chance remark. In 386 BC after Rome had been sacked by the Gauls, the Romans were debating whether or not to move their capital elsewhere. A company of soldiers halted in the marketplace, on the order of their officer, who cried out 'Let's stop here!' The words were believed to have been divinely inspired.

One of the most famous prophecies concerned the city of Pompeii. When the earthquake of 62 AD hit the Campania region, damaging many of the city's public buildings which then required costly and extensive repairs, the local magistrates were concerned that the city would never regain its original prosperity. A local soothsayer, named Biria Onomastia was consulted about Pompeii's future, and she soothed the fears of the magistrates by telling them that she had seen into the future. She could see the city thriving 'visited by people from all over the world, even more than a thousand years from now'. She was certainly correct, though as with most prophecies the future did not appear quite as the prophecy had suggested, and it was certainly not in a way that the city fathers would have liked.

Many signs and portents were bewildering and needed the interpretation of a trained Auger. By the time of the Emperor Augustus there was a good deal of literature available to explain the various meanings of the signs, even though the methods used by the Augers were supposed to be secrets. The books turned Augury into a science.

Many authors tackled the subject, including Appius Claudius, who was the predecessor of Marcus Tullius Cicero as Governor of Cilicia. One Aulus Caecina wrote a book on it, as did Marcus Messalla, the consul of 53 BC. Cicero also wrote on the subject. Cicero's *On Divination* took the form of a dialogue between Cicero and his brother Quintus.[61]

Gradually, the inner appearance of the intestines of animals became all-important for divination. This science was originally used by the Etruscans, and the best 'Haruspices' were always believed to come from Etruria. They never formed an official priesthood in Rome, and never held the authority of an Auger. No Roman citizen could become a Haruspex in the early days, although by Cicero's time that rule no longer applied. If a doubtful point of interpretation needed a second opinion, the Haruspex was on hand to assist. There are carvings showing a Haruspex examining the liver of a sacrificed animal, and little bronze models have also been found that showed what an ideal liver should look like. One of these was found at Piacenza, with details giving instructions. It is divided into two halves, each containing on its margin eight regions, and marked on the back with 'of the sun' and 'of the moon', meaning use for either day or night.[62]

The sixteen regions were the way the Etruscans divided up the heavens and indicate the correlation between the cosmic and terrestrial life. Inside these are further inner segments, sixteen on the side of 'day' and eight on the side of 'night', each bearing the name of the God who controlled that segment.

A Haruspex could be called in to explain other things than the good or bad appearance of an animal's liver. Another matter which involved Publius Clodius Pulcher, this time concerning his great enemy Cicero, needed the advice of a Haruspex. Cicero had returned to Rome after a year in exile to find that his house there had been destroyed by Clodius. Not only had Clodius pulled down his house, but he had deliberately had the area consecrated as temple land. Therefore, when Cicero tried to rebuild, he was greatly disturbed to hear strange noises in the area, having to call in a Haruspex to explain them. The Haruspex told Cicero that the gods were displeased that he had profaned an area dedicated to the gods by trying to rebuild on it, as Clodius had hoped.[63] Cicero was furious, but fully aware that it was a serious matter and one which could not be ignored. He was to devote a long and vitriolic speech in the senate to rebutting Clodius's claims.[64] He was fully aware that Clodius was intent on making a fool of him by building a 'temple of liberty' in the ruins of his house. Was he also responsible for the strange noises? It was not the first time Clodius had tried to play games with the gods, but he could not expect to remain unpunished for ever. When he was finally killed by Milo's men, it was generally considered to be his just deserts.

Clodius's death would have been seen as a necessary sacrifice to atone for his disrespect, for sacrifice in Roman religion was just as important as prayer. Sacrifice means literally to make something holy, 'sacer', setting it aside from normal life and normal use, as an offering to the Gods. As with the October Horse, it was necessary that the gods be offered something precious, for only the very best was good enough, or certainly the best that could be afforded. It was not just that something beautiful, precious and the best of its kind should be offered, but preferably something that had life.[65]

In fact, for most everyday offerings, particularly those in household shrines, the usual item offered was a handful of grain. This was usually in the form of small 'cakes' made with spelt, or sometimes just flour mixed with salt (mola salsa). Ovid describes during the family meal a small piece of food would be broken off to be thrown into the flames of the brazier.[66] Other regular offerings most often given in sacrifice were flowers, honey, cheese, fruit, wine or milk. All these items were considered to have had life and were therefore suitable. However, animals large and small were the most effective and most conspicuous sacrifices, as well as being the most expensive.

The idea of giving something animate or quasi-animate is understandable. The gods were alive, therefore their vitality had to be acknowledged and at intervals renewed, in order for them to function. Without this, the crops would likely fail, disease could spread and life for everyone would stop. The very existence of the gods depended on the devotion of humans, on whether or not they were neglected: 'The gods do not die while ever men speak their names.' The prayers to the gods, the repetition of their names, the offerings given to them, all served to keep them alive and strong, and they in their turn could keep the people alive and strong. The 'contract' between gods and men had never been clearer.

In the temples, the sacrifices were made by state officials or by private individuals at their own expense. The choice of sacrificial victim was laid down in the 'manuals' of the Pontiffs and depended partly on which god was involved and on the reason for the offering.[67] Male animals were usually offered to male gods, and female ones to goddesses. Colour also mattered, white creatures for Juno or Jupiter, the deities of the upper air, and black animals for the underworld Gods. Size was also regulated in the manuals, whether the creature was a suckling, 'lactentes', or full-grown, 'maiores'. There were traditional animals specified for certain festivals, goats at the Lupercalia, a red dog for Robigus, a horse for Mars, and the most special and expensive of all, the triple sacrifice of the 'Suovetauralia', which required a white bull, a white ram and a white boar, performed only on special occasions such as at the conclusion of the census.

Anyone needing to make a sacrifice would have to fix a convenient date with the temple custodian, the 'aedituus', to arrange for the people who cut the animal's throats, the 'poppae', and the ones who dissected the slain animal, 'the victimarii', to be in attendance. There was also a need for a flute player, a 'tabicen'. All these people had standard fees for their services. The details are recorded in collections of Latin inscriptions.[68]

The necessary beast had to be perfect, as any deformity would be an insult to the god. On the day, dressed in his best toga, the supplicant would tie ribbons to the animal's horns or even gild them. It would then be led through the streets to the relevant temple. It was considered a very good sign if the victim went willingly to its death, and for this the animals were usually drugged to make them compliant. If it did not, if it struggled or even ran away, it was not auspicious. If it even managed to escape, the owner would have to sell it back to the vendor at the animal market, buy another and start all over again. Despite Juvenal's proud boast that his white ox pulled eagerly towards the priest, in effect offering itself, there must have been very many occasions when things went wrong.[69]

On re-reading the instructions for the process, the first question arising is where did these animal sellers have their premises? The Forum Boarium or meat market was down near the Circus Maximus, a fair walk from where most of the temples were in the centre of Rome. It must also be assumed that the vendor kept the chosen animal until the date for the sacrifice, as the buyer could hardly have taken it home with him, therefore the vendors must have had premises close to the centre of things, as having to walk all through the noisy and crowded streets would be impossible with any large animal, let alone one that was unwilling. A bull is of course a very dangerous animal, a fully-grown male pig is also strong and perhaps even more bad-tempered. Even a ram is strong and can be determined, and smaller creatures can be highly strung, and all would be subject to the stresses and change of routine of the sacrificial day, when they might be expected to be recalcitrant – a far cry from the quiet, obedient creatures standing patiently covered in flowers, as suggested by the carvings and paintings.

We are aware that the animals were drugged before the event, but this is an inexact science, particularly with large animals. The reports that animals did indeed kick the altar over or try to gore someone, or actually manage to run away, show that it quite often went wrong. The amount of sedative consumed must have varied greatly, to account for the aberrations. It all sounds a worrying and exhausting business.

The manual actually has instructions on what to do when things did go wrong. It must have been humiliating to stand before the crowd of grinning neighbours and have the priest reject a recalcitrant or imperfect animal as being not good enough for the gods. Even the official instructions that one should 'sell it back' to the vendor and casually 'buy another' seem airily complacent and fraught with potential difficulties. The original vendor might be offended at the idea that his animal was in some way unsuitable. He might be reluctant to take it back, and one can almost hear the argument ringing down the centuries, with the haggling going on, disputes about the amount of money owed or the cost of the new one – could the original one be part-exchanged for another? The idea of the purchaser having to argue about this with the vendor, still in his glad rags, is worthy of a comedy by Terence,[70] or something that might have happened to Petronius's character Trimalchio.[71] No doubt the return of unsuitable animals was fairly commonplace and with this possibility, the initial expenses, the priest's fees, the unused flute-player still wanting his money for turning up, the trampled flowers and the all-round opportunity for money-making for everyone concerned except the buyer, it must have been a sore trial to the ordinary man, who was merely trying to do his best and perform this devotion to the deity. One can almost hear the gods laughing.

Religious festivals took up a fair amount of time in the Roman year, quite apart from personal ceremonies, such as burial games put on by wealthy families in honour of their deceased.[72] The earliest festivals, based on the agricultural seasons, still tended to follow those seasons, even though Rome itself had become far more urbanised. Some of the festivals were fixed and others were, within certain limits, moveable. The Romans had a calendar giving dates of the festivals for the different gods – 'feriae stativae' – which also indicated the periods within which the non-fixed festivals could take place.

In 46 BC Julius Caesar, on expert advice, issued the improved calendar whereby the dates better coincided with the seasons, and this Julian calendar was kept until the Gregorian calendar was introduced by Pope Gregory XIII in October 1582.[73] Incidentally, the date 46 BC was, for the Romans, 709 AUC (Ancient Usage Calendar).

The Romans always loved a show, particularly if it cost them nothing, and funeral games were a time when gladiator fights could be enjoyed while still feeling that one was doing the right thing and attending a religious occasion. The fighters at these events might not necessarily be killed, but the idea of such games did stem from a period when the blood of the combatants was in itself a form of sacrifice, spilled to honour the gods in the name of the deceased. Some funeral games were necessarily quite modest, but others could employ many pairs of fighters and entertain a large audience.

Purely religious festivals might be generally less well attended, except for the most important ones. These were scattered throughout the year and some religious festivals lasted for more than one day, so that there was plenty of opportunity for people to join in, if they were free to do so.

January was the time of sacrifice on behalf of the incoming consuls for that year. It was also the month of the Compitalia, a celebration for the Lares of the crossroads (the compitum), which lasted three days and often became rowdy. It was twice suppressed due to this, but Augustus revived the festival in order to encourage a sense of Roman identity.[74]

February takes its name from februm, meaning an instrument of purification. The two main festivals were the Parentalia and the Lupercalia. Parentalia was a festival of the dead, while Lupercalia, which was held at almost the same time, (13th-24th) was a fertility festival and a chance for people to let off steam.

March was when the Vestal's fire was re-lit, and for the month of Mars the streets would be busy with the dances of the Salii in honour of that God. Anna Perenna was celebrated on 15 March, a rite of spring and renewal, when picnics in the countryside were popular.

April was a busy month, when on the first day working class women could use the men's public baths and pray to Fortuna Virilis for success with men in the coming year. The 4th brought games in honour of Magna Mater, and the 19th was the Festival of Ceres. Three other festivals came close together after that, the Parilia on the 21st, the Floralia on the 28th and the Feriae Latinae at the end of the month. The Parilia was in honour of shepherd deities, the pales, and associated with the early history of the Palatine Hill. The Floralia was for Flora, goddess of flowers when from 28 April until 3 May there were games and horse racing in the Circus Maximus. Plays presented at this time tended to include nude scenes, and the Floralia appears to have been as much a celebration of spring-like resurgence of sex as it was of the flowers themselves. Cato, always strait-laced, had once famously walked out of one of these performances.[75] The Feriae Latinae was more serious, a joining of Romans and Latins on the Alban Hills. Magistrates were obliged to attend the sacrifice there and the communal meal which took place afterwards.[76] This festival was usually at the end of April, on a date fixed by the Consuls for the general holiday.

May, named for Maia the mother of Mercury, was considered unlucky. The main festival was the Lemuria on the 9th, 11th and 13th days, dedicated to ghosts. The most dangerous and potent spirits were believed to be those of people who had died young. The Roman attitude towards death was that expressed by Cicero, when he said: 'That long night, when I shall not exist, troubles me more than this brief life, which yet seems to be too long.'[77]

June was more cheerful, with the boundaries of Rome walked in procession and married women were allowed into the storerooms of the Vestals, bearing small gifts of food on the 5th of the month. This was the Vestalia, a baker's holiday, when small cakes were exchanged. The Ides of June (the 13th) was one of the rowdiest nights of the year, when the guild of flute-players, essential for all sacrifices, held their dinner at the temple of Minerva on the Aventine. They then roamed around the city wearing masks and usually drunk. It was a time when decent citizens locked their doors and stayed at home. The 15th was the day when the Vestals swept out their storehouses, and this ended the 'unlucky' period which had begun in early May. Also in June was the Fors Fortuna on the 24th, which was always very popular, as the festival was one attended by slaves as well as by the citizens.[78]

In July the games of Apollo had a good deal of support, and these were held from the 6th to the 13th days. They had lost much of their religious flavour, with plays and gladiatorial games being staged. Cicero commented on them that 'it is indeed something for one's mind to relax, both at the spectacle and at the impression of religious feeling.'[79] Although, by his time, an impression was about all the religious feeling that remained. July's other festivals were rather quieter, with the Lucaria on the 19th to the 21st, which was celebrated only by the priests, and the Neptunalia on the 23rd which saw bonfires being lit upon which were thrown small fishes as a sacrifice to the god of the sea. On the 25th, the Furinalia was another festival mainly for the priests.

In August the well-attended festivals began again, with the 12th day being when the Praetor offered a heifer to Hercules in the Forum

Boarium. On the 13th Diana was celebrated and slaves could also attend, with that day becoming a summer holiday for them. The Portunalia was on the 17th for the God, Portunus, who represented gates, harbours and ports. His delightful little temple is also in the Forum Boarium. On the 19th of that month the gardeners had a holiday, and the 21st was for Consus, the god of the granary, which took place in an underground barn beneath the Circus Maximus. This event was closely associated with horse-racing, due to its position, and the Vestals attended with the priest of Quirinas, who made a sacrifice there before the races began.[80]

September was the month of the Ludi Romani, the main games event of the year. This took place between the 5th and the 19th and always attracted huge crowds. On the 13th the dedication of the temple of Jupiter Optimus Maximus was celebrated, with the Consul making a sacrifice followed by the usual banquet. The most important day of the games was the 15th, when statues of Jupiter, Juno and Minerva, beautifully dressed, appeared as if to enjoy the games with the people. They were surrounded by musicians, incense, clowns and delighted crowds of people [81]

October had horse-racing again with the 15th being the date of the chariot races after which the October Horse was sacrificed, with its genitals being used as part of the ashes for the Parilia in the following year.

November was usually fairly quiet, except for the Plebeian Games from the 4th to the 17th and a feast of Jupiter which took place on the Ides.

December was busy again, with the all-important festival of Bona Dea, the 'putting the goddess to sleep', although Juvenal said that this particular worship was only for drunks and perverts, continuing the male belief that unsuitable behaviour was a part of it. As a male he could never have attended one of the goddesses' festivals, therefore he had no real idea what went on, and his remarks were purely spite.[82]

The year ended with the Saturnalia, originally on the 17th but later lasting over several days. A sacrifice and public feast were usual to open the holiday, which everyone could attend. Shops and schools were closed, as were the law courts, and everyone dressed in the best they could afford. Slaves were given special privileges at this time, with a tradition of reversing the natural order within households, allowing the slaves to be served by their masters. Parents gave gifts of toys to the children, and friends exchanged candles. People generally made it a time for visiting friends and family, although not everyone enjoyed it, Pliny retired to a private room for the duration of the holiday,[83] and Seneca said that it should be observed with 'frugal contemplation', which was surely one of the earliest complaints about the 'commercialisation' of the event. Most people simply enjoyed the festivals, the relaxation of normal rules, and looked forward to the new year, when it all began again.

The continuance of public respect for the gods and temples is shown by the response of the Emperor Domitian (51-96 AD) when Suetonius reported that he had ordered the destruction of a tomb, built by one of his own freedmen, to honour the man's deceased son. Apparently, the stones used to build this tomb had been intended for the temple of Jupiter on the Capitoline Hill. Domitian was horrified that these had been used and intended to make an example, offended that the sanctity of the god had been abused by the thoughtless use of the stones. He had the bones and ashes of the deceased young man flung into the sea, to prevent anyone in the future thinking that such disrespect to the gods could go unpunished.[84]

This attitude towards the gods might be best summed up by Marcus Aurelius:

> ...to them that ask thee, where hast thou seen the Gods? I answer first of all that they are in some manner visible and apparent ... neither have I seen my own soul, and yet I respect and honour it ... so then, for the Gods, by the daily experience that I have of their power and providence towards myself and others, I know certainly that they are – and therefore I worship them.[85]

5

Wealth and Poverty

Rome was certainly not a classless society, even during the years of the Republic. It didn't pretend to be, nor did it want or need to be. The whole of Roman society was based on the premise of each man and woman being in their place, performing in a correct manner their appointed task. That the rewards for these tasks were often so highly divergent was just the way things were – the 'mos maiorum' again. 'Mos' meant established custom and in this context 'maiorum' meant the ancestors or forebears, therefore it represented not just the way things had always been done, but the way in which they should continue to be done.

This way of life naturally depends heavily on the acquiescence of those people at the bottom of the pile, whether they are prepared to continue to accept their lot. In any society the poor always vastly outnumber the rich, who use more than their fair share of any available resources. Occasionally the poor will make their opinions felt, and also occasionally there emerges a person or small group of people who do their best to reset the balance a little. These attempts are usually accompanied by riots, social disorder and quite likely also with the deaths of the chief protagonists, as with the Brothers Gracchi.[1] After these disturbing interludes, the situation inevitably slides back into inertia, with little gained by either side, until the next time.

The stratification of society was strengthened by the way in which Roman society had been formed. The old nobility, the Patricians, had the experience of generations of rule. They also had practically a monopoly of real political power, and the three hundred seats in the Senate were very nearly filled from their ranks. The Consuls, once elected, also had near-regal authority while in office. They controlled the machinery of the state, but just as importantly they controlled the state religion, with Patrician status being a pre-requisite for holding the highest positions.

The Pontiffs were fully aware that control of the religion also meant control of the law, which had for a long time been preserved by an oral tradition which had left a good deal open to the interpretation of a presiding magistrate and his often arbitrary decisions. The Plebeians were to a large extent held down, firstly by a sense of obligation to the great Patrician families, and also by the fact that any presumption on their part could be dealt with by direct intimidation.[2]

The Patricians often had vast personal wealth at their disposal, and they commanded a majority in the Centuriate Assembly, as well as being the natural leaders of the people in times of war. They also had the leisure to practise the arts of war from an early age, and the funds with which to provide themselves with arms when necessary.

The Plebeians, apart from a few prominent families, tended to be a mass of people of mixed descent, with few natural leaders, little wealth, and they also tended to lack real political ambition, being largely satisfied to have freedom, even at a price that occasionally meant explosion. Gradually, this mass of people, with few natural advantages and quite untrained in public life, learned the business of politics and gained confidence in demanding their rights. After many generations, they moved on from being merely 'the Plebs' to become 'the Populus', but even then they remained far behind the Patricians in almost everything that mattered, particularly the control of the state and the acquisition of personal wealth.

For many Patricians, even a show of sympathy for the sufferings of the poor caused some suspicion. In the case of Spurius Maelius, a wealthy knight who, in 439 BC during a time of great scarcity, had provided food for the hungry. This act of generosity and kindness caused him to be accused of 'aiming at kingly power' and he was summoned to hear the charges being brought against him. When he refused to be brow-beaten, he was stabbed to death in public by Servilius Ahala.[3] This attitude was a very long time in changing. Three hundred years later, when Gaius Sempronius Gracchus met his own end, the suspicions against him had been exactly the same. It was never allowed that any man engaged in attempting to make things more equal could be entirely altruistic. He must always be assumed to be aiming at that almost-mythical 'kingly power' under the guise of helping the unfortunate. Obviously, the idea of sharing resources more fairly between the haves and the have-nots had gained no credence during the intervening centuries.

Even Cicero was to class Spurius Maelius and the Gracchi brothers as traitors. Not merely to their social class, but to the state which they should have supported unquestioningly. It would prove to be a problem that many men in public life would struggle with, as the Plebs' consciousness of their inferiority grew. They would need to be kept not only quiet and pliable, but also be convinced that the Roman state had their welfare in mind, whether it actually did or not.

After the expulsion of the kings of Rome[4] by 509 BC, the power passed to two Consuls on certain conditions. They were not allowed to wield power outside the city walls, and their position as chief magistrates would last for one year only. A new feature appeared with the institution of the Tribunate, which was designed to protect the Plebeians from the abuse of Consular power. Rome grew into a world power, but the social and political ties began to loosen, with the deep patriotism which had been a feature and the foundation of the common cause giving way to a personal selfishness, setting people one against the other.

The Lex Liciniae Sextiae was a series of laws proposed by the Tribunes of the Plebs, Lucius Sextus Lateranus and Gaius Licinius Stolo. These were intended to address the economic plight of the Plebeians by providing a limit on the interest demanded for loans, and also a restriction on the private ownership of land.[5] A further advance was that one of the Consuls in office should always be a Plebeian. Later, there would be other attempts to limit the powers of the magistrates, and their acquisition of wealth – for example, the Lex Acilia Repetundarum of 123 BC and the Lex Iulia Repetundarum of 59 BC, which were both intended to confirm (or limit) the levels of payments due to magistrates and judges in respect of their public duties.

Gradually, nobility of office should have succeeded nobility of birth, but the 'new' nobility quickly developed the same tenacity and jealous exclusivity regarding wealth and privileges as the Patricians had always exhibited.[6] The Plebeian noble expected to have the same marks of dignity that the hereditary families enjoyed – the purple-striped toga, the gold ring of office, and particularly the wax portrait masks of the ancestors who had themselves held office. Unfortunately, there was nothing at all for the seething masses of the poor, left behind by their upwardly mobile Plebeian leaders. They had proved to be just as keen to advance themselves at the expense of the poor as anyone else, tending to think of 'the people' only when support was needed at election time, as politicians of all persuasions have always done from time immemorial.

Despite the very large numbers of the urban poor, the way the voting system worked would work against them ever being able to have much of a voice politically. The 'tribes' was not an ethnic grouping of people, but a purely political grouping which served the purposes of the state. There were thirty-five 'tribes' in Republican Rome, thirty-one of which were rural with only four being urban. The sixteen really 'old' tribes bore the names of the various Patrician 'gens', which indicated that people who belonged to those groups were either members of that family line, or perhaps lived on land owned by that family. During the early and mid-Republic when Roman-owned territory began to expand, tribes were added to accommodate the new citizens within the body politic. Full Roman-citizen colonies also became the nuclei of fresh tribes. The four urban tribes were popularly believed to have been founded by King Servius Tullius, though they were probably founded later, during the early Republic. (The last date of a tribal creation was 241 BC). The four urban tribes took their names from areas of Rome – Collina; Esquilina; Palatina and Suburana. The final one, Suburana, was named after the Subura, one of the poorest, most crowded and most notorious areas of the city, where crime was rife. Freedmen were put into only two of these tribes, either Suburana or Esquilina.

Every member of a tribe was entitled to one vote in the tribal assembly. However, this vote was in itself quite insignificant. The votes were counted first in each tribe, then the tribe as a whole cast its one single vote, which meant that in no tribal assembly, however large, could the huge number of citizens of the four urban tribes effect the outcome of any vote! Each of the other thirty-one rural tribes was also entitled to register its single vote, so even if only two people had turned out to vote for each rural tribe, the result was the same.

Members of 'rural' tribes did not have to come from the country, and almost all senators and knights belonged to the rural tribes, but the four urban tribes were outnumbered before they started, irrespective of how many people placed their votes, or how few of the rural tribes' citizens had turned out.[7]

As Rome expanded its hold over other territories, keeping up the numbers in the legions began to be a problem. The use of the urban poor had never, in the early days, been considered, as a soldier was then obliged to provide his own kit, which would be quite beyond the abilities of the poorer citizens and prevented them fighting for Rome. The traditional idea of the young man's family kitting him out with all he needed was still the norm, and also the soldier was expected to return home between campaigns, to continue his normal life, costing the state nothing in upkeep. This was also impossible for the urban poor.

It was Gaius Marius, himself a 'new' man and not from one of the ancient Patrician families, who first broached the idea of using all those thousands of poorer men in the legions by the simple expedient of providing them with kit at state expense. This idea met initially with great opposition, and even though Marius was elected to his first Consulship in 107 BC it took him some time to be able to push through his excellent plans. From then on, men without the support of family property were allowed to join the army, providing the legions with thousands of willing men, glad to have some provision made for them, and glad to have been given a purpose.[8]

These men would, in their turn, give a great deal back to the state, as the rewards of Rome's expansion became enormous and could not have been accomplished without the regular supply of men that admission of the 'head count' classes had permitted.[9] The monetary rewards of the poor soldier and his commanders were as far apart as ever. The soldiers received wages and food, plus a 'family' of sorts, as the legions melded together. A man who took up this life could gain many advantages over his previous life in a slum area, although putting his life on the line for Rome, and his absolute loyalty, was expected in return.

The commanders did not expect to be killed while on active service. For them each achievement and each year completed was a stepping-stone to higher office and to the means of greater wealth. Commanders were expected to continue to equip themselves and the costs could be large, depending on how much 'grandeur' he intended to exhibit to his subordinates. However, his rewards could be enormous. A successful general, if that rank was reached, could expect to take as captives any surviving enemy men and women, and these unfortunates were not normally killed as they could be sold as slaves, with the proceeds of such sales going to the commander. A man of substantial private wealth, such as Gaius Marius, might on occasion donate some, or even all, of these proceeds to his legions, which was always a useful popularity booster, but it was not to be automatically expected. Some commanders never did it, it was certainly not mandatory.

Most commanders intended to make all they could out of campaigns, as did the governors of provinces. These men were paid relatively little, and it was understood that they would increase their income by whatever means came to hand. In this way, a man could accumulate a good deal in a fairly short time, and very few commanders ended their term of office as poor as when they had started. While the legions might expect friendship, a sense of purpose and usefulness, and a good deal of pride in being at the forefront of Rome's expansions, the officers would have an eye on their political career back in Rome, and their term of service was expected to raise at least some of the funds to pay for it.

Women, of course, had no place in the legions. They either waited at home, or became camp followers, trailing behind the soldiers looking for protection. Worse even than that, if they were a member of a subject or conquered people, they could easily find themselves sold into slavery. The life of a camp follower was not enviable, whether the woman was Roman or otherwise. If her man was killed, then she would be left with very little, possibly dependent on the charity of his friends, if their partnership had been a recognised one, otherwise quite without resources. There could be children to feed, and the urgent necessity of finding another male protector. Without a one-to-one relationship of this kind, the woman could all too easily become a prostitute, struggling to survive on the periphery of army camps. The Emperor Augustus restricted the ability of soldiers to marry, or take their women with them, thereby creating a need for them to find 'wives' and perhaps create families wherever they were posted.

The most senior members of a Roman general's military staff were his legates, and in order to be classified as 'legatus' a man needed to be of senatorial status and was quite often consular in rank. Legates answered only to the general and were senior to all other types of military tribunes.[10] It would be difficult indeed for any man without money to be able to make his way up the ranks of the military command, but for any young man of decent birth it was an essential, to provide him with the grounding necessary for political life. This was the dilemma facing one of Rome's greatest generals, Lucius Cornelius Sulla.

Sulla was born a Patrician, but without money. For a Patrician, family backing and family resources were essential to set a man on his way along the 'cursus honorum', or sequence of offices which could lead to the top. This sequence of offices could not even begin until the young man had completed his military service, but the idea of a man of high birth enlisting as an ordinary soldier was not something that could be contemplated. For Sulla, it also meant that he was excluded from making those important friendships and connections which would assist his progress later. Young people need to make friends somewhere, and for Sulla that meant 'unsuitable' relationships with people of the theatre and the circus. These people were on the fringes of decent society, and while admired and sometimes even feted, they were always considered slightly bizarre. To his credit, when a series of fortunate events allowed him to enter the legions and begin his rise, he did not entirely drop those people who were considered unsuitable, who had befriended him when others would not, though he would later be criticised for it.[11]

Once military service was completed, a young man could start his political career. The Lex Villia Annalis of 180 BC gave the minimum ages required before a man could stand for election to each magistracy. Quaestor was at thirty years, Aedile or Tribune was thirty-seven years, Praetor was forty years, and Consular rank was expected at forty-three years, if achieved at all. It was considered fortunate if a man could reach each level at the correct age, 'in suo anno' or 'in his year'. Not only did it mean that he had been ready to move upwards at the correct time, but also that he had been elected to each office at the first time of trying.

It was considered rather unfortunate if a man lagged too much behind each correct year, which could mean that he wasn't liked, but it could also mean that he lacked something more important than mere popularity; this happened to both Gaius Marius and Sulla. For Sulla, as we have seen, he had the family but lacked the money – for Marius the problem was reversed, he had plenty of money but lacked the family.[12]

The career path could be fast-tracked if one had an established politician as a friend or relative. For Marius it was a marriage arranged with the family of the high-born Julia Caesaris (Gaius Julius Caesar was her nephew).[13] The family were of the highest possible status, but over the years had lost political 'clout' due to lack of money. The marriage with a Julia altered everything for Marius. For Sulla, the death of his stepmother, who left him a substantial legacy, did the same. He had been born in 138 BC but failed to be elected Praetor in 98 BC at the age of forty, becoming city praetor the following year. Fortunately for him, his natural ability, great charisma and boundless ambition allowed him to make up for the rather wasted younger years.[14]

Had either of these men not been granted more than the usual amount of luck, they would never have broken through the barriers holding back other men. It would have been Rome's loss – militarily with Marius, and legally with Sulla, who was far more than a mere soldier. When in power he was responsible for a great deal of reform, legal, constitutional and administrative. He reformed the criminal process by establishing a system of jury courts to try particular categories of crime; he considerably restricted the power of the tribunes, whose power of veto was too often allowed to paralyse the legal process and was also too easily bought. He also ensured that the senate recovered some of its lost power and prestige. He doubled the size of the senate (from 300 members to 600) by introducing supporters from the equestrian order consisting of wealthy citizens of Rome, rather than Patricians, thereby transferring power from the old families and placing it in the hands of some new men with new ideas.[15]

Sulla's presumably childless stepmother must have been fond of him to leave him everything, but when young he was very charming and attractive, and his natural attributes brought him attention from both men and women, not always for the best reasons. In Rome, a man who was rather 'pretty' was always considered suspect, and Sulla certainly had to prove himself worthy of his military standing to gain acceptance.

The middle-aged and unprepossessing features of Gaius Marius may have been less appealing to Julia Caesaris, who found herself a bargaining counter in the arrangement between him and her family. As a member of the status-proud but purse-poor faded nobility, a marriage to a man derived from a farming family in Arpinum, who was marrying her to further political ambitions, was the best she could expect. She gained security, but he gained important contacts with families who were themselves connected to the Caesars, such as the Metellii. His finances benefited Julia's family in general, re-establishing them as power players. Julia's opinions were not recorded, as she would have been raised to understand that such marital and political manoeuvres were the norm, and that the standing of the family came before personal considerations.

For a woman lacking personal ambitions who could subsume herself to the needs of her birth family, to be followed by her marital family, the rewards could be pleasant enough. A comfortable home, friends in similar situations, servants to attend to every need, children who could be a joy without having to become a burden of care, perhaps a villa outside the city for when Rome became too hot, and sufficient freedom to indulge herself at the fabric or jewellery markets without having to worry much about the costs of it all, could make life very pleasant indeed, even if one's husband was not necessarily of one's own choosing.

Roman women were great collectors of jewellery, the easiest way to display wealth. Pearls, greatly prized, were to be found in the Porticus Margheritaria in the Forum. Julius Caesar was known to have given his mistress, Servilia Caepionis, a pink pearl of such enormous size that it was worth six million sesterces. The Roman world of course had wide contacts – Egypt for gold, always its greatest lure, so much so that the neighbouring kings would plead blatantly with Pharoah to 'send us gold, you have so much,' as if it could be picked up on the streets.

Aegyptus was certainly the source of wonderful luxury goods, not only due to its gold supplies from Nubia. There was ivory from Africa. Carnelian and malachite were used for the tops of the popular small tables and were enormously expensive. There were ocean pearls from Taprobane (Sri Lanka), along with rubies, sapphires and spices. Other precious stones came from Arabia, including diamonds. The 'adamas' stone was known to be the hardest substance, and India also produced fabrics and spices, with Egypt being then the centre of the trade in emeralds. These were sometimes polished into cabochons, but were more usually made into beads, which, along with smaller pearls and beads of gold, became necklaces and earrings. Emeralds had been coming out of Egypt since around 500 BC and several examples of this type of jewellery were found at Pompeii. The Media lands, between Assyria and Persia, were sources of lapis-lazuli, turquoise, jasper, carnelian and rock crystal, plus more gold.

By the time of the early empire, luxuries in Rome were not lacking, and the empire's desire for unusual foods and good wines is also well recorded. As Rome expanded and prospered through its military achievements, beautiful things of all kinds found their way into the city, supplying increasing demand. The old Republican ideals of a simple life would, except for the Stoics,[16] drown under a sea of expensive consumer goods.

But not for everyone – in the midst of all the wealth and the eagerness to embrace foreign products to the full, there were still the poor. Not for them the jewellery markets attended by pampered and excited women choosing ornaments for themselves while attended by servants. Not for them the Epicurean feasts or enormous fish wearing jewels on their fins, nor the delights of cool salads, or even fine wines, though the area excelled in viniculture.

The wines of the Alban Hills were particularly noted for their excellent quality, Caecuban and Falernian were famous, and two-thirds of the larger villas in and around Pompeii had their own vineyards. Some of the more expensive wines could cost as much as the price of a slave, just for one amphora, and wine was often used as currency.[17] Some of the best Roman vineyards trained the vines up olive trees. Profit margins on the production of wine could be small, unless produced and sold in bulk, but from the first century AD it was also being imported from Gaul and from Spain, who were producing excellent wines of their own.[18] Rich full-bodied red wines were usually drunk watered down. These and the finer white wines would not have been available in the street bars, where a rough red was all that was available.

The Popina (pl. popinae) the Roman wine bar, would only serve wine of a lower quality. The Thermopolium would offer drinks but also a limited menu of simple foods; olives, bread, stews and so on. The proliferation of these bars, some with a small area for tables, was due to the need to cater for local people who had no cooking facilities at home.

Most of Rome's poorer people were literally piled above each other, living in insulae or apartment blocks. These insulae could be built five or seven storeys high, often around three sides of a courtyard, with a wall on the fourth side, to prevent intruders from gaining access. Apartments could be behind workshops or above shop premises, often brick-built, then covered with concrete. Laws which limited them to 68 feet high under Augustus, or later to 58 feet high under Trajan, were often ignored and some blocks even reached nine storeys high, with each successive layer becoming flimsier, to reduce the weight and also the building costs. They were usually surrounded by roads, hence the name,[19] and were often extremely dark and cramped, uncomfortable dwellings with small rooms. Some had facilities such as shared lavatories, or running water, while others had nothing and were mere shelters. Though life could often be largely lived in the streets in Mediterranean countries, during winter weather, or with a family tightly sharing space, they would have become unpleasant, particularly as the upper storeys were usually made of wood, which made them a fire risk. There are remains of some of the insulae still in Rome, and rather more survive at Ostia, where they might at least have had the benefit of sea air and a little more space. The remaining insulae at Ostia are also rather better built and more solid, with sewage systems beneath the streets.

In Ostia, as in Rome, urban development was linked to the evolution of building materials. In the Imperial period Ostia was to undergo a complete transformation with regard to town planning. Even in Republican times, Ostia was known as the Emporium, or commercial centre of Rome. The beginnings of Ostia had coincided with the beginning of Rome's maritime and commercial policy. It was, at first, a fortified citadel, which later became a large and commodious city, surrounded by new walls and with a perimeter wide enough to accommodate its development as Rome's port.

Lining the main streets were rows of shops, with the modest houses and apartments of the people alongside, above and behind them. More luxurious houses of the atrium and peristyle type were built slightly further out of town, to give them more privacy and space. Under Trajan, building activity would become more intense, with large storehouses being built to contain grain, oil and wine. New buildings were added to the town centre, such as a basilica and senate house. A new port was built by Trajan between 100 and 106 AD, with a hexagonal form and links to both Rome and Ostia by new roads. It also had a new waterway, to take goods easily and directly into the city, and this was named the Fiumicino, or little river. This was close to where Rome's airport now is.

This need for expansion makes clear that the volume of road and waterway traffic in the area, due to increased population, was in need of an increasing level of imported goods.

Under Hadrian (76-138 AD) and Antoninus Pius (117-161 AD) Ostia was transformed by town-planning projects, which took into account not only its fine public buildings, but also the residential areas. Due to the pressure on space, this again had to take the form of vertical developments, with dwellings on several storeys. Many of these had received daylight by means of windows on the façade or opening onto small internal courtyards. With these, noise and lack of privacy often added to the discomforts. Later, larger properties would have been more comfortable, but it would appear that the desire to provide model dwellings for the people soon took second place to civic pride, when attention turned to the building of a Forum complex containing a temple to Ceres.[20] The renovation and enlargement of the Theatre, or the offices of the Ostian commercial organisations, along with those of other cities of the empire whose names can still be seen on the mosaic pavements outside their business premises, took priority.[21] These up-to-date commercial buildings were to attract further trade and further profits, but at the expense of the poorer people, who had to confine themselves to cramped apartment living in order to save space for more important business ventures.

As might be supposed, in a bustling and thriving town, wealth and incomes varied enormously. As a rough guide, it is likely that a cash income of around 300 denarii per year would keep a reasonably sized family above subsidence level, in all but the largest cities. A denarius a day was probably the standard wage, although plenty got by on half of that. In addition to low wages, underemployment and a widely fluctuating demand for labour meant that most labouring people could not guarantee to always be in employment at all, and many lived on the edge for much, if not all, of the time.[22]

This again needs to be compared with the enormous wealth of the elite, at the apex of the Roman heap. To qualify for membership of this group, a person would need to be worth over four hundred thousand sesterces for an equestrian, or over one million sesterces for a senator. Among the approximately fifty to sixty million people in the Roman Empire, there were perhaps five thousand adult males possessing such wealth. The elite of local towns would be beneath them, producing perhaps thirty to thirty-five thousand very wealthy families. The Romans themselves were fully aware of this breach between the classes and recognised it by naming the super-wealthy as 'honestiores' or honourable ones, and the rest of the free people as 'humiliores', or lesser beings. The lesser beings made up 99.5% of the population.[23]

Living in such an unremittingly secernated world, most people dealt with equals as equals, deferred to those people above, and took whatever advantage they could of those who were unfortunate enough to be below, whenever possible. There was actually a prejudice against the poor from those who were better off. Graffito on a wall in Pompeii reads, 'I hate the poor, if anyone wants to have something for nothing, he is a fool. He should have to pay for it.'[24] It was an unsympathetic and uncompromising attitude from someone more fortunate, who should have prayed that Fortuna's wheel would not turn against him. It is very like the attitude in Victorian England, regarding its own poor as somehow being at fault, not just lazy or unfortunate, as if the very poverty they suffered was some form of condign punishment. Even Cicero, who might be expected to have had rather more sympathy bearing in mind his close friendship with his own favourite slave Tiro, said that working for a wage made any man into a kind of slave, and he unfortunately showed the same attitude towards those less fortunate that most well-heeled Romans did. The poor were a nuisance, an embarrassment, to be dismissed and put out of mind.

Unfortunately, the poor did always pay, though not necessarily in coin. They paid in the general insecurity and stress of their lives. In trying to find work when no work was available, and even when jobs could be found finding that employers were unwilling to pay the correct rate, offering only the absolute minimum, yet expecting every ounce of effort from people who might be already hungry and exhausted. They paid in ill-health, in shortened life spans and in marriages that buckled under the strain.

Not all marriage failures can be laid at the door of poverty, the rich certainly had break-ups too, but theirs were usually for gain, or because a husband was too busy to give his wife the attention she needed, then found that a lover had taken his place. Another example is the usual one of a marriage partner getting a better offer than the one they presently had and deciding to make a change. In each case there would be a dowry involved, which was of course intended to be returned to the wife should the marriage end, for her future support. It is in reading the details of some of these dowries that the true inequalities of life for these women are made clear.

When the daughter of Gaius Julius Caesar was married to Gnaeus Pompeius Magnus, her dowry was one hundred talents of silver, which amounted to approximately twenty-five million sesterces![25] She had previously been betrothed to Marcus Junius Brutus, the son of Caesar's mistress Servilia Caepionis. On breaking the original betrothal, for the 'better offer' of Pompeius Magnus (Caesar needed him politically), he paid off Brutus by giving him another hundred talents of silver, which was the amount of dowry he would have received had his marriage to Julia Caesaris gone ahead. Brutus was one of the richest men in Rome at that time, so he certainly didn't need the money. Both of these large sums had to be borrowed, as Caesar was heavily in debt at the time, with no free funds. His 'backer' was Marcus Licinius Crassus, already mentioned as 'Dives' or 'the rich'.[26]

Crassus's great wealth had begun largely from the profits of Sulla's proscriptions, when his enemies were deprived of their goods and in some cases their lives. Crassus had bought property very cheaply at that time, and in the crowded life of Rome soon found that his investments were hugely profitable. He had often made fabulous displays of generosity to the populace, but had still been sidelined, so he needed Caesar's support and gained it by settling his enormous debts for him and offering other monetary support whenever Caesar needed it. Through this further investment in the rising man, he made sure that he rose with him. Caesar had been so deeply in debt that he could never have paid off all he owed at that time, which was very dangerous for his career. In 73 BC he was elected Pontifex Maximus, which must have been a huge relief, because it not only gave him the extensive Domus Publica to live in, along with a substantial salary, it meant he could not be prosecuted for debts, which for him was the most important aspect of the position.

Crassus was notorious for lending people money without interest, but then foreclosing almost without warning, so they had to hand over property to meet his demands. He also began a fire-service in Rome, where so many buildings had upper storeys of wood, and were likely to catch fire due to people using braziers in them for warmth or to cook food. Often the men employed by Crassus would helpfully turn up at these disasters, but demand payment before the fire was extinguished. Damaged properties could also then be bought cheaply, repaired, and let out again for higher rents.

Caesar's daughter was said to be happy in her marriage to Pompeius Magnus, and she certainly lived surrounded by every luxury, as Magnus was also super-rich and would hardly have noticed the hundred talents of silver that Caesar had borrowed to secure the marriage alliance. However, it is wise to compare the dowry of this fortunate young woman of the highest class with the dowries of ordinary women, for many of whom the amounts concerned were pathetically small. There are a number of Egyptian records extant which give details of these dowries arranged for humble families.[27]

One village family, document number 252, gives a dowry valued in clothes and jewellery of 200 drachma. Document 127 refers to a contract for marriage of around the same amount, which was quoted to include both jewellery and dress. Number 128 had a dowry amounting to 200 drachma, but property had to be sold to raise this amount, should the marriage fail and the wife demand her marriage portion be returned. Document number 129 refers to a dowry of a little over 240 drachma in clothing and jewellery, plus 120 drachma in cash. One lady had nothing except 75 drachma in cash and a pair of small gold earrings. It seems very little to start married life on, though presumably even that was better than nothing at all. If the marriages should fail, and the woman got her portion back, it would be worryingly little for her to try to re-start her life with, and that is even if the ex-husband could find the money to pay it back at all.

Within these extremes, life went on. If one was poor, there was the hope that things might improve. Perhaps a better job might be offered, or children who might before long be able to earn something to keep the family afloat. Marriage did not require love as a necessity but working together with loyalty and sympathy could make all the difference, especially in a poor family.

Apart from health, financial considerations always head the list of worries, especially with life so precarious. While ordinary working-class and hard-working people could always hope that Fortuna would smile on them and make dreams happen, there is no real way of finding out how many of these people achieved some kind of security, and how many of them fell by the wayside.

The woman's main task within the home, apart from producing children, was to keep the household functioning. There was basic domestic work, which could take up the larger part of her day, but if her husband had a small shop or business then she would also be expected to help him in his work, perhaps keeping the books for him. Women also had to find jobs outside the home when money was tight, hiring themselves out wherever they could, even to farms. Despite this necessity, the home was still the centre of most women's lives, with food preparation, childbearing and rearing, and the chaste, modest and frugal wife was still the celebrated ideal. But the stark reality of life often meant that she would have to do rather more to help keep the family afloat.

The famous wool-weaving, for which the diligent Roman woman was praised, could extend beyond her own household, as a hard-working woman could produce a surplus that could then be sold. For many poorer households, this kind of 'cottage industry' could be crucial to survival.[28] There are contracts and documents from Roman Egypt showing that women participated in weaving both as such a cottage industry and also in a manufacturing environment. A woman could even own and run such a weaving establishment, and women who did piecework at the loom to earn a wage were mentioned in the Iliad,[29] although it is not possible to estimate how many women worked outside the home in this way. In Artemidorous of Daldus's 'Dreambook' women's occupations are mentioned far less frequently than men's.[30] Work as an actress, a nurse, a midwife, a priestess or a cleaning woman were mentioned, along with prostitution.

Work itself was not seen as being a part of any woman's identity, although they were always well represented in the service jobs. Production of cloth and clothing, craft-type work, hairdressing and sometimes the luxury trades such as perfumery or working with gold-leaf, were considered to be acceptable. There are pictures of women serving in shops, selling fruit, vegetables or fabrics. One image of a Roman butcher's shop shows the husband slicing meat for customers, while the wife sits nearby keeping a record of purchases, so husband and wife partnerships were not unusual. An inscription from Tunisia laments the death of a woman who had been her husband's associate in his business:

> Urbanilla, my wife, lies here, a woman of complete modesty. At Rome she was my companion and associate in business dealings, sustained by her frugality. With everything going well, she returned with me to my homeland – ah! Carthage – ripped my wretched

> companion from me – there is no hope of living without such a wife. She managed my household and gave me good advice. Taken from the light, pitiable she quiet lies, enclosed in marble. I, Lucius, your husband, covered you in marble here. Fate's chance gave this woman to me on the day we were born.[31]

This man's anguish at the loss of his wife is palpable and shows her value to him, not only as his marriage partner but also as a working woman on whom he could rely.

Evidence from Pompeii shows that women regularly worked there too, a woman named Faustilla being a moneylender who took small items of jewellery in pawn for loans. 'July 15 – an earring left with Faustilla as collateral for a loan of two denarii (32 asses)'. She took as interest one bronze 'as' from the sum of thirty-two.[32] And again – this time scribbled on the wall of a bar: 'November, from Faustilla, eight asses in interest for fifteen denarii.'[33]

There were many contracts for wet-nurses, for nurses to look after foundlings, and for doctors. Domestic help, other than that provided by slaves, was generally female. However, this raises another point, in that the preponderance of slaves to do all the household work in better-off households naturally meant that there would be far less work available in that sphere for poorer women who were freed or born free. The cleaning, cooking and laundry work, along with the dressing of hair and the care of children, jobs which in our own time offer employment to many women who need to earn money outside the home, were not as widely available in Roman times, with slaves performing the majority of these tasks.

There was a habit in Egypt of trading the services of a woman, usually a daughter, for a monetary loan, although it is not entirely clear whether this was done in the Empire as a whole.[34] Also from Egypt, there is a contract extant for a dancer and castanet players:

> Sosos, son of Sosos ... has hired himself to Olympias ... dancer, acting with Zopyros ... as her guardian. To work with her as a flute player for twelve months ... for a wage of forty-five bronze drachmas per month ... and Sosos has received from Olympias in advance fifty bronze drachmas. He shall not fail to appear at any festivals or other engagements at which Olympias is present and shall not provide services for anyone else without the authority of Olympias.[35]

There was always work for the prostitute, which sometimes led on from inn-keeping or bar work, but for those women not attracted to this kind of life yet still needing work, there could be fortune-telling, magic or the mysteries of the 'wise woman'. Pliny the Elder thought that the knowledge of charms, potions and magical herbs was the speciality of women, and certainly ordinary people who were superstitious – or merely desperate – had great faith in such gifts.[36] Magic was frequently resorted to for the solving of problems and lovers went to wise-women for advice about their relationships, although the expertise of such women often went far beyond this. An expert sorceress could make a good living, curing people's emotional and physical problems, or attempting to, and even curing sick animals by divination.

Women were probably only very rarely allowed into trade guilds, but they were certainly allowed to be members of funeral associations, sometimes even as officials. One all-female group is recorded at Lanuvium in Italia[37] although this is quite likely to have been a household burial group or cult association with a limited membership.

Rich and poor, masters and slaves, men and women, could all work together in the membership of some of the religious cults, and women could also be teachers, until Christianity took a hold, bringing its restrictions against females with it.

Despite a lack of pictorial evidence, we know that outside the towns a number of fortunate women were landowners, actively engaged in agriculture. In Roman Egypt, they owned between sixteen and twenty-five per cent of the available land, but this has to take into account that Egypt had always had a totally different opinion of women's capabilities than did Rome. In Rome, all women still needed to have a guardian to actually conduct the business matters for them, even if they were the actual owners, as they needed a man to make the legal contracts.

Some women did actually collect their rents, although most used agents to deal with their tenants. They were, however, as likely to be defrauded by these agents as by the tenants themselves. It was probably thought that a female owner was easy prey, so they took what advantage they could. Poorer women did work in agriculture for wages, for work such as winnowing, but were also hired to work directly in the fields.

Not every woman was fortunate enough to have family support, or a devoted and protective husband with a thriving shop or other

WOMAN WITH CHILD – Capitoline Museum. Shows the ideal Republican female, mother of a healthy son, to follow in his father's footsteps.

MIDDLE AGED NOBLEMAN – Vatican Museum. The male ideal: calm, assured, fairly austere.

ROMAN OFFICER UNIFORM – Gladiator Museum, Piazza Navona. Every man of status was required to help carry civilisation to the outposts, a necessary step towards a future political career.

FORUM IN ROME – The half mile that ruled the known world, originally a malarial marsh.

Above left: ORIGINAL LUPA – Believed to date to 600 BC. The Romulus and Remus figures are medieval additions.

Above right: YOUNG GIRL BURIAL – Capitoline Museum. Rare remains of a four-year-old female child, dating 8,000– 10,000 BC. Buried with offerings of pottery, jewellery, a bowl of grain and the jawbone of a lamb. High status burial from the Trastavere area.

PORTICUS OF OCTAVIA – Between the Theatre of Pompeius Magnus and the Circus Flaminius. Built around 27 BC by Augustus to honour his sister Octavia Minor. It was once the gateway to a large piazza lined with temples and shops, decorated by several equestrian statues by the Greek master, Lysippus.

DOMESTIC LARS ALTAR – Pompeii. The Lararium was the centre of domestic religious life, and was the responsibility of the wife.

MOTHER AND TEENAGED SON – Palazzo Altemps Museum. Pride in family and continuation of service to the State.

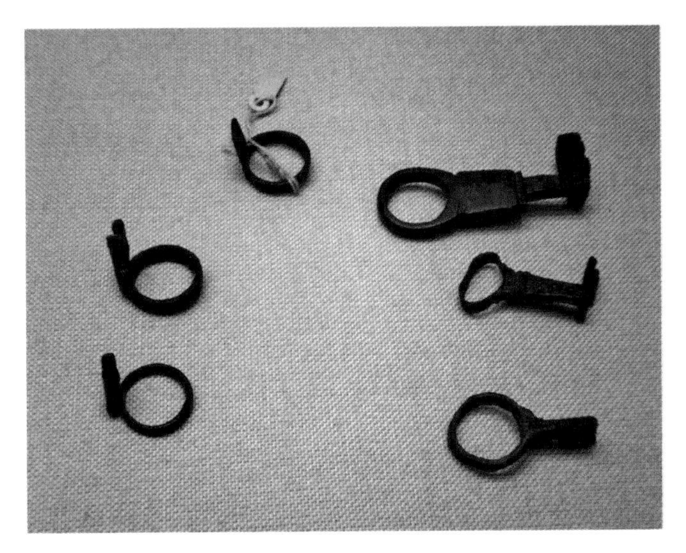

KEY RINGS – Marie-Louise Museum, Seville. The holding of the household keys was an important part of the wife's responsibilities.

MARRIED COUPLE SARCOPHAGUS – Capitoline Museum. Duty often became affection, and despite increasingly easy divorce, many marital links held.

FAMILY GROUP WITH DAUGHTER – Palazzo Altemps Museum. Burial memorial showing parents and daughter.

JUPITER OPTIMUS MAXIMUS – Barracco Museum. The Chief of the Gods, whose temple stood on the Capitoline Hill.

Right: CHIEF VESTAL VIRGIN – Domus Vestae, Rome. One of only six high-born and privileged women, whose celilbacy was essential to the continued welfare of the State. One of the few women in Rome who held power.

Below: TEMPLE OF ISIS, POMPEII. The 'foreign' religion was originally disapproved of, but became very popular, supported by many wealthy families.

Left: AREA SACRA – Largo di Torre Argentina, Rome. Sacred area with four of Rome's oldest Temples, very close to the later Theatre of Pompeius Magnus, in the Curia of which Julius Caesar was assassinated.

Below: RECONSTRUCTION OF THE HOUSE OF LIVIA – Palatine Hill, Forum. An example of a wealthy home in an elevated and pleasant area. The Palatine was a favourite place of residence long before the Emperors built palaces there.

ROMAN INSULAE – Capitol Hill. An example of poorer housing, dark and cramped. Situated at the foot of the Capitoline, close to Santa Maria in Aracoeli, which stands on the site of the Temple of Juno Moneta.

EUMACHIA – The Eumachia Building, Forum, Pompeii. The Corporation of the Fullers. Statue of a wealthy and influential woman who was also a priestess of the Imperial cult.

GOLD SNAKE BANGLES – Marie-Louise Museum. Seville. Examples of the type of jewellery found throughout the Roman world. Complete with a gold headband.

GARDEN OF THE HOUSE OF MENANDER, POMPEII – Larger houses enjoyed cool and pleasant spaces, giving peace and privacy from the street.

ASELLINA'S BAR, WITH LARARIUM – Pompeii. Poorer people ate and drank at such bars and thermopolia, as many had no cooking facilities. Asellina's and its painted Lararium is on the Abbondanza.

Above: POLITICAL SLOGANS, POMPEII – Graffiti is nothing new, outer walls were written on. Games, advertisements, slogans for political parties, vulgar comments and also drawings.

Right: LADY WITH PAINTED HAIR – Capitoline Museum. Reputed to be Calpurnia Pisonis, the last wife of Julius Caesar. She was 17 years old when they married, probably younger than his daughter Julia. Calpurnia was daughter of Lucius Calpurnius Piso Caesoninus.

STADIUM OF DOMITIAN – below Piazza Navona. The present-day Piazza follows the ground plan of Domitian's Stadium of 80 AD. Used for athletic contests, it could seat 30,000 spectators. The remains are 15ft below present ground level.

COLOSSEUM – view from the Temple of Venus and Rome. Inaugurated in 80 AD the Colosseum was the scene of executions, gladiator fights, battle recreations and exotic animals. It seated more than 50,000 spectators.

GUARD AND CLIENT – carving from Pompeii. Is the man with the sword a guard, or perhaps a robber? Wealthy people rarely went out alone.

CAPTURED PRISONERS – Arch of Septimius Severus, Forum. Such unfortunates may have been intended to be the midday entertainment when executed in the Colosseum.

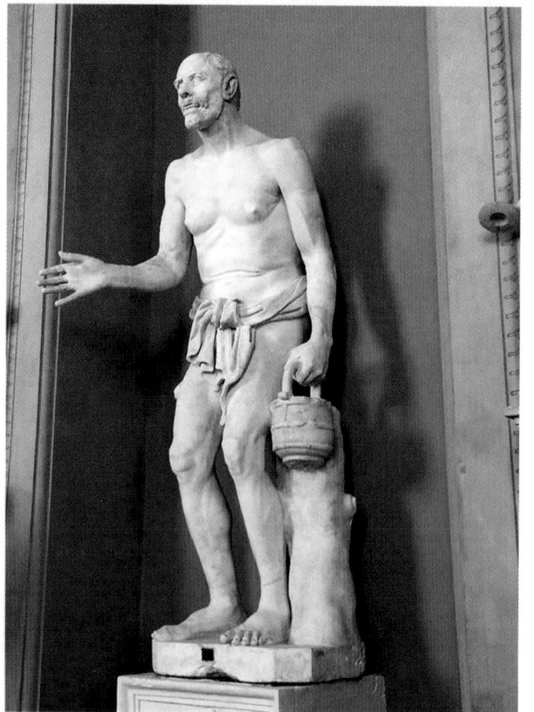

Above left: HOPLOMACHUS GLADIATOR – Gladiator Museum. Piazza Navona. Gladiators were expensive to train and keep, they were not intended to die but to become famous and generate income.

Above right: GLADIATRIX – University of Granada. Recently reappraised statue of what appears to be a female gladiator in a victory pose. (Alfonso Manas)

Left: STATUE OF AN OLD MAN – Vatican Museum. The difficulty of growing older when poor.

Above left: STATUE OF AN OLD WOMAN – Capitoline Museum. The prototype of the Crone Goddess, Anna Parenna, patron of the Plebians.

Above right: JEWISH HEADSTONE – Capitoline Museum. Headstone showing two young boys, sad reminder of high child mortality. Note the pet dogs carved above. The prosperous Jewish quarter was close to the Theatre of Marcellus.

Right: GLADIATOR MEMORIAL – Galleria Doria Pamphilij. Memorials were often paid for by burial clubs, or donations from friends. Some gladiators became famous and wealthy, but others were buried in mass graves.

Above: ODEON OR SMALL THEATRE – Pompeii. The Odeon was intended for poetry readings and recitals, a respectable place for women.

Left: YOUNG AUGUSTUS – Vatican Museum. Gaius Julius Caesar Octavianus, adopted son of Julius Caesar. Later the Emperor Augustus, whose images always appeared youthful.

business, like the grieving Lucius, in which they could immerse themselves. Many free and freed women had no choice but to hire themselves out where they could, in effect becoming little better than slaves themselves, being obliged in the workplace to accept the dirtiest and most tedious types of work, quite likely suffering various types of abuse also, yet fearful of losing even that level of work if they failed to please.

Very many of Rome's poor lived a hand-to-mouth existence, without much prospect of their situation ever being able to change for the better. Their main problem was the simplest – mere survival. The astrological work 'Carmen Astrologicum' defined poverty as 'not having the bread to fill the belly, or the clothes to clothe oneself…' This level of hardship stops short of the 'ordinary' person who had some small cushion of resources but found this insufficient to allow them to break into the economic layer above. A poor family, living on their own plot of land, might well be regularly on the edge of starvation, but they at least had access to a small food supply of their own working. The definition of a peasant was one who worked on the land, living in squalor and with only the most basic foods to eat, and an income supplemented by sale of his garden produce in the markets.

A good tenant farmer was one who paid his rent on time, but he still did not own the land he worked and lived on. Therefore, he was always in danger of suffering eviction. Non-slave agricultural workers, of both sexes, had to rent themselves out as best they could, making themselves useful where needed, and this in exchange for only a subsistence level of living. Many such people could often wait all day for an offer of work, as those seeking work always greatly outnumbered the people needing to hire. They could easily end a day's waiting with nothing at all to show for it. In our own time, when the state at least provides a basic level of support, however meagre, it is hard to visualise having absolutely nothing. For those people at that level, it must have been easy to envy even a slave, in a decent household, who at least had food and shelter, and may even have been able to save a little money.

Naturally, the lack of written evidence about the poorest of the people makes it difficult to give a full account of the lives they led, or indeed how they were viewed by their fellow humans, when they had sunk so low as to become destitute. In some towns, a public dole might help a little to alleviate the plight of these poorest people, but such charitable provision could only have reached a fraction of those needing it the most.

For the poor in the larger towns, life could actually be even harder. The poet Martial refers to a number of examples,[38] particularly beggars. These people are recorded as asking 'in hoarse voices' for the bread that would be thrown to the dogs. Martial also writes of a 'beggar's bridge' under which homeless people regularly sheltered, as they would under any covered spaces such as aqueducts, although there was a law which forbade the homeless to squat in tombs. It was common for the poorest to live in lean-to huts, placed against any available wall. However, if these thrown-together and often flimsy shelters were deemed by the authorities to be a fire risk, they would order them to be demolished. If the home-made structure was sturdier, then the squatter could very likely find himself being charged rent for the privilege of being allowed to stay.[39]

The outskirts of many large Roman towns must have been littered with these 'shanty-towns' inhabited by the very poorest people. Roman moralists, in their references to beggars, believed that they should be ignored, but not everyone could be so hard-hearted. A painting from Pompeii, showing life in the local Forum, shows a scantily dressed beggar with his dog on a lead, being given alms by a lady who is attended by her servant.[40]

There are few traces of this borderline level of destitution, but unfortunates at this level tend to leave few traces of their existence. Their desperate situation often solved itself in the only possible way, with the death of the person concerned. Generally un-mourned, they would end up in the lime pits outside the town walls. Martial spoke of the homeless person being shut out of the archway where he had sheltered, miserable in the winter weather. The dogs set upon him, and even the birds try to steal what little food he has. The image of the homeless beggar is therefore of one who is effectively already dead yet remains unburied.[41] Beggars used to congregate at the town gates, as there they could not only to ask for alms, but hopefully find some kind of work. A day, or even an hour or two, on some construction site, might hopefully lead to a longer term of employment and some future improvement. Any kind of day labour would at least enable them to buy a decent meal. Failing the chance of a full day's work, they could offer themselves as porters, or messengers, or show themselves able and willing to do anything which might earn them a coin.

Children were also expected to work, and they started their life of labour very young indeed, not for the poor child the tutors or even a spare coin to pay for a school place. Skeletons of the very young have been found in graveyards outside Rome and their bones and joints show the kind of damage caused by hard labour, which they had not survived for long. The reality of the life of the poor was that they would have to continue to work, where they could, until they died, whether their life ended tragically while still a child, or whether they struggled on until middle age. One cemetery outside of Rome, near to where an ancient textile and laundry works used to stand, had several skeletons of young people, whose bones also show signs of very hard wear. Laundry work was not as clean or pleasant as it might have seemed, as the cloth was 'fulled' to cleanse it, requiring much stamping and treading, meaning a great deal of heavy and smelly work. Not only the bones which can be seen, but the lungs which now cannot, would have suffered from this kind of work. One of the main ingredients of the process was human urine, which was used in cleaning the woollen materials. Pots for the collection of this urine were left available at various places in the streets, particularly outside bars. The Emperor Vespasian was said to have used this trade as the subject of a joke about 'the smell of money', but it would be far from amusing for those obliged to work in it, daily breathing in the miasma of stale ammonia.

Many smaller headstones show children hard at work, carrying the tools of their trades, but the greatest of these 'trade' tombs is probably that of Marcus Vergilius Eurysaces, which is designed to represent his business as a baker. He may have been an ex-slave, or descended from one, but his rather grand tomb, built around 30 BC near to the Porta Maggiore for himself and his wife Atistia, shows how much his business thrived, due probably to his contracts for supplying bread to the legions. Around the top of this large and impressive tomb is a frieze carved to show the various processes of making bread, ranging from weighing the flour, to kneading the dough, to putting the loaves into the ovens, which look like modern pizza-ovens. Watching and instructing the slave workers is a man wearing a toga, which probably represents Vergilius. His may have been a rags-to-riches story, but his good fortune could hardly be expected for everyone.

Lucien[42] noted that typical work for the poor could include selling fish, cobbling shoes or sandals, or merely begging for food or coins. There is very little data from the ancient world that helps us to determine the relative size of these groups of the poorest people, which would in any case tend to differ from place to place and from time to time. Based on studies of early modern Europe, it is quite possible that around 65% of the population, both slave and free combined, were at risk of death due to the disruption of their subsistence existence, through illness, famine, or any other natural catastrophe; their continued survival was so fragile that almost anything could tip them over the edge.[43] These are horrifying statistics, given the vast wealth of the elite, living in the same place and time.

It must also be borne in mind, however, that these large numbers of people found their own ways of coping with the life they lived and that the very commonality of the experience led to shared outlooks. They would certainly have wished for more than they had, but they did not expect to receive it. Their lifestyle was one of subjection, to the landlord, to the tax collector, or the moneylender or any state official. They were never, in any sense, free agents, but the very inevitability of that status quo provided a kind of constant. As their options were very few, this in itself must have encouraged an attitude of acceptance and resignation, which could allow them to cope with the difficulties and apparent futility of their lives. Having said that, the suggestion that they could, and probably did, learn to tolerate and even cope with their destitution, is in no way intended to minimise the hardships they undoubtedly suffered.[44]

The need to recognise and even accept the inevitable ongoing state of crisis tends to concentrate focus on activities rather than beliefs. The wisdom of the poor is what to do and what not to do, although this did not make the poor person an automaton, without creative ability, it merely suggests than in extremity the creative level of thinking tends to be in abeyance or more limited, due to the constant need to focus primarily on overcoming challenges. The poor need to be very practical in order to survive at all.

From the late Republic, a number of public assistance programmes were maintained by the government, but most of these were aimed at free men and boys. The doles were generally motivated not so much by humanitarian concerns, but by the desire of the politicians to keep the males quiet and to curry a certain amount of popularity with the crowds.

Publius Clodius Pulcher proclaimed a free grain dole, in order to gain such favour, in 58 BC. He also initiated a programme of legislation aimed at providing the Plebs with free food supplies, and with legalising the guilds of craftsmen, and he went so far as to have himself 'adopted' as a Plebeian away from his ancient, very wealthy and impeccably noble Patrician family, in order to become Tribune of the Plebs, and increase not only his street credibility but also his political power with the masses.[45]

The grain dole, while already a long-standing custom, was not entirely philanthropic. Famous politicians often subsidised grain (wheat) and the reputation gained for such generosity was always useful when votes were needed. However, it had a deeper purpose as the proletarii, the lowest caste of impoverished Roman citizens, were always liable to riot and the dole of free grain was a part of the 'panem et circenses', or bread and circuses, which helped to control them.

When, in 58 BC Clodius legislated his free grain dole, it provided five modii of free wheat per month to all Roman citizen males. This amounted to a ration of around 13 lbs per modii, providing approximately one large loaf of bread per day. Clodius applied no means test for this dole, with the result that many men who did not need it could still claim their share of it. When Caesar became Dictator, he cut the free grain dole from three hundred thousand recipients, down to one hundred and fifty thousand, simply by introducing a means test.

It begs the question why, if the rich were relatively so few (only approximately 300,000 seriously wealthy men in the Empire), was there not far more social unrest than seems to have been recorded? The answer is that there probably was a good deal of conflict and general unrest, but that it was on a fairly small scale. Thefts, assaults and such disorders went on in Rome and all the other large towns just as they do now, and the authorities were keen to keep such incidents to a minimum, although we know that even the emperors were often very wary of the reception they were likely to receive when they attended the public games. General acclamation by the crowd could by no means be guaranteed, even for the apparently all-powerful.

However, the graffiti which is still to be seen in the bars at Pompeii show something surprising, which is that a certain level of basic education seems to have been the norm for most people, at least in urban areas. There are good levels of Latin which show that reading and writing were fairly common, and that craftsmen, traders, and even slaves, were expected to have had a decent basic level of literacy, and quotes from literature and the poets also show that most people had at least a passing familiarity with the famous stories. On the walls of Pompeii, the graffiti shows at least fifty quotations from Virgil. This is the equivalent of most people in modern times being familiar with a few lines of Shakespeare. It does not mean that they were highly educated, but it certainly suggests that most people had a smattering of the basics. The walls of one Pompeiian laundry were decorated with a scene from the story of Aenid and close by someone had written a parody of the first line of the poem 'Fullones ululamque cano, non arma virumque' meaning 'the fullers and their arm I sing, not arms and the man.' This referred to the owl being the mascot of the laundry business. It shows that there was a shared frame of reference between the world of classical literature and the life of the street.

Women, as a rule, were less likely to rise up in revolution against their leaders and so were less feared by the authorities, who felt less need to exercise control. Although technically citizens, they were not allowed to vote, so there seemed little point in including them in grain doles, primarily a vote-winning exercise. In any case, the grain dole was only enough to support one man and was designed to supplement other sources of income, it was certainly not intended to support a family.

Occasional distributions, assistance programmes and public feasts given by private benefactors were usually on the same lines, in that women if they were included at all would generally be given less. This discrimination was the same even if the donor was female and there is only one public dinner recorded for women. This was for the Curia Mulierum of Lanuvium in the late second or early third century, and although men were excluded from that event, there was for them a cash distribution.[46] Children were supported by some special programmes, in keeping with the state's policy of increasing the birth and child-survival rates. These also heavily favoured boys over girls, as they were aimed at future army recruitment. The Emperor Augustus included boys under the age of eleven in those eligible for irregular distributions, 'congiaria', that were made on special occasions. The Emperor Trajan also added five thousand boys to the list of adults who were receiving the grain dole in the city of Rome.[47] Regular distributions for the support of children in Italy were also established by Trajan. According to inscriptions at Veleia in Southern Italy,[48] the monthly allowance was sixteen sesterces for boys and twelve for girls, twelve was given to illegitimate boys and only ten for illegitimate girls. Boys may have been supported until they were seventeen or eighteen, but girls only until they were around fourteen, when they were expected to marry.

Private schemes were initiated earlier than state ones, with the first recorded one being late in the first century AD by Tiberius Helvius Basila. His gift was for the children of Atina, also in Southern Italy. However, his was not discriminatory either by sex or by legitimacy. Pliny founded a fund at Comum in Northern Italy to help freeborn boys and girls and approximately seventy-five girls and one hundred boys were assisted by his foundation.[49] A woman named Caelia Macrina at Tarracina provided monthly allowances to one hundred children, giving twenty sesterces to the boys and sixteen to the girls.[50]

Unfortunately, generous as it was to try to support other people's children at all, the usual favouring of males over females could not have encouraged poorer families to raise girls well. This practice was short-sighted in the extreme, as those girl children would become the mothers of the next generation. Some benefactors did begin to realise this, and a few public and private funds were then created solely for the benefit of young girls.

In memory of his wife the elder Faustina, Antoninus Pius established the 'puellae Faustinianae' and in the second century AD a daughter of Gaius Fabius Agrippinus created a fund for girls at Ostia in her mother's memory. This probably supplemented the state fund at Ostia, which had been intended to only help boys. However, all the funds for girls were on a rather small scale.

With financial considerations so small, the main reason for marriage among the lower classes was likely to be simple affection. The basic human desire to feel needed and supported by another person made these marriages rather less likely to end in divorce. Nor did they have the need to be 'upwardly mobile' and find a richer or better-connected spouse, which drove many changes in marriage partners in better-off families.

The many divorced partnerships are less likely to be commemorated on tombstones, but even with non-Romans or Romans of the lower classes, the ideals of marriage held strong, with marriages of long duration being celebrated and women praised for being married only once.[51]

For the poorest people there would be no tombstone at all, potter's fields would be the resting places of those without resources and a burial without ceremony was usual for them. A pottery vessel plunged into the ground could mark the spot of burial and perhaps receive an occasional libation from those who still remembered the deceased.

Another area where rich Romans could meet and do business with Romans lower down in the social scale was in clientship, although to be someone's client did not necessarily mean that the client was poorer than his patron. A person of free status (or freed, which was never quite the same thing), who did not necessarily have to be a Roman citizen, could pledge himself to another man, and they would then be in the position of patron and client. The client undertook, in the most solemn and binding way, to serve the wishes and interests of his patron, which would be in return for certain favours. These might include small gifts of money, recommendation for jobs, or legal assistance with general support and advice.

The client and patron relationship was an important one and there were formal laws governing it. Whole towns, cities and even countries could become clients, sometimes of Rome itself. Great and famous Romans could number kings and satraps among their clients, each side hoping to gain something from the relationship. On a smaller scale, a man seeking some political 'clout' would encourage other men to become his clients, and these people would usually attend him at his house at dawn, where they would be greeted by their patron with varying degrees of warmth and familiarity, the 'salutatio', after which they would likely follow him to the business of his day, forming a support group of admirers around him, thus increasing his public prestige. Sometimes the more important clients would be asked to dine with their patron, while the less important could easily be dismissed with a thanks and a small coin. For the poorer of them, this coin would be hoped for and necessary, but from the patron's point of view, the more important the client, the more likely he was to be welcomed and cultivated for what he could do in exchange for the patronage.

A man up and coming in the political sphere was very likely to be approached by other men who wanted to become his clients, in the hope that they could rise with him, banking on his success and using the fact of their familiarity with him as a matter of pride. Each side was supporting but also using the other. Conversely, if the patron seemed to be losing his position, and likely to fall in stature in his public life, then he would find his clients deserting him and trying to attach themselves to someone who could do more for them. Sometimes the first clue a man had that his career was slipping, was that instead of finding a group of eager clients waiting for him each morning, he could find his rooms empty, and realise that they had become aware of his imminent downfall, quickly abandoning his cause to avoid sharing his ruin.

Cicero, when his period of influence was waning, discovered that the client's morning call was often no more than politeness, and with the Empire this call on one's patron lost its importance, being considered nothing more than a tedious chore, although during the Republic it had been a time for unofficial transactions of both public and private business, when political manoeuvres were devised by the politicians and support arranged for the candidates at forthcoming elections.[52] The Tribunes Gaius Gracchus and the younger Livius Drusus were reputed to have devised a system of grading their morning callers, in order to give each group a different kind of attention. First, they received the private callers, then the small groups, and then finally the public were admitted. From the point of view of the client, particularly if he was a poorer man of no importance, it meant a good deal of waiting around, from early morning until midday, with little or no breakfast and no prospect of being offered anything. If he were lucky, he might gain a few minutes of his patron's attention, either to present a plea or merely show his patron that he had turned up. The coin he received for this could mean the difference between getting a meal or not, although sometimes men had more than one patron and collected a coin from each.

In private houses, the wealthy, even sometimes childless widows, would receive callers in this way. Some people of standing, even Consuls, might call out of courtesy or old friendship towards the family and confirm ties. Unfortunately, other callers would be on the make, hoping for gains far greater than the usual 'sportula' offered, which was usually only around twenty-five asses per day.[53]

A few houses still retained the old type of patron and client relationship, when the clients had been real dependents of the family and would attend the patron with real problems, which the patron would feel duty bound to try to solve. Initially, the candidates for public office would have their clients canvass for them, as much grafitti in places like Pompeii shows, and this is exactly how the relationship was originally intended to work, although sometimes it did not.

Seneca wrote:

> Consider the people who keep a whole programme of official calls, a nuisance to themselves and everyone else, mad but quite resolute in their madness, doing their round of calls every day, never seeing a door opened without going in. Now when you consider the vast size and infinite distractions of the city, answer this question – after they have completed their stipendiary round of calls at a whole variety of mansions, just how many people will they have succeeded in seeing? Several of them will have been pushed out of the door after being told their patron is asleep, or because he is amusing himself, or out of sheer bad manners. Or, after teasing them for so long he will then pretend to be in a great hurry and walk straight past them. Often, when his hall is crammed full of his clients, he will avoid going out that way and will instead slip out of the house by an obscure back door. Would it not be better to exclude them altogether than deceive them like that? They, the poor creatures, have cut short their own sleep in order to attend somebody else's. The patron's name is whispered a thousand times, but he is drowsing or half-drunk from the previous night's debauch – so in reply he scarcely raises his lips, but just gives an insolent yawn.[54]

Some people were still willing to put up with the inconveniences and petty humiliations of such behaviour, in exchange for the belief that they were consorting with great men, but many others were intent on finding more material advantages from their clientship. A poet, such as Martial, naturally needed patrons and as a number of his 'Epigrams' on the subject show, he found clientship an unpleasant experience. Some of it was particularly degrading but still useful for his work, however patronising it might have been at the time.

Although a patron was flattered by having many clients, it did not mean that they had any particular liking for him personally. 'Nobody is interested in you, only in what he can get out of you. Once clients wanted to have a powerful friend, but now they only want someone to rob. Let a lonely old man alter the terms of his will, and the next morning he will receive no callers.'[55]

Some clients found their way into the history books, such as Iturius and Caluisius 'who had run through the whole of their fortunes'. They informed against Agrippina in 55 AD (probably hoping for a large fee), and also Publius Egnatius Celer who was prepared (again for a fee) to produce the evidence necessary to send Barea Soranus to his death.[56]

Because of the attention given to this aspect of Roman life by such writers as Juvenal and Martial, it might be wrong to assume that a very great number of Roman men passed their mornings in this apparently wasteful and degrading manner. Generally, for the upper classes, midday marked the end of the working day, due to people's habit of rising at first light. It was one reason why libraries were built facing East, in order to take full advantage of the morning light, and libraries were most often used in the mornings.[57]

One group of people who were expected to maintain a traditional patron and client relationship, despite the general growing impatience with it, were the manumitted slaves. For them, the relationship with their previous masters – now their patrons – would last for a lifetime.

The manumitted slave would take the name of his patron added to his own, and he and his former master would often go into business together once he was freed. During this business venture the patron would expect to take the lion's share of the proceeds, in recompense for him setting his client up in the business. However, the same subservient position was not expected from the children of the freed slave once he had died. Thereby the client could assure himself that his work had at least guaranteed a decent life for his offspring, along with a way of making a respectable living. The fact that so many freedmen had their former slave status carved on their tombstones showed their pride in the achievement of manumission and also the respect they felt towards the patron who had made their change of status possible.

For the less fortunate poor, some families developed relationships with other families in a similar position, to help them with the general struggle for survival. This gave both sides support in the most difficult times, evoking the positive traits of bravery, friendship, opposition to mutual enemies, hospitality, honesty and trust. People would be expected to help each other, without expecting anything in return except the hope of reciprocation in the future when it became necessary. Daily life was essentially competitive, but many found genuine support from friends, who could make life more tolerable with their backing. The idea that everyone was out to harm everyone else in order to ensure his own survival is not borne out by the evidence; many people did try to help each other, both inside and outside of their class divisions.

As their family units increased with the births of children, the poor would have come under greater pressure. Also, older relatives, less able to work and earn their keep, would become frailer and more vulnerable. Life became a very difficult juggling act.

Some people believed that the poor were only interested in working until they had fulfilled their basic needs, which some people believed were mainly in the wine bar. Anything beyond that was wasted effort because it would not measurably improve their general condition.[58] No doubt a few people, worn down with work and struggle, did feel that way, but it was by no means the norm. The evidence does show that most people did try to get on, were interested in their children having a better life, and also tried to help each other when difficulties arose. People were not without natural affection, and poor people are often amongst the most caring and most eager to try to make something of life, particularly when they have children to work for.

Many more people occupied the next level up from actual destitution. It was remarked that the higher up an apartment block one lived the poorer one tended to be, with the best apartments at lower levels, and the cheapest and poorest, often without facilities, on the higher levels. Juvenal joked about someone living on the top floor of such a block 'with nothing to keep him from the rain but the roof tiles.'

Evidence from a cesspit excavated from beneath a small block in the town of Herculaneum gives us information about the regular diet of the possibly one hundred and fifty residents of the building. The block contained both shops and apartments, so that the cesspit contained a good deal of broken crockery and also broken glass, thrown down the lavatory from the upper floors, showing that people did own these items. Their food seems to have been based on fish, including sea urchins, with also traces of chicken, eggs, walnuts and figs. There were also some small items of jewellery which had been lost down the chute, so these must have been fairly decent flats, as the cheaper and even smaller ones would have had no cooking facilities at all. In such cases the residents were obliged to use the public lavatories and baths which were usually run by old women.[59] Even this might have seemed like luxury to the poor child worker from Spain, whose carved image shows him holding a basket and a pick, whose short life was spent doing heavy and possibly dangerous manual work, and whose inscription reminds us he was only four years old.[60]

People at the bottom levels are generally hopeful of sudden improvement, as thousands are even now when buying lottery tickets. A few people did get lucky, as is shown by a graffito from Pompeii, whose lucky winner's pleasure and surprise is apparent … 'I won at Nuceria, playing dice. Eight hundred and fifty-five and a half denarii … honestly, it is true!' At four sesterces to the denarius his win came to almost four thousand sesterces, which was roughly four times the annual pay of a soldier, so it is no wonder that he was so excited. This was a potentially life-changing amount, as an example five hundred sesterces would buy a good mule, while one sesterce, according to a Pompeiian bar's price list, would buy a pitcher of the best Falernian wine, far better than the rough red that the bars usually served.[61]

This indicates the social world which is totally separate from that of senators and other officials. However, except for the most destitute of people, everyone needed some sort of social life, and theatres and great public ceremonies were things that for most people could only be viewed at a distance. They and their friends would visit the bars or the lunch places, mixing with others of their class, where they would probably pull the politicians to pieces and give their opinions on everything. There they could drink and dice and get a little pleasure out of life, always with the hope that, like the excited man from Pompeii, they, too, would one day get lucky.

Poorer areas such as the Subura were very much a law unto themselves, and during the Republic public order regularly broke down with people taking to the streets to shout at, throw things at, and sometimes manhandle – even occasionally kill – unpopular public figures. During the Empire there was more physical protection for the emperor, whose main threats tended to come from his closest associates, yet officials did sometimes have to face attacks. In 51 AD the Emperor Claudius was pelted with bread in the Forum and had to be smuggled back into his palace by a rear door. At around the same time, in Aspendus in Turkey, one local official very narrowly escaped being burned alive by an angry crowd, who were protesting against landowners locking up all the available grain in order to get better prices by exporting it.[62]

Apart from the most unfortunate people who in any society seem to fall through the net, the majority of Romans appeared to live their lives in much the same way we do today. However, there was certainly a greater level of callousness, particularly in their attitude towards animals, to the victims of the games, in their apparent coldness in forcing marriages on family members, and the exposure of unwanted children. In their basic needs and in their enjoyment of simple pleasures, their hopes of the 'big win' that could change their lives, and even in their sense of duty, responsibility and their place in the world, they were perhaps more brothers under the skin to us than we might care to admit.

In their world, to be rich was desirable. There was no sense of dignity in poverty for the Roman, everyone wanted that step up, to be higher-up than, or better than, others. But for the poor of all ages there is only the desire to be less poor, it was certainly not a life choice as it could be for the later Christians, whose ideas of austerity and humility would have been incomprehensible to the Roman mind. The idea of a simple life might appeal to the Stoics, but their idea of simplicity was still based on Roman foundations and was never an abstract concept of pleasing some god by self-denial.

The last word on the subject might be best left to one Ancarenus Nothus, an ex-slave who died at the age of only forty-three. He must have had hopes of his freedom and the possibilities of advancement that it might bring as a stepping-stone to better things. For him the modest prosperity he desired never came, and his ashes were found in a shared tomb just outside Rome, with a poetic inscription which echoes with the futility of his life's hopes.

> I'm no longer worried that I'll die of hunger, I am rid of aching legs and getting a deposit for my rent, I am now enjoying free board and lodging for eternity.[63]

6

The Outcasts

The term 'outcasts' can be variously applied. They might be exiles, vagabonds, pariahs, or a 'homeless, rejected and abandoned wretch.'[1] The Collins Dictionary gives a more reasoned definition: 'a person who is excluded or rejected from a particular group or from society.'

This is rather more reassuring, as many of the 'outcasts' dealt with in this chapter were neither wretches nor vagabonds, and though in some senses they may have seemed to be pariahs, they were not necessarily reprobates either. They were people on, or just beyond, the fringes of respectable society, whose lifestyles or jobs caused them to be looked down on by others, who felt able to consider them in some way inferior. In many cases, they were people who lacked the start in life that could give them choices, or people whose skills – or lack of skills – led them towards the type of work that brought them notoriety, perhaps even fame, without an equal measure of acceptability.

Anyone – absolutely anyone – could find themselves changing status and slipping down the greasy pole that was public life. They could exchange high status, security and wealth for sudden exile, confiscation of property, and even risk to life. Any politician who made the wrong decisions too often, any military leader who backed the wrong general in one of the many civil disputes or changes of leadership, could find himself becoming outlawed. Some of them were able to return to public life when the political climate changed again, some were not, and some paid with their lives for an unfortunate run of luck or a bad decision made.

This is why Fortuna, in one of her many guises, was always such a popular Goddess. She was to be placated, due to her control of the ups and downs of life. Good luck or bad, a fortuitous decision or a stupid one, the ability to sway with the prevailing wind of change, and enough determination to keep going whatever the Fates threw your way, were all necessary. Although some of the skills needed to survive could be learned, some events were dependent on outside forces beyond one's control, hence the need for Fortuna's help and the help of any other gods it might be wise to have on one's side. The general about to go on campaign, with his ribbon of imperium tied across his breastplate[2] and his legions behind him, would be wise to stop and ask Fortuna Huiusce Dei to give her blessing to his venture, lest some unexpected disaster strike.[3]

However, many people on the fringes of Roman society had never had any status to lose, so their world was far removed from the struggles for supremacy that occupied their betters. The early life of the general Sulla had caused him to draw closer to the very people who could be referred to as outcasts. The world of the theatres and the circus has always exerted a pull of its own, and in these days actors and actresses can become famous and wealthy in their own right, as a few of the Roman ones did. Yet it must be remembered that well into the nineteenth century theatre people were considered to be 'low' and their women usually without virtue, 'infra dig'[4] and not to be permitted within one's family circle, however entertaining they might be outside of it. The idea of a young man of good family consorting regularly with such people (as Sulla certainly did) was unsuitable, and even the writer Charles Dickens, who had a lifelong love of the theatre, was obliged to hide his long-standing affair with an actress, although the lady in question was not a prostitute or in any way promiscuous.[5] Her professional life still put her beyond the pale and any recognised relationship with her would damage Dickens's career, and the respect and affection in which he was held.

For Sulla, his contacts with the recognised yet never quite respectable world of entertainment in some ways defined his life. It certainly defined the way in which others regarded him for many years, until he had carved out a new persona that was more acceptable. With the people who became his friends, when others of his own class had no interest in a man without money to support his rank, he was always hugely popular. He had a love of the bizarre which easily embraced the mimes, the transvestites, the singers, dancers and clowns who were employed by others, but who were socially inferior. Sulla was bisexual, he wrote bawdy plays and had a long-standing affair with the actor Metrobius, who was still with him at the end of his life, despite a military career, great power, four marriages and five children. Sulla and Metrobius had long periods when they were unable to see each other, yet still their relationship held, although it would have been foolish to parade openly that he had a male lover. However, in certain circles it was never a secret and it didn't actually matter, so long as he performed his duty as a Roman male, married and produced children. It was no more or less than other men did, without feeling any need to 'come out' openly about it, which would have been counter-productive, although nobody could claim that he was less of a man, or less than a general, due to his personal choices.[6]

When he became well-known his refusal to entirely turn his back on these rather shady friends is hugely to his credit; such an aberration has continued to ruin lives throughout the centuries. There was no place for a mention of Metrobius on Sulla's tomb on the Campus Martius after his death, and so the actor disappears from history, although the inscription recording that the deceased was 'No better friend, no worse enemy' to those with whom he shared his life gave a clue to his attitude towards friends and other associates, false or otherwise.[7]

Another well-known performer who got off less lightly for his association with the powerful was Mnester. He was a dancer, a comedian, and a pantomime actor of peasant stock, who was immensely popular during the reigns of the Emperors Gaius Caligula (37-41 AD) and Claudius (41-54 AD). The Emperor Caligula was devoted to Mnester. His 'insane passion' for the actor was such that he was known to stop performances so that he could 'shower kisses on Mnester, even in the theatre'. Also, 'if anyone made the slightest noise during a performance, the Emperor was likely to drag them from their seats and beat them with his own hands.'

To a knight who had created some disturbance while Mnester was on the stage, he sent a centurion with instructions that the man was to go immediately to Ostia, he was then to convey a sealed message to King Ptolemy in Mauretania. The message that the unfortunate knight carried said 'Do nothing, either good or bad, for the bearer.'[8] This was basically a death sentence, meaning that the offender could be offered nothing, not food or water, shelter or help of any kind.

According to Suetonius's *Twelve Caesars*, Gaius Caligula firmly 'believed that he was a good singer, dancer and actor and was so proud of his voice and his dancing ability that he could not resist the temptation of supporting the tragic actors at public performances, where he would repeat their gestures by way of praise or criticism.' He often danced at night, and on one occasion summoned three senators of consular rank to the palace. These three men arrived 'half dead with fear' wondering what they had done wrong to account for the unexpected summons. They were led into a room which contained a small stage, and suddenly amid a 'tremendous racket of flutes and clogs' the Emperor appeared, bursting out from behind curtains, dressed in an ankle-length tunic and a cloak. He performed a song and a dance, then without a word he disappeared again, according to the account of Suetonius. The astonished senators were then sent home again, though whether they had the self-preservation to applaud the Emperor's efforts we do not know. Neither do we know whether his singing and dancing abilities were as good as he believed, or whether his unwilling audience were unsure whether to laugh or cry at his antics. Probably they were just delighted to get away in one piece.

Caligula loved chariot racing, and often dined with the 'Greens' team and spent the night at their stables. On one occasion he gave the driver Eutychus presents worth twenty thousand gold pieces. His favourite among the horses was Incitatus and to prevent him being disturbed in his stable at night, would picket the area with troops the night before the races, so the great horse could get enough sleep.

Incitatus had a marble-lined stable, an ivory stall, and royal purple blankets as if he, too, were an emperor. He wore a collar of jewels. The horse owned a house, a team of slaves and had his own furniture, so that he could provide entertainment for the guests that Caligula invited on his behalf. Was it true that he intended to give Incitatus a consulship? Or was that merely a warning to the consuls already in office?[9]

For Mnester, the eventual murder of the Emperor meant that, at first, he had even more fame and fortune at the court of the successor, Claudius. However, his real problems started when the Empress Messalina imagined herself in love with him. She demanded that he sleep with her and although he resisted for some time, fearing the wrath of the Emperor, Messalina persuaded Claudius to order Mnester to 'obey her in all things' and she made it clear that her sexual demands were included. Mnester already had a mistress of long-standing, Poppaea Sabina, of whom he was very fond. She was the mother of the Poppea who would later become Nero's empress. Messalina and Mnester did become lovers, although it must have been a very uncomfortable relationship for him, knowing the risks he ran and what might eventually happen.

Things appeared to ease a little when Messalina turned her attentions to another man, the extraordinarily handsome but rather stupid Gaius Silius. The Empress started an affair with him, but unfortunately for Mnester she also kept him as a part of her intimate circle, so he was unable to escape her completely. She decided to marry Silius, considering that her own impeccable descent from Augustus was good enough to give her new lover the authority to become Emperor in place of Claudius. However, Claudius had a faithful servant in his freedman Narcissus, who had never liked Messalina, whose reputation had by then sunk to the lowest possible level. Narcissus heard about the proposed marriage to Silius and knew what it could mean for Claudius. The Emperor was warned and was afraid, asking repeatedly 'Am I still the Emperor?' Messalina's wedding party was broken up and the guests scattered. The Empress was captured and was very nearly forgiven by Claudius, who was prepared to listen to her excuses on the following day, being conscious that she was the mother of his children. However, others took the matter in hand and Messalina was executed in the Gardens of Lucullus, ostensibly by order of her husband. When he was informed of her death, Claudius made no protest and she was not mentioned by him again.

Unfortunately, Mnester had been a member of the ill-fated wedding party and when captured he pleaded his innocence in the matter. He reminded his questioners that the Emperor had instructed him to obey the Empress, which was why he had to be present at her new wedding. However, his pleas regarding the Emperor's order of compliance did him no good, and he was among the people executed. The story of this unfortunate man, whose fame and popularity might have been expected to give him a good life yet were the very things which drew him into danger, highlights the problems of dealing with the fickle imperial families, and is a reminder that even being a favourite of theirs did not guarantee personal safety.

Women were not allowed to perform as actresses in the Roman Republic, nor in the early Empire, although they were certainly present around theatres as the wives and girlfriends of performers, and the handsome actor was just as much of a draw for women then as now.

There would certainly have been 'hangers-on', though with the lack of respectable reputation that went with theatre connections, having a relationship with one of the performers was not really acceptable. Not until the more decadent emperors, with their own love of performing in public, did the theatre gradually become considered fit for decent people.

Another emperor who believed his own publicity was Nero. Born Domitius Ahenobarbus in 37 AD, he was the stepson of Claudius (son of his last wife Agrippina and her husband Gnaeus Domitius Ahenobarbus), and became emperor at the age of seventeen. Nero's horoscope, read as was usual for any newly born child, gave so many ominous predictions that his father remarked that 'any child born of himself and Agrippina was bound to have a detestable nature and become a public danger.'[10] Nero grew up in poor circumstances after his father's death, when the Emperor Caligula had taken all that the family had and banished Agrippina. Nero was raised by his aunt, Domitia Lepida, who chose a dancer and a barber to be his tutors, although when Claudius became Emperor the family inheritance was restored. Nero reputedly gave a good performance in the 'Troy Game' at the circus at the age of ten, for which he was loudly applauded, which may have been when his lifelong love of Greek culture and the theatre began. Claudius became Nero's stepfather, and after his rather suspicious death (with rumours that Agrippina had poisoned him), Nero was acclaimed as Emperor.

His reign started very promisingly, but he began to give a wide variety of expensive entertainments, and actually raced chariots pulled by four camels at the games. He created a series of plays called The Great Festival devoted to the eternity of the Empire, and in these plays parts were taken by both men and women, still considered a scandal. One well-known knight was said to have ridden an elephant down a sloping tightrope, and when Nero staged the play 'The Fire' by Afranius, the actors were allowed to keep the valuable furnishings they rescued from the actual burning house that was used as a prop. Throughout the Festival gifts were scattered freely, one thousand assorted birds daily, quantities of food parcels, vouchers for grain, clothing, and even gold, silver and precious stones, pearls, paintings, slaves, pack animals and trained wild beasts were given away.[11] Naturally, such generosity caused his immediate popularity to soar, as such games and festivals were already a cherished part of Roman culture. When he inaugurated the 'Neronia', which was a festival of competitions in music, gymnastics, singing and drama to be held every five years, he took part personally, accepting the wreath for Latin oratory and verse. He was also offered the wreath for a lyre solo, but modestly asked for it to be placed on the statue of Augustus.

Less modestly, in the ballet 'Minotaur', an actor disguised as a bull, actually mounted another who played Pasiphae, and supposedly occupied the hindquarters of a hollow wooden heifer. The audience were unsure whether the sexual performance had been real or not. In another ballet, 'Daedelus and Icarus', the actor playing the part of Icarus, while attempting his first flight, fell beside Nero's couch and splattered the Emperor with his blood.

At an athletic contest, Nero shaved his chin for the first time, put the hair into a pearl-studded gold box and offered it to Capitoline Jupiter. He invited the Vestal Virgins to attend his shows, saying that the priestesses of Ceres at Olympia had that privilege, therefore Roman priestesses should have it too.

Despite all this, he began to impose heavy penalties on excessive personal expenditure, even while building the Domus Aurea (Golden House) outside the city centre. This was to be the largest and most sumptuous palace ever seen, with its collection of Nymphaeums, banqueting halls, bath-houses, terraces and gardens, all intended to be unique. There was to be hot and cold running water in the bathrooms, and one of the rooms would shower visitors in flower petals and perfume as they entered it. The grounds covered a square mile and contained vineyards and game.[12] He preferred to remain in this fantasy world of play-acting and believing he was a serious performer, taking part in the chariot race at the Neronia but this time not with the camels, but with ten horses (according to Suetonius) instead of the usual four. It is highly unlikely that any chariot could be successfully driven with so many horses, being too difficult to manoeuvre around the Spina in the centre of the track. Even using four took enormous skill and the near-wheeler, the left-hand horse, had to be well-trained and biddable, as he took all the strain on the ends of the anti-clockwise course – this is why this nearside horse was the one sacrificed as the October Horse, because he was the best of the team.

Whether or not Nero did attempt a ten-horse team, his chariot turned over and he was thrown out and injured. True to form, he then claimed that had he not suffered an 'accident' he would certainly have won the race.[13] He was to continue with his playing and singing and promoted the kind of applause used by the Alexandrians, teaching others the 'threefold' method. This was the 'bees' made by a humming noise, the 'roof tiles' or clapping with hollowed hands, or the 'bricks', which was clapping with flat hands.

He sometimes chose to play the female part in tragedies, working with professional actors and often wore masks, either modelled on his own face, or on the face of whichever women he currently admired. Again, nobody was allowed to leave the theatre during a performance, however pressing the reason. We are told of one woman in the audience going into labour and actually giving birth, which must have put even Nero off his stride. Other stories are of men pretending to faint, or even die, so they could be carried out.

However, as with most Romans, the great passion was horses, and he continued to risk his life in chariot races. On his way back from Olympia he insisted on a processional entry into Rome, using a chariot once used by the Emperor Augustus for a triumph. He wore for this occasion a Greek mantle spangled with golden stars over a purple robe. The Olympian wreath was on his head and others were carried before him, and an escort shouted out what he had won, and against whom he had triumphed.

If he had lived entirely in this world of make-believe then he might have been forgiven his excesses, but unfortunately, he was also fond of robbing shops and stealing from his subjects, believing his imperial status allowed this. People were even stabbed on the streets at night. Once he was badly beaten by a senator whose wife he had molested. This only taught him not to go out at night without an escort. He delighted in visiting the theatres during the day, watching the quarrels of the actors backstage, and when they came to blows he would join in by throwing things, encouraging them to fight it out with large stones, or parts of broken benches. Once he fractured a praetor's skull with a well-aimed missile.[14]

Eventually Rome became sickened by him, and he was obliged to commit suicide, although his courage failed him and he had to have a slave help him to do the deed. He died in 67 AD at the age of only thirty. It was reported that as he died, he exclaimed, 'Oh, what a great artist dies in me.'

Despite support from people such as Nero, theatre people were still considered beyond the pale by decent people. Even if wealthy and successful, they remained low status and were referred to as 'histriones' from the Etruscan word 'hister' meaning dancers. It was often said that the theatre was made up only of foreigners, bought slaves, or those born into it.

In the year 364 BC, Rome was visited by a plague. The Romans tried to avert the anger of the Gods by scenic plays, 'ludi scenici', which had not been performed before. As nobody in Rome knew how to prepare such a performance, they sent to Etruria where dancers moved to the music of the flute. Roman youths began to imitate these dancers, while reciting rude verses, and this was the basis of Roman drama until Livius Andronicus introduced a slave onto the stage, to sing or recite, while he performed a dance or gesticulation. The next step was dialogue, also attributed to Livius. Livy tells us that such histriones were not citizens, could not be entered into the Tribes, and could not be in the legions.[15] If any Roman citizen took to the stage as a profession, he could be excluded from his Tribe, and many Roman writers state that the theatre people were generally held in contempt.[16] Towards the end of the Republic, only men such as Cicero, who had had a Greek education, valued them for their talents.

Despite this, the most famous of them, such as Roscius, could earn one thousand denarii for each day that he worked. Aesopus left his son and heir a fortune of two hundred thousand sesterces, acquired solely by working in the theatre. An ancient law empowered magistrates to coerce histriones at any time or place, and the Praetor had the right to scourge them, 'jus virgarum in histriones', although this was partly abolished by Augustus. However, severe punishments could still be inflicted on actors who, in their private life or their conduct on stage, were considered to have committed some kind of impropriety.[17] After Augustus, the only legal punishments permitted to be inflicted on actors appear to have been imprisonment or exile.[18] However, the great favour shown to actors by some of the Emperors caused increased arrogance and loose conduct among them, and in the theatres there were many bloody fights. Tiberius was on one occasion obliged to expel all histriones from Italy temporarily.[19]

During the Empire it seems that the average pay for one performance was five denarii, or sometimes as much as seven drachmae. Several Emperors prohibited the people from paying actors 'immodest sums' of money, and Marcus Antonius, who was also fond of the theatre, stated that each actor should receive five aurei, but that none of them should get more than ten. Beside their regular pay, they did receive gifts, and the audience were known sometimes to throw gold and silver coins onto the stage as signs of their appreciation.[20]

Much later, one woman did rise from the ranks of entertainers and actually became royal. This did not happen until the Western Empire had given way to the Eastern one, centred in Constantinople. Theodora was a harlot, born into the circus, a daughter of low-class people who worked at the Hippodrome. The father, Acacius, was a bear keeper who had died after being mauled, and the widowed mother, Macrina, along with her daughters Comito, Anastasia and Theodora, went as suppliants to kneel in the sand and beg for alms. The mother had already chosen her husband's successor, one Basilius, and wanted his position as bear keeper confirmed. The Blues party decided to employ him, and Theodora had had her first experience of the power of the crowd.

She grew up beautiful, but there was nothing for her except to become a prostitute and after a few years of serving men around the Hippodrome she decided to make more of a name for herself. She made friends with another woman who had access to the Blue and Green teams, and before long Theodora owned her own house and knew richer clients. She had many adventures and travelled, facing many reverses of fortune. In Antioch she had a son, named John, who was left in the care of a friend while she journeyed on.

Back in Constantinople, the Emperor was Justin, who was crowned in 518 AD[21] and the appointed heir was his nephew Justinian. Legend tells us that by then Theodora lived decently, supporting herself by spinning wool. The truth may have been quite different, but she met Justinian, who was then thirty-nine years old, a scholar, and on the point of becoming co-Emperor. Eventually she made it clear that she wanted marriage, although the law did not allow any member of the nobility to marry an actress, so even Justinian could not ignore her past. It was said that he finally tricked his uncle into signing the decree allowing 'men of all ranks to marry with actresses and similar' and people began to make jokes about Empresses behaving like harlots, but now they would have a harlot as Empress. Justin died in 527 AD and Justinian and Theodora were crowned at the Hippodrome where Theodora had once worked as a prostitute. On either side of the Imperial Box were four magnificent bronze horses, sculpted by the Greek master Lysippos. These are now in Venice, while copies of them adorn the front of St. Mark's Basilica.

Theodora would reign with Justinian for twenty-one years. She always retained her rather earthy interest in sexual matters, asking friends and servants about their experiences. Rumours were rife that she had lovers, and Justinian's secretary, one Priscus, particularly suspected her morals. He was reportedly kidnapped while walking by the sea and was never seen again.[22]

Apparently, Justinian was told she had been visited by a young man. Jealous and angry, he had the man traced and arrested. Theodora realised he was missing and heard, to her horror, that he was being tortured to reveal details of their relationship. She begged Justinian for his life, telling him that the man was not a lover, but her son John, born many years before. Word was sent to protect the man, but was too late, her son had died. Many thought it was a punishment for her behaviour, and Procopius of Caesarea heartily disliked both 'Theodora the Harlot' and Justinian, whom he described as 'treacherous and incapable of being faithful to any friend, a man who bends and breaks his own laws, to suit any purposes of his own.'[23] Theodora died in 548 AD aged about fifty, and although she had a daughter still living, born during her years as a prostitute, she had no children with Justinian. He did not remarry and lived another seventeen years after her death; for him the spark had gone.[24]

Entertainers were there to be hired when needed, watched when bored, people who only occasionally caught the public imagination. It was, however, the one place where anyone of low status could hope to fit in. People such as chariot drivers or animal keepers were proud of their strength and courage. In doing their jobs, they could also show stoicism in the face of injuries and receive some honour for their 'virtus' – and be acclaimed by men and desired by women.[25]

Contrary to common belief, these people did not always expect to die in the arena, as training gladiators, for example, was a very expensive business, and nobody would want to lose their investment as soon as they performed. Julius Caesar had a gladiator school outside Pompeii and the amphitheatre at Pompeii was the first permanent one in Italy. Previous performances had taken place in town Forums, with grandstands erected at the sides, or sometimes temporary wooden arenas were used. It seemed more respectable to have only temporary places of such entertainments. The amphitheatre at Pompeii was constructed shortly after the town became a Roman colony, after being besieged by Sulla in 89 BC. It was then named 'Colonia Cornelia

Veneria Pompeianorum' referring to Sulla's family name, Cornelius, and the town's patron Goddess, Venus.[26]

This amphitheatre was built at the expense of Gaius Quinctius Valgus and Marcus Porcius. They were also responsible for the building of Pompeii's small covered theatre, more precisely an Odeon, erected at around the same time. This Odeon could hold around one thousand people, and was next door to the much larger theatre, which held around four thousand people. This was built during the early second century BC and is still occasionally used for performances. The Odeon was intended for musical recitals, singing, poetry competitions and so on. The amphitheatre staged everything from gladiatorial contests to wild beast shows and was considerably rowdier than the Odeon. In Pompeii in 59 AD a famous riot erupted between local people and those from the neighbouring town of Nuceria. This riot spread out from the amphitheatre itself into the streets and incensed the authorities in Rome.

> At about this time, there was a serious fight between the Pompeiians and the people of Nuceria. It arose out of a trifling incident at a gladiatorial show given by Livineius Regulus, whose expulsion from the senate has been mentioned. During an exchange of taunts, characteristic of the disorderly country towns, abuse led to stone throwing, and then swords were drawn. The people of Pompeii, where the show was held, came off the best. Many mutilated and wounded Nucerians were taken to the capital, and many bereavements were suffered by parents and children. The Emperor himself [Nero, reigned 54-68 AD] instructed the senate to investigate the affair, and the senate passed it on to the consuls. When they reported back, the state debarred Pompeii from holding any similar gatherings for ten years. Illegal associations in the town were dissolved and the sponsor of the shows and his fellow-instigators were exiled.[27]

Although the amphitheatre in Pompeii was relatively small compared to the one which would be built in Rome between 72 and 80 AD (construction of which began with the Emperor Vespasian and was completed under his successor Titus), it still held around ten to fifteen thousand spectators. That was more than the male population of the town, so it was obviously intended to be a centre for visitors from the towns nearby. The idea of a good many armed members of a crowd of that size rioting in the streets is terrifying. The famous wall painting in a house in the town clearly shows fighting not only within the arena but also spilling into the nearby streets.

During the ten-year ban, Pompeii held games that featured only 'athletes' standing in for the gladiators. The ban was lifted, probably by Nero, in 64 AD. Grafitti in the town reflects the passions aroused in the spectators by the games in general. Their loss must have had a significant impact on the economy and status of the region. 'Bad luck to the people of Nuceria' from the Via di Mercurio and 'Good luck to the people of Puteoli, good fortune to the people of Nuceria and the hook to the people of Pompeii' from the Vico del Lupanare. The hook was the tool used to drag the defeated fighters out of the arena.

The external arches of the amphitheatre in Pompeii, which are no longer in existence, were where food and drink stalls were set up, along with advertising signs: 'Gnaeus Aninius Fortunatus occupies this spot with the permission of the aediles.' These stalls are clearly visible on the wall painting of the riot. There were also many shops and bars close to the amphitheatre and they would profit hugely when the games were taking place, although they also probably suffered occasional damage when the customers became over-excited and a fight started.

The games were originally far smaller, and tended to have only two types of fighters, Gauls and Thracians. This did not necessarily mean that they came from Gaul or Thrace, but described the style of equipment they used. In Republican Rome a gladiator would fight for four to six years, and he might actually fight only five times in any one year. It was unusual for him to be killed, although he would certainly suffer injuries and his training and care would be supervised by a 'doctor'. The 'lanista' was the head of the training school. The gladiator could originally have been a criminal, a deserter from the legions, or slave, or even a freedman who had signed himself up voluntarily. In all cases, he had to have had some desire to become a gladiator; a reluctant or frightened man would not be worth the considerable expense of his training.[28] The 'Neronians' were gladiators who were trained at the Imperial School at Capua (the Ludes Neronianus.)[29]

Later on, the fighting styles would expand to include a Murmillo, a Samnite, a Retiarius, and the usual Thracian. The schools tended to be owned by businessmen or wealthy nobles, much as rich men own racehorses in our own time. They could expect to make healthy profits from hiring out 'pairs' of gladiators all over the country, as the fights were not merely for entertainment of the masses but were a major part of funeral games. Many senators and knights also owned some gladiatorial schools, and some of these were large enough to house over a thousand men at a time. In Pompeii itself we know that there were several different types of gladiator, as the armour for these styles has been found. There are also paintings and graffiti and the evidence of literary sources of the time.

The Thracian tended to be the most popular, fighting with a short, curved sword or 'sica' and carrying a small square shield known as the 'parmula'. He wore an arm guard and two leg guards, which were often highly decorated. His helmet could be spectacular, ending in a griffin's head or tall crest. He tended to fight the Murmillo, another Thracian, or the Hoplomachus, who carried a straight sword, had high leg guards and a helmet similar to that of a Thracian or a Murmillo.

The Retiarius fought with a trident and a net, or with a short sword. He wore an arm guard and had a rectangular bronze plate, the 'galerus', tied to his left shoulder. The Retiarius fought either the Murmillo or the Secutor. The Secutor fought with a short sword and a large rectangular shield. He wore a metal greave or 'ocrea' and an enclosed plain helmet. He tended to fight with the Retiarius.

The Murmillo fought with a short sword (the gladius from which the word 'gladiator' derives, and he carried a three-feet-high wooden shield, covered with leather. He had a visored helmet and a square-shaped crest. He wore armguards and possibly a left leg guard and could fight with the Thracian, the Hoplomachus, or the Retiarius.

The Eques fought on horseback with a lance and a small round shield. Their helmet had a visor and they wore a short tunic with guards on their thighs and arms. They only fought with another Eques. An Essedarius fought from a cart or a chariot.

By the Pompeiian amphitheatre is a large palaestra, or training ground. This was built at public expense and several houses were demolished to make space for it. It is surrounded on three sides by a portico and there was in the centre a swimming pool, supplied with constantly flowing water from the public aqueduct. It was not Pompeii's first palaestra, as near to the Doric Temple is one from the second century BC, which is far smaller. The later one was a real exercise ground and graffiti suggests that it was also open to the general public.[30]

The smaller and earlier one had been connected to the Republican baths and possibly to a gymnasium, all constructed at the same time in the second century BC. Before the end of the first century BC the baths had been demolished to make way for houses, leaving only the palaestra standing, and this had been much reduced in size to allow for the building and extension of the Temple of Isis in 6 AD.[31]

The structure of the seating of the amphitheatre, known as the 'cavea' was supported by the embankment of the town walls, plus another embankment built up artificially using the earth excavated from the arena. Spectators may, in the early days, have been separated by military rank, and later some public officials paid for permanent sections of seating that formalised the divisions according to social status in different areas.

The names of the magistrates who paid for the constructon of sections of the seating are inscribed on the balustrades:

'The magistrates of the Pagus Augustus Felix Suburbanus, in place of games, by decree of the town council.'

'Titus Atullius Celer, son of Gaius, Duumvir, built a section of seating in place of games and lights, by decree of the town councillors.'

'Lucius Saginus, duumvir for lawsuits, built a section of seating, in place of games and lights, by decree of the town councillors.'

'Marcus Cantrius Marcellus, son of Marcus, duumvir, built these seating sections in place of games and lights, by decree of the town councillors.'

The donors were all concerned to show that they had contributed to the cost of the seating at the amphitheatre, but they preferred to pay for seating to be constructed 'rather than games and lights' not only because it might prove cheaper than subsidising the games themselves, but also because they gained a permanent record of their donations.

So much of the evidence in Rome itself has been destroyed by centuries of deliberate destruction, by sheer thievery disguised as 'collection' of artefacts, and unfortunately by generations of popes, who regularly gave permission for the fairly extensive remains of ancient buildings in Rome to be demolished, re-used for housing, altered beyond recognition or even deliberately pulled down and burned to be used as a source of lime. Rome's incomparable treasures have been lost and mercilessly pillaged until what is now left is a pitiful fragment of the remains that were still in place until fairly recent times.[32]

The tomb of Barbatus is an example of this vandalism. In May 1780, several underground chambers containing carved sarcophagi were discovered outside the Porta San Sebastiano in Rome. The tomb belonged to the immensely important Scipio family, famous for having triumphed over Hannibal. The oldest sarcophagus was that of Barbatus, who conquered the Etruscans in 298 BC and was praised in his epitaph as 'Lucius Cornelius Scipio Barbatus, the son of Gnaeus, a courageous and wise man. He conquered Tourisia and Cisauna, in the Samnium, and subjugated the whole of Lucania, whence he brought back hostages.'

When this labyrinth was fully explored, it yielded a dozen more sarcophagi dating between the third century BC and the first century AD. Pope Pius VI had the Barbatus sarcophagus and its inscriptions transported to the Pio-Clementine Museum, but all the others were simply smashed. The funerary objects in them were sold and the bones of this most eminent and fascinating family were lost.[33] The idea of such wholesale destruction of such important and rare ancient evidence is enough to make one weep. However, such destruction continued unabated until recent times, when in the 1920s the Dictator Mussolini, in attempts to create a new Roman Empire, made a new processional way, the Via del Fori Imperiali, stretching from the Piazza Venezia to the Colosseum, which went across the Forum of Julius Caesar, the Forum of Trajan, and the Forum of Augustus. Archaeologists are now desperately attempting to recover what they can of the ancient structures lying under the road, hoping to excavate a series of tunnels underneath the main road to create some access to the important areas which had been so casually covered by concrete in the 20th century.

Pompeii has also suffered destruction, with its share of 'collectors' and the bombing of World War II, but there has been less modern road building and some of Pompeii's secrets are still buried. What we are now able to see is not so much a time capsule, as a jewel, like a fly caught in amber. We are able to see the streets, the bars, theatres, shops, temples and baths and even its people. It is hugely rewarding to see how closely the lives of these inhabitants feel to our own, and easy to imagine the streets filled with noisy, smelly, and crowded life. The people, their love of all kinds of sport, their voting slogans and their tombs outside the city walls, all came to an end when Vesuvius erupted.

Among the skeletons found during excavations were those in the gladiatorial barracks. One of these was a woman wearing expensive jewellery. Was she meeting a lover among the gladiators, who were known to be very attractive to women? We shall never know. However, these men would often boast about their sexual conquests: 'Girl's heartthrob, Thracian gladiator Celadus, belonging to Octavius, fought three, won three!' or 'Celadus, the Thracian, fancied by all the girls.' The darker side of this was also discovered, when excavators found the skeletons of sixty-three men at the barracks, some of whom had been shackled together at the ankles.

It was Julius Caesar who had the idea of digging a long underground passageway under the Forum in Rome, after a fire in 52 BC had allowed improvements. At that time Caesar was actually in Gaul, but he ordered that the rebuilding after the fire should include the passageway, with steps or ramps in a number of places so that gladiators could suddenly emerge into the daylight in different parts of the Forum. This idea was expanded on when the Colosseum was built in the 70s AD (it was opened in 80 AD) as it had beneath it a maze of tunnels, rooms, lifts, ramps, cages, and accommodation for humans and animals to provide the exciting entertainment that kept the people happy.

When a performance was due, the walls in the city would be plastered with posters, several of which were found, again at Pompeii:

> Twenty pairs of gladiators owned by Decius Lucretius Sater Valens, lifelong priest to Caesar Augustus, and ten pairs of gladiators owned by his son Decius Lucretius Valens, will engage in combat in Pompeii on the 8th, 9th, 10th, 11th and 12th of April. There will be wild animal hunts, as permitted by law. The seats will be shaded by awnings.[34]

We do not know the daily ticket prices, but the ordinary people turned up in huge numbers. The sponsor, who could be the emperor or a rich senator, might make free tickets available. People were keen to see the shows as they were less frequent than the chariot races. In the Circus Maximus in Rome up to two hundred thousand spectators could be accommodated, while the Colosseum held around fifty thousand people.

The standard daily programme had an established routine. In the morning were wild beast hunts, 'venationes'. At midday, criminals and runaway slaves would be executed, and also at lunchtime there could be comic interludes with clowns, or athletics. Sometimes female gladiators took part in these noon diversions, but the real business of the day came in the afternoons, when the gladiators fought.

They were the stars of the show, with followings that a present-day celebrity might envy. We do not have any accounts of actual fights. Martial certainly entered into the spirit of the thing, but in his Book of Spectacles or 'Liber de Spectaculis' he concentrates on the animal fights, or fights between men and large animals, rather than the gladiators. The visual artists give an idea of the power, vulnerability and sometimes terrible despair of the drama. Martial[35] tells us of a fight between an elephant and a bull, when, after the elephant had thrown the bull, it apparently knelt to Caesar: '...piously and in suppliant guise, the elephant kneels to thee oh Caesar, the elephant which erstwhile was so formidable to the bull his antagonist, this he now does without command and with no keeper to teach him – believe me, he too feels our present deity.' On a woman fighting with a lion he remarked, 'That the warrior Mars serves thee in arms, suffices not Caesar. Venus too serves thee.'

On one occasion, a criminal was forced to act out the part of Daedalus; this was a common way of entertaining the crowd with a simple execution, by making a drama out of it. Due to the failure of the man's wings, the unfortunate victim was precipitated into a group of hungry bears, in the arena below him. Martial remarked gleefully, 'Daedalus, while you were being thus torn by a Lescanian bear, how much you must have desired those wings of yours.'[36]

Animals were brought from all over the known world to die in their tens of thousands and although fewer Christians died in the arena than was once supposed, plenty of other people did, providing amusement through their agony and terror.

A terracotta figurine of a naked woman with her hands tied behind her riding on a bull while at the same time being attacked by a large cat, which is tearing at her flesh, is particularly horrifying. Perhaps fortunately, the figurine is no longer sufficiently detailed to be able to see her expression.[37]

However, the mosaics at El Djem, Tunisia, are depicted in great detail. These show condemned prisoners, victims of the noon executions, being taken into the arena with arms bound. Some are propped up and probably forced forward by the men behind them. A leopard has jumped onto the thigh of one of the victims and is tearing at his face, and the man's blood pours onto the sand.[38] Another is held upright by two men, while the instrument of his death, another leopard, leaped towards him – the man's expression of helpless terror is quite clear. In another of these mosaics a different refinement is being used, as the victim has been wheeled into the ring tied inside a small chariot. Again he is being attacked by wild animals.[39] Several of these incidents appear to be taking place in the arena at once, so whether the 'supporters' who pushed the victims towards the animals managed to escape the general carnage, or whether they were also intended to become part of the show, is difficult to determine.

Seneca described these shows as sheer slaughter, and perhaps the crowds also began to find them tedious and predictable. Possibly that is why the organisers felt the need to make a 'drama' or mythological narrative of them to add excitement to build up to the inevitable death It was all a far cry from the image of a few Christians calmly praying in the arena, before the lions were released.

A story often used and described by Martial was that of Parsiphae and the bull. Parsiphae (wife of King Minos) fell in love with a beautiful bull and concealed herself in the replica of a heifer to be mated by him, resulting in the half-human, half-bull Minotaur. In the arena this was played out by a female victim being draped in cowhide and smeared with the blood of a cow on heat. We can assume that the woman was badly maimed by the excited bull, before she was put out of her misery.[40]

These unfortunates were merely the interval, to keep the audience in their seats before the main bouts, and when they started it was impossible to predict how long each fight would last. The spectators cheered on their favourites among the gladiators and if both of the combatants were tiring without a clear winner emerging, the umpire could stop the bout, and step in to declare a short break to let them catch their breath, but if the fight resumed still without a clear winner, the emperor and public could be asked to declare their preference. Gladiators who fought bravely were granted an honourable exit. However, most fights did have a winner and the Zliten mosaics (Tripoli) show the outcome of several fights. One between two Murmillones has ended, and the umpire declares one man the victor. Another image shows a Retiarius who is gravely wounded in his leg, with blood spurting onto the sand, who is sticking out his right index finger to ask for mercy.

A Pompeiian frieze shows several fights taking place, including one of two men reaching the conclusion, where the Hoplomachus is thrusting his sword into the body of the Murmillo. The Murmillo is clearly aware that it is a fatal blow and is putting his hand on his chest in despair.

Tertullian[41] tells us that at the end of the fights a strange character appeared in the arena. Dressed in tight-fitting clothes, wearing leather shoes with pointed toes, and a mask on his face resembling a bird's beak, he represented the ferryman Charon, who transported the dead across the River Styx. He held a long-handled hammer with which he struck each fallen man to make sure that they were dead. This was to make sure that the loser was not faking in order to avoid fighting to the death. Alongside 'Charon' was another man, representing Mercury, who jabbed at the victim with the point of his staff. He had the role of accompanying the souls as the dead were removed with hooks by the Colosseum staff.

After this brutal and undignified end, it may come as a surprise to realise how many tombstones to gladiators there are. Like the tens of thousands of slaughtered animals who suffered in the arena, they in one sense had great value, but in another were expendable, and their role was simply to entertain. When they could no longer do that, their usefulness was at an end.

The animals slaughtered presented a problem. Birds and small animals could be carried away on carts. Lions and tigers were harder to remove, not to mention elephant, hippopotamus or rhinoceros bodies. These could be dumped in remote places, ravines, or specially dug pits. Some of the surviving predators could consume some of the meat of deer, antelope and other creatures. However, bodies would still mount up, start to decompose and present a hygiene problem, so human consumption of at least some of the meat was one answer.

The great mass of poor Romans usually lived on a diet of bread, barley porridge, olive oil, vegetables and fruit, flavoured with the pungent garum fish sauce.[42] They would have been grateful for doles of fresh meat when the games were on. We do not know how this was shared out, but lottery tickets were often thrown to the crowds with the name of the article to be claimed, so there may have been a similar way of distributing the usable meat. Whether a recipient found himself with hares, ostrich, boar or a piece of a lion probably didn't matter much.[43]

Not all gladiators ended up in the lime pits, and there is considerable evidence, even from England, that there were cemeteries quite close to the amphitheatres in London, York and Chester. These cemeteries have revealed many skeletons of young men, probably gladiators, along with female skeletons which show similar injuries.

At Driffield Terrace in York, now a residential area, over eighty complete skeletons were found in 2004 in a cemetery dated to the end of the second century AD. Pottery confirms the date and that they are Roman burials. The skeletons were subjected to ten years of investigations led by Kurt Hunter-Mann of York Archaeological Trusts and a team from York University. 60% of the skeletons had been decapitated, apparently by a single blow. A few of them had grave goods, mainly food, and one man aged between eighteen and twenty-three years was found with the remains of four horses and some cow and pig bones. Some of the dead also had silver coins. The decapitations suffered by a large number of these men were probably a form of coup-de-grâce, or perhaps the action of a 'Charon' character, as in Rome, to ensure that the man was indeed dead. They had all been muscular, and the cemetery was in a prestigious site not far from the military headquarters at the top of Stonegate.

One of the skeletons had most unusual shackles around his ankles. These were not the usual type of removeable ones, but a pair of custom-made leg weights, of two solid iron pieces which had been actually forged around his ankles while still hot enough to be fixed together permanently. This was a very rare find, and the man having these rings fitted around his legs while they were still hot enough to be malleable must have suffered untold agony. He was the largest and apparently most muscular of the skeletons, and it has been suggested that the iron rings may have been intended as a handicap, to slow him down in the ring, or a method of preventing escape. The bones of this man's legs showed distinct injuries from the irons, which fitted closely to the leg bones, and must have been quite tight when his legs were fully fleshed, causing terrible burns when first applied. There was new bone formation around the shackles, showing that he did survive the suffering, and he had also suffered several blunt force injuries to his bones, which, though painful and incapacitating, would have been non-fatal. Some of the other skeletons in the same cemetery had even suffered skull-penetrating wounds that had healed.

Dr Janet Montgomery, a Bioarchaeologist from Durham University, examined the teeth of the various skeletons, and isotope analysis determined the origins in many of the cases. Very few of these people were native to York. They were migrants from Spain, Italy, Gaul and even the near-East, probably from Turkey. Their teeth showed evidence of deprivation during childhood, along with stress lines. However, infant malnourishment had been followed by a high-protein, high-maintenance diet of meat, fish and vegetables which was far better than that enjoyed by the average person. It was suggested by the team that these men had been from poor backgrounds and were later selected for gladiator training.[44]

One of these men had at one time been in combat with a wild beast, while another, one of the smaller men, had suffered deep puncture wounds on his pelvic bones, which were consistent with being gripped by claws. Other deep punctures fitted the profile of lion or tiger bites and these injuries had not healed, so they were probably peri-mortem. They were severe enough to have been unsurvivable.

Most of the ante-mortem wounds on the skeletons had been skilfully treated, showing that effective medical care was available each time they were injured. Despite the fact that approximately 700,000 people were killed in the Colosseum over time, they were still valuable enough to merit good food, proper medical care, and professional training to make them fit for purpose. All of this was hugely expensive, without adding the costs of importing exotic wild beasts also intended to die in the arenas.

Even in York (Eboracum) and far from Rome, people and animals were imported because York was twice the centre of the Roman Empire. This was due to the actual residence there of the reigning Emperor, as during his presence in the city the Roman Empire was ruled from Eboracum. The city as we know it began with the Romans in 71 AD when five thousand men of the Ninth Legion (Spania) marched from Lincoln to set up camp there. The facilities of York were good enough for Septimius Severus (Lucius Septimius Severus Pertinax) to bring his wife with him, Julia Domna, and their sons Caracalla and Geta. Septimius Severus actually died in York in February 211 AD. He had been Emperor since 193 AD.

The other Roman Emperor actually to live in York was Constantine, who arrived in York in 305 AD with his father Constantius. Constantine ruled as Caesar from 293 to 305 AD and as Augustus from 305-306 AD. He was the junior colleague to Augustus Maximian under the Tetrarchy and succeeded him as senior co-Emperor of the Western Empire. He was acclaimed Emperor in York in 306 AD.

The presence of these men was crucial to the status of York itself. And anyone who served the Imperial household rose in status, even the gladiators. These men, although young when they died (the eldest was in his early forties), had all been buried in a respectful manner and many had been left with grave goods. They had not been buried casually, or face down, as might be expected if they had been criminals.

This is in direct contrast to a find at Saintes in Aquitaine, in 2014. The amphitheatre there was large and important, fitting for the capital of Gallia Aquitania (Saintes was then known as Mediolanum Santonum). The arena was capable of seating around fifteen thousand spectators, and archaeological digs at the necropolis, around 250 metres to the west of the amphitheatre, showed hundreds of graves. These dated to the first and second centuries AD and are believed to hold the remains of those who died in the arena there.

These people were not buried respectfully, in individual graves, but put into pits resembling trenches. Some of the finds there were particularly unsettling – of skeletons still wearing iron shackles of various kinds, which suggested they had been slaves or prisoners, and several were children. Three of four adults found together had their ankles bound by iron chains, while the fourth was shackled at the neck. The child found with them, whose sex was undetermined, had a chain attached to its wrist. They were all lying head-to-toe in their shared pit. These were naturally compared to the skeletons found at York and are believed to have been slaves.

Slaves were often forced to fight each other to the death, and some of these battles pitted an armed man or woman against another without armour. Archaeologists are eager to find the causes of death of these individuals, as well as their status during life.

Many at Saintes were buried in pairs, laid out side-by-side, and while sometimes these people were given grave goods, the graves at Saintes contained no artefacts, except that one man had several small vases beside his body. One skeleton, again of a child, was found with coins placed over the eyes to pay the Ferryman to cross the Styx.

Female gladiators certainly existed and were known in their own time as 'Ludia' or female performers at the Ludii, or games. They were sometimes referred to as 'mulieres' or women, but very rarely as 'feminae' or ladies. As 'Ludia' could also refer to actresses during the Empire, this can be confusing, although there is enough evidence to show that some of them were certainly female gladiators. The term 'Gladiatrix' was not then used, only coming into being in the 1800s. Roman writers such as Juvenal certainly mentioned them, also Tacitus, Suetonius, and Cassius Dio, but they were always spoken of critically.

Some evidence suggests that only lower-class women took part, and they appear to have chosen this career for themselves. Was it because of money, to find some kind of fame, or merely to have independence? Whatever their reasons, they immediately gave up any claim to respectability, though they could achieve a certain amount of honour, like their male counterparts. The option to enter this unusual profession seems to have been available to women for a long time.

In 11 AD the senate passed a law forbidding freeborn women over the age of twenty years from taking part in the games. This might suggest that it had previously already been done for some time. It does say 'freeborn' women, not slaves, who may have continued to appear. In Nero's time, women regularly fought in his shows, and they were not always slaves, foreigners or even lower-class women, sometimes even being of the senatorial class. Such fights were probably not a serious part of the programme, to judge by a show in Puteoli (Pozzuoli) in 63 AD. These were organised by Patrobius, a slave who had been freed by Nero, and the games were intended to honour the visit of King Tiridates of Parthia. The King had brought men, women and even children with him from Parthia, to fight in public.[45]

The Emperor Domitian, who also had some strange tastes, once staged a nocturnal performance in which female gladiators fought either each other, or fought against dwarves, by torchlight.

Women did not train with the men in the schools, and there is no record of a woman having fought against a male gladiator. They may have been trained by their fathers, if ex-gladiators, or paid for private lessons from a 'lanista'. Wooden swords were used in training (certainly after the slave revolt led by Spartacus), and also a wooden sword was awarded to mark a gladiator's retirement from the arena.

Juvenal found the whole idea of female fighters amusing and also slightly disgusting, and he wrote cuttingly of the female athlete:

> Purple dressing gowns and ladies' oil, who does not know this? But who has never seen a woman behind her defiant shield, repeatedly striking at the exercise pole with her sword, according to the rules of the game? Such a woman deserves a clarion call, but just imagine she has more in mind, that she is training for the real circus. A helmeted woman thinks she can do anything. She is fleeing from her own femininity too, she loves power, although she doesn't want to be a man either, she feels that too cold. But if you ever have to sell

> your wife's belongings, then you will make a great impression with a plumed helmet, dagger belt, gauntlets and a left-shin plate. Or if your darling wife switches to other weaponry and so throws away her leg protectors, you can be proud! And look – although they are often unable to tolerate the finest, most expensive robes, and even seem sensitive to silken cloth, look how they repeat the thrusts they have seen demonstrated, their breath heaving, and look how their little heads strain, under such weighty helmets and how the thick bandages of coarse bark support their knees.[46]

This patronising and misogynistic view was held by many Roman men and surfaced whenever a woman tried to break free of male ascendancy. However, given the loss of status of this particular move, one can also sympathise with the male view that if the woman wanted to do a male job, she could hardly have picked a worse one from a husband's point of view.

In 200 AD, Septimius Severus outlawed any woman from taking a part in the arena, arguing that such spectacles encouraged a lack of respect for women in general. He also did not want them to appear in the Olympic Games in Greece, believing the whole thing distasteful and a threat to good social order. This may have been prompted by some high-born women who did want to do it, much to the disgust and offence of their husbands.

However, some certainly did, although they never received the adulation and popularity of the male fighters, and it remained a disreputable choice for a woman. Women still fought in the arenas in the third century AD, and an inscription near Ostia (the port of Rome) says that a magistrate named Hostilianus was the first to allow women fighters since Ostia was founded. Although he may have got around the official prohibition by using slaves rather than freeborn women.

The noon executions were described by Seneca:

> These noon fighters are sent out with no armour of any kind. They are exposed to blows at all points, and none ever strikes in vain. The crowd demands that the victor, who slays his opponent, shall then face the man who shall slay him in his turn, and the last conqueror is reserved for another butchering. The outcome for all the combatants is death, and the fight is waged with sword and fire.[47]

He was obviously disgusted, but then the noon shows were just execution, not skill, and their only purpose was the death of the victims. With regard to dying, the famous 'thumbs-down' gesture is thought to have derived from the 'munerarius' drawing his thumb across his throat when asking, and considering, the opinion of the crowd. The commands of 'missio' or let the victim live, and 'stans missus' or sent away standing, meant that the bout was considered a draw. It must not be forgotten that far more people were spared in actual gladiatorial bouts than were killed.

As each fight ended, the victor walked to the emperor's box to receive his prize of an olive branch, along with a sum of money. He also sometimes received a laurel wreath. He then bowed to the emperor, waved to the crowd and left the arena via the Porta Sanavivaria or 'the gate of health and life' to the cheers of the spectators. His value would have risen from his victory and the sponsors would have to pay a higher price to include him in future shows.

The exit of the loser, carried off on a stretcher through the Porta Libitinaria (the gate of Libitina) was less honoured. He was taken to the 'spoliarum' where his weapons were taken from his body and, to ensure that he was actually dead, his throat was cut. Or perhaps in some regions it was the custom to behead the corpse?

The fights would continue all afternoon, with scribes keeping a record of the events. They wrote a 'V' for victor, alongside the name of the man who won, beside the loser's name went an 'M' for missus, if he left the arena alive, or a 'P' if he perished.[48] The 'P' was for periit, or missus periit if he, after fighting bravely and escaping death through the intervention of the Emperor and the crowds, was later to die of the wounds he'd received.

In the case of female gladiators, it was the idea of 'decent' women degrading themselves that so much incensed the men, nobody seemed to object when female slaves fought. However, Cassius Dio even disliked the idea of women playing a musical accompaniment:

> There was another exhibition that was at once most shocking and disgraceful, when men and women, not only of the equestrian but even of the senatorial order, appeared as performers in the orchestra, in the circus, like those of low esteem. Some of them played flutes, and some danced in pantomimes, or acted in tragedies or comedies, or sang to the lyre. They drove horses, killed wild beasts, and even fought as gladiators.[49]

His feelings of disgust were echoed by Tacitus, who said 'Many ladies of distinction, and senators, disgraced themselves by appearing in the amphitheatre.'[50]

Most of the dead gladiators, both male and female, were not burned, nor would the dumping of so many bodies be practical for long. Gladiators who had friends and relatives to mourn them, and who wanted their body kept separate from the others, would escape the lime pits. These were outside the city limits, as with all burial places, and there was a large pit at the necropolis on the Campus Esqualinus, which had been used for victims of the proscriptions of the Triumvirate of Antonius, Octavianus and Lepidus in 43 BC.

The most humiliating thing was not to be buried at all, thrown into a ravine, or left in some remote spot to be eaten by animals, or thrown into a river, as many defeated political enemies were. They believed they would never find peace if they were treated without respect in this way. Having one's body thrown into a river had been done for centuries if one was a murderer, as the water was believed to have a purifying effect. Everything reminding anyone of the deceased would be swept away. Caligula is said to have occasionally ordered condemned men to be thrown into the wild animal pits to be eaten as food. He is also reputed to have watched while it was done.[51]

Gladiators who were given the coup-de-grâce, or who merely died of wounds, might, if they were lucky, have saved enough to pay for a tomb, or sometimes friends would contribute. Everyone wanted a tomb, that way they weren't entirely gone and forgotten, and loved ones would have some focus for grieving. It seems clear that many gladiators, of both sexes, joined a 'collegium', a cross between a trade union and a burial club. Contributions could then provide some kind of memorial stone for each member. This could be a simple headstone, or a niche in a communal burial chamber among comrades.

A very few gladiators were given high-profile funerals, with the deceased lying in state on a bier, covered with the usual spices and scented oils and flowers, followed by cremation with the ashes later interred in a grave that the successful gladiator could have providently bought during his life.[52]

A cremation like this was found in 1996 at Great Dover Street, in Southwark. A woman who came to be referred to as 'gladiator girl' was found there. All that remained of her body was her pelvis, but an abundance of expensive oil lamps, the evidence of a lavish feast, and the presence of pine cones (which were used in the arena to purify it for the games), show that the grave where her ashes were interred was that of a respected female gladiator, who had been buried with all the proper mourning rites.

A second century AD relief from Bodrum in Turkey shows two women, obviously gladiators. A shard (possibly a pendant) from Leicester was inscribed 'Verecunda ludia Lucius gladiator' which may have meant that Verecunda was a performer and Lucius was a gladiator, but of course 'ludia' also refers to a female gladiator, who may have been the friend or girlfriend of Lucius.

A statue in the Museum fur Kunst und Gewerbein in Hamburg shows a woman gladiator holding aloft a 'sica', the curved sword, triumphant to the end.[53] A headstone showing two other women, working under the 'stage names' of Amazone and Achillia, who are facing each other and bearing shields, is on a relief which came from Helicarnassus, dated to the first or second century AD, which is now in the British Museum. It states that they fought 'stans missus' to a draw. Based on the style of their shields, they both appear to have been either Murmillo or Samnite fighters. That the two women had drawn in conflict is indicated by the removal of their helmets.

People connected with the games were unfortunately not the only kind of outcasts in the Roman world. Many men were cast out of society due to some crime, although the legendary punishment for the most serious of these – treason against the state – was from the time of Romulus and involve the 'original sin' of a woman. During the earliest days of Rome, around the time of the Sabine abduction, Rome was about to be attacked by Sabine men in retaliation. It was then under the command of Spurius Tarpeius, whose daughter was a Vestal. She is said to have been on duty and going to collect water for the sacred rites, when she met with a group of warriors, led by the Sabine King, Tatius. The king bribed her to open the doors of the Arx (the shrine of Juno was on the peak of that hill, close to the shrine of Jupiter.) The girl must have been very sheltered to not know what had been going on in the city, or perhaps she was impressed by the heavy gold bangles worn by the warriors on their left arms, but she agreed to let them into the city for 'what was on the left arms' of the men,[54] hoping for a share of the gold they wore. Once they were inside the city, they crushed Tarpeia with their shields, and then threw her body from the rock face. It is said that she was buried beneath the rock that from then bore her name. The Tarpeian Rock was then around eighty feet high and is situated on the southern summit of the Capitoline Hill. From then on, traitors, perjurers and larcenous slaves were killed by being thrown from the rock onto the stones below, which was considered to be a terrible disgrace.

Rome's only prison during the early Republic was the Tullianum, which was intended only for holding people pre-trial, or for the execution of prisoners, which took place down a hole in the floor leading to a bottle-shaped cell below, accessible only by a ladder. This is where the strangulation of important prisoners took place after they had taken part in a general's Triumph.

During the Empire, the Mamertine Prison became notorious more for the tortures and other abuses going on there at the whim of deranged Emperors, rather than its actual role as a prison. Rome did not see imprisonment as a punishment in itself, merely a holding tank before punishment. Nor did Rome have an organised police force, with special military personnel enforcing laws on behalf of the state. The Urban Prefect was a senator responsible for policing ordinary crime in the city and up to one hundred miles around it.[55]

The Twelve Tablets (between 451-449 BC) were bronze records that formed the basis of the Roman legal system. The law code was intended to represent the interests of everyone, covering most areas of private law and relationships between individuals, more as a list of civil actions than all-encompassing law codes. They dealt with many items relevant to the agricultural state Rome had been, with damage to crops by using magic meaning death by crucifixion. Arson had its homeopathic death penalty, by burning. These punishments reflect the general fears of a people dependent on their crops and living in a city vulnerable to fire. Property damage was punished by banishment from Rome and loss of citizenship, while confiscation of property was the penalty for being an accessory to a crime. Settlement could sometimes be made by paying compensation to the victims.

Also covered by the Twelve Tablets was 'ius vocatio' or a private summons, whereby a plaintiff could have a defendant forced to appear before the magistrates. The Tablets covered marriage, guardianship, inheritances and funeral payments.

During the Empire rulers often tried to rule by will, but the legal system did tend to hold, with prosecutors and lawyers arguing cases and records being kept. In some cases, the convicted could appeal to a higher authority, which is something modern nations did not achieve for another two millenia. Men such as Cicero gained their fame as trial lawyers, and their skills were prized and highly respected.

While imprisonment was not in itself a punishment, an accused living in the provinces could wait a fairly long time until a judge visited the area on his circuit. The governor could, in the meantime, order the accused to be chained if circumstances warranted it. Certainly, within Rome a trial could be swift, with punishment equally so. There was a definite division between the classes with milder punishments for senatorial or equestrian class people than for ordinary citizens. By the late Republic and early Empire, citizens had milder punishments than 'peregrines', aliens or foreigners. A citizen's right of appeal was also denied to foreigners.[56]

By the second century AD, the distinguished (honestiores) and the humble (humiliores) were also treated differently. For a serious crime, beheading or exile could be the penalty for a distinguished person, while the humble might die by burning, by being thrown to wild beasts, or even crucified. Another option was to be reduced to the status of a slave, and perhaps end life in the mines or quarries.

In Cicero's time, the early first century BC, there were two Urban Courts in Rome, one for citizens and one for non-citizens. These were presided over by Praetors. Gradually, the distinction ended, the number of courts increased and each began to specialise in certain types of cases. The local courts throughout the provinces of Italia could only hear civil cases with an upper limit value of fifteen thousand sesterces, and litigators could demand a transfer to the courts in Rome for their trial to be heard.

In the civil courts many offences that we would now consider criminal matters were tried. Most violent crimes and all property crimes involving lower-class people were considered to be 'civil' matters. By the second century AD permanent criminal courts for upper-class offenders were established, and the juries selected from an annual list of men of standing. Their majority verdict did not carry the right of appeal. Usually, political crimes such as treason or bribery, especially if used to influence political leaders or elections, were also dealt with there. By the third century AD crimes involving senators were tried by a jury of peers in the senate itself, and sometimes the emperor would act as a judge.[57]

There were two recognised types of treason, 'maiestas' or little treason, or 'perduellio' for great treason. By the early Empire the use of perduellio had fallen into disuse and maiestas then covered all types of treason. Although a man convicted could hope to keep his life, and perhaps in some cases even his citizenship, he would certainly lose his money, his property and his right to live in Rome, becoming an outcast from his city.

In the provinces, a governor would have sole authority and no limitations on how he could treat non-citizens. During the Republic limitations had been set for citizens by right of appeal, 'provocatio ad populum', which transferred their cases to Rome, and in the early Empire this would mean that the appeal was directed at Caesar. Governors tended to inflict whatever penalties they chose when they felt it necessary to maintain order in their provinces, but even then, excessive corruption or too blatant abuse of power could mean that on his return to Rome the Governor might also face a trial, particularly if his victims had been citizens.[58]

The list of possible crimes was longer in the case of slaves, foreigners and non-citizens. Slaves could be executed for forgery, whereas citizens could not. Certain murders and treason meant the death penalty whether one was slave or free, but for slaves, torture would be automatically applied. This was not intended to be a penalty but was the standard method of interrogation to ascertain the truth, which, although optional for other non-citizens, was mandatory in the case of slaves if their evidence was to be admissable in court. There must be some prior evidence for them either to refute or corroborate, but if a master were killed then all his slaves were tortured to find out if they were involved in the murder. Even if their innocence could be verified, they could still be executed for having failed to prevent the murder.

Lucius Pedanius Secundus, a former consul, was stabbed by a slave in 61 AD. The senate led by Gaius Cassius Longinus demanded the execution of all the four hundred household slaves, and this was permissible, although not mandatory. The common people protested at the huge waste of innocent lives and wanted the slaves released, but Nero finally used the army to ensure that the full sentence was carried out. Capital offences were deliberately punished brutally as a deterrent. Roman citizens could appeal against being tortured, but in a case of treason it was standard procedure, even for them.

For parricide the 'poena cullei' was used. This was the punishment of the sack, which meant being put into a sack with a rooster, a dog, a snake and a monkey, and then thrown into the sea or nearest river.

In some cases the punishment did not involve the animals, which seemed rather pointless anyway. When Aulus Fulvius was killed by his father for his involvement in the Catilinarian Conspiracy in 63 BC, the Paterfamilias was not prosecuted for the killing of his son, as the conspirators had plotted to kidnap and kill the consul Cicero, so the father's action was deemed to be correct.[59]

Livy recorded that in 101 BC Publicius Malleolus, who had killed his mother, was the first man actually to undergo the sack punishment and was thrown into the sea, although no animals were mentioned as having been included. In 80 BC Cicero defended Sextus Roscius on a charge of parricide, but again no animals were mentioned in his defence speech, although they were mentioned in the writings of the jurist Modestus (mid-third century AD) an excerpt of which survives and was quoted in Justinian's *Digest* of the sixth century AD.[60]

One crime of which the Roman authorities took a dim view was unlawful assembly. During the Republic, any meeting with possible political overtones had to be presided over by a magistrate. Unsupervised gatherings, particularly if political in tone, were always suspect, and guilds, 'collegia', and associations, 'sodalicia', needed a licence from the senate from the 50s BC onwards, even then they could not meet more than once a month.

Avoiding the census meant losing one's property and being sold into slavery, according to King Servius Tullius, the sixth king of Rome. This law was either not enforced or quickly became obsolete. Livy recorded that failure to comply with a census meant imprisonment or death, although Romans did usually comply with the census requirements, as their citizenship was precious and they did not intend to risk losing it. However, Cicero reported that one Publius Annius Asellus, who failed to be entered on the census and had avoided it in order to circumvent an inheritance law, lost only his right to vote.[61]

These are crimes and punishments usually involving the elite, people who had something to lose. For ordinary people the streets themselves were a dark and dangerous place, and at night people tended to stay indoors unless accompanied by others, as gangs roamed freely, particularly in the poorer areas. In such areas, residents did not have their own bodyguards and a cry for help was likely to be ignored. Minor crimes such as stealing and public disorder tended to be punished by physical labour. A perpetrator might easily find himself working on one of the many public projects for a fixed amount of time, building roads, maintaining sewers, cleaning public latrines or bath-houses. A man would not lose his citizenship for this and would be freed when his time was ended.

For more extreme offences, there could be a quick death after being sentenced to 'summa supplicia' which was applicable to any non-citizen, either free or slave, and referred to penalties carried out in atrocious or ignominious ways, such as exposure to wild beasts, or gladiators in the arena, 'damnatio ad bestias', which meant that the convicted would become part of the lunchtime entertainment in the arena. 'Damnatio ad gladium' meant becoming a public slave and being sent to a gladiator school. Forced labour in perpetuity 'damnatio ad metalla' would strip him of his citizenship and he could then spend the rest of his life labouring in the mines or quarries. Hanging, 'ad furcam damnatio', or even crucifixion, 'damnatio in crucem', were final options, and there were others, such as being burned alive, 'vivi crematio', or beheading, 'capitis amuputatio'. In the early Republic the sentence of crucifixion was used for treason or incest, and Nero was later to make use of it for executing dissidents such as Christians and Jews, sometimes adding the refinement of burning them as they hung on crosses, using them as living torches.

Exile was always a Roman favourite, 'exilium', and was applicable to almost anyone at one time or another, with many famous Roman citizens having an enforced period of time of being outcast from Rome. It could be voluntarily undertaken, or it could be imposed as a mandatory sentence. It could be designated for an individual, for groups of people, even whole families, and could also apply to an entire region. Cicero said of his period of voluntary exile: '[It] is not a punishment, it is a harbour from punishment. Those who leave their native soil take refuge, as in sanctuary, therefore citizenship is not taken from them, it is merely for a time discarded, as no one can live as a citizen of two states at once.'

As Cicero wisely said, the option of taking voluntary exile for a while allowed a person not only to avoid punishment but gave him time to reflect, to consider his course of action without pressure. Many voluntary exiles did not stay away long, in Cicero's case it was for only one year.

Exile had different definitions, and when applied by the state could have different lengths of time connected to it. There were also different distances imposed that the exile had to travel before he could settle.

Some exiles were full-life terms, and 'exilium' or banishment was often expected and, in some ways, prepared for. Quintus Servilius Caepio, proconsul in 105 BC, was reputed to have found (and hidden) the Gold of Tolosa (now Toulouse), a huge treasure which mysteriously disappeared, and which had belonged to the combined German and Gallic tribes and had been taken with them on their mass migration towards Italy. The family was later considered one of the richest in Rome. Caepio was always suspected of stealing it and was later stripped of his proconsular imperium and his seat in the senate. He was fined fifteen thousand talents, had his property confiscated and was sentenced to exile – forbidden 'aquae et ignis interdicto' – or fire and water for any place within eight hundred miles of Rome. He died in Smyrna, still an exile, but had lived there very comfortably for the rest of his life.[62]

The banishment of 'eight hundred miles from Rome' was quite severe, as it was often only for fifty miles from Rome, or one hundred miles. This often allowed the exile to comfortably sit out his term of banishment in his villa near Naples! However, the victim lost all civil rights and his property was supposed to be confiscated, and this sometimes even happened to self-exiles. However, it was not usually a death sentence, and not often a life sentence either.

'Relegatio' was the removal of undesirables, often foreigners, for a certain period of time. This did not involve loss of any rights, but they were required to leave the city by a certain specified date. 'Deportatio' was more severe, which meant forcible removal, often to an island. This happened to the daughter of the Emperor Augustus when she was accused of immorality, and was often a lifetime term that also required the loss of rights.

During the reign of Augustus the poet Ovid (born in 43 BC) was also exiled and forced to live at Tomis on the Black Sea. His offence is not known, perhaps Augustus had taken a dislike to him, or he had made a foolish mistake. He died at Tomis (now Constanta), in around 17 AD aged about fifty-eight. It was said that he found life in Romania uncomfortable and had sent endless pleas to the Emperor, begging to be allowed to return home. He attributed his exile to 'carmen et error', a poem and a mistake. As the Emperor's granddaughter was banished at around the same time, speculation was rife that he had had an affair with her. To mark the two-thousandth anniversary of the poet's death, and to 'repair the serious wrong suffered by Ovid', politicians of the anti-establishment 'Five Star Movement' pressured the government to have Ovid reinstated. The Mayor of Rome's Council, Virginia Raggi, officially revoked his sentence of exile.[63]

Many famous Romans did not have to wait two thousand years for their reinstatement. Even Julius Caesar had found it sensible to absent himself from Rome for a time in his youth, while the conflict between Marius and Sulla was played out. The Stoic philosopher Seneca (4 BC-65 AD) was banished in 41 AD by the Emperor Claudius, accused of adultery with the Emperor's niece Julia Livilla, and while away he wrote three treatises. He was recalled in 49 AD due to the influence of Julia Agrippina, the Emperor's then wife. He later became tutor to her son, the future Emperor Nero.

A sentence that one had become 'inimicus' (or unfriendly) meant the confiscation of one's property, even for the Pontifex Maximus Marcus Aemilius Lepidus, when he joined with Marc Antony after the death of Caesar in 44 BC. He could not be stripped of his religious office as High Priest, nor could the senate refuse him the large salary which went with it. Had he been declared 'Hostis' (enemy) he would have lost everything, probably even his life, but inimicus was a much lesser description, deserving of criticism but not necessarily death.[64]

Sextus Pompeius was another who fell foul of the increasing emnity between Marc Antony and Gaius Octavianus (later the Emperor Augustus). He was a naval commander and the son of Gnaeus Pompeius Magnus. He had risen to become admiral of the fleet in order to conduct the senate's war against Antony, and he seized Sicily and its all-important grain. In 40 BC, he made an alliance with Antony against Octavianus, was declared a pirate and finally defeated. He died in Asia in 35 BC after having to flee and was murdered there, a sad ending for the son of the man who had defeated the Cilician pirates in 67 BC.

Piracy was always a problem in the Mediterranean, which for a long time was too large to patrol effectively. Over the years the pirates had become extremely confident due to their repeated successes. They regularly took hostages from captured ships and demanded large ransoms for anyone of status. Their outrages included attacks on Brundisium and Caieta and the kidnapping of a noblewoman from inside her own house at Misenum. They finally had to be dealt with after their attack on the Roman port of Ostia in 68 BC, when they had sailed into the harbour, only fifteen miles from Rome, and destroyed the consular war fleet, burning ships and part of the port itself. Nineteen war triremes were destroyed, grain warehouses were lost, threatening Rome with famine, two Praetors were kidnapped, still in their official robes along with all their retinues, still carrying the symbolic fasces. It was an insult that could not be tolerated.

Pompeius Magnus had then established himself as the most powerful man in Rome, and he was asked to take charge of the fleets and try to eradicate the pirate menace. Marcus Licinius Crassus also wanted the honour, but Pompeius was appointed. He divided the Mediterranean Sea into thirteen different areas, each one under a different commander, then swept along the sea with his own fleet, driving the pirates ahead of him, flushing them out of their hiding places into the path of the other commanders. By great vigilance, and at great cost, most were captured and those few who managed to escape fled East, where they had originated. Pompeius rounded them up, completing the first part of the campaign in the western Mediterranean in a record forty days.

He then turned his attention to the Eastern Mediterranean, giving mild terms to those who surrendered to him personally. He knew that most of these men had taken to a life of piracy due to desperation. He found out where others were hiding in Asia Minor. He had a victory over them at Corasesium and the Romans confiscated their wealth and created settlements in Cilicia and other places, with many settling at Soli, which was renamed Pompeiopolis, in his honour. The Eastern part of the campaign had lasted only forty-nine days, a total of eighty-nine days for the whole remarkable campaign.[65]

Exiles of all kinds were barred from entering the city of Rome, whose official boundaries were marked by stones named 'cippi' and this boundary or 'pomerium' was reputed to have been made by King Servius Tullius, although it had various changes over the centuries. Religiously, the heart of Rome was inside it, while all outside of it was merely Roman territory. This virtual boundary was the official barrier to anyone not considered 'suitable' to live within it. This meant outcasts and their wives and families.

Although women played a lesser part in the history of Rome generally, that was because they were considered to be legally less, not because they did less. They could not fight in the legions, but they could marry a soldier, or at least until Augustus changed the rules of ernlistment and made his men serve for twenty years without being officially allowed to marry. This prohibition was not lifted until the reign of Septimius Severus[66] but in the meantime they tended to form 'attachments' anyway, and it was common for soldiers to have families no matter where they were posted.

The families of the men who struggled with ostracism or exile had to endure it with them, and for the wives the everyday problems were then exacerbated by the additional loss of respectability. The need for acceptance seems to have been a greater factor in the lives of women, although some men certainly regretted their loss of homeland. Other women, the trainee gladiators about whom men like Juvenal enjoyed being so scathing for example, were probably just glad to escape the usual 'feminine' constraints and become responsible for themselves and make their own choices. The female gladiator might have a difficult and dangerous line of work, but she could still feel pride in her achievements, even if her tough life might also be short.

The wives of men sent into exile for political reasons would have to get used to the changes, whether they went with them or were able to stay with their own families. They could reassure themselves that changes were always a risk in the topsy-turvy world of politics, and that things often changed back again eventually.

For all those women, a consolation of which they may have remained unaware was that their lives were part of the foundation stock of Rome. They would die, some of them horribly in the arena, but if they had children those children would continue to take Rome forward. Whether they came from a foreign land, from the slums of the Subura, or the comforts of the Palatine Hill, whether they were slave or free, they *were* Rome, just as much as its soldiers, heroes and administrators.

7

Slaves and Prostitutes

The most famous slave in history was surely Spartacus. He led a slave revolt that gave Rome a serious fright. However, his was far from being the only serious revolt of slaves that Rome had to deal with. The first Sicilian Slave War lasted from 135-132 BC and the second Sicilian Slave War was from 104-100 BC. The Spartacus war, otherwise known as the third Servile War, began in 73 BC and lasted until 71 BC.

Unlike the two earlier serious slave uprisings, which were comfortably far away across the Strait of Messina, in Sicily, the third one actually came within a week's march of Rome itself. It involved approximately 60,000 rebels, who were a mixed bunch of slaves, feeedmen, and some free but poor Sicilians. It also involved a large number of women and, we must therefore presume, also children. Not since Hannibal had so much damage been done to the countryside. With roughly one to one and a half million slaves in all, the revolt involved around four per cent of the servile population.[1]

Earlier revolts had centred around gang-leaders, even mystics, but in this case they were led by trained gladiators. At that time gladiators trained with real weapons, while the members of the legions trained with wooden ones. The wooden weapons were heavier than the real thing, and the legionary was expected to be able to march up to 30 km per day while carrying a 5 kg shield, a 2 kg sword, and a pack weighing 30 kg, in addition to his body armour.[2] The legions relied on collective fighting, although they were equally skilled in single combat. They were not inferior to the gladiators, although the gladiators were chosen for size and weight, and exceptional physical strength.

However, the fights of the gladiators were relatively short, while the legions were trained to endure. Organisation usually trumps chaos, however brave the undisciplined opponent might be.

Spartacus appears to have had some military training, and the other gladiators with him may have been intelligent and capable. His 'army' once collected had a majority of Celts and Germans, who tended to be big and strong, although it also collected a substantial number of field and farm slaves and even some free farmers as the numbers grew.

The legions had greatly improved since the reforms of Gaius Marius and soldiers had become long-term professionals rather than the short-lived civilian levies of earlier times. Soldiers would have very likely been veterans of several previous battles, so were perfectly capable of dealing with large numbers of opponents and even accustomed to winning against larger numbers.[3]

So what went wrong? How could this ragtag army of escaped slaves and disaffected farmers manage to do so much damage to the Italian countryside and the country's economy? How could it hold off all attempts at pursuit, apparently so easily, for so long?

The answer must surely be that in this case the legions were inefficiently led. Probably the senate did not take the uprising seriously enough initially, allowing it to grow and ravage the countryside. This is confirmed when one sees that Crassus, in taking over command, was able to alter things dramatically and get the rebels on the run. Pompeius Magnus then met the fleeing survivors on his march back from Spain and wiped out the five thousand who were fleeing north.[4] Magnus was good at 'mopping up' operations, and as we have seen in the 60s BC would go on to eradicate the pirate menace in the Mediterranean.[5]

Spartacus had chosen his timing well, as Mithradates in the east was still causing problems and in 88 BC had not only initiated a massacre of Roman and Italian residents in Asia Minor but offered freedom to any slave who would kill, or inform on, his master. In 73 BC the legions were also fighting in Spain against Quintus Sertorius, an army officer who had fled there in opposition to Sulla after the Social War of the 90s.[6]

Spain's native population had long been oppressed by a series of corrupt Roman governors, so they had been happy to make common cause with a young and competent man who had his own issues with Rome. Pompeius had been sent to deal with the matter, but even he had found Sertorius a difficult opponent to beat, and Sertorius very nearly drove the Romans out of Spain altogether. He finally went the way of most of Rome's opponents, but he had not been beaten by Pompeius Magnus – he was assassinated by his own subordinates who were jealous of his successes and the almost spiritual hold he had over his followers. He had believed he had divine guidance from Artemis and was undefeated on the battlefield. His subordinates quickly fell foul of Pompeius, lacking not only his military prowess but also his charisma.[7]

With Rome fully occupied in both east and west, Spartacus had certainly caught them on the hop. About the man personally we know little, although he was possibly a Murmillo, living at the gladiator barracks owned by the Lanista Gnaeus Cornelius Lentulus Vatia at Capua, fifteen miles north of Naples. He was probably from the Balkans originally and in his native Thrace had served in an allied unit of the Roman army. The Romans called these troops 'auxilia', which literally meant 'help'. They were separate from the legions as they were not Roman citzens, but they would have seen something of Rome's training methods. It is possible that Spartacus had been a cavalryman, as Thracians were known to be good horsemen. Cicero wrote about the slave revolt in his 'Orations'[8] and according to one writer, Spartacus had deserted his unit and become a 'lastro', which means thief or bandit, but can also mean guerrilla soldier or insurgent. Perhaps he had hoped to join Mithradates and fight against Rome, or perhaps his grievance was a personal one? Either way, after a time he was captured, enslaved and sentenced to fight in the arena as a gladiator. Rome usually used this punishment only for serious criminals; perhaps he did not deserve such a harsh sentence.

The Roman writer Varro, who lived at that time, believed that Spartacus was innocent of any serious wrongdoing and if that were true it would have inflamed his resentment further when he was sold to Vatia and sent to the Capua barracks. Capua was then a gladiator centre training fighters for Rome. It was an ideal place for training. Julius Caesar's own training barracks was nearby, 130 miles from Rome but connected to the city by two good roads, the Via Appia and the Via Latina.

At that time an estimated twenty per cent of the population were slaves. Some of these had been soldiers, some were born free, and some of them still had enough freedom to live as herdsmen, or as farmers, as they did not all have to return to a slave barracks at night. In the town, slaves took part in every type of work, in shops, schools and in kitchens, and they even collected the five per cent tax owed when other, luckier, slaves gained their freedom.[9] Some of the fortunate ones even prospered.

Among the men Spartacus would meet at the training school were Germans. They would play a large role in his revolt. Like the Celts, they had been captured in large numbers thirty years previously by Gaius Marius. Like the Thracians, they were warlike, and Tacitus wrote of them that 'peace is displeasing to their nation.' Anyone suitable could volunteer as a gladiator, so the school also held free Italians, even Roman citizens who may have joined for a taste of adventure, so it was a multi-ethnic group of around two hundred men. The oath they took there was very serious, as a new inmate had to swear to 'be burned (perhaps tattooed?) chained, beaten and killed with an iron weapon' should his owner choose. The gladiators were in a strange position, being valuable athletes who received treatment far superior to that of most slaves, and if lucky could survive and even gain their freedom one day, but they were also demeaned and brutalised. They lived well, were given good food, some money, had celebrity and access to women, yet they were not free and their lives could be short.

At Ephesus in Turkey, 120 skeletons were studied, and they had almost all died before the age of thirty-five, many before twenty-five. Almost half of these men had died of wounds bad enough to cut or shatter bones, and others quite likely died of infections or blood loss. The Thracians, Celts and Germans took pride in their contempt for death, but they needed a leader to revolt, and they found him in Spartacus. He not only had the charisma to carry them along with him, he also had a woman with him, a Thracian who claimed to be a wise woman. Gladiators often did have families, their 'wives' or girlfriends accepted by their owners as it was believed that these relationships stabilised the fighters, although their 'marriages' were not, of course, valid under Roman law. Spartacus's woman claimed to know that he would have 'a great and fearful power'[10] and Romans generally had faith in seers.

Even Gaius Marius had believed in Martha, the Syrian prophetess, and Sulla had been told, when in Mesopotamia, that he would be 'the greatest man in the world'. After that revelation he took the extra title of 'Felix', or lucky.[11] Particularly among Celtic and German people, women were honoured and a female slave often took on the role of 'vilica' or housekeeper of any farm or plantation, dealing with the female side of its organisation, as many owners did not run their businesses themselves but left the running of the estate to a steward (or 'vilicus') and the domestic side of things to the housekeeper. The vilica did not just deal with food and clothing but also acted as a teacher and as a truant officer. These two key workers were slaves but had earned positions of trust and were respectable.

However, they were still capable of choosing to take part in the revolt and this they did, helping to free other slaves from estates in the area. At some point the runaways had armed themselves with whatever was available from the barracks. Sidonius Apollinaris claimed that Spartacus preferred to use the 'sica', the Dacian/Thracian/Illyrian sword with a blade which curved sharply forward. At around eighteen inches long, this blade could be used to hook weapons or shields from opponents. It was a more tactical weapon that the usual Roman gladius and was considered a weapon of criminals. Anti-Roman groups such as the 'Sicarii' had used these and taken their name.[12]

One of the leaders of the second slave war in 104-100 BC had been a vilicus, tough, hard-working and capable, and as such a vilicus would make a good quartermaster. The free men who also joined the revolt were small farmers who had been deprived of the best land in order to create latifundia estates.[13] Some of these small farmers were struggling to survive, so were ripe for revolt. There may also have been a few diehard Italian nationalists within the group, still bitter over their defeats in the Social War.[14] When these people left home, whether a struggling farm or a slave barracks, they took their women with them.

They probably moved along the Via Appia leading towards Pompeii, although they would have avoided the city itself. City slaves were not likely to rise up in support, they were usually better treated and were both softer and lazier. They knew little of their rural brethren and would be less likely to survive the trials ahead. The group headed for Vesuvius, which was then believed to be extinct. It was an area of rich soil, lush and fertile, an area of olives, figs and Italy's famous 'Vesuvinum' wine. Other slaves joined them there.

Not long after their arrival, they faced an armed group from Capua, probably hired by Vatia. The gladiators drove them away easily and seized their weapons. One ancient writer claimed that they were glad to be rid of their gladitorial weapons, as they considered them 'shameful and barbaric'.[15] This first engagement may have been small, but it sent a message. While camped on Vesuvius several thousand more runaways from other estates joined them, and they took the opportunity to drill and practise fighting together as a unit. They also turned to crime, raiding the rich villas in the area, not only for food but also gathering silver and gold, jewellery and anything else saleable.

Fifty years later, the poet Horace could still make a joke when sending his slave for his wine, saying 'If Spartacus has left us a single jar!' Spartacus insisted that everything be shared equally. With the Mithradates problem[16] and the the pirates attacking Roman shipping in the Mediterranean, this new revolt may have seemed a minor irritation, and the senators decided to send an obscure Praetor to deal with it, one of that year's eight. He was Gaius Claudius Glaber, who had three thousand men with him and was probably confident of success. Romans did not expect slaves to fight with real courage and commitment. With only one road up the mountain, Glaber had it guarded, then made camp. He was then attacked by Spartacus and was thoroughly beaten. There must have been casualties, but the sources agree that the Roman soldiers fled, probably leaving behind useful food, clothing and even letters from the senate.

The woman would probably have been cheering on their men, as was traditional for Celts and Germans. This shocked Roman writers but is well attested. An immense mass grave of Gallic warriors in northern France, dating from 260 BC, revealed that one-third of the bones were female. Most of these women, like their men, had been killed in the prime of life.[17]

The first major success of the Spartacus group was not due merely to Roman incompetence. The men were by then organised and disciplined and even though only the gladiators would have been in full fighting trim, the others were tough and had been moulded into a team. More recruits appeared, possibly Celts, known to be good herdsmen, and they would also have their women with them. Romans had always believed in supplying herdsmen with women to satisfy their needs, not only sexual. Spartacus was to use the herdsmen as scouts and lightly armed troops, possibly along with some of the women.

When news of Glaber's defeat reached Rome, another leader was sent, one Publius Varinius. Then shortly afterwards a third praetor was sent to assist, named Lucius Cossinius. It was the autumn of 73 BC when

Varinius's legate, Lucius Furius with two thousand men was attacked by Spartacus and trounced, but worse was to come. Spartacus had his scouts watching Cossinius, who was staying in a villa near Pompeii. He and his men had to flee back to his camp, chased by the rebels. Some of the Romans ran away and the others were slaughtered, including Cossinius. Spartacus raided two more of the Roman camps, each time collecting useful supplies, weapons and valuables, but the greatest blow was dealt to Roman morale. Varinius's camp was overwhelmed, with some of his men also running away. Sallust wrote that 'the height of their disgrace is that they were shirking their duty.'[18]

Such a disgrace was very likely due to Rome not having taken the threat posed by Spartacus particularly seriously and having sent out its commanders in charge of untried men, not veterans who could have faced the opposition with more equanimity. Rome had not expected to lose, nor had the senate expected Spartacus to prove so efficient a leader.

Varinius pitched camp near the rebels with four thousand men, but Spartacus then had ten thousand. Granted, some of these were women and children, and they had more men than they had weapons and were also running out of food. The logistics of providing for such a host, some of them non-combatants, was always going to be a problem. However, the greater numbers did help to give the impression that the camp was more ocupied than it actually was, and it was only when Vatinius became aware that the area was too quiet that he realised that his foes had already slipped away. The Celts had been 'taunting' the Romans, a typical practice, and by the time Varinius sent his cavalry out to check on them, they were far enough away. The rebels could move surprisingly quickly and 'they roved throughout all of Campania.'[19] raiding and devastating all the farmlands and the territories around Nola and Nuceria.

Crixtus was in favour of attacking Varinius directly, but Spartacus wanted to avoid a battle, believing that sooner or later the Romans would wipe them out. He needed to leave Campania and move north in an attempt to reach 'homelands' either in Thrace or Gaul. Unfortunately, he was to find himself at odds with his followers over this intention, the problem being that most of the men with him had been born in Italy, and they had no friends or families to go to outside of it. For them, there were no 'homelands' elsewhere. They decided they had to fight Varinius, but not immediately, so headed south hoping for shepherds as recruits. These people had made up the hardcore of previous slave revolts, and the current rebel leader in Spain, Sertorius, drew recruits from shepherds. The Romans could easily afford the mistakes they had made, but the rebels had no margin for error. They headed first for the Picentini Mountains, then towards Lucania, a landscape of plains, thick forests and crags, until they reached Forum Annii. There the men burned houses, raped women and encouraged local slaves to force their masters to hand over treasure, 'Nothing was too holy or too heinous for the anger of the barbarians or the servile natures.'[20]

Spartacus opposed atrocities, knowing they set a dangerous precedent, so they moved on again, this time with new recruits who would also need weapons and food. They had no choice but to follow the Via Annia, heading south, using local guides. They did not have the equipment to allow for a pitched battle, but they managed to ambush as guerrillas, capturing Roman standards and taking control of Varinius's lictors and even his horse, although Varinius escaped. 'After this, even more came running to join Spartacus.'[21]

The numbers concerned are approximate and sometimes wildly exaggerated, but it seems that Spartacus and Crixtus probably had forty thousand by spring 72 BC and more by that autumn. Close to the Ionian Sea they were remote from Rome but were not welcome and had difficulties with the locals, leading to fights. The news of their arrival was liable to cause panic and they moved to Bruttium, a mountainous region, fanning out into the hills and attacking Roman farms. At Thurii they finally took a city and slaughtered the inhabitants before settling down to train their recruits. The chains of the slaves were forged into weapons and Spartacus tried to turn a rabble into an army. He seems to have planned to go north again, clinging to the idea of leaving Italy, where they would be safe from Rome. In Rome the news had spread that Spartacus and Crixtus had split into two groups, with Crixtus staying in the south. They had disagreed, and perhaps there was rivalry, but an army needs food and the numbers had become too unwieldy.

The consuls for 72 BC were Lucius Gellius and Gnaeus Cornelius Lentulus Clodianus. At sixty-two Gellius was old by Roman standards, but with his praetor Quintus Arrius he crushed the army of Crixtus in Apulia. Two-thirds of the men died, including Crixtus. The next target was Spartacus. The consul Lentulus blocked the road ahead and Gellius moved up rapidly hoping to create a trap, but Spartacus, still holding the trust of his men, decided on attack. He had some cavalry and used it efficiently, then struck with fury. The sight of the Germans, Celts and Thracians must have been terrifying, and again the Roman troops panicked and fled, disgracing their traditions. The army of Lentulus was destroyed and his baggage train captured. Then Spartacus turned against the forces of Gellius, defeating them too, an astonishing triumph.

Spartacus then gave Rome the greatest possible insult by giving funeral games in honour of Crixtus, but instead of slave fighters he forced the captured Roman soldiers to fight each other as blood sacrifices. So the Romans assumed the status of gladiator slaves and the real gladiators, the audience, were free men. The whole performance shamed the Romans utterly. Cicero, in a speech he was to give fifteen years later, was so horrified and disgusted, still so aware of Rome's humiliation at what had happened, that he said 'Nothing could have been more polluted, deformed, perverted or disturbed.'[22]

They continued northwards, towards Mutina (modern Modena), where the Governor Gaius Cassius Longinus had two legions to call upon, around ten thousand fighting men. He had a successful career and was from an eminent family. He was at that point the only real defence Rome had between Spartacus and the Alps. There was an engagement, but few details of it survive. Unfortunately for Rome, Longinus lost and he barely escaped with his life.[23] He was never again to play a major role in public affairs.

The road to the Alps was then open, but Spartacus did not take it. Was the move vetoed by the men? They had never intended to leave Italy, so were they hopeful of taking Rome? Spartacus and his army turned south again, back into danger.

Terror began to spread through Rome at the news, but it is doubtful whether Spartacus could really have threatened the city. According to ancient sources, after his defeat of Longinus, 'many deserters approached him...'[24] These were surely not deserters from the Roman army but slaves working for them. Spartacus could not afford to turn them away, despite the possibility of spies, as Gellius and Lentulus had regrouped and were prepared to attack again. Experts say that Spartacus might have had sixty thousand troops by late 72 BC and some put it even higher, but a large number were still women, children and old men.

The showdown came at Picenum with a pitched battle. Lentulus expected reinforcements to defeat the enemy, but they arrived too late and the rebels were too strong. The Romans yet again had to flee the field. But Spartacus did not attempt an attack on Rome, 'because his forces were not appropriate for the operation, nor was his whole army prepared as soldiers should be, since no city was fighting with him, save only slaves, deserters and rabble.'[25] He knew he was not capable of laying siege to Rome. The slave army returned south, having travelled about 1,200 miles in four or five months, a punishing trek with non-combatants present. They had fought battles and amassed loot but had also lost Crixtus and buried many old comrades, and they were then fast running out of options.

Rome was facing disgrace. One of the few men to serve with distinction was Cato. He was offered honours but refused them, saying his family pride could not accept honours for a defeat. Cicero, in exasperation at his friend, wrote that Cato thought he was living in Plato's Republic.

However, things were finally set to change. The senate appointed yet another commander, Crassus. Marcus Licinius Crassus was son of Publius Licinius Crassus who had committed suicide in 87 BC when Gaius Marius took over Rome and began to massacre his opponents. Crassus Senior's head was displayed on the Rostra. His son Marcus had to flee to Spain to escape the civil war, and then went to join Sulla in Greece. He returned with him to victory when Sulla fought Marius at the Battle of the Colline Gate.[26] Crassus distinguished himself in that battle against the army of Marius, made up largely of slaves who had been promised their freedom for killing Romans. After the Colline Gate, he concentrated his energies on getting rich. By the time of the Spartacus war Crassus wished to improve his public image. Even though a campaign against mere slaves could never be considered high-profile, it had already broken three of Rome's leaders. Crassus did not intend to run away, or allow his men to run away, being a pragmatic man rather than a moral one. This was shown by the way he had evaded a charge of seducing a Vestal Virgin by claiming he was far more interested in her money than in her body.[27] He was to recall many veterans to fight by saying that age did not matter, '...everyone who has a soldier's heart, even if the body is old,' knowing that their experience would stiffen the resolve of the younger troops who had been found wanting. His immense wealth was also a factor in his appointment, as the senate was struggling to pay so many troops and they hoped Crassus would pay for his own, at least with a long-term loan.

Crassus entrusted the legions to one Mummius[28] telling him to follow the slave army closely but not to engage. Mummius unfortunately took advantage of the first opportunity to fight – and lost, many of his men 'throwing down their weapons and fleeing' and it became yet another disgrace, an even worse one, as dropping one's weapons defined cowardice. Crassus was furious and decided on the most extreme punishment to teach them a lesson – decimation. Five hundred Roman troops were rounded up and fifty of these (one in ten) would be clubbed to death by nine other comrades. The victims were drawn by lots, and by insisting on this terrible humiliation Crassus ensured that his men would fear him more than they feared Spartacus. They would not run away again.

According to one account, Crassus's army then met with around ten thousand of the men belonging to Spartacus encamped. The Romans attacked and won a great victory, nobody ran away and some claimed that two-thirds of the rebels had been killed. It was their largest defeat since the death of Crixtus and it proved a turning point for the Romans.

Spartacus marched to Regium, to the sea, only the Strait of Messina separated it from Sicily and safety in Rome's most important province.[29] It would be a good place to stop, where they could interfere with Rome's grain supplies and was always a haven for runaways. It might not make a permanent home but would grant them a respite.

Spartacus would have known that the pirates who lived there had fought for Mithradates in the east and for Sertorius in the west and had originally hailed from Cilicia. According to Cicero, the Governor of Sicily, Verres, had blackmailed wealthy locals and looted artworks while leaving Sicily itself defenceless.[30] Verres had also crucified a man who had turned out to be a Roman citizen, and thus secure from such a punishment. This man, Publius Gavius, might have been a spy for Spartacus. Was he one of the 'free men of the fields' who had joined him? Many Sicilians had already lived through two slave wars and could be forgiven for being anxious, although Verres had certainly exceeded his powers.

Spartacus arranged with the pirates to have two thousand of his men ferried across the Strait and although this was only a small part of his army they would serve to establish a base. In any case, the Sicilian ships were small and could not hope to carry all at once. The pirates demanded payment in advance, which Spartacus paid, and also gave them several gifts, but then 'once the pirates had made the agreement, they sailed away and did not return.'[31] Was Spartacus naïve to trust them, or did the idea of the Roman pursuit put them off? Thucydides had described the narrow Strait of Messina: 'The narrowness of the passage and the strength of the current of water that pours in from the vast Tyrrehenian and Sicilian mains have rightly given it a bad reputation'[32] It is one of the most dangerous bodies of water due to its riptides, despite being only two miles across at one point, near the city of Villa San Giovanni. A car ferry now crosses regularly, but for Spartacus with tens of thousands of people to care for, it was impossible. They even tried to build rafts by 'placing wide-necked jars under beams, tied together with strips of hide or vine branches'.[33] They must have foraged locally for supplies as well as keeping an anxious watch for Crassus. Florus tells us 'They tried to launch the rafts of beams and large wide-mouthed jugs, tied together, into the very swift waters of the strait, but in vain.'[34] They had not only wasted time in attempting that doomed crossing but probably also lost men.

Spartacus turned round again and headed back through Italy. Crassus appears to have done nothing to stop the attempt to cross the Strait,[35] leaving him to Verres, but Cicero praised Crassus, '... that bravest of men, whose courage and good judgement saw to it that the fugitives were not able to tie the rafts together and cross the Strait.' He speaks of efforts made to stop the rebels from crossing, but tantalisingly gives no details. Was there a skirmish on the beach? Crassus was then to show some reluctance to engage with the rebels. Cicero had made these remarks in 70 BC when prosecuting Verres and was determined to undermine any claim that Verres had stopped the rebels. Did Crassus encourage Spartacus to attempt a crossing, knowing he would be trapped if he did manage to get to Sicily? Crassus would then attempt to trap the fugitives between the Strait and the mountains. The rebels needed food. The city of Regium was walled and defensible and the Via Annia was blocked by Roman troops. Spartacus then had no choice but to take to the Aspromonte Mountains.[36]

In those mountains, in early 71 BC, on a ridge about two miles wide, two armies waited. The Romans, behind a defensive network of deep trenches lined with sharpened poles and an embankment topped by a dry-stone wall, closed off three sides of the ridge, leaving only the southern approach open, to force the rebels to attack from that side. The attackers reached for fortification but could not break through. Crassus had gambled on the defensive line and was determined to beat Spartacus, knowing that failure would drag down his own career. The Romans were to claim a huge victory on that day, saying that twelve thousand rebels had been killed, for only the loss of three Romans and a few wounded. Even if that were true, they knew the rebels would be back, for they had no choice but to fight to the end.[37]

Some present-day scholars not only discount the Roman figures but also doubt that they could have built any strong defensive structures in the time allowed. They also believe that Spartacus should have been invincible in his 'natural habitat' in the mountains. However, it is perfectly feasible that they did do it, being natural builders and also very swift to act, and the natural terrain would have been a help to them. In some places the slopes were so precipitous that no fortifications were needed.

There has also been a suggestion that Crassus would gain nothing by forcing Spartacus into the 'toe' of Italy, where he could live indefinitely. This is not likely, as the terrain was very difficult, as well as poor and infertile. The rebels were already short of food and one of Crassus's best reasons for having the band confined to that area is that he could perfectly easily cut off their supplies.[38]

Several placenames in the area suggest the conflict. A section of the Melia Ridge is known as Marco's Ridge (Marcus Licinius Crassus?) and there is a town named Scrofario; Crassus's lieutenant was named Scrofa. Local hamlets are named Casa Romano and Contrada Romano, and there is even a 'slave's tower', the Torre lo Schiavo.[39] These give tempting clues to the history of the area. At the heart of the Melia Ridge are areas named 'Tuna Trap' and 'Grand Enclosure', mysterious appellations.

Spartacus still had cavalry due to reach him, so may not have despaired, and Crassus was almost as trapped on the ridge as the rebels were. Spartacus continued to annoy, throwing bundles of burning wood into the Roman trenches and distracting the soldiers by moving from place to place, but he had to make sure his men kept focus. Were they already beginning to desert? To prevent any idea of them leaving to join the Romans, he crucified a Roman captive in the space between the two armies, to show his men what they could expect if they fell into Roman hands.

Back in Rome, there was disappointment at how long it was all taking, and it was voted that Pompeius Magnus, who had just completed the defeat of Sertorius, should step in to help Crassus settle the matter. The was the last thing Crassus wanted, as the campaign was intended to benefit his own career, not add another accolade to Pompeius; but he asked for Marcus Terentius Varro Lucullus. Having two generals working together would serve to downgrade the importance of Pompeius.

Spartacus also heard that Pompeius was expected back from Spain, and saw it as an opportunity, knowing that Crassus did not want Pompeius to steal his thunder. He made a very unexpected move, offering Crassus a peace treaty, but not in any way a surrender. He asked Crassus to take him and his people into Rome's 'fides', which meant not only faith and trust, but also protection. Had that been agreed, it would have created mutual obligations and rights. The two sides would be bound by moral ties that were obligatory. Acceptance would have meant that the slave army would become the 'clients' of Rome, and Rome itself would become their protector and ally.

Rome might regard the matter as a form of surrender, but it would be a perfectly dignified one, confirming that Spartacus and his people had rights and could even hope for freedom and safety eventually. It was a desperate move, and Crassus declined it.

Spartacus's cavalry reinforcements arrived on a windy and snowy night, probably in February of 71 BC, and Spartacus finally made his move. Some writers say that his men filled in part of the trenches with earth, wood and branches, sometimes with corpses. Spartacus and most of his men escaped the ridge and Crassus was again obliged to take up the pursuit, this time in the direction of Samnium.

Samnium had always been inimical to Rome, and Sulla destroyed its elite at the Battle of the Colline Gate in 82 BC.[40] The rebels may have had hopes of support from the area, but the slave army was to fracture and split apart. It was said that 'they began to disagree among themselves' and some of the Celts and Germans went off on their own.[41]

One morning in March 71 BC a group of women had gone out early to make sacrifice. They were Celts, whose women sometimes went off in small groups to 'call on the Gods'. The power of women was very important to Celtic people, and Caesar was to write of them 'the whole of the Gallic people is passionately devoted to matters of religion.' Plutarch said of the incident, 'The women were sacrificing on behalf of the enemies of Rome.'[42] While away from the main camp, they spotted Romans – six thousand men were circling round the same mountain. They did not panic but hurried back to the camp to raise the alarm. 'Celtic women were always ready to help beleaguered husbands by charging into battle, where they would bite and kick the enemy.' Archaeological evidence shows many Celtic women were buried with weapons and even with chariots.

Crassus had been cheered by the splitting of the rebels and he hoped to pick off the two smaller forces individually. The breakaway group had camped near Lake Lucania near Paestum. Archaeologists have found thousands of 'acorn' missiles there, probably dated from the Crassus campaign. These were made of stone, clay or lead, the size of small nuts. They were fired from slings and were often used against cavalry. Crassus turned up from another direction taking attention from the troops on the hill, who suddenly attacked from the rear. The rebels broke and ran and would all have been slaughtered had Spartacus not arrived. His appearance caused Crassus to break away and the rebels were saved. Crassus attacked again a few miles away, and although Spartacus had not moved off, Crassus distracted him and his men, leaving the other rebels under the command of Castus and Cannicus. They were weak from the first attack but also ashamed. Failure to stand and fight was a violation of their beliefs. Crassus intended to tempt Spartacus into a feigned battle under Lucius Quinctus, which worked well. The others were to lead the men of Castus and Cannicus into a trap and this also worked, with the rebels finding they were facing the Romans in battle formation.

For the Celts, battle was religious. If they won, they would sacrifice animals and kill any captured chiefs. If they lost, then they were the sacrifice. Plutarch said 'It was the most valiant battle' of all that Crassus fought. The rebels fought to the death and Plutarch reported that only two dead men out of twelve thousand three hundred had back wounds. They certainly did not run away.[43]

The Celts were granted heroes' deaths as they believed that suicide, in the form of a hopeless fight, was far preferable to surrender. There were probably some prisoners and a few might have escaped the battlefield in order to make it back to Spartacus carrying the grim news. After the battle, the Romans found a rich haul of trophies the rebels had taken. These included five fasces with rods and axes, tokens of a magistrate's power and right to punish, usually carried by his lictors. The lictors had been shamed by their loss and their recovery was a great honour for Crassus and his men. They also recovered five Roman eagles and twenty-six battle standards. Officers named Aquilifers carried the standards into battle, and they embodied the whole Roman unit. Losing a standard was a disgrace but recapturing one from an enemy was a distinction.

Castus and Cannicus would have been mourned, but this time there were no funeral games, Spartacus and his men 'retreated towards the Peteline Mountains'[44] presumably the mountains near Petelia in Bruttium. They were pursued by Lucius Quinctius and Gnaeus Tremelius Scrofa, although neither of those leaders took the sensible precaution of keeping well back. Spartacus suddenly turned on them and the Romans fled in panic, leaving Scrofa wounded.

Spartacus was aware that he needed to leave Italy as soon as possible and that Brundisium, on the Adriatic coast, was their best bet to head east.[45] He said 'Freedom was better than the humiliation of being on display for others' and also 'It is better to die by iron, than by starvation!' If they could not find find ships to take them to Thrace, there was always Apulia, with its further possibilities for food supplies and even recruits.

Then the rebels heard that Marcus Lucullus had already landed his troops there, fresh from his own successes in Thrace, and they realised that after their success against Crassus they had become over-confident. Plutarch was to write 'Success destroyed Spartacus, because it aroused insolence in the group of runaway slaves.'[46] Despite all they had achieved, they were still referred to as runaway slaves by the Romans, and still considered beneath contempt.

The rebels knew that Pompeius Magnus was on his way and Spartacus's men were becoming mutinous. He decided to move, and another fifty miles would take them to Venusia (Venosa) which city had been a Roman colony for two hundred years. Word of their approach horrified Venusia: 'They will indiscriminately mix murder, arson, theft and rape.'[47] However, Spartacus then turned south, towards the Roman camp.

He now knew that the odds were against him and that his people would prefer to end it with a fight to the death. They were exhausted by continual travelling and had run out of options. Crassus also wanted a fight, and he wanted it before Pompeius Magnus appeared to take the credit for it himself. Due to repeated losses, it is doubtful if the rebel army then had more than half of the original sixty thousand members. Crassus probably had about forty thousand men.

The rebels needed to avenge their fallen men and each man also needed what was considered to be a hero's death. A group of slaves from the second Sicilian slave war had opted for suicide, while others who were captured killed each other, rather than become noon-time entertainment for Rome. It was probably April 71 BC when they were in the Silarus Valley, and various towns now claim to be the site of Spartacus's last battle, but it is unverifiable. When Crassus's scouts located the rebels, he pitched his camp provocatively close by, possibly acting a little rashly in his urgent need to beat Pompeius. He had his men start to dig trenches, but they were attacked by rebels. Plutarch claimed that they had attacked on their own initiative and forced his hand.

As they prepared for battle, each commander usually addressed his troops, but Spartacus went one better – he killed his precious horse! This made it clear to his men that he did not intend to leave the field. It also prevented him from overseeing the conflict properly, but his men probably appreciated the symbolism. Thracians regarded horses as sacred, so it was an impressive gesture. Plutarch claimed that he then said, 'If he won he would have many horses, but if he lost he would not need any.'[48]

It would be an epic fight and Spartacus had only one aim – to get close enough to kill Crassus.

> He made his way through showers of darts and heaps of slain. He did not, indeed, reach him but he killed with his own hand two centurions who had ventured to engage him. He exposed his body to danger. [Crassus] availed himself of every circumstance which Fortune favoured him, performing every act of generalship. Yet he was only wreathing a laurel for the brow of Pompeius.[49]

Spartacus ran the greatest personal risk by fighting on foot. His charge, brave but foolhardy, with a group of picked men, is one of the main events, but he was charging the legion intent on protecting Crassus and Spartacus never reached him. 'At last, those that seconded him fled. He, however, stood his ground and though surrounded by numbers he fought with great gallantry until he was cut into pieces.'[50]

Another report claimed that Spartacus was wounded in the thigh by a short javelin. 'He got down on one knee, thrust his shield before him, and continued to ward off those who were attacking him until he fell, and the large number of men around him were surrounded and fell.'[51]

For all their hatred of the slave rebels, Spartacus's enemies were in awe of his courage on that day. Sallust reported that 'He did not die quickly, or unavenged.' [52] Florus wrote of him, 'He died almost an Imperator' which was a very special honour, only awarded by one's own men on the field of battle.[53] For Spartacus the struggle was finally over. It was later said, referring to his bravery, '...as befit an army led by a gladiator, it was fought "sine missione", to the death.'[54]

Unfortunately, for his surviving followers, it was not over. The army fell into disorder and the legionaries forced their way into the rebel lines. 'They were cut down en masse.'[55] Another wrote, 'They met with a death worthy of real men.'[56] They probably owed some of their courage to their women, rallying wavering men with cries and taunts. The Cimbri women were said to have killed any men who fled. The rebel army was crushed at the cost of around a thousand Romans killed. They had inflicted carnage in return, with one estimate of five to ten thousand dead rebels.

Many survivors took to the nearby woods, taking women with them rather than leaving them to the Romans. The corpse of Spartacus was never found as the tide of battle had flowed over it, leaving just another disfigured body. Romans normally cremated their dead on the field, giving comrades a final salute by marching around the funeral pyre in armour, blowing trumpets, while the rebels would be hurried into mass graves.

Crassus marched six thousand captive slaves about seventy-five miles back to Capua, where he intended a mass crucifixion. In 86 BC Alexander Janeaus, King of Judea, had crucified eight hundred men and had their wives and children killed before their eyes. In 332 BC Alexander the Great had crucified two thousand rebels from Tyre. The Roman official Quintilius Varrus in 4 BC would crucify two thousand rebels in Judaea and supposedly five hundred a day were crucified during the six-month siege of Jerusalem in 70 AD. So Crassus's mass killing would not be the first, but was probably the largest. Most people considered the revolts of slaves were crimes inflicted on Italy, and the slaves had to be warned not to try it again. Crassus intended to crucify 'all along the road from Capua to Rome'.[57]

Roman crucifixion consisted of three elements, first the scourging of the condemned, then the carrying of the crosspiece to the appointed place, finally lifting the crosspiece into place with the victim attached. This might have included women, as Roman jurisprudence allowed for the crucifixion of females. Slaves were probably crucified low, close to the ground, while people of higher status were lifted around three feet off the ground. Death could take several days, and the corpses would not be cut down but left to the vultures and animals to tear at. The road to Rome was always busy, so everyone could see what had been done. If passing slaves or gladiators saw the rotting bodies, so much the better.

Crassus had defeated the slave army within six months, but Pompeius Magnus had followed a group of survivors and exterminated them. He then wrote to the senate claiming 'Crassus had defeated the slaves in open battle, but he, Magnus, had torn up the very roots of war.'[58] Magnus expected to be awarded a Triumph, and would get one, but Crassus was only entitled to an Ovation because he had only fought slaves.[59] Crassus was not happy about the distinction, but had to accept it, receiving only the concession that he could wear a laurel wreath like Magnus, instead of the Ovator's usual myrtle.

For several years, bands of survivors of Spartacus's army lived as bandits in the hills of Bruttium. They had learned not to fight Rome openly, but in 63 BC the Roman aristocrat Catilina tried to raise another revolt of slaves and debtors, which was crushed by the senate. Again, the survivors joined the bandits, but Octavianus would 'put an end to them on his journey'.[60] There are few details, but no doubt there were further crucifixions. Perhaps some of those men had once trained with Spartacus, but no large revolts would follow. The senate was too aware of the danger posed by gladiators and made moves to stop them being housed anywhere close to Rome. The best-known revolt afterwards came from Sextus Pompeius, son of Pompeius Magnus. He ran a successful pirate fleet out of Sicily between 43 and 36 BC, which included thirty thousand runaway slaves.[61]

It had been a salutary lesson and resulted in a heightened general suspicion of slave workers, particularly those engaged in field work or anything connected to the arena. There was a general tightening of security around slaves. Spartacus became a legend, an example of fortitude and determination that Rome could not have expected from one whose life was the entertainment business of the circus. The most frightening part was that he had behaved almost like a Roman.[62]

Not all slaves were gladiators or field workers of course. Around 10% of the inhabitants of Rome were slaves, and the Ponte Galera slave cemetery at Ostia has many remains of people presumably employed in the salt works near the mouth of the Tiber in the first and second centuries AD. Around 72% of the bodies in one cemetery were male, while another urban cemetery had 50% females. These were all poor burials, in a cemetery covering around 3,000 square metres and holding 270 individuals. One boy, approximately eight years old, had a small necklace of beads, but very few of the others had even the usual coin in the mouth. They all showed signs of heavy fatigue, with limb fractures and vertebrae lesions common.

One man appeared to have had a disease which blocked his jaw, preventing him from eating. It appeared that teeth had been removed to allow him to take food and drink. As this was not likely to be a concern for the gang owner, the slaves may have been trying to help each other. Professor Angelo Bottini, Superintendent of Archaeology for Rome, observed: 'Here we are seeing a poor community that did what it could to save the life of another person, permitting him to be able to breathe and eat again.'

Conditions for some slaves could be very different, with highly educated Greek tutors (pedagogues) teaching children in Greek and Latin. Many men of this type sold themselves into slavery in order to increase the prospect of a good career, with freedom as the final prize. Some of the more privileged 'household' slaves might be able to buy themselves freedom using the 'peculium', which was payment for work done for anyone else, with their master's permission, or small sums of money given from time to time by an owner. Florentinus said in his *Institutes*, 'A peculium is anything a slave has been able to save by his economies.'[63]

In a normal, prosperous family, a slave was part of the household, known as the 'familia' and subject to the 'dominica potestas' of the master. They could be acquired as property by inheritance, gift, purchase or sequestration, or bred at home from household slaves. These would, when young, play freely with the master's children and were potentially very profitable. They had the advantage of Latin as their first language and were trained from an early age. With good treatment, they would become amiable and loyal. Cicero's friend Atticus would not have any other kind of slave.[64]

In any large household slaves could specialise in certain crafts. The elder Pliny knew one owner of vast estates who died in 8 BC leaving a household of over four thousand slaves. The younger Pliny, at his death, made provision for the support of a hundred of his own freedmen, which also implies a large family of slaves. However, the majority of these would be farm workers or employed in industry, with the number of house slaves being smaller.

Augustus was to fix the number of slaves permitted to be taken into exile with a freedman at twenty, and this was probably no prohibition at all. The tomb of the Statilii in Rome, a prominent family from 40 BC to 65 AD, suggests that Tiberius Statiliuis Taurus Corvinus, consul in 45 AD, had eight slaves. People of moderate means would have only one or two and many families would have none at all.[65] Within the city, there was little room for the housing of slaves and the wealthier houses would have slaves sleeping in attics, or even boarded out. Rooms specially provided for slaves were only known in rare cases, for example the Villa Rustica of Agrippa Postumus near Pompeii, which provided small single rooms. In the younger Pliny's expensive Laurentine villa, the slave quarters were some distance from the house, but were good enough to be used as spare rooms for guests. When used by slaves they were probably shared.[66]

In around 100 AD the ex-praetor Larcius Macedo, an unpleasant man with slave ancestry, was assaulted in his baths by his slaves and left for dead. He revived long enough to see the slaves who had assaulted him recaptured and executed. He finally died but had had the rare pleasure of seeing his murderers killed. From the first century AD there was increasing public disapproval of the ruthlessness of the law and the power of masters over their slaves, and during the Empire a greater humanitarian sense came into being. An edict of Claudius stated that if a sick slave was abandoned by his master, and then recovered, he was to be freed. If a slave fled from his master and took refuge by a statue of the Emperor, the local governor should hold an enquiry, and if convinced of a master's brutality, could force the sale of the slave household.[67] Stoic teaching had always urged kindness towards slaves, and most Romans realised that, apart from the truly idle or vicious, kindness would produce dividends.

Not only Pliny and Cicero had friendly relations with their slaves, many families relied on and trusted them. Cicero's relationship with Tiro is well known but deserves repetition to emphasise the closeness of their friendship. In a letter to Tiro, dated 7 November 50 BC, Cicero said 'Your services to me are beyond count, in my home and out of it, in Rome and abroad, in private affairs and public, in my studies and in my literary work.' Cicero finally gave Tiro his freedom after many years, when Tiro was about fifty, in 53 BC. Cicero's brother Quintus wrote to him:

> I have just heard about Tiro. He ought never to have been made a slave and now you have decided that he should be our friend instead. My delight at the news is matched only by the longing I have to see you, your children, and my own boy. After reading your letter and Tiro's I jumped with joy. Thank you for what you have done and many congratulations. The loyalty which I receive from Statius is a sheer delight to me, so how much you will gain, in the same way, from Tiro and more, because Tiro is a scholar, a conversationalist, a humane man, and these are qualities which count for more than material values. I have innumerable reasons for loving you, especially because, as was right, you wrote to send me the news. I read the letter and it was you all over.[68]

Quintus has taken a sly dig at his brother, because Marcus Tullius had never approved of his brother's manumission of his slave Statius. However, Tiro was such a general favourite that his new status gave pleasure to all who knew him. There had always been a need for men of education and talents in the fields in which, for social reasons, the freeborn Romans could not engage. The financier Crassus, with all his extensive real estate, also had money tied up in slaves, of whom he had great numbers, trained as readers, secretaries, connoisseurs of silver, accountants, waiters and others. He supervised their education and training, believing nothing had a greater claim on a master's attention than his slaves. They were the human factors of his prosperity.[69]

Public service also used a great many educated slaves in the Imperial household, and in commercial life there was a need for men with a good grasp of languages, for shorthand writers ('notarii') for clerks and for men with a good literary education. Surprisingly, inscriptions commemorate brilliant slave children who had died young. One was a shorthand writer who could take rapid dictation. Another was a 'calculator' aged only thirteen, 'whose ample knowledge would fill volumes'. With a need for such specialists, two great Imperial training schools were set up in Rome, one on the Palatine and another in the

Caelion. To judge from inscriptions, education continued at least until the age of eighteen.

Many were apprenticed as shorthand writers, as weavers, and in other useful trades. Though many people lived and died as slaves, the intelligent and hard-working slave could always hope to receive freedom eventually or buy it from his saved peculium. By law, strictly speaking this sum would also be his master's property, but in practice it was treated as being the slave's own. He might receive his freedom as a gift from his master, or under the terms of a will at his master's death.

However, it could cause problems for an heir if too many slaves were manumitted at once. Augustus placed restrictions on the freeing of slaves, under the Lex Fufia Caninia of 2 BC and the Lex Aelia Sentia of 4 AD. By the Lex Fufia Caninia a limit was placed on the number of slaves to be freed by testament. In a household of between three and ten slaves, only half could be freed. Between ten and thirty slaves, the limit was a third. In a household of more than thirty but not more than a hundred, the limit was a quarter and after that the limit was one-fifth, with an absolute maximum of one hundred manumissions.[70]

By the Lex Aelia Sentia, except in circumstances of the utmost formality, no slave under the age of thirty years could be freed, and no master could confer freedom at all if he was under the age of twenty years – possibly to prevent the young and impulsive from giving away their patrimony. However, the law did allow for exceptional cases.[71] There was also a tax payable on slave manumission, to be paid by the masters. This also prevented a master freeing too many at once, although if the slave was buying himself, an owner might add the price of the tax to the price of freedom. Some slaves of high value could never hope to save enough to buy themselves free. Full manumission brought with it not only freedom but the all-important Roman citizenship. Men such as Juvenal opposed this, complaining that Rome was becoming a city of mongrels.

There was an intimate association between a newly freed slave and his master's family. He would take the family name as part of his own, and if he had a woman, he would also wish to free her so they could legally marry. He might continue to live in his master's household and may have had no alternative, or he might set up a small business with his master's help, then becoming one of his 'clients'. He might also find that his master's friends began to treat him differently. Certainly not as an equal, and there could be a good deal of prejudice to overcome as the stigma of slave blood was very real, and freedom did not always eradicate it. The freedman's children still could not marry freeborn children, if they were descended, even three generations back, from a senatorial family. However, once a man had made that transition from slave to free and had hopefully been able to free the woman he considered his wife, he could then marry formally to legitimise any family they may have. That allowed him to look forward to future generations being born free and having Roman citizenship automatically, even if the elites still looked down their noses at the family background. Petronius in his *Satyricon* featured the wealthy ex-slave Trimalchio who was considered above his station by freeborn men. Much fun is made of his attempts to 'fit in' and make friends by overly extravagant gestures, and the sarcastic sniping must have gone on in the real world against men who gave away their lack of culture and education accidentally.

Slaves did, of course, create problems while still within the household. Some of these men were young, handsome and highly sexed, and a great temptation to the ladies of the household, particularly wives who were much younger than their husbands. Petronius also made fun, saying that pretty slave girls only wanted the master in their beds for the benefits they might get from the liaison. However, the ladies of the household were often only too eager to share their beds with a handsome young male slave.[72] If a woman did lose her head where a handsome slave was concerned, it was very dangerous.

If she should have a child to the slave, the child would be born free and a Roman citizen. By Roman law the mother's status determined the status of the child. If the slave who sired the child belonged to the mother of the child, all would be well, but if she had a child sired by a slave owned by someone else, there were serious problems. If the slave's owner knew of the liaison and approved it, then the woman sank to the status of a freedwoman, by a law of Claudius in 52 AD.[73]

If the male slave's master disapproved, or had not been consulted, then the woman could become a slave herself, and her child with her. Some masters might be eager to increase their household by taking the child into it, and this move would keep the woman's status unaffected, but Hadrian would forbid the practice, giving the guilty woman no way out.[74]

It was usually a male slave who was manumitted, as he could still be useful to his master as a client. Female slaves could be bought free by another but were far less likely to be freed without a husband to go to, they would they be adrift and alone. And a woman could be useful within her master's household into old age, although the variety of her work was far more limited, and she was less likely to have received an education. She took on domestic work and if she found a partner among the male slaves could cohabit with him in 'contubernium', although their relationship had no legal standing and their children remained illegitimate and were the property of the master to be disposed of at his whim. Many masters preferred their slaves to establish families, not only to produce more slaves, but because it was believed that it created stability; but there was no security in it for the slaves, for if the master's situation changed, or he died, the family could be broken up and sold separately. Some were lucky, and inscriptions survive showing that slave 'marriages' could be stable, and although they brought some comfort and affection to the slaves themselves, they were always subject to their master's will.

Many men had relationships with their female slaves, willing or not. For the female slave sexual abuse must always have been a real fear and very common. The law did allow a man to manumit a slave in order to marry her and some did this to legitimise the children born of the union, to ensure they were born free and had citizenship.[75]

The owner of a pregnant female slave might even be a slave himself – don't forget that Cato encouraged his slaves to buy slaves of their own – he might be able to arrange for his own master to free the woman in 'contubernalis vicaria' on his behalf, so the child would be freeborn. However, it would still be illegitimate. Since a slave who was manumitted still had obligations to the ex-owner, the freed 'wife' would remain bound to her 'husband' not by the bonds of marriage, but by patronus, and could not desert him or 'remarry' without his permission. All slaves wanted freedom, but strangely that did not mean that they wished to abolish the slave system. On the contrary, they often went on to buy slaves of their own, continuing it, so long as they were on the right side of it.

For women, it was taken for granted that a master would probably expect to use his slaves sexually, as his property. Fortunately, not all men took advantage of this, but there was always the fear of being sold to another who would. That also brought with it the reality of greatly declining value as increasing age brought loss of looks and desirability. Any woman who spent her life with domestic work had far less opportunity of receiving tips or gifts which could be saved for buying freedom.[76] Her only way to acquire money or valuables was as her master's mistress, but he would very likely already have a wife, so her position in the household could be made unpleasant. Although a man might occasionally free a slave mistress to marry her, it was very much looked-down on if a woman should free a male slave for that purpose, and such marriages were outlawed by Septimius Severus.

The motive for any free or freed woman wishing to marry a slave could, surprisingly, be financial. Male slaves in important families could hold posts of prestige and security. If a free woman married an Imperial slave, she could technically secure her own status while also improving his. For the owner of such a slave it would not make such financial sense, for any children of the union would still belong to the free mother. Again, the prejudice against any free woman consorting with male slaves extended even to slaves in such a privileged position. The Senatus Consultum Claudianum of 52 AD successfully discouraged such unions by reducing the woman to slave status, thereby giving the male slave's owner rights over her children.[77]

None of these considerations applied if the unfortunate female slave had been sold directly into prostitution, as so many were. Much later, in 428 AD, the Emperor Justinian would make amendments to the slavery laws. He would decree that any slave forced into prostitution by her master would automatically be given her freedom. Unfortunately, this reform was too late to save very many girls and women from abuse in the centuries between. Justinian also decreed that the maximum power any master could have over his slaves was 'reasonable chastisement' and this was a very long way from the absolute power over slaves of the early days.

One way for girls to grow up as prostitutes was the practice of exposing unwanted children, who would be mainly girls. This had been very common in Rome's earlier times, allowing the exposed child to be picked up by anyone, to become a useful servant or field hand, but she would have more financial value as a prostitute. The slave markets were often used by brothel keepers to find new girls, and slave workers were far easier to control than free women, who could easily run away.

The prostitute's life was often involuntary, dangerous and degrading in a culture which carefully protected the virtue of upper-class girls and respectable married women. This left a huge mass of men, and sometimes women, who had the power and means to exploit another person for the use of their body. Most references are to women, though male whores were well known, and catered to both male and female clients. The legal authority Paulus noted that a male prostitute could be killed by a husband if he was found having sex with the man's wife.[78] There are no special laws or notices applying to male prostitutes only, or to differentiate males from females separately. It is important to know that they did exist and plied their trade just as the women did. Some of them would be unrecognisable in daily life, appearing to be a 'regular' male, while others were more blatant, appearing as a 'saltatrix tonsa' or barbered dancing girl, referring to a male homosexual who dressed as a female to sell his sexual favours.

For every person who sold themselves willingly, there were many more forced into it. These also included children, both male and female. Any master selling a slave could insert a clause into the contract restricting them from future prostitution, but they may not have done this often, as masters would have value in mind and the value of an attractive young person would drop drastically if this were excluded. Many were bought specifically for the work and children were very vulnerable to this exploitation.

A free woman, often desperate from poverty or even due to family pressure to earn money, might also have to offer herself as a sex worker. Slave owners or brothel owners might step in to prevent the worst type of rapes purely in order to save the worker from excessive damage, but any free woman venturing into the profession might work alone and not even have that small amount of protection.[79] If she found herself taken up by a pimp or 'leno' she might have physical protection of a kind, but also might find herself becoming far more professionally involved that she had intended. Physical abuse from customers was common, and led to vaginal and anal injury, sometimes severe enough to prevent work. It was a very hard life, often frightening and without options, whether the prostitute was a slave or was free.

High-class courtesans were also a presence in Rome, and Suetonius wrote a book about them.[80] Unfortunately, this is now lost, but he and other writers were fascinated by these exotic courtesans, bringing sex into a world that, supposedly, held morals in high esteem. It was an irresistible combination of debauchery, intrigue and sex and Suetonius wrote of the Emperor Gaius (Caligula) setting up a brothel inside the palace.

> And lest any plunder go untried, he set up a number of small rooms, just like in a brothel, and decorated them sumptuously. He had both married women and freeborn stand in the cells, again just like in a brothel. Then he sent heralds around to the markets and places of public business to invite both young and old to indulge their lusts. He had money to offer, at interest, to all those who came, and men at the ready who openly wrote down their names as contributing to Caesar's income.[81]

Suetonius and Tacitus both tell lurid tales of Imperial women engaged in something very like prostitution. Their emphasis on the scandal caused by such behaviour shows it was uncommon, but it did happen, certainly in the case of Claudius's wife Messalina, for whom adultery was said to be an everyday matter, leading eventually to her death. Her dissolute lifestyle, with sudden attractions to different men, followed by equally sudden rejections of them when she was satiated, was well known. She behaved, in fact, just as many men did. Julius Caesar had become famous as the 'bald adulterer' and had as many sexual partners as anyone else, but the usual double standard applied. For the bored and spoiled Messalina, who thought she could do as she pleased, the double standard worked against her. She once competed with Scylla, Rome's most notorious prostitute, with Messalina servicing twenty-five lovers in twenty-four hours.[82] (Her record was nothing compared to a modern-day prostitute in Mayfair, one Martha Watts, who on VE Day in 1945, took home forty-nine clients that day, in a mood of celebration.)[83]

Claudius naturally had mistresses of his own, Calpurnia and Cleopatra, who worked against Messalina, informing on her to increase their own power. They told the timid Emperor of Messalina's fatal marriage ceremony with Gaius Silius, which terrified him, and he kept asking 'Is Silius still a private citizen?'[84] His favourite freedman, Narcissus, also played up to his timidity, asking the Emperor 'Are you aware that you have been divorced? If you do not act quickly, her new husband will control Rome!' However, once Messalina was punished, Claudius showed no further interest in her fate.[85]

The Emperor Augustus was more strait-laced, and enacted extensive laws regarding marriage and adultery. He was fortunate in his own contented marriage, but became concerned about laxity elsewhere, and reluctance on the part of young men to commit themselves to proper marriage. He read out a speech in the senate in support of his legislation to encourage marriage and childbearing:

> If we could survive without a wife, citizens of Rome, all of us would do without that nuisance. But since nature has so decreed that we cannot arrange comfortably with them, nor live in any way without them, we must plan for our lasting preservation, rather than for our temporary pleasures.[86]

Can't live with 'em, can't live without 'em. It was evident that not everyone was as keen on monogamous marriage as Augustus was, judging by the wealth of legislation he instigated in attempts to halt moral decline. His own daughter, Julia, was banished for adultery to the island of Pandeteria, and he was equally strict with others. The Lex Julia Adulteriis of 18 BC permitted fathers to kill adulterous daughters, and their paramours too. It also allowed betrayed husbands to kill their wives' lovers, in certain circumstances. He also insisted that adulterous wives must be divorced. These moves were not popular, and in 9 AD were modified by the Lex Papia Poppaea, which was named for the two bachelor consuls of that year. The later laws were often referred to by juristic sources as the 'Lex Julia et Papia' but these nearly all fell into disuse, or were repealed under first Constantine and later Justinian, until only the prohibition against marriages such as between senators and actresses remained.

Although the Lex Julia Adulteriis was an effort to control laxity, it only made adultery by the wife an offence. This was triable by special adultery courts and had serious consequences. There was nothing at all attempting to control the lustful urges of the men, and one section specifically exempts men from punishment if they only 'use' household slaves: 'Sexual intercourse with female slaves, unless they are deteriorated in value, or any attempt is made against their mistress through them, is not considered an injury.'[87] Any man who knew of his wife's adultery was placed under a duty to divorce her and also to prosecute her. If he failed to act within a required time (within three days he must declare with what adulterer and in what place the offence happened),[88] then he was required to dismiss his wife. If he did not, he could be prosecuted for being her pimp, 'Lenocinium'. In the same section of the Lex Julia it states that it is permissible to detain for up to twenty-four hours any adulterer caught in the act, and to get neighbours to be witnesses. It also stated that 'two adulterers may be accused at the same time with the wife, but no more.'

Women convicted of adultery were to be further punished by loss of half their dowry and one-third of their goods, as well as being banished to an island. The adulterer should also be deprived of half his property, and also be sent to an island. This stipulation is from the 'improved' version, as originally the cuckolded husband had had the right to kill him! It further makes the point, sensibly, that the two guilty parties should be sent to different islands. Fathers could again exercise their right of Paterfamilias to kill adulterous daughters, but men were not supposed to kill adulterous wives, although in practice those few who did were not often convicted for it.[89]

There is a good deal of legislation on the rights of a husband in killing a lover, if the man is caught in the family home, provided only that the lover is of inferior status to the husband, such as a dancer or an actor. It was also legally 'lenocinium', or pimping, for anyone to 'aid the commission of any adulterous act', for example by acting as a go-between or allowing one's premises to be used by lovers for their meetings.

It also attempted to deal with the problem of incest. 'For the case of incest, of which the man is deported to an island, this shall not be inflicted on the woman, that is to say when she has been convicted under the Lex Julia regarding her adultery.' Was that suggesting that only wives committed incest – or perhaps that there was a shortage of suitable islands? However, the husband was to be further reassured on two points:

> Anyone who has sexual relations with a free male, without his consent, is to be punished by death [and] It has been decided that adultery cannot be committed with women who have charge of a business or shop.

That presumably gave the married man security if he was chasing after shopkeepers or businesswomen, and he could also have boyfriends so long as sex with them was consensual. However, his wife had to be careful not to appear to be too fond of her brother.

The Lex Julia had a sensational impact on Roman society and the satirists had a field day with it. The element of compulsion, forcing a husband to divorce an errant wife, was ridiculed as being detrimental to the very family life that Augustus professed to uphold. The Emperor was much castigated for apparently conflicting aims. However, the law remained the cornerstone of Rome's matrimonial law for centuries, although erratically enforced, and there is 'little evidence that Augustus changed his opinions or standards of behaviour in his own time'.[90]

None of the legislation altered the world in which the streetwalker lived. The Luparia in Pompeii is as far removed as one can get from the adulterous wife of a man of status, with its cramped and squalid cells and their concrete beds. Its paintings of sex acts, probably to inflame the customers, were probably a depressing background to the work, especially when the prostitute knew that she did not have a choice regarding the clients.[91] Even the coy patterned soles of the sandals of the street whore, with their tempting 'follow me' message, cannot give a true impression of the life of 'the woman who openly makes money by the selling of her body', which was the legal definition of the prostitute.

The law did not punish prostitution, it was legal, and sexual relations with any prostitute, male or female, did not count as adultery, nor could an unmarried whore be a party to any adultery, much less be guilty of it herself. 'Stuprum' or illegal intercourse was the term used for sexual relations with an unmarried girl or widow (or indeed boy) but did not apply to sex workers. The key is the inviolability of the family unit, and sex with a prostitute did not damage the family bloodline, nor could it compromise the sexual purity of a potential wife or the legitimacy of the children.

There were some legal distinctions – the fact that a prostitute was 'probrosae' and could not marry a freeborn Roman citizen. They also suffered from 'infamia' so that they could not leave a will or receive a full inheritance. But if a prostitute did marry, within the degrees allowed, the stigma disappeared.[92] The authorities did not appear to care about any moral implications or the morals of the clients that the prostitutes serviced. For the woman there was a certain amount of social disgrace but without it incurring any legal penalty, it could be lived with. However, the fact that cash was changing hands, albeit in small amounts, was a very different thing. By the mid-first century AD the prostitutes were taxed, and it is likely that the idea for such a tax originated in Greece. The first documentary evidence came in the reign of the Emperor Nero, but Caligula was the first to enforce it. 'On the proceeds of the prostitutes at a rate equivalent to the cost of one client fee, and it was added to this section of the law that those who had practised prostitution or pimping in the past, owed the tax to the treasury and even married persons were not exempt.'[93] Suetonius commented that the tax could not be evaded by claiming to have left the profession. To collect the tax, officials would have been familiar with the whores in their area and have some idea of how much business they were doing. Special collectors, public officials or even soldiers would have had to collect it, and it is always possible that in the course of their work there was some extortion, too. Independent prostitutes could have been difficult to keep track of, but those in brothels would have been easier to trace. That would not stop collectors demanding more than their due, or perhaps freebies? The Romans, with their passion for order, somehow managed to make it work. On festival days, or a day of special markets, a legal one-day pass was issued to prostitutes to allow them to work the crowds, no doubt with a fee attached. From Upper Egypt one such permit exists:

> Pelaias and Sokraton, tax collectors, to the prostitute Thinabdella, greetings. We give you permission to have sex with whomsoever you wish in this place on the day given below – year 19, third day of the month Phaopi. Signed Sokatron, Simon's son.[94]

A document from Palmyra gave three levels of taxes, a 'per-client' rate of one denarius or more paid one denarius in tax. A client rate of eight asses (eight-tenths of a denarius) paid that rate in tax, and a per-client rate of six asses (one-sixth of a denarius) paid that amount in tax. We do not know how often the tax was collected, whether daily, or less often.

The pimp or brothel owner might have to have paid the tax, rather than the employed prostitute. The streetwalkers were quite likely harassed by officials hoping for bribes, in cash or in kind, and so would the part-time prostitutes who had regular jobs in bars or some kind of entertainment. Unless there was some disorder, the taxes were the only way the state interfered in a prostitute's business.

There was no red-light district as such and no districts from which they were banned. There would naturally be more of them in areas like the notorious Subura, or around the Forum or Circus on busy days. Despite some prostitutes working independently, as the tax receipts show, the system was more geared to those within a brothel or towards the pimp. He (or she) organised, controlled and exploited the prostitutes, most of whom were freedwomen, so they must at some point have been able to buy themselves free. About 20% of the eligible women worked, at least intermittently, as prostitutes, and although an elite man could not marry one, other men did and sometimes the woman's husband was her pimp. Slave owners usually did very well out of the profession, and the sex industry had a steady source of workers, not merely from slave owners looking for the best profits but also the pimps employing free women, with their business centring around the brothels, various inns, or the public baths.

> A person is a pimp if he has slaves working as prostitutes, but he is also a pimp if he provides free persons for the same purpose. He is subject to punishment as a procurer whether he makes it his main business or whether he conducts it as ancillary to some other business, for example as a tavern owner or stable master. If he has that sort of slave working and taking advantage of their opportunity to make money, or if he were a bath manager, as happens in certain provinces, having slaves to guard the clothes people leave and who offer sex in their workplace.[95]

In cases where lodgings, rooms used for sex, clothing or other benefits were received from a pimp, these were all paid for out of earnings. Despite seeing several clients in a day, it is reasonable to assume that any prostitute earned little take-home pay, although even then some managed to struggle up from the lowest rungs of the profession...

> Vibia Chresta, freedwoman of Lucius, set up this monument to herself and her own, and to Gaius Rustius Thassalus, freedman of Gaius, her son, and to Vibia Calybe, her freedwoman and brothel manager. Chresta built the memorial from her own profits without defrauding anyone.
>
> This grave is not to be used by the heirs.[96]

The above inscription comes from Benevento, Italy.

In a risqué poem in honour of the Phallic god Priapus, a slave prostitute is celebrated.

> Telethusa, famous among whores of the Subura district, has gained her freedom, I think, from her profits. She wraps a golden crown around your erection, holy Priapus, for women like her hold that to be the image of the greatest god.[97]

It has been estimated that one in every hundred people, men, women and children, in Pompeii was working as a prostitute, with much higher figures for women in the prime ages of 16-29 years. Pompeii was then a busy port, so there was plenty of demand. Many taverns and places to eat would have a room or two at the back, serving the customers. Even in the House of the Vetii, there is a back room off the kitchen decorated with explicit erotic art. At the entrance to the house is a graffito saying 'Eutychis, a Greek lass with sweet ways...2 asses'.[98]

Disgruntled or dissatisfied customers also often left their mark. 'Successus the Weaver loves the bar girl named Heredis, who certainly doesn't give a damn for him.' But a rival scribbles on a wall that she should have pity on him. 'Come on, you're just spiteful because she broke off with you. Don't think you can better a more handsome man – an ugly man can't best a pretty one!'[99]

Public baths were a favourite haunt of prostitutes, both male and female. The historian Ammianus Marcellus (330-400 AD) describes a typical scene there.

> If they (the bathers) suddenly learn that a previously unknown prostitute has appeared, or some whore of the common herd, or an old harlot whose body is up for cheap, they rush forward, jostling, pawing the newcomer, and praising her with outrageously exaggerated flattery, like Egyptians laid on their Cleopatra.[100]

Not only the baths attracted sex workers, they hung around anywhere with discreet spaces for clients. Tombs outside the city were favourites and the theatres and amphitheatres also gave opportunities, so much so that the supporting arches, the 'fornices' gave us the word 'fornication'. Some theatrical productions were very provocative and put clients in the right mood. In the tavern of the Via Mercurio in

Pompeii is a series of highly erotic scenes painted on the walls. These appealed to both theatregoers and drinkers. Mimes, like prostitutes, performed on the streets and were highly popular. These told tales of ordinary people, tailors, fishermen, sailors, both in adultery and other compromising situations. They played to the basic instincts of the audience, usually with a nude final scene, when the audience would shout 'Take it all off!' and the actresses complied. These were particularly enjoyed in May during the Floralia, when parades of mimes and prostitutes were central to the celebrations. Tertullian was disgusted at the performances and freely criticised them:

> The very prostitutes, sacrifices on the altar of public lust, are brought out on stage quite unhappy in the presence of other women, who are the only people in the community from whom they keep out of sight. They are paraded before the faces of every rank and age, their abode is proclaimed, their price and their specialities, even before those who do not need to be told. Yet more is shouted out, what ought to lie hidden in the shadows, and in their dark caves, but I'll keep silent about that. Let the senate blush! Let everyone be ashamed! These women themselves – assassins of their own decency, blush this once a year, fearful of having their deeds brought to light before all the people.[101]

Prostitutes also frequented temples, that of Venus particularly. South of Rome, at the eighteenth milestone on the Via Latina, at an ancient sanctuary of Venus, four women set up a cookshop. 'Flaccia Lais freedwoman of Aulus, Orbia Lais freedwoman of Aulus, Cominia Philocaris freedwoman of Marcus, and Venturia Thais freedwoman of Quintus, built a kitchen at the shrine of Venus in a leased space.'[102] These freed women have the sort of names associated with prostitutes, and may have made enough money to set up an eating establishment of their own, choosing a site where customers were likely to gather, with the combination of a food shop next to where sex was available.

The prostitutes' 'toga', supposedly a mark of shame, was intended to differentiate them from decent women who wore the 'stola'. It was at one time suggested as suitable wear for women taken in adultery but that was considered a step too far. Although this 'toga' was mentioned by ancient writers, (Horace in *Satires* and Sulpicia Tibullus in *Elegies*) there is no pictorial evidence of them wearing such a garment.

In brothels, women are usually pictured naked, wearing what appears to be a bra even when engaged in sex, or fully clothed, using bright colours to stand out in the crowds.

A prostitute in the Tavern of Salvius in Pompeii is pictured wearing a long gown of bright orange-yellow, with fancy slippers. Her client is saying 'I don't want to with Myrtalis.' The next picture shows a barmaid wearing a similar long dress, although in plain white, and with normal footwear. A prostitute's main attraction was that he or she might be willing to do something that 'nice' women didn't. Wives were not expected to have much interest in sex, and routine coupling becomes boring. More adventurous sex available was shown in the brothels pictorially, but such skills were degrading for a wife. That is presumably why Augustus was lenient with men who visited brothels regularly.

A character from the play *The Weevil* speaks cynically when entering a brothel:

> No-one says 'No' or stops you buying what is openly for sale, if you have the money. No-one prohibits anyone from going along the public road, make love to whomever you want, just make sure you don't wander off it onto private tracks – I mean, stay away from married women, widows, virgins, young men, and boys of good family.[103]

Prices charged varied for the same acts performed, but it was usually two asses. The 'as', a tenth of a denarius, was the small coin usually used on the streets. Two asses would buy bread or a cup of decent wine, or a chunk of cheese. Ordinary people carried asses, or its dividers, a quarter ass, or a half ass. Whores naturally priced their services according to this coin. A sestertius was two and a half asses, and the denarius was ten asses. If a person wanted to splurge on a good time, eight asses (which was close to a good wage for a full day), would purchase a room, food, and a girl in a public house.[104]

A prostitute working regularly could earn twenty or more asses per day, while a man paid for a day's work could expect to earn five to ten asses per day, but such daily regular work might be hard to find, so the prostitute earned far more than any woman could in a more 'respectable' trade, and often more than most men. However, the brothel or her pimp would take most of her money and without their 'protection' she was subject to attack or abuse on the streets. Gaius Plancius, a friend of Cicero, was a young man involved in the gang rape of a female mime, and Cicero's reaction to this is revealing: 'They say that you and a bunch of young men raped a mime in the town of Atina – but such an act is an old right when it comes to actors, especially out in the sticks.'[105]

No thought was given to the woman concerned, and to modern eyes Cicero was defending the indefensible, but it was a widespread attitude towards theatre people. Ulpian in the *Digest* says, 'If anyone proposition a young girl, and all the more if she is dressed like a household slave, there isn't much harm done, or even less so if she is dressed like a prostitute or not in the garb of a respectable matron.'[106]

Practical problems were more important than shame for a female prostitute, as getting pregnant could mean loss of earnings for a long time. There were magical spells of course, or the rhythm method, but the doctors got it wrong, and recommended the 'safe' period to be in the most fertile time. Potions were recommended such as willow, iron rust, fern root in wine, and even iron slag. Pessaries and ointments were a bit more useful, with olive oil, honey, lead or even frankincense and there were sponges soaked in common vinegar (still used in the medieval period), or the final resort of having an abortion, extremely dangerous. Apart from such physical intervention there were the vaginal suppositories or oral poisons. If these didn't work, there was nothing for it but to have the child, and once it was born it could be exposed and abandoned, or killed. Of course, if the child was a girl, it could be raised to become a prostitute, in which case the round started again.

The one problem the Roman prostitute did not have to worry about was the fear of diseases such as Aids or HIV, and syphilis was also unknown. Gonorrhoea may well have existed in the ancient world, but as it leaves no evidence on the bones, osteoarchaeology cannot help. Medical writers are also inconclusive regarding sexual diseases, as it appears that genital warts and herpes existed, but writers of the time do not appear to connect these with sexual activity. In that one way at least, the prostitute was free of anxiety and also of the most damaging and dangerous of the risks to the professional sex worker in modern times.

8

Age, Disease and Death

During the Spartacus slave war, Marcus Licinius Crassus had referred to 'Everyone who has a soldier's heart, even if his body is old…' He emphasised that he preferred seasoned men, the veterans of several campaigns, who had already seen everything that battle could throw at them and were unlikely to flee when faced with an enemy. He was paying tribute to their courage, which had been earned and bolstered by experience. He was to prove correct in his choice of such men over raw recruits.

In Rome, as in all societies, increasing age was only respected while it continued to be useful. Old age could be pushed back if the person concerned, whether male or female, was still able to make a contribution for the general good. However, increased age brings with it the problems of disability, immobility and loss of faculties. If the person concerned keeps busy and is useful, then their experience is also useful, whether in a veteran soldier or a midwife. Their contribution can still earn them respect and acceptance, preventing them from becoming a burden to their society, which many did sink into, through no fault of their own. This fact is regrettable but inescapable.

Once the life reaches its end, there was a desire to have a 'good death', particularly prevalent in Roman males. This did not mean an easy one, it meant one with dignity. When Caesar was assassinated in 44 BC his last concern was to pull a fold of his toga over his head, to prevent the assassins seeing his expression as he died. He also pulled some of the fabric over his legs, to make sure his genitals were decently covered. Thus, although he died a violent death, he was able to retain the necessary dignity of his position.

The death of Marcus Porcius Cato, as we have noted earlier, was also one of choice. Equally violent, though by his own hand, he attempted suicide, which failed. The doctors tried to save him, but he responded by pulling off his bandages and tearing open his abdominal wound, refusing to live in the Rome that Caesar was then creating. Not for him a pointless death, but one of defiance and honour, entirely in keeping with his rigid principles, so considered a 'good' and dignified act.

To many ancient peoples, once helplessness was reached, it was considered not only more practical but also more merciful to kill those members of the tribe who could no longer keep up with the others or contribute in any way. It was far preferable than to have to abandon old relatives to die alone, and also a saving of valuable and sometimes scarce resources. That not everyone is rendered helpless by increasing age has been shown in 2020 by the example of Colonel Tom Moore, who in his hundredth year raised £33million for the NHS during the pandemic and was rewarded with a knighthood. It could be said that, in any emergency, old soldiers can still step to and do what they consider to be their duty. Likewise, old women have often come out of retirement to help in times of need and to teach younger ones useful skills, showing that despite increasing age they do not deserve to be overlooked.

Older people have often proved themselves to still be achievers. Gaius Julius Caesar was around fifty-six when he was murdered. Far from beginning to slow down, he had planned to go on a new campaign to the East within a few days of the date of the attack.

Gnaeus Pompeius Magnus was fifty-seven when he was murdered; he had already proved himself an able and capable general and had hopes of doing so again.

Gaius Marius was a famous and highly respected commander and had repeated terms of office as Consul. He died aged seventy-one of a stroke, possibly brought on by the immense stress he was then experiencing. None of these very able men had any intention of retiring at the age they died, and they were still respected and powerful, even feared, at the time of death. The Emperor Augustus, another man of immense achievements, died at the age of seventy-six. Pythagoras was credited with having lived to eighty or even ninety years old. The tombstone of one fifty-year-old male in Algeria, dating from the third century AD, states that 'he died in the full flower of his youth.'

So when did 'old age' actually begin? It is easy to take for granted the idea that people in ancient times lived far shorter lives than people of the present day, but the evidence does not confirm this. To die young was then seen as a harsh and unnatural fate, one where talent and promise was wasted, hence the fear that the spirits of the young might be more malevolent than those of older people, resenting their shortened lives. There was regret at ambitions being unfulfilled, accomplishments uncompleted, family heirs unborn. Seventy was considered a reasonable age to aspire to, but just as many people exceeded this figure as failed to attain it.

We know that very high rates of infant mortality were the norm. However, if these are removed from the general death count, the 'average' age at death rises enormously, and becomes far closer to what is considered the norm in our own time. The main exception to this, of course, was the death of young males in battle.[1]

It is known that 6 to 8 per cent of the Roman population in the first century AD was over sixty years old. A few of these people, even then, might live to be a hundred. The average span would be somewhere in the sixties and seventies, although the Empress Livia Drusilla lived to be eighty-five. It appears that the human lifespan, contrary to common belief, has not changed dramatically over the past two thousand years. Certainly, a greater number now appear to reach a good age, but that is in proportion to the general increase in population. The old belief that our ancestors were smaller, weaker, sicker and more prone to disease, likely to be carried off by early middle age, is not borne out by the facts available, and by the lives of distinguished people whose biographies are recorded by the early writers.

Gaius Marius, who died of a stroke in 86 BC, had fought brilliantly in Numantia, Further Spain, and in the East against Jugurtha, against the Cimbri and the Teutones. He went East to negotiate with Mithradates of Pontus and fought in the Italian Social War. He was Consul for a record seven times and a re-organiser of the Roman army in many vital respects.[2] He was representative of the type of man Rome bred and encouraged, and these were not the sort of people to succumb easily to either misfortune or disease. Rome was justly proud of these people, with their proven courage and resilience, they were the Roman ideal, strong, healthy, capable and enduring.

Based on skeletal remains, the Roman male then averaged around 5 ft 5 inches in height, with Roman women being around 5 ft 1 inch.

Their diet largely consisted of wheat-based produce for the average citizen, with vegetables and fruit, and it is now believed that the rather low protein content tended to limit height.

The well-documented lives of famous Romans give the impression that becoming older meant, for them, an increase in respect paid in homage to experience, but these accounts mainly concern the upper classes, and the experience of poorer people could be quite different.[3] The upper-class gentleman could still be shown respect, provided he remained useful and in possession of his faculties. These men still felt themselves able to chase after (and sometimes marry) much younger women, and even breed new families with very young wives. They did not usually consider it necessary to cultivate or continue an amorous relationship with their own, equally ageing wives, as it was believed to be foolish to sleep with an older woman at all, as no children could possibly result.[4] It was generally believed that men aged more slowly than women, therefore elderly men frequently discarded old wives in favour of someone younger and more likely to have that second family that gave the illusion of youth. However, that hope ran contrary to the idea that too much sex was deleterious to an 'ageing frame' and that the silly old fool was likely to shorten his life by it.

Older women were treated far more harshly than men, whose peccadilloes of age were more likely to be tolerated, particularly by other males. Older women were expected to give up any idea of a sex life once fertility was at an end, and with the loss of their looks they merely aroused contempt, at best amusement, if they still had any interest in the opposite sex.

Men could still expect to take part in normal life as they aged, but women whose childbearing years were over tended to concentrate on their grandchildren, or perhaps on religion. With their physical power over men eroded, they were largely passed over, and sometimes even replaced. This double standard is one we are all familiar with, as matters have changed little in the intervening centuries. Therefore, the key to how older people were generally regarded in Roman times was clearly connected to their perceived usefulness to others.

'Hearken to the father than begat thee, and despise not the mother when she is old.'[5] In the male-oriented world of Rome, it is understandable that the man might still be listened to, but the old woman was disregarded. However, even older men could find themselves ousted by the pushy new generations, keen to make their mark and impatient of those who demanded respect but represented the past. Only the very high achiever could still win admiration, while the younger people found little to esteem in those who were no longer productive.

Naturally, wealth played a large part in whether a person was treated well or badly. Cicero was to stress the boon of wisdom and experience, (he was then sixty-two years old) but artistic representations and literary perceptions do not always give a realistic picture. Most of the wealth in Rome tended to percolate downwards to the younger generation, sometimes leaving their seniors relatively powerless. If poverty was also a factor, then life could become very uncomfortable indeed. The wealthy man, with slaves at his bidding, could command all the help he needed as age crept on, and children could be just as much help in some cases, although not all. Women certainly came off worse as the care and attention given to elderly men was not extended to older women, often resulting in loneliness and even destitution.[6]

A son was expected to support his aged father when in a position to do so, but that duty was seen as being a moral one, rather than one strictly required by law. Ulpian stated that it was the duty of a filius to support his parents in 'ratione naturali', but that certainly did not extend to the payment of a father's debts.[7] The legal duty of a daughter is far more difficult to trace. It was certainly in line with the 'pietas' that she should support parents if she could, although if she was married her ability to do so would be heavily dependent on her husband's views, and he might prevent her. The care of older people within the Roman family might certainly be expected to fall on the children, but if they failed in this respect there was no safety net, and direct legislation on the point was never introduced in Rome. The institution of 'patria potestas' meant that the Paterfamilias could expect support from descendants, but this might continue only so long as he was in control of the purse strings. The position of the mother, or even the maternal grandparents, who did not hold such sway in legal terms, was less straightforward.

The idea that extended family members should receive any support relied heavily on the individual's feelings of duty. What this might consist of is not explicit, although it may have been limited to some financial aid, to be expected only if the children were themselves financially capable and the parents or grandparents in dire need.[8] Therefore, the Paterfamilias may well have been catered for, but the needs of other elderly relatives would depend on circumstances, and they could easily fall by the wayside if the children or grandchildren saw no need to show interest. The Roman legislators saw no need to intervene on their behalf.

One example of maintenance at Roman expense is of a Plebeian woman whose mother had been imprisoned but received no food. The daughter is supposed to have visited her mother and fed her with her own milk. Being caught in the act, the mother was then freed and both women received 'perpetua alimenta', or food supplements, as a reward for this extreme act of 'pietas'. This was a tale told during the Republic, so belongs to the far past, and may have been used as an example to extol the virtues of Romans of earlier times. However, the site of that prison is said to have been consecrated in 150 BC and a Temple of Pietas build there, close to where the Theatre of Marcellus now stands. Whether the story is apocryphal or not, it certainly appealed to Romans, as there are depictions of it in Pompeii.[9]

Pliny mentions that the winner of the crown, the 'Corona Civica', also won a lifelong honour, in that he, his father, and his 'avus' or grandfather were to enjoy a 'vocatio munerum omnium', or exemptions from further duties.[10] With no provision being made for those people without wealth, or even without children who were financially secure enough to help support them, where would people turn? It was natural for elderly people of wealth to suddenly acquire a large circle of 'friends', but the poor had no such bait to offer.

Membership of a collegium might give some support, but not everyone was a member. Sometimes aged slaves could be seen as a liability, and they would then be sold off. Their value could have greatly diminished, sometimes enough to make them worthless in financial terms, and in that case they might even simply be dumped. Within Rome, sick or feeble slaves were quite often left on the Isola Tiberina, which was a callous practice that Claudius attempted to counteract in an edict of 47 AD.

For the freeborn poor, marriage was one solution to the problems of an isolated old age. A couple, even a poor one, could at least offer each other mutual support, and the idea that people should have made some provision for old age was still prevalent. Those who could do remunerative work did so with that in mind, often enduring great hardships in order to provide themselves with a small nest egg. Many others lived in poverty all their working lives, living very frugally in fear of not having enough to see them through to their life's end. Cicero, in his consolation, 'On old age', has Cato admit that age is only tolerable due to wealth and a respected position.[11]

> If moreover, poverty happened to befall a man when he became old, he would pray to be freed of life ... because of his deprivation in all respects, not having anyone to guide him, nor a source of support, not having adequate clothing, lacking shelter and food. There are times when he does not even have anyone to draw water for him.[12]

Galen was to ask 'Why do people become demented? It clearly damages all the activities of the soul. Old age destroys everything.'[13] Seneca agreed, remarking that 'Old age is an incurable disease.'[14]

Rome's way of dealing with illness was far more geared to prevention than curatives. It could be proud of the fact that Rome was the first state to provide hospitals, at least for the army. However, almost anyone could refer to himself as a 'doctor' although there were also experienced men, and women, with years of treating and dealing with people, so they were far more likely to be able to help the genuinely sick than the fakers with their claims of cures. The female doctors did tend to specialise in women's ailments, although not exclusively, and the best trained male doctors came from Greece, and were probably brought to Rome as captives initially. Eventually, Greek medical knowledge became prized and many doctors from Greece, or trained in Greece, turned to Rome to practise their profession. Surgical skills also improved due to the necessity for doctors to be able to treat wounds. But it was the Roman passion for hygiene that marked the city out from others. Strabo stated, 'The Greeks are famous for their cities, and in this they aimed at beauty. The Romans excelled in those things that the Greeks took little interest in, such as the building of roads, aqueducts and sewers.'[15] Romans certainly had more interest in providing public baths and latrines, with an impact on hygiene and public health, than in concentrating merely on pretty public buildings. Rome was throughout the Republic and into the Empire a rather cramped and scruffy city. It was Augustus who said 'I have made a city of brick into a city of marble,' but even then he had had economy in mind, and the marble was only a facing over the bricks.[16]

In Rome, in 293 BC, the first Aesclepium was built, and the healing snakes were taken there from Epidaurus, although the 'healthy mind in a healthy body' theme was to continue, with great emphasis on fresh air and exercise. Celsus considered that 'A person should put aside a part of each day for the care of his body. He should always make sure that he gets enough exercise, especially before a meal.' The individual's own input was considered important with regard to bodily and mental health, and each person was responsible for his own wellbeing.

Between its seven hills, Rome had always been marshy, a place of mists in winter and malaria in summer. Richer people built higher up in the surrounding hills, seeking fresher and healthier air, away from the city miasma, which bred disease. Caesar had followed the lead of earlier officials by attempting to drain the swamps surrounding Rome, work that has continued into the 20th century. The Pontine Marsh or 'Agro Pontino' was only reclaimed in the 1930s, a very low-lying area stretching from the Tyrrhenian Sea to the foothills of the Apennines, south-east of Rome.[17]

Rome's greatest sewer, the Cloaca Maxima, was one of the marvels of engineering in the ancient world. There were no facilities within the city for the disposal of waste, so it was thrown out onto the streets, or very often into the light wells between apartment buildings. There it would fester in the sun until, hopefully, a heavy shower of rain might eventually wash it away. The sewer system under Rome had been under construction since the sixth century BC, and the huge Cloaca Maxima was intended to cope with everything that, literally, was thrown at it. Any city of a million or more people has sewage disposal problems. The Cloaca Maxima was intended to be the main repository of several smaller sewers which ran into it. It ran from the Temple of Minerva in the Forum of Augustus, passed the Basilica Julia and went out of the central part of the city via the Piazza della Bocca della Verita, finally discharging into the Tiber close to the Ponte Rotto (now the Ponte Palatino), through an arched opening five metres in diameter.[18]

Ordinary insulae (apartments) did not appear to have been connected to sewers via any form of plumbing, and their latrines emptied into cesspits, if they had latrines at all. Most people will have used the pottery jars which served as chamber-pots, and the 'plostra stercoraria' or night-soil carts did the rounds at intervals, although it is unlikely to have been a regular or reliable service. It was quite common to throw out the pottery jar as well as its contents, and Juvenal complained that 'You are truly negligent and careless if, before leaving the house to go out to dinner, you do not make your will!' as it was common for people to be hit by falling jars, along with their noxious contents.[19]

Eleven aqueducts would eventually supply the growing city with its clean water, eight of which entered in the region of the Esquiline Hill. After popes replaced the emperors, four more were added, but even without the later additions no ancient city had anything like Rome's efficient supply of clean water, which earned the city the title of Regina Aquarum, or Queen of Waters.

The best water came from the Claudian Aqueduct, begun by Caligula in 38 AD. The Aqua Marcia, begun in 144 BC created the most technical difficulties, as it had a total run of 91 km, of which 80 km was underground.[20] It appeared that the inhabitants of Rome had more incentive to keep themselves clean, and had more fresh water to drink, than any other city of its time. These elementary precautions against disease went alongside the general opinions of the causes of diseases. Varro blamed 'tiny creatures, far too small to be seen' for the spread of illnesses. Columbella blamed poisonous vapours from the swamps and marshes. These were in contrast to the astrological preferences of Crinas of Massilia, who believed that illness was caused by an adverse conjunction of the stars. The Four Humours were the basis of much early medicine – fire, earth, water and air corresponded to yellow bile, black bile, phlegm and blood, and any imbalance of these could cause imbalance within the body.[21]

The hazards of city life, where disease more easily spread, encouraged those who could afford it to have a house in the country. In his letters, Pliny the Younger often yearned for the tranquility of a rural life. To a friend from his native town he wrote:

> Are you reading, fishing, hunting, or all three? You can do all together on the shores of Como...I can't say that I begrudge you your pleasures, I am only vexed to be denied them myself, for I hanker after them as a sick man does for wine, baths and cool springs.[22]

Seneca deplored the fact that women indulged in the same vices as men, to the detriment of their long-term health. 'Nowadays they run short of hair and are afflicted with gout,' he said sourly. General health could be affected due to the lack of knowledge regarding transmission of germs. Despite the fresh water, a decent sewer system, public latrines and bathing, these often had less effect than might have been wished, because they had been built to take away evil sights and smells, rather than from any real idea of tackling the spread of germs. Latrines, even those flushed through with clean water, as in the richer houses, were still not germ-free if the individual then cleaned himself with a sponge on a stick, which would be rinsed through ready for the next user. Sometimes lavatories were situated within kitchens, as in the grand houses of Lucius Gaius Secundus and Gaius Trebius Valens in Pompeii.[23]

These certainly contributed to the spread of disease, particularly bowel disorders such as internal parasites, usually whipworm and roundworm. To judge by the frequency with which the medical writers mention diarrhoea and dysentery, they must have been endemic in most places, and although many people will have developed some resistance, for anyone weakened by other ailments or simply by old age, they could have been fatal.

Both men and women often went to great lengths to retain the hair on their heads, while carefully removing all the hair from their bodies. Roman satirists such as Juvenal and Martial made fun of this vanity, but it did help prevent infestations of body lice. It also had the beneficial effect of reducing rashes and itching, and more importantly, would help to decrease the chance of contracting such parasite-borne diseases as typhus.

Ageing women tried to look younger by the use of cosmetics, which often contained white lead, with charcoal or powdered antimony to blacken eyebrows or eyelids. They also used much false hair, and false teeth were available to those who could afford them. Unfortunately, sometimes these illusions of beauty only served to make them look ridiculous...

> Your tresses, Galla, are manufactured far away. You lay aside your teeth at night, just as you do your silk dresses. You lie stored away in a hundred caskets, and your face does not sleep with you, yet you wink with an eyebrow which has been brought out for you this morning.[24]

Vitruvius warned against the dangers of using mineral-based cosmetics, such as stibnite and white lead, and Celsus had a remedy to deal with lead poisoning, but their use continued, either through vanity or sheer ignorance.

Halitosis was another common problem, often due to wine drinking and the pungent fish sauces (garum), and there was little attention paid to oral hygiene. Some people ate pastilles to try to sweeten the breath, or even drank perfume. Martial again had something to say: 'That you may not smell strongly of yesterday's wine, Fescennia, you devour immoderately Cosmus's pastilles. That snack discolours your teeth but is no preventative when an eructation returns from your abysmal depths.'[25] The excessive use of perfumes to cover all kinds of unpleasant smells was often condemned. Senena claimed 'I have, throughout my life, avoided perfumes, because the best scent for any person, is no scent at all.'[26] The sale of perfumes continued to be a flourishing trade, which ran alongside an extensive drug market blamed for all ills, including moral lapses.

People in rural communities might avoid these urban problems, but they also had to contend with lack of sanitation and lack of doctors. They then had to rely on prayers to the gods or the occasional visit from a 'circuit' doctor. Largely, it was up to the individual to do his or her best to maintain good health, by moderate diet and drinking, and by getting some exercise. This obviously depended on common sense and the avoidance of poor lifestyle choices. However, there is plenty of evidence that ill health was an ever-present problem and one which poorer people were least able to resist.

Quite apart from the private physicians of rich families, there was another group of physicians employed by the civic authorities. These were intended to provide medical treatment for all who required it. They were privileged by immunity from taxes and sometimes from compulsory service, though many doctors complained that they had to struggle to avoid the latter. Premises were provided for them, and although they were not supposed to charge fees they often received gifts from grateful patients, so could achieve a comfortable standard of living. One or two of these people became famous, such as Criton the physician of the Emperor Trajan, who wrote the History of the Dacian Wars, and of course Galen, who was once given four hundred gold pieces for performing an operation. However, doctors at this level were very much in the minority. By the fourth century AD, doctors in

Rome had to be selected by at least seven other doctors, but they were not without their critics:

> There is no doubt at all that these physicians, in their hunt for popularity, by means of some novelty, did not hesitate to buy it with our lives, hence those wretched, quarrelsome consultations at the bedside of patients, with no consultant agreeing with another, lest he appear to acknowledge a superior, hence too, that gloomy inscription on monuments, saying 'It was the crowd of physicians that killed me!'[27]

Martial, ever acerbic, said 'Lately, Diaulus was a doctor. Now he is an undertaker, and what the undertaker now does, the doctor did before.'[28]

The apprenticeship system was deeply rooted in Rome, and this also applied to the study of medicine. It partly arose due to restricted access to written works, understandable in an age when every 'book' needed to be laboriously copied by hand, ensuring that only the wealthy could afford to collect texts, and then only in the larger cities. There were great public libraries in Alexandria, Pergamum, Athens, Ephesus and in Rome, but again, access to these was a luxury mainly for the rich.

Stress was laid upon a physician's relationship with his patients. 'The intimacy between physician and patient is close. Patients in fact put themselves into the hands of their physician, and at every moment he meets women, maidens and the possessions which are precious indeed. So towards all of these self-control must be used.' This point is reiterated in The Oath: 'Into whatsoever houses I enter, I will enter to help the sick. I will abstain from all intentional wrong-doing and harm, especially from abusing the bodies of men or women, slaves or free.' Because of the bad press doctors often received, guidance was given by a code of practice which already existed in several parts of the Hippocratic Corpus, where it was recommended that a physician should

> ...look healthy, and as plump as nature intended him to be, for the common crowd consider that those who are not of excellent bodily condition to be unable to take care of others. He must be clean in his person, well-dressed and anointed with sweet-smelling unguents... In appearance let him be of serious but not of harsh countenance, for

> harshness is taken to mean arrogance and unkindness, while a man of uncontrolled laughter and excessive gaiety is considered vulgar, and vulgarity must be avoided.[29]

The basics of this was in the Oath taken by all physicians, which is also the foundation of the Hippocratic Oath: 'I swear by Apollo, physician, and all the Gods and Goddesses, making them my witnesses, that I will fulfil according to my ability and judgement this oath and covenant.'[30]

Doctors are often portrayed as serene, attentive, sober, scholarly men, either of middle age or sometimes even of advanced age, full of knowledge and experience. However, in Martial and Pliny's time the stock figure of a doctor was that of an adulterous swindler, a charlatan, who was quite likely to poison his patients. Although these cynical accounts make interesting reading, Seneca took the trouble to praise his own physician, for his patience and sympathy and the man became a friend. 'He sat beside those in distress, and was always present in times of crisis. No duty burdened him and none sickened him, he heard my groans with sympathy and amid a crowd of patients my health was his first concern ... I was bound to him, not as to a doctor, but by ties of friendship.'[31]

Health was, hopefully, restored by correcting the diet, by careful use of drugs, and by blood-letting. Serious operations could only be attempted as a last resort. The place where treatment was given was naturally dictated by wealth and position. The wealthy or influential client would be attended in his own home, and he would sometimes have a resident physician. Many doctors, even the public ones, would provide treatment at premises in the town, or sometimes they used rooms in their own houses. 'Tabernae medicae' were small street-shops where medical attention could be found, though there is no evidence of any general hospitals, except for those connected to the army.

The House of the Surgeon in Pompeii is a good example of what appears to be a local physician working from home. It is a substantial house, in which was found a very considerable number of medical and surgical instruments. It is situated on one of the main streets (now known as the Via Consolare). There is no clue to which room or rooms were used for treatments. Unfortunately, the house was one of the earlier ones to be excavated, before modern archaeological techniques were available. The exact location of the finds was not recorded and the method of making casts of objects made or organic materials had not been developed, so that a great deal of vital evidence was either missed or accidentally destroyed.[32]

Although the medicines themselves have long since deteriorated, their containers are occasionally found. One characteristic type of rectangular box with a sliding lid and internal compartments allowed the storage of several different medical substances, without contamination. These boxes are often made of bronze, but sometimes are ivory, and there must have been others made of wood. Often several are found together, and a specialised type of stacking system of cylindrical bronze pots was also common. Glass vessels were used for liquids, with slender glass phials and small squat jars being usual, but very small 'dropper' juglets are also known.[33]

With the great expansion of the Roman Empire, it became possible for exchange of ideas and comparisons between the approaches of different countries. Galen assembled some six hundred remedies, while Pliny in his *Natural History* recorded nine hundred substances. Pliny was very concerned about the quality of herbals, which painted pictures of plants and described them and their properties. But Pliny complained that the colours were often very misleading: 'Much imperfection arises from the manifold hazards of the accuracy of copyists, and in addition it is not enough for each plant to be painted in only one period of its life, as it alters its appearance with the fourfold changes of the year.'[34] The Herbal of Dioscorides, *De Materia Medica*, comprised five books written in Greek around the year 64 AD and was the product of a lifetime's study. Its systematic layout ensured its success, along with its detailed observations and rejection of superstition and magic. It was to become a standard work and its influence was felt until recent times. Once printing was invented the *Materia Medica* went through seventy editions in Europe.

While the more educated people could appreciate a non-superstitious approach to medical matters, the majority were still fearful of the gods and reliant on their goodwill; or perhaps they were merely hedging their bets, just in case? Greek medicine was eased into Rome along with the cult of Aesculapius and was quickly absorbed into another culture which looked to the gods for the preservation of health. Some physicians were sceptical about healing sanctuaries, while others accepted them as another way of combatting disease. The cult of Aesculapius spanned around a thousand years and he was usually represented as a middle-aged, powerful man, with a long cloak over his left shoulder, carrying or leaning on the distinctive snake-entwined staff. His daughter Hygieia was also shown with the staff, and her cult ran alongside his, with the resident snake being a beneficent deity, and quite without the sinister connotation later given to it by Christians. Snakes in ancient times were a symbol of rebirth, rejuvenation and restored health, and were very appropriate for a healer god.[35]

Followers of the god performed the ritual cleansing, the offering of a sacrifice and ritual bathing and then the afflicted person went into the 'dormitory' to rest. It was through this 'temple sleep' that the cure was decided on and treatment was given only after priestly interpretation: whether drugs, diet changes or supplements, or exercise was required.[36] Votive offerings of plaster or terracotta 'body parts' could be bought, and they showed the diseased areas, consisting usually of arms, legs, ears, eyes, breasts, genitals and even in one case a representation of a uterus. These were left in the temple, or would be inscribed on votive columns, describing the cures received by grateful patients. Legs and feet were very common among these votive offerings, showing the vital importance placed on mobility. Models of heads and chests had flattened bases so they could be displayed upright, but many others were perforated, so that they could be hung on the walls. Female parts were usually coloured white, male ones were red. These anatomical votives offer intriguing evidence of people's reactions to diseases, and we are unable to be sure whether they were offered before treatment, in hope of a cure, or after it, when they would be tokens of gratitude. They also give a fair idea of the usual problems that people worried about, as many of the 'body parts' were mass-produced.

At the Republican healing sanctuary of Ponte di Nona, studies of over eight thousand of these votives have led to the conclusion that the area specialised in foot and hand disorders.[37] The shrine was established in the early third or late fourth century BC and appeared to serve a rural area as some of the hand and feet votives are made to show the stresses that farm labourers are subject to. They show fallen arches, ingrowing toenails, torn ligaments, arthritic joints (which appear to have been very common), even a club foot.

The healing sanctuary at Campeti in the city of Veii had a large proportion of votives depicting male and female sexual organs, showing testicular tumours, breasts and wombs (possibly offered in gratitude for a successful birth), and there are models which attempt to show the symptoms of cystitis, urethritis, and gonococcal disease.

The presence of these votives does not, of course, necessarily indicate that a cure was effected.[38]

Hot and cold mineral springs became increasingly popular in later Republican Italy, showing a marked predilection for hydropathic treatments, commonly used as 'safe spaces' or havens from plagues and epidemics such as typhus and malaria.[39] Hot water springs may have inspired wonder in some superstitious minds, with belief in the limitless powers of the divine spirits, though natural springs did indeed bring relief to some sufferers.

Most revered of all were the thermal springs and the sulphurous baths at Baiae and by the first century BC this had become the most fashionable of the holiday resorts. Rich invalids travelled there to take the waters, and people who were not ill also took holidays there, giving the area a reputation for riotous and licentious living. The Romans developed thermal springs wherever they found them, including in Britain, putting them under the protection of the local god or goddess. The custom of dedicating anatomical votices, which went out of fashion in Rome by the first century BC, continued far longer in the provinces of Britannia and Gaul, where votives made of stone or metal continued to be made, many showing eyes, confirming the prevalence of eye diseases.

The hot springs near Puteoli (now Pozzuoli), were also famous for their successes with eye complaints, while the waters of Sinvessa in Campania were said to cure 'barrenness in women and insanity in men'. The waters of Albula near Rome were well known for their ability to heal wounds.

Despite all this, the poor, however ill they may have been, were unlikely to be able to afford to visit these healing springs, or even to find reliable medical help. It had long been realised that good diet and residence in a decent area had a profound effect on bodily and mental health, but for the poor and sick it meant nothing.

The god Aesculapius was usually depicted with a small, hooded figure alongside him, which represented Telesphorus, the God of Convalescence. This was considered to be an important part of the healing process, and Pliny the Younger, who was fond of his wife and attentive to her needs, sent her to Campania to recuperate from illness. He also rested at his country villa to restore his own health. For the poor, the local shrine or town baths would have to suffice. However, even the most powerful could suffer from debilitating and painful ailments and comparatively few diseases were completely curable. The Emperor Marcus Aurelius tried to 'cure' his chest pains only through the patience of Stoicism:

> Pain is neither unbearable nor unending so long as you remember its limitations, and you don't add to it with your imagination. What we cannot bear takes us away from life, what lasts can be borne, pain in the hand or foot is not against nature, provided that the hand and foot are still fulfilling their own tasks.[40]

But any drug that could help a little was acceptable, and the Emperor was given 'Theriac' by Galen. This was formerly known as Mithradatum and its most powerful ingredient was opium.[41]

Pain and suffering could drive people to suicide, particularly if it was in the head, stomach or bladder.[42] The use of suicide as a way out of suffering became all too prevalent, and Pliny the Younger wrote of this in the case of his friend, Titius Aristo:

> His patience throughout his illness, if you could see it, would fill you with admiration. He fights the pain, endures thirst and unbelievable heat of fever, without moving or throwing off his coverings. A few days ago he sent for me and some of his intimate friends, and told us to ask the doctors what the outcome of his illness would be. If it was to be fatal, he would put an end to his life, although he would carry on the struggle if it was only to be long and painful. He owed it to his wife's prayers and his daughter's tears, and also to us, his friends, not to betray our hopes by a self-inflicted death, so long as those hopes were not in vain. This, I think, was a particularly difficult decision to make, which merits the highest praise. Many people have his impulse to forestall death, but the ability to examine critically the arguments for dying and to accept or reject the idea of living, or not, is the mark of a truly great mind.[43]

People were fortunate if they could end their days at healing shrines, or at a spa, and some of these catered for those with terminal illnesses. Vitruvius recommended sites for healing shrines, remarking that a salubrious situation could help the sick as well as glorify the deity. At times of epidemics they naturally proved very popular. Roman medics had little idea how disease spread, although they were aware that illnesses such as phthisis (pulmonary tuberculosis), psora (scabies), and lippitudo (opthalmia) were infectious. They believed that infection was due to putrid air, although Galen suggested that 'bad seeds' could enter a body, and lie dormant until some stimulus activated them. At least his theory strove to explain the uneven susceptibility of certain individuals in cases of epidemics.[44] One sensible doctor in Rome, Celsus, said that anyone who went to use the public baths risked being the victim of infections, particularly if there was any kind of an open wound, however small, and gangrene might be the result. This cast a surprisingly defamatory light on the cleanliness, or lack of it, of these establishments.

One of the most severe epidemics ravaged the Mediterranean in 165 and 166 AD, casting its shadow over the reign of Marcus Aurelius. Galen had sensibly left Rome to avoid it, but Marcus Aurelius was still troubled by the effects of it when on his deathbed in 180 AD. At this distance in time it is difficult to guess what type of illness it might have been. Galen gave detailed eyewitness accounts of the symptoms, which included diarrhoea and a blistered skin rash. Death estimates ranging from ten per cent to a rather too high thirty per cent of the population of the Empire have been suggested, and the Emperor Lucius Veres (co-ruler with Marcus Aurelius) was probably a victim in 169 AD.

Livy mentions several outbreaks of pestilence in Republican times, and in 65 AD an estimated thirty thousand people were said to have died in Rome, while an epidemic which broke out in 189 AD was said to have been responsible for the lives of up to two thousand people each day.[45] That particular disease may have been taken into Rome by the army, which had been involved in the Parthian Wars in Mesopotamia. The infected troops spread the disease widely, causing terror and panic in Rome. These epidemics were, of course, in addition to the usual threats to life such as cancer and strokes, which were common. Pneumonia was generally fatal, and even Poliomyelitis stalked Rome during the summer weather. A description of a plague during the time of Marc Antony and Cleopatra had symptoms which sound very much like the Black Death.

These disabling and life-threatening ailments were likely to prevent many Romans from having the 'happy and peaceful retirement' which was the Roman ideal. 'The first two stages of a man's life should be devoted to his country, but the third and the last to himself.'[46]

In Rome, a man was considered to have become a 'senior' at the age of forty-six, for voting purposes, when election time came round. It normally signified the end of his liability for military service, although in a crisis he could still be called up to serve. This fairly low age is in direct contrast to the achievements of service of many of the great generals of the Republic, who were still active with the legions well into their sixties or even older. For educated Romans, however, retirement from public life was never intended to be a time for idling. If a man was no longer making a useful contribution to the life of the community, then he should at least be improving himself. Naturally, the nearer one came to that point of retirement, the more one tried to push it further back, and for some people the moment of actual retirement never came,[47] although under the Republic the reward of a successful career was 'cum dignitate otium', or the privacy of the elder statesman.

Even Vestal Virgins could, and did, retire in their late thirties, with what must have seemed like a long stretch of years ahead. Perhaps that is why many of them chose to continue, far better to take the plum role of Chief Vestal for life than to relegate oneself to the sidelines for the decades that were left. Many older women who were widowed, if wealthy enough to have no worries about their comforts, may have looked forward to a villa on the coast or in the country, rather than continuing to live in the noisy, crowded city, once their sons had married. A happy retirement was considered to be the reward of a life well led, and people would say 'multo labore hoc otium meruit' or 'he has worked hard to earn this respite.'[48]

Cicero had written that there was no better relaxation than in farming one's own land, saying 'Nothing is better, nothing is more profitable, nothing is more becoming to a gentleman.' If a man retired to the country he could then interest himself in experimental agriculture, and other gentle pursuits.

The younger Pliny, on being invited to visit the country to dine with Terentius Junior, who had finished a successful career then retired to the countryside to farm, expected to have a boring visit. Pliny had primed himself for this by reading up on various agricultural questions in order to keep the conversation flowing, yet had resigned himself to tedium. He was then amazed to be challenged to a literary talk by a man whose Greek was just as fluent as his Latin! He responded wryly 'You might have thought that we were in Athens.'[49]

Naturally, a 'good retirement' was not only heavily dependent on having enough money, but also on one's state of health. Vestricius Spurinna was, for Pliny, the very best example of serene old age. At seventy-seven years old, with a distinguished public career completed, he retained all his faculties. He lived very comfortably in his country house, and Pliny reported that he called for his shoes in the mornings and proceeded to walk for three miles. After a rest he went for a seven-mile drive, accompanied by his wife, and later walked another mile. After a quiet period of writing, he would, at the ninth hour of the afternoon in summer, or slightly earlier in winter, go to the baths, undressed and walked naked in the sun on hot days. After that he could still play ball strenuously. He took his bath, and after a short interval reclined for his dinner, which was a cultured meal that might sometimes be prolonged until after dark, even in summer.

In all levels of society there were men who, after retirement, surprised their friends by taking an unexpected course, as when the boxing champion, Horus, retired from the ring to take up philosophy.[50] One Servilius Sulpicius Similis, who was a Prefect of the Guard under the Emperor Hadrian, eventually retired to his farm, where he lived for a further seven very happy years. He composed his own epitaph, which said 'Similis died at so many years old, but he had lived for seven.'[51] His feelings may easily be understood if, after a lifetime of service, he considered that his 'real' life only began after his retirement.

After the establishment of the Aerarium Militare in 6 AD (a department for the payment of military gratuities), a guardsman's honourable discharge, or the 'honesto misso,' would normally come after sixteen years. The discharge of a legionary from full service was usually after twenty years, although there would be a further five years on active reserve, or 'sub vexilis' and the auxiliary soldier could retire after twenty-five years of service. Until the reign of Septimius Severus, it was a condition for the legionaries (although this did not include the auxiliaries), that they could not marry. Thus nearly all the surviving gravestones of soldiers in the early Empire were erected by parents, brothers or fellow soldiers. With no widows' or dependents' allowances available, he would have had no officially accepted family to worry about. If he kept a woman in the settlement attached to a camp, and if he was killed, his savings in the unit's bank could be transferred to her, so long as he had made a will to that effect. His contributions to the unit's burial fund would cover his burial expenses.

If he had a son, even illegitimate, that son would be welcomed into the legions once he was eighteen years old, so long as he was fit and active. For the existence of these soldier's sons, born out of official wedlock but acceptable, there is ample evidence.[52]

There are numerous discharge certificates, or 'diplomata', of auxiliaries showing that they received Roman citizenship as did their sons. Therefore, in his forties, the average legionary would face civilian life unmarried, with his gratuities and whatever booty had been shared out after any victory he had taken part in. If his unit was under strength, as was often the case, he could be pressed to carry on longer. If he had been commissioned during his service, he could sign on again as a Centurion. There are numerous inscriptions showing the careers of these veterans, so Juvenal's description of 'a centurion at sixty' was no fantasy. In fact, the inscriptions show records of men who had died aged seventy-one years old, after forty-eight years of army service, or died at sixty-four after forty-six years' service, and another who died aged seventy, after completing forty-five years of service.[53]

At the end of the Civil War, it had been the practice to settle veterans in new colonies. Under Nero in 60 AD there was an attempt to revive this practice, to repopulate cities in Antium and Terentum, but the scheme failed. 'The men slipped back to the province where they had done their service, they left no children because marriage and the bringing up of children was outside of their experience.' For Antium (Anzio) Tacitus's account of the failure of the scheme was shown by the funeral monument of an ex-Centurion who had settled down and become a municipal magistrate. When he died, he had no family to make his heirs, so he left his property to four other ex-Centurions.[54]

In Cologne, the settlement of veterans was more successful, with a far better integration of the veterans and the natives. They intermarried and within twenty years were conscious of themselves as being a single society.

After the settlement of 6 AD, the gratuities were often given in land rather than cash, although there were regular complaints about the quality of the land grants. If a retired soldier did not wish to farm the land, he could sell it and with that money, plus his savings, could return to his home town, marry and settle down there. Soldiers from the Rhine tended to settle in Spain or Provence, for a kinder climate, while men of commissioned rank usually went home, but they would have had families to return to, and could hold magisterial posts or belong to the local senate, marrying women of their own race and class to raise families.

When an aged man, who as Paterfamilias still controlled the economic life of the household, became incapable due to mental incapacity or began to act recklessly with the family property, there were serious problems. It was a well-known feature of Roman law that the Paterfamilias could control the family, the finances, and the property until death intervened, without being under any obligation to hand any responsibility to his heirs. This could cause great conflict between the generations, but however much the sons complained, there was very little they could do. In Athens a young man became independent at the age of eighteen, but this did not apply in Rome. There must in many cases have been a temptation to help the old man out of the way, when the adult sons were still obliged to ask him for money, as if they were children, when they had wives and children of their own. This contrasts with the idea of the elderly male being marginalised purely due to his age.

For the truly marginalised, who were the very young, the fatherless children, the infirm, and women of any age or condition, they could only hope to invoke pity. In Livy's account[55] it was the sight of an elderly invalid soldier who had been whipped by his creditors while in prison that provoked sufficient outrage to begin the Plebeian Revolt of 495 BC.[56]

One of the most common identifiable diseases of the Roman world was osteoarthritis and it has been suggested that over eighty per cent of adults could have suffered this debilitating illnesss. Sometimes known as the 'wear and tear' disease, there is a progressive deterioration of the articular surfaces of the free-moving joints through repeated trauma or overuse. A common result is the development of a 'flange' of newly formed bone around the margin of the joint. Though this does not cause death directly, in the advanced stages in involves intense pain, deformity of the affected joints, and ultimately immobility. People badly affected by this are often unable to take any active part in family life, or in their community, and are increasingly likely to become a burden. Pliny the younger described the state that an elderly invalid, Domitius Tullus, had reached:

> Crippled and deformed in every limb, he could only enjoy his vast wealth by contemplating it. He could not even turn in bed without

> assistance, he had to have his teeth cleaned and brushed for him – a squalid and pitiful detail. When complaining about the humiliations of his condition, he was often heard to say that every day he licked the fingers of one of his slaves.[57]

One can sympathise with the distressing way in which the life of Tullius ended, but for people at subsistence level the difficulties, compounded by lack of help and lack of money, would have been totally insurmountable. The occurrence of osteoarthritis in particular joints often reflects the uneven stresses to which the body is subject during its working life, and evidence from Cirencester, where spinal arthritis was not only very common but also not differentiated by sex, suggests that women as well as men often did back-straining work such as digging or carrying heavy burdens.[58]

This ailment was not confined to the damper and colder regions of the Empire. Joint pains and disorders were commonly referred to by medical writers of the time[59] including a more specific joint disease – gout – which was caused by an excess of uric acid in the blood resulting in deposition of urate crystals in the joint tissues, which then gradually degenerate, with destruction of the joint surfaces. This also causes swelling, inflammation, pain and restricted movement of hands and feet. Both of these problems, referred to by ancient writers under the names of 'podagra' or 'cheiragra' to describe both ailments, seem to be part of a range of diseases caused by drinking lead-adulterated wine. In the Roman period, wine syrups or 'sapa' were prepared in lead containers, which were believed to improve the flavour. Their toxicity would often have been sufficient to cause kidney failure.[60]

Both Pliny and Galen described a new form of 'podagra' or gout which had become prevalent in their time and which they believed was attributable to the consumption of luxury foods and drink. Pliny described the agony of a friend, Corellius Rufus, who had suffered from joint pain for many years.

> At the age of thirty-two years, I have heard him say, he developed gout in his feet just as his father had done, like other characteristics illnesses can be hereditary. As long as he was young and active he could keep it under control by temperate living and strict continence. Latterly, when he grew worse with advancing age he bore up through

> sheer strength of mind, even when cruelly tortured by unbelievable agony, for the disease was then no longer confined to his feet, but was spreading through all his limbs.[61]

The doctors attending Rufus were unable to do much for him, and eventuallly, driven to suicide, he starved himself to death.

These degenerative diseases were all too common, while epidemics, though terrifying, were sporadic. The real killers of the ancient world were the infectious diseases such as meningitis and pneumonia. Diphtheria may equate to a disease which Aretaeus of Cappadocia attempted to describe, likewise there is uncertainty around typhus, an acute disease of war, famine and catastrophe, whose infecting organism is spread by fleas, lice and ticks. Typhus may have been a regular visitor and may have been the plague that struck Pireaus and Athens during the Peloponnesian War (430-429 BC) that killed a quarter of the Athenian army.[62]

Poliomyelitis, a viral infection of the central nervous system, is commonly caught during childhood, and creates deformities due to muscle wasting and limb atrophy. Tetanus was another killer for those sustained injuries, and Aretaeus described the convulsions which '... arch the patient's back like a bow, dragging the head between the shoulder blades... an inhuman calamity, a spectacle agonising even to the beholder, and a malady beyond all cure'.[63]

Pulmonary infections were the greatest problem in towns, made worse through poor ventilation, lack of hygiene and crowded quarters. Tuberculosis was a scourge of the poor, and being a lingering disease with a long infectious phase, it remains endemic even in dispersed groups. The bacilli are transmitted directly, exhaled in coughing and excreted in sputum, with the primary infection site in the lung. It is often contracted in childhood, and those who do not become immune suffer chronic ill-health, coughs, pain and emaciation. 'The malady usually arises in the head, thence it drips to the lungs, there ulceration supervenes and from this feverishness is produced, which even after it becomes quiescent nevertheless returns. There is a frequent cough and pus is expectorated, sometimes bloodstained.'[64]

This disease rarely shows itself in the bones, so may have been far more common than is believed from osteoarchaeological records. Where bone infection does occur, it is often at the knee or hip, but most commonly at the upper part of the vertebral column, and angular distortion of the spine may have been the inspiration for the many Roman and Egyptian 'hunchback' figurines.

Leprosy is another chronic infectious disease of the same genus of bacteria as tuberculosis, but its mutations inspired terror and led to the shunning of its victims. A disease normally identified as leprosy in classical writings is elephantiasis. Pliny remarked that it was common in Egypt but rare in Italy. Celsus also believed it was almost unknown there:

> Whilst almost unknown in Italy, it frequently occurs in certain regions, the whole body becomes so affected that the bones are diseased. The surface of the skin shows a multiplicity of spots and swellings, which are first red, then gradually change to black. The skin is thickened and thinned in an irregular way, hardened and softened, roughened in some places with a sort of scales, the body wastes while the feet, calves and face swell. When the disease is of long standing the fingers and toes are sunk under the swellings.[65]

This description is probably of the most severe form of leprosy, afflicting those with low resistance. It is a disease with a long incubation period, allowing the infected victim to spread it widely. The increasing mobility of the Roman Empire allowed the disease to reach northern Europe, with evidence of it in early Britain. A body buried at Poundbury Roman Camp in Dorchester, a mature adult from around 400 AD, was a victim, but the body was not segregated from others in the cemetery, implying that ostracism was not customary at that time, or at least that any segregation was not continued after death.[66]

When death occurred for any Roman of reasonable means, there were usually five elements essential for the 'accepted' form of funeral. These were a procession, cremation (or later burial), a eulogy, a sacrifice and a feast. Lastly there would be some form of commemoration. Burials were not allowed within the city and undertaker's premises were also kept outside. The preferred locations for the tombs of the wealthy were on the best roads leading into the city, for example the Via Appia outside Rome, or the Herculaneum Gate at Pompeii, where the monument commemorating the deceased could be seen by the most people.

The procession for a wealthy person could be expensive. Men of standing would have their 'imagines' or wax masks worn by actors, to suggest the presence of revered ancestors. Women did not have these masks, but in certain circumstances the ones belonging to a distinguished matron's family could be used and worn at her funeral, and this also happened in the case of a Vestal. The deceased took part in the procession seated on a chair or bier, surrounded by noise, music playing, and the wails of hired mourners. Tacitus described the funeral procession of the widow of Gaius Cassius and the sister of Marcus Brutus in 23 AD: 'There were twenty masks of ancestors, Manlii, Quinctii, and all the rest, with Brutus and Cassius outshining them all ... from the fact that their masks were not included!'[67] This referred to the missing masks being of two of the murderers of Julius Caesar.

The funeral procession would make its way to the Rostra in the Forum, where the eulogy would be given by a close relative, followed by a sacrifice and the feast. If the family already had an imposing tomb, the ashes of the deceased would be included, however many people had new tombs made, with provision for the passers-by to stop, rest and read the inscriptions, and reflect on death.

One such useful tomb was that of Aesquillia Polla, outside the Nola Gate at Pompeii. This consisted of a marble half-circle of seating, with a small column, on top of which was an urn containing her ashes. The inscription on the base of the column, set up by her husband, read 'Numerius Herennius Celsus, son of Numerius, of the Menenian Tribe, Duumvir with judicial power for the second time, Praefectus Fabrum,[68] dedicates this to his wife Aesquillia Polla, daughter of Gaius. She lived twenty-two years. The burial place was given publicly by decree of the Town Councillors.'[69]

Tombs built at public expense were another way of honouring powerful families, often including women. Another such at Pompeii was that of the priestess Mamia. An inscription, unfortunately badly damaged, found in the Forum suggests she was responsible for the dedication of a temple, though its location is now uncertain. Mamia seems to have been from an old Samnite family, and her tomb was also an 'exedra' with seating, like Polla's. It had a prominent location, outside the Herculaneum Gate. The inscription read 'To Mamia, daughter of Publius, public priestess, a burial place was given by decree of the Town Council.'[70]

Less wealthy or important people had far smaller tombs, such as those at the Isola Sacra at Ostia. This cemetery includes the famous tomb of the midwife delivering a child.[71] The cemetery was extensive and although some tombs there were for the poor, the majority were built by middle-class families, many of them appearing as small houses, with facilities for sharing festivals with the deceased. These burial grounds were from the second century AD and the first half of the third century AD, and they show the gradual transition from cremation to inhumation.

Some women were able to build their own, as in the case of Eumachia. She was from a wealthy family in Pompeii, and amphorae suggest that her father exported the famous Pompeiian wine. She was married to Marcus Numistrius Fronto and was able to construct a substantial building in the Forum in Pompeii. An inscription on the building says 'Eumachia, daughter of Lucius, public priestess, in her name and in the name of her son, Marcus Numistrius Fronto, built at her own expense the chalcidium (porch), the cryptum (covered passageway), and the porticus, and dedicated them to Augustan Concord and Piety.'[72] Another inscription, on the base of a statue, shows her influence in the town, saying 'To Eumachia, daughter of Lucius, public priestess, from the Fullers.'[73] Eumachia is shown in her guise of priestess, emphasising piety and womanly virtues. Her tomb outside the Nuceria Gate has an inscription recording that she built it for herself and her family, at her own expense. It seems odd that a lady of such influence did not receive it as a public gift. However, it is large, consisting of a terrace with a seating area and an enclosure for burials. It sufficiently eclipses all others in the area by its size alone.[74]

Interestingly, one imposing tomb was that of a freedwoman, Naevoleia Tyche, married to a freedman who had become an Augustalis, an order ('sodalitas') of Roman priests originally instituted by Tiberius to attend to the maintenance of the cult of Augustus and the Julii. He had built a fairly simple tomb for himself and his wife and was buried there. However, his wife who inherited his business interests and property wanted something better, and she built another. This new tomb, in altar style with relief sculptures, referred to an honour given to her husband during his life (a magisterial bench at the games and performances) and its carvings also show some public ceremony along with a portrait of Naevoleia. The inscription is dedicated to her and her husband.

> Naevoleia Tyche, freedwoman of Lucius, set this up for herself and for Gaius Munatius Faustus, Augustalis and country dweller, to whom an account of his merits the town council, with the approval of the people, decreed a bisellium (honorific chair). Naevoleia Tyche

> built this monument for her freedmen and freedwomen and for those of Gaius Munatius Faustus during her lifetime.[75]

Inside this tomb were a number of glass cremation urns, each accompanied by a lamp. It showed the importance of the freedwoman and her family and may have given inspiration to other freed people, showing how much could be achieved.

There was no obligation for any family to give funeral games, fortunately, as they could prove very expensive indeed, and some people bankrupted themselves to pay for them. A benefactor, during life or by instructions in his will, could put aside money for a single celebration of games, or he could bequeath a sum to his municipality which, after investment, could be used for the holding of regular games. People locally might even expect them and be resentful if a well-known family did not wish to stump up. When a rich centurion died at Pollentia, the local people held up the funeral until the heirs promised to provide money for gladiatorial games. News of this so incensed the Emperor Tiberius that he sent troops to arrest the local senate, and others, for allowing such a scandalous thing to happen.[76] In the second century AD in the north of Italy, one man tried to avoid appearing mean, by drafting his will to say 'annual games to be held in due accordance with all the laws, plebiscites and decrees of the senate.'[77]

When the Greek historian Polybius lived in Rome in the second century BC, he stated that of all the impressive sights Rome had to offer, nothing had impressed him more than a statesman's funeral, especially the parading of the death masks of the ancestors and the funeral orations when the man's achievements were commemorated. It would probably have surprised him to know that within half a century a woman could be considered worthy of such public recognition, when the first public oration was given for a woman in 102 BC. It was spoken by the consul Quintus Lutatius Catulus for his mother, Popilia. This precedent was followed and by the end of the Republic several ladies had been similarly honoured.

The most famous of these speeches was given by Julius Caesar in 68 BC for his Aunt Julia, the widow of Gaius Marius. He started the eulogy in an unusual fashion:

> My Aunt Julia was descended on her mother's side from Kings, and on her father's side from Gods. Her mother was a Marcia, and

> the Marcii Reges go back to Ancus Marcius. Our own family, the Julii, traces its descent from Venus, so she combined therefore the sanctity of kings and the holiness of gods, who have kings for their servants.[78]

There is no record of funeral games being given for these women, but 'Ludi Funebres' had been held since 264 BC when gladiator fights were arranged for the first time, and they rapidly became an important part of funerals, when they could be afforded. They could last for as long as three or four days but were usually only for one day. On one occasion 120 gladiators fought for three days, and the whole Forum was covered with triclinia and tents in which people could feast.[79] Women were not allowed to attend these displays of manly skills, as in the early Republic it was considered shameful. Publius Sempronius separated from his wife owing to the disgrace she had brought on him by being present at one without his knowledge.[80]

As the funeral games were given by private individuals, they were not, strictly speaking, public games, although the public certainly watched them. They derived from the blood sacrifice to appease and 'feed' the gods but were also to please the deceased and ease them gently into the afterlife. In 264 AD, on the death of Decimus Junius Brutus Pera, his son selected three pairs of slaves from among prisoners of war to fight in his father's honour. When the Pontifex Maximus Publius Licinius Crassus died, Livy reported that 'One hundred and twenty gladiators fought and funeral games were given for three days, then after the games there was a general banquet.'[81]

The games given by Julius Caesar for his beloved daughter Julia had featured 320 gladiator matches, an enormous number; not only was there competition and an obligation to give the best, there was also a need to gather political support and show political strength.[82]

After these ceremonies were completed, the deceased was taken for cremation, (or later inhumation). It was believed that the deceased would not leave the earthly body until the cremation or inhumation was done, only then would they pass over the River Styx. Until then they lingered around friends and family and were quite likely to take offence if anything derogatory was said about them.

The deceased were then remembered at certain times of the year, when the Parentalia came around, or when the Mundus was opened to allow spirits to rise from the Underworld, or at the Lemuria when the ghosts of the dead were expected to be at large. Families gathered at burial sites to make offerings and activate the shades, or else the deceased might lose all memory of their existence on earth. Once the family had ensured that their departed relative had had a good send off, usually by spending more than they could afford and even getting into debt, their minds could then turn to the final stage – the inheritance.

For the heir it could be a worrying time, wondering how he would pay for it all, but for the heir who had lived under the iron rule of his Paterfamilias, it could be a relief. Even allowing for heavy new responsibilities, he would have the freedom to make his own choices, deal with the family's property, or choose husbands for sisters or daughters, looking first to his own preferences.[83] If the heir was too young for responsibility, the deceased could have given his wife authority to appoint a tutor or guardian to guide the boy. If the wife had been fully under her husband's authority and had not been emancipated by him, he might have appointed a guardian for her, too, or perhaps allowed her to appoint one for herself. The widow would succeed to the estate on her husband's death, but she would share it with their children.

If they had been in a 'free' marriage, she had no rights of intestate succession to her late husband's property and he would need to leave her provided for, but only so far as her legacy did not exceed that left to his heir.

Sometimes the widow could be left in poor circumstances if her late husband had neglected to provide properly for her, or had had insufficient means. The legislation of the Emperor Augustus, in operation from his reign until the fourth century AD, stated that she could only inherit one-tenth of her husband's bequest if she was over the age of twenty-five but under the age of fifty, if her husband had been between twenty-five and sixty at his death, and there were no children of the marriage to be the direct heirs. A man could leave up to a quarter of his estate to his mistress, and only a tenth of it to his wife, with perfect legality.[84] The rich widow, particularly one without children to complicate matters or take a dim view of a fortune-hunting stepfather, could easily attract men. If she was still in possession of her faculties and not easily taken in by the blandishments of the hopefuls, she could derive amusement from the situation, as they put themselves out to please her and brought her expensive gifts, always in the expectation that they would shortly get them back through marriage.

Pliny the Younger had entertaining stories to tell of Marcus Aquilius Regulus and his search for a wealthy wife. At one time he had forced himself into the bedroom of the rich Verania, widow of Lucius Calpurnius Piso, who had been adopted as son and heir by the Emperor Galba, rather than Otho, who had then rebelled. Under Otho's influence the Praetorian Guard were enticed to seize both Galba and Piso, who were killed in 69 AD, when Galba had only been Emperor for six months. Marcus Aquilius Regulus must have thought the widowed – and ill – Verania a good prospect, and apparently did a calculation of her horoscope, assuring her that her illness was grave but she would recover. Later he returned with news that a soothsayer had confirmed his diagnosis. The lady believed him, and added a codicil to her will, then realising her mistake, called down curses on the head of Aquilius as she died. On another occasion, the same man found a woman named Aurelia making her will and begged her to leave him the rich clothing she was then wearing, but he was to be disappointed as although she made the codicil, she did not die.[85]

The Lex Voconia de Mulierum Hereditatibus (law of women's inheritance), passed in 169 BC, severely curtailed the rights of women to inherit from wills. Even if the woman concerned was her father's only child, she could not be designated the main heir. The nearest agnate relative (on his father's side), would take precedence.

Cicero argued a case where the Lex Voconia could not apply because the deceased man's property had not been assessed at the Census. The then praetor, Gaius Verres, overruled Cicero's argument and refused to let the woman in question inherit her father's property. She may have been an innocent victim not only of the strictures of the Lex Voconia itself, but of the ongoing hostility between Cicero and Verres, whom Cicero prosecuted for extortion while he was Governor of Sicily in 73-70 BC.

This law could, presumably, be got around by careful fathers, as we know of several women who managed to inherit vast sums from parents. One of these was Cornelia, mother of the Gracchi, daughter of Scipio Africanus. Another was her granddaughter Fulvia, daughter of Sempronia (the sister of the Gracchi brothers) and her husband

Marcus Fulvio Bambalio. Fulvia inherited a large fortune from each of her parents and married three times, first to Publius Clodius Pulcher, secondly to Gaius Scribonius Curio, and finally to Marcus Antonius, and in each of her marriages was able to spend money freely.[86] Both these Patrician ladies were 'in sui iuris' and able to control their own finances, which along with their bloodlines probably formed the greater part of their attractions.

For lesser people the Lex Voconia must have been a great inconvenience, and a father who was fond of his daughter and wished to provide for her properly must have been frustrated to know that the fruits of his own hard work were likely to fall into the hands of a distant nephew. However, Roman inheritance was not merely about transferring property from one generation to the next, as there was often little or no property worth passing on. In Rome the 'damnosa hereditas', or ruinous inheritance, could have no financial benefit, passing on only debts and obligations. That was the point of the Roman legislation, to appoint a successor to legally step into the shoes of the deceased and deal with all legal matters.[87] This was known as the principle of universal succession, and in appointing an heir the testator was choosing a suitable person to carry out not only the family's legal requirements but also the religious duties. In some cases it was difficult for a woman to perform such duties, particularly if she was under the control of a husband or guardian.

In a case where a freeborn man died leaving a small child as his heir, he would have appointed a guardian who would take over all legal responsibilities until that child came of age. However, unlike medieval laws in England, where the child would be expected to live with the guardian, in Rome such an heir would remain at home with its mother if she still lived. In cases where a freeborn man died without leaving a properly witnessed will, the estate would go first to persons who were 'sui heredes', that is 'own heirs', and these people would become 'sui iuris' or 'in their own hands' on the death of the man who had control over them while he was the Paterfamilias. These would be his own children, remoter issue through the male line, and any wife of a 'manus' marriage, who would legally be regarded as a daughter for these purposes. A number of amendments were made regarding succession on intestacy, in attempts to clarify and improve the situation of women in these cases, as unless a woman was a part of a 'manus' marriage, she would have no rights to her children if her husband had died intestate.

The S.C. Tertullianum of 130 AD, and the S.C. Orphitianum of 178 AD intended such clarification. The Tertullianum applied to women who had borne three or more children (four for a freedwoman), and its aim was not to give any person (apart from the mother) greater rights than previous law.[88] The Orphitianum was intended to protect the rights of children if their mother died intestate and represented a major departure from the old principle of only agnate succession, because it gave the mother's children, whether legitimate or not, the legal right to succeed to her estate. These two 'Senatus Consulta' were the first time that the blood tie was recognised in the 'ius civile' law of intestacy, but the reforms were still quite narrow in scope, and it was remarked by Schultz in his *Classical Roman Law* that 'What puzzles us concerning these two enactments, is not that succession is granted to blood relations, but that this was done so reluctantly and so incompletely.'[89]

Most women would have been puzzled, if they'd had time to consider the matter, by the idea that it had taken so long for her rights over herself and her offspring to be considered at all, however reluctantly it was done. The key word is that 'reluctance' of men to accept that any woman had enough competence to deal even with herself or her children, let alone any legal matters, despite the evidence of many perfectly competent women throughout Rome's history.

The further tragedy would be that such attempts to ameliorate the lot of women in general would be relatively short-lived. Even Justinian's reforms of the sixth century AD did not give full attention to the rights of a surviving spouse, and these problems would certainly increase with the later Christianisation of Rome, after which the rights of women would again take very much a secondary place. Their situation would gradually sink to a position unprecedented in the Ancient World. For the average woman, her legal status would by the medieval period relegate her to the level of an infant.

Although the concept of slave-keeping would very gradually die out, the strictures upon women would tighten over the coming centuries, leaving the woman of intelligence, education and ambition open to criticism, if not actual censure. The Cornelias, the Julias, and the Fulvias of Rome, whatever their faults, had lived their lives if not in total equality, then certainly in balance with their men, as had the marketwomen, the businesswomen, and the highly respected medical women of the Roman world.

Augustus was unfaithful to Livia, despite his expressed views on adultery, but was still reputed to have continued to love her and their bond held firm. Perhaps the final word should be left to him:

> My ideal is that we may have lawful homes to dwell in and houses full of descendants. That we may approach the Gods together with our wives and children, that a man and his family should live as partners, who risk all their fortunes in equal measure and likewise reap pleasure from the hopes they rest upon one another.[90]

Endnotes

Chapter One

1. J.P.V.D. Balsdon. 'Roman Women'
2. The statue of Jupiter Optimus Maximus (Jupiter Best and Greatest) on the Capitol was originally terracotta. A general awarded the privilege of a Triumph coloured his face with minim on the day, to honour the god. Minim was a vermilion pigment, made of cinnabar or mercuric sulphide.
3. Balsdon. 'Roman Women'
4. A. Momigliano. J.R.S. 112 (1957)
5. This power to take life altered over time, but a Paterfamilias could still lock up or disown members of his family, or force a divorce in certain circumstances.
6. Caecilia Metella Dalmatica bore Sulla twins named Faustus and Fausta. This break from the traditional names was to commemorate Sulla's luck.
7. For the traditional account of the scandal see Mommsen, otherwise reported by Dionysius of Helicarnassus.
8. Titus Livius (Livy). 'History of Rome'
9. Lynda Telford. 'Sulla, a Dictator Reconsidered'
10. Livy. 'History of Rome'
11. Sir James Frazer. 'Ovid's Fasti' Vol. III. On the introduction to Rome of the cult, see H. Graillot 'Le Culte de Cybele'
12. Balsdon. 'Roman Women'
13. H. H. Scullard. 'Roman Politics'
14. Balsdon. 'Roman Women'
15. Brian Caven. 'The Punic Wars'
16. H. H. Scullard. 'From the Gracchi to Nero – History of Rome 133 BC to 68 AD'
17. Ibid
18. Lynda Telford. 'Sulla, a Dictator Reconsidered
19. David L. Stockton. 'The Gracchi'
20. H. H. Scullard. 'From the Gracchi to Nero'

21. One 'iugera' was approximately half an acre, therefore 500 iugera amounted to 250-300 acres, depending slightly on the quality and productivity of the land.
22. Keith Richardson. 'Daggers in the Forum'
23. Ibid
24. D.L. Stockton. 'The Gracchi'
25. H. H. Scullard. 'From the Gracchi to Nero'
26. Keith Richardson. 'Daggers in the Forum'
27. By the early Republic 'tribes' was not an ethnic grouping but a political one. There were 35 tribes, 31 of which were rural and only 4 urban. The 16 oldest ones bore the names of the original patrician 'gentes' indicating either membership of that family (Julii, Cornelii etc), or that one lived on land owned by the family. By the middle Republic further tribes were added to accommodate new citizens. Each member of a tribe was allowed one vote, but this only counted in determining which way the tribe voted as a group, as each tribe delivered just one vote. Most senators and knights of the first class belonged to rural tribes, considered a mark of distinction.
28. Keith Richardson. 'Daggers in the Forum'
29. D. L. Stockton. 'The Gracchi'
30. Homer. 'The Odyssey'
31. Plutarch. 'Lives – Tiberius Gracchus'
32. Ibid
33. Slaves were generally tortured while being questioned, although it often meant that the evidence given was then questionable.
34. Keith Richardson. 'Daggers in the Forum'
35. Plutarch. 'Lives – Gaius Gracchus'
36. Lynda Telford. 'Sulla, a Dictator Reconsidered'
37. The 'public horse' was a horse belonging to the State, and in the days of Kings 1,800 knights of the 18 most senior centuries were given a horse at state expense. Despite later knights being businessmen rather than soldiers, the right to be given a public horse was highly regarded and hotly defended.
38. Plutarch. 'Lives – Gaius Gracchus'
39. Rome replaced the destroyed Fregallae with the town of Fabrateria Nova on the opposite bank of the River Liris to the original town.
40. 'Tribune of the Plebs' began early in the Republic, when the Plebeian order was at loggerheads with the Patricians. The Tribunes vowed to defend the lives and property of members of the Plebeian order. By 450 BC there were ten Tribunes of the Plebs, elected by the Plebeian Assembly and their power was in the oath of that order to defend them. They were not elected by Patricians but had the right to exercise a veto against any law, election, or decree of the Senate, even during war. This meant that their tribunician function was often more obstructive than useful, especially when they were easily bribed to use the veto, which became increasingly common.

41. Plutarch. 'Lives – Gaius Graccus'
42. D.L. Stockton. 'The Gracchi'
43. Keith Richardson. 'Daggers in the Forum'
44. The denarius (pl. denarii) was the largest coin denomination under the Republic.
45. Rome's actual Treasury was beneath the Temple of Saturn in the Forum.
46. H. H. Scullard. 'From the Gracchi to Nero'
47. W. K. Lacey. 'Cicero and the end of the Roman Republic'
48. H. L.Havell. 'Republican Rome'
49. Ibid
50. Cannae, on the Aufidius River, was the scene of a battle between Carthaginians and a Roman army. Lucius Aemilius Paullus was one of the commanders. The Roman army was annihilated, with the survivors being made to pass beneath the yoke, a terrible disgrace. It was the worst Roman defeat until Arausio.
51. He had crushed the Fregallae revolt. Lucius Opimius was the first man to persuade the Senate to pass the Ultimate Decree, the 'Senatus Consultum de Republica Defendenda', effectively martial law. While in force this Ultimate Decree overrode everything and was to be used in civil emergencies.
52. Sallusts 'Jugurtha' refers to the beating and execution of a junior commander who was a Roman citizen.
53. Games and displays were commonly held in the Fora of towns and cities. It was considered rather decadent during the Republic to have a permanent place for these, and Pompeii had an amphitheatre before Rome did.
54. Keith Richardson. 'Daggers in the Forum'
55. Plutarch. 'Lives – Gaius Gracchus'
56. Ibid
57. The Temple of Castor and Pollux ('The Dioscuri') was on the other side of the Sempronian Hall, later to be replaced by the Basilica Julia. Castor's temple was very old, indicating that worship went back to at least the time of the kings. It was a favourite place for meetings.
58. Keith Richardson. 'Daggers in the Forum'
59. This is the standard version of the story. The servant goes by various names and it cannot be determined whether Gaius died by his own hand or that of his servant. It is also possible that his enemies caught up with him and killed him at the Grove of Furina.
60. Plutarch. 'Lives – Gaius Gracchus'
61. W.K. Lacey. 'Cicero'
62. Plutarch. 'Lives – Gaius Gracchus'
63. The Grass Crown or 'Corona Graminia' was the most prestigious of the several 'crowns' awarded to military men and the most difficult to win. It was awarded only to a man who had saved a whole legion, and was decided on by the soldiers. It was traditionally made of grass stalks, straw,

or whatever was available on the field of battle, and was given after the engagement.

64. Sarah B. Pomeroy. 'Goddesses, Whores, Wives and Slaves'
65. Cicero. 'Cato'

Chapter Two

1. Sarah B. Pomeroy. 'Goddeses, Whores, Wives and Slaves'
2. Livy. 'History of Rome'
3. Lynda Telford. 'Sulla'
4. Sarah B Pomeroy. 'Goddesses, Whores, Wives and Slaves'
5. Ibid
6. Lynda Telford. 'Sulla'
7. Balsdon. 'Roman Women'
8. Ibid
9. Ovid (Publius Ovidius Naso). 'Ars Amatoria' or Arts of Love.
10. Encyclopedia of Technical Chemistry.
11. Ovid. 'Ars Amatoria'
12. Lucien of Samosata. 'Amores'
13. Now in the Palatine Museum, Rome.
14. Balsdon. 'Life and Leisure in Ancient Rome'
15. Seneca. 'Letters from a Stoic'
16. Balsdon. 'Life and Leisure in Ancient Rome'
17. Suetonius. 'Lives of the Caesars'
18. Kathryn Tempest. 'Cicero, Politics and Persuasion in Ancient Rome'
19. Balsdon. 'Life and Leisure in Ancient Rome'
20. W.F. Snyder. J.R.S. 17 (1936)
21. R. Ross Holloway. 'The Archaeology of early Rome and Latium'
22. G.G. Bruns. 'Fontes Iuris Romani Antiqui'
23. The Palatine Hill today contains the ruins of the palaces from the Imperial period, with the Forum on one side and the Circus Maximus on the other. In Republican times this area held streets of large houses, the homes of the wealthy. Even earlier, it was the area of the origins of Rome, where the first village was situated. Even during the Republican era, a small round hut was preserved and known as the 'Hut of Romulus'.
24. Cassius Dio (155-235 AD) was a statesman and historian. He published 80 volumes of the 'History of Rome' beginning with the arrival in Italy of Aeneas, the son of Venus and King Anchises. When Troy fell, he fled to Latinum and founded the race from which Romans believed they descended. His son Iulus, by his Latin wife Lavinia, was believed to be the ancestor of the Julian family, allowing Julius Caesar to claim descent from Venus.
25. In 78 BC Sulla died and Marcus Aemilius Lepidus attempted to overthrow Sulla's constitution. Pompeius Magnus crushed a rebellion in Gaul, and there

was trouble in Etruria when veterans settled on allotment land met with resistance. In 52 BC Milo killed Publius Clodius Pulcher and was prosecuted for murder. He later retired to Massilia. That year also saw the rebellion of Vercingetorix in Gaul.

26. Balsdon. 'Life and Leisure in Ancient Rome'
27. Lynda Telford. 'Sulla'
28. The Praetors were the second highest magistrates after the Consuls. By the end of the Republic there might be six Praetors in one year, otherwise eight, with varying duties. The Praetor Urbanus had authority within Rome. It was a legal position and was confined to civil rather than criminal suits. He had authority as far as the fifth milestone from Rome and could not leave the city for more than ten days at a time. The Praetors Peregrinus travelled around Italy dealing with non-citizen cases. There were also two dozen young men elected as Tribunes of the Soldiers and they represented (and normally commanded) the legions.
29. A Triumph was a successful general's greatest day. He had to have been hailed as 'Imperator' by his troops, after which he could petition the Senate for the privilege of a Triumph. It was sometimes withheld, and at other times he might have to wait for months, with his troops, on the Campus Martius before he was given a date. He could not enter Rome itself while he still held Imperium (official authority) and must stay outside the Pomerium (the official boundary of the inner city, marked by posts). If he gave up his Imperium he could no longer claim a Triumph, so he waited for Senatorial approval. If granted, it was an impressive procession, displaying campaign spoils and sometimes high-born prisoners, followed by a banquet.
30. G.O. Hutchinson. 'Cicero's Correspondence – a literary study'
31. Balsdon. 'Life and Leisure in Ancient Rome'
32. Lucien of Samosata. 'The Parasite'
33. Albulae was on the road from Rome to Tivoli. During the Empire, it was a favourite place for villas and even had a palace of the emperor.
34. Plutarch. 'Lives – Caesar'
35. Balsdon. 'Roman Women'
36. Ibid
37. Richard Holland. 'Augustus, Godfather of Europe'
38. Providing furniture for the marital home was the duty of the husband. It continued to belong to him, as did everything else, except his wife's personal property. Houses were sparsely furnished, but the Roman woman's lack of input in this aspect of family life may seem strange to us.
39. Pliny the Elder. 'Natural History'
40. Pliny the Elder 'Letters'
41. Balsdon. 'Roman Women'

42. Ovid 'Ars Amatoria'
43. Livy. 'History of Rome'
44. Marcus Porcius Cato 'of Utica' (95-46 BC) known as Cato the Younger.
45. The marriage arrangement between Cato and his friend, whereby Cato's wife was passed from one to the other, was supposed to be in line with Stoic principles, which considered deep emotional attachment to be a mistake, and that one should never allow one's feelings to be overwhelmed.
46. He was unfortunately proved correct when Caesar made himself Dictator in Perpetuity, king in all but name, an idea anathema to Republicans. Also, at Thapsus, Caesar had broken the code by executing 10,000 Roman prisoners who had fought for Pompeius, but had been unarmed and attempting to surrender.
47. Lynda Telford. 'Women in Medieval England'
48. Ralph Jackson. 'Doctors and Diseases in the Roman Empire'
49. Soranus. 'Gynaecology'
50. Marcus Valerius Martialis, a poet during the reigns of Domitian, Nerva and Trajan.
51. Galen was born around 130 AD in Pergamum (now in Turkey). He studied widely in Greece and became the Chief Physician to the Gladiator School of Pergamum, where he became very experienced in the treatment of wounds. He is well known for his medical experiments and his literary output was prodigious. He died in Rome in 210 AD.

Chapter Three

1. Balsdon. 'Roman Women'
2. Sarah B. Pomeroy. 'Goddesses, Whores, Wives and Slaves'
3. For the Lex Claudia de Tutela see G. Rotondi's 'Leges Publicae Populi Romani'.
4. I.L.S. 7213.12 (Inscriptiones Latinae Selectae, edited by H. Dessau).
5. Sarah B. Pomeroy 'Goddesses, Whores, Wives and Slaves'
6. Lynda Telford. 'Sulla'
7. Balsdon. 'Roman Women'
8. Plutarch. 'Lives – Tiberius Graccus'
9. Livy states that the marriage of first cousins was legitimised between 241 and 219 BC. Cassius Dio stated that it was legitimate for a man to marry his brother's daughter, but not his sister's daughter. Dio also said that the marriage of uncle and niece was rescinded by the Emperor Nerva.
10. P.E. Corbett. 'The Roman Law of Marriage'
11. This was quite different to the rules of wardship in medieval times, when it was customary to marry off a ward to one of her guardian's family, to secure the inheritance. The Roman custom was, in this case, more sensible.
12. P.E. Corbett. 'The Roman Law of Marriage'
13. Cassius Dio. 'Roman History'

14. Balsdon. 'Roman Women'
15. Plutarch. 'Roman Questions'
16. Balsdon. 'Roman Women'
17. Plutarch. 'Roman Questions'
18. L.M. Wilson. 'The Clothing of the Ancient Romans'
19. H.A. Sanders. 'A Latin Marriage Contract'
20. Pliny. 'Lives of the Emperors'
21. Frank Ezra Adcock. 'Marcus Crassus Millionaire'
22. Marcus Tullius Cicero (106-43 BC) was married to Tarentia who had far more money than he did. Their daughter Tullia married Publius Cornelius Dolabella in 50 BC. She was to die in 45 BC leaving her devoted father devastated by the loss.
23. Cicero. 'Letters'
24. Balsdon. 'Roman Women'
25. By Cicero's time the legal complications regarding retention and repayment of dowries was so daunting that the jurist Servilius Sulpicius Rufus felt obliged to write a book on the subject, in order to clarify the situation.
26. Richard Holland. 'Augustus, Godfather of Europe'
27. Lynda Telford. 'Sulla'
28. Plutarch. 'Lives – Cato the Younger'
29. Balsdon. 'Roman Women'
30. Suetonius. 'Lives of the Caesars – Domitian'
31. Juvenal. 'Satires'
32. Pliny. 'Natural History'
33. Balsdon. 'Life and Leisure in Ancient Rome'
34. A. Watson. 'The Law of Persons in the later Roman Republic'
35. Pliny. 'Natural History'
36. Balsdon. 'Roman Women'
37. Pliny. 'Natural History'
38. Pliny was Gaius Plinius Caecilius Secundus (61-112 AD) son of Caecilius Clio. His mother's brother, Pliny the Elder, adopted him after the death of his father. He became a lawyer, administrator and writer.
39. Pliny the Younger. 'Epistulae'
40. Plato. 'Republic'
41. Soranus. 'Gynaecology'
42. Ibid
43. Ralph Jackson. 'Doctors and Diseases in the Roman Empire'
44. Lynda Telford. 'Women in Medieval England'
45. Soranus. 'Gynaecology'
46. Ibid
47. Ralph Jackson. 'Doctors and Diseases in the Roman Empire'
48. Balsdon. 'Life and Leisure in Ancient Rome'

49. Pliny. 'Natural History'. This was said to have been the highest price ever paid for a slave, and in the case of Lutatius Daphnis it was actually paid twice.
50. Augustine of Hippo. 'Confessions in Thirteen Books'
51. Balsdon. 'Life and Leisure in Ancient Rome'
52. P.E. Corbett. 'The Roman Law of Marriage'
53. Stacy Schiff. 'Cleopatra – A Life'
54. Plutarch. 'De Amore Prolis'
55. Pliny the Younger. 'Epistulae'
56. Seneca. 'De Matrimonio' – one of the fragments of Seneca's lost essay on matrimony.
57. Aulus Gellius. 'Noctes Atticae'
58. Tullia married first Gaius Calpurnius Piso, then Furius Crassipes, thirdly Publius Cornelius Dolabella, and had two sons with Dolabella, but they both died.
59. W.K. Lacey. 'Cicero and the end of the Roman Republic'
60. Valerius Maximus. 'Nine books of memorable deeds and sayings.'
61. Martial (Marcus Valerius Martialis). 'Epigrammata'
62. Soranus. 'Gynaecology'
63. Lawrence Totelin. 'Roman Childbirth'
64. Caroline Rance. 'The History of Medicine in 100 Facts'
65. The Kahun Papyrus – 1850 BC – or Kahun Gynaecological Papyrus. Egypt's oldest known medical text.
66. This burial is very important in relation to the attention given to a young child at a very early stage in Rome's development, particularly as the child was a girl.

Chapter Four

1. Lar (pl. Lares) these original deities share with other 'faceless' gods and goddesses the modern term 'numen' and these disembodied numinae governed everything in daily life, from the state of the weather to the functioning of a doorway.
2. The 'Silanus' head, usually found at fountains, is a satyr-like face, leering with open mouth. It was often used to direct water into the fountains set up by Cato the Censor.
3. The Pantheon in Rome takes its name from the pantheon of Roman gods and goddesses whose statues originally occupied it. These have now been replaced by Christian altars to saints.
4. The Temple of Ops was on the Capitol, close to that of Jupiter Optimus Maximus.
5. Positioned at the end of the Via Sacra just before the slope leading to the Capitol.
6. Unfortunately, he didn't respect Rome's remains enough to prevent him driving the wide road named the Via dei Fori Imperiali through the Imperial Fora it is named for.

7. It is also the area where Gnaeus Pompeius Magnus would later build his immense theatre complex.
8. Plutarch. 'Lives – Sulla'
9. Sekhmet, the Goddess of War and Destruction, also Goddess of Healing, Truth and Justice. One of the oldest and most powerful of the gods, companion of Ptah and mother of Nefertem, still revered as a deity of immense power by followers of the Kemetic religion.
10. Paul Jacobs II and Diane Atnally Conlin. 'Campus Martius, the Field of Mars in the life of Ancient Rome'
11. David Watkin. 'The Roman Forum'
12. Ibid
13. Ibid
14. Soprintendenza Archeologia di Roma. 'The Palatine'
15. Lynda Telford. 'Sulla'
16. R.M. Ogilvie. 'The Romans and their Gods'
17. Balsdon. 'Life and Leisure in Ancient Rome'
18. David Watkin. 'The Roman Forum'
19. Under the Emperor Augustus the social qualification was lowered and by 5 AD the Emperor was obliged to accept the daughters of freedmen as candidates. This could not have happened during the Republic, when only the daughters of the highest families were considered eligible.
20. Balsdon. 'Roman Women'
21. Tacitus. 'Annals'
22. Balsdon. 'Roman Women'
23. R.M. Ogilvie. 'The Romans and their Gods'
24. Balsdon. 'Roman Women'
25. R.M. Ogilvie. 'The Romans and their Gods'
26. Tacitus. 'Annals'
27. L.R. Taylor. American Journal of Philology, 1942.
28. Livy. 'History of Rome'
29. Pliny the Younger. 'Epistulae'
30. Livy. 'History of Rome'
31. Dionysius of Halicarnassus. 'Roman Antiquities'
32. Marcus Licinius Crassus (115-53 BC), known as 'Dives', was always alive to every possibility of increasing his fortune.
33. Livy. 'History of Rome'
34. Plutarch. 'Moralia'
35. Balsdon. 'Roman Women'
36. Domitian was not, in 83 AD, then involved with his own niece, an affair which resulted in her pregnancy, abortion and death, so he was free to judge others despite the reluctance of the Pontiffs at the time, one of whom died of a heart attack probably caused by stress.

37. Suetonius. 'The Twelve Caesars'
38. Pliny the Younger. 'Epistulae'
39. Cassius Dio. 'Roman History'
40. R.M. Ogilvie. 'The Romans and their Gods'
41. 'Inscriptiones Latinae Selectae' edited by H. Dessau, for priestesses of the Imperial cult.
42. R.M. Ogilvie. 'The Romans and their Gods'
43. Plutarch. 'Lives – Caius Julius Caesar'
44. Balsdon. 'Roman Women'
45. Cicero. 'Letters to Atticus'
46. Ibid
47. W. Jeffrey Tatum. 'The Patrician Tribune – Publius Clodius Pulcher'
48. William MacQuitty. 'Island of Isis'
49. Leonardo B. dal Maso. 'Rome of the Caesars'
50. Joanne Berry. 'The Complete Pompeii'
51. Ibid
52. An Aedile was one of the four Roman magistrates, two Plebeian and two Curule. They were responsible for the city's streets, drains, public buildings, and for weights and measures and the public grain supply.
53. Joanne Berry. 'The Complete Pompeii'
54. Lynn E. Roller. 'In search of God the Mother – the cult of the Anatolian Cybele'
55. R.M. Ogilvie 'The Romans and their Gods'
56. Ibid
57. Marcus Calpurnius Bibulus (died 48 BC) was in opposition to Julius Caesar, being a traditional Republican. He opposed Caesar's agrarian law and, when forcibly prevented from vetoing it, retired from political life to 'watch the heavens' for omens. He spent so much time staring at the sky that nothing could be done, and he successfully blocked all further legislation. He was married to Porcia, the daughter of Marcus Porcius Cato the Younger.
58. Livy. 'History of Rome'
59. Lucan. (Marcus Annaeus Lucanus – 39-65 AD) who wrote an epic poem on the civil war. Quote from 'Pharsalia VII'
60. Pierre Grimal. 'The Civilisation of Rome'
61. Cicero. 'On Divination'
62. Weinstock. Journal of Roman Studies no.36 (1946)
63. Publius Clodius Pulcher had confiscated, then destroyed, Cicero's house on the Palatine, after Cicero was exiled in 58 BC. Cicero's exile was short, and he was back in Rome in 57 BC and started rebuilding his house, although Clodius had had the area declared a holy space.
64. Cicero. 'On the answers of the Haruspices'
65. R.M. Ogilvie. 'The Romans and their Gods'

66. Publius Ovidius Naso (Ovid – 43 BC to 17 AD) 'Fasti'
67. Cicero. 'On the Laws II'
68. The two standard collections of Latin inscriptions are C.I.L. (Corpus Inscriptionem Latinarum) and I.L.S. (Inscriptiones Latinae Selectae)
69. Juvenal. 'Satires'
70. Publius Terentius (Terence) 195-159 BC. A famous writer of comedies.
71. Trimalchio was a character from the novel 'Satyrica' by Petronius, who was a senator, suffect-consul (in 62 AD), and previously a governor of Bithynia. His name could possibly also have been Gaius Petronius Arbiter or possibly Titus/Publius Petronius Niger.
72. Balsdon. 'Life and Leisure in Ancient Rome'
73. The Gregorian Calendar has three fewer days every four hundred years. The year numbers evenly divided by one hundred are NOT leap years, those evenly divisible by four hundred remain leap years.
74. The Compitalia was suppressed in 64 BC until 58 BC, then suppressed again in 45 BC, due to political exploitation.
75. Valerius Maximus. 'Memorable deeds and sayings – Book II'
76. Pliny the Elder gives a list of forty-seven names of attendees.
77. Cicero. 'Letters to Atticus - XII'
78. This was considered a concession, as normally the presence of a slave was believed to pollute a religious ceremony. One statue of Mars had a notice attached to it, saying 'This statue is not to be touched by a slave.'
79. Cicero. 'Letters to Atticus – XIII'
80. The Circus Maximus was built by King Tarquinius Priscus before the Republic. It filled the whole area of the Vallis Murcia between the Palatine and Aventine Hills. Only Roman citizens were admitted to the Circus and there is some evidence that even freedmen citizens were classified as 'slaves' in this instance, and also refused admission, very likely because everyone else wanted to get in.
81. The Emperor Augustus took credit in his 'Res Gestae' for restoring the couches upon which the holy statues were placed.
82. Juvenal. 'Satires'
83. Pliny the Younger. 'Letters II'
84. Suetonius. 'The Twelve Caesars – Domitian'
85. Marcus Aurelius – 'Meditations'

Chapter Five

1. H.H. Scullard. 'From the Gracchi to Nero'
2. Geddes and Grosset. 'Ancient Rome – the Republic'
3. Gaius Servilius Ahala was considered a patriot due to his killing of SpuriusMaelius in 439 BC. Maelius had been feeding the poor but was accused of 'attempting kingship' by seeking personal popularity.

4. The Eruscan king, Lucius Tarquinius Superbus, was expelled around 509 BC by Lucius Junius Brutus (545-509 BC)
5. The Lex Liciniae Sextiae, legislation passed by Lucius Sextius Lateranus and Gaius Licinius Stolo, in the fourth century BC, attempted to balance Patricians and Plebeians by decreeing that one Consul per year should be Plebeian and that there should be regulations of interest and capital of debts. It also stated that citizens should be restricted to holdings of no more than 500 iugera of state land.
6. Geddes and Grosset. 'Ancient Rome – the Republic'
7. Lynda Telford. 'Sulla'
8. The 'headcount' or people of the lower classes were not originally used as soldiers in the legions. Soldiers had to provide their own kit, which was beyond the ability of poorer people. Gaius Marius had to persuade the Senate to begin to utilise these poorer men and provide kit for them. Also, a 'landed' soldier could go back home and work on the family holding between campaigns, costing the State nothing. Marius's reforms revolutionised the army by allowing thousands of poorer men to fight for Rome.
9. Lawrence Keppie. 'The Making of the Roman Army'
10. Ibid
11. Lynda Telford.'Sulla'
12. A.H. Beesley. 'The Gracchi, Marius and Sulla'
13. Gaius Marius (157-86 BC) married the sister of Gaius Julius Caesar, who was the father of the more famous Julius Caesar, enabling the families to support each other, Marius with money and Caesar with increased status.
14. Arthur Keaveney. 'Sulla, the last Republican'
15. Andrew Borkowski. 'Textbook on Roman Law'
16. Stoicism was a Hellenistic philosophy founded by Zeno of Citium in the third century BC. Cato the Younger and Marcus Aurelius are the most well known Roman Stoics.
17. Mark Cartwright. 'Wine in the Ancient Mediterranean'
18. Ibid
19. 'Insulae' means island.
20. The Goddess Ceres protected cereals and other foodstuffs.
21. Leonardo B. Dal Maso. 'Rome of the Caesars'
22. Robert Knapp. 'Invisible Romans'
23. Ibid
24. Corpus Inscriptionum Latinarum.
25. A 'talent' was a unit of weight defined as being the load a man could carry. Bullion and large sums of money were expressed in talents, but the term was not confined to money or precious metals. In modern terms, a talent weighed approx. 50 to 55 pounds (25 kg).

26. Marcus Licinius Crassus (115-53 BC) was a statesman and general and member of the First Triumvirate made up of himself, Julius Caesar and Gnaeus Pompeius Magnus, whom he disliked.
27. Jane Rowlandson – editor. 'Women and Society in Greek and Roman Egypt'
28. Robert Knapp. 'Invisible Romans'
29. Homer 'The Iliad'
30. Artemidorous of Daldus wrote the 'Interpetation of Dreams' in the first or second century AD. He was a professional dream interpreter.
31. C.I.L. 8.152. Sommet el Amra, Tunisia.
32. C.I.L. 4.8203
33. C.I.L. 4.4528
34. Robert Knapp. 'Invisible Romans'
35. Jane Rowlandson. 'Women and Society in Greek and Roman Egypt'
36. Pliny the Elder. 'Natural History'
37. C.I.L. 14.2120
38. Martial 'Epigrams'
39. Mary Beard. 'S.P.Q.R.'
40. Painting from the House of Julia Felix, Pompeii.
41. Martial
42. Lucien of Samosata
43. Robert Knapp. 'Invisible Romans'
44. Ibid
45. W. Jeffrey Tatum. 'The Patrician Tribune'
46. Angela Donati. 'Revista Storica dell' Antichita'
47. Suetonius. 'Augustus'
48. Veleia is now Elea, an ancient city in Lucania. It became a World Heritage Site in 1998.
49. Pliny. 'Eppigramae'
50. I.L.S. 6278. Caelia Macrina of Terracina
51. Sarah B. Pomeroy. 'Goddesses, Whores, Wives and Slaves'
52. Balsdon. 'Life and Leisure in Ancient Rome'
53. The 'sportula' was a small basket and gave its name to the 'dole' given either in food or money to clients. Sometimes food would be given, in a small basket, in place of cash.
54. Seneca the Younger. 'De Brevitate Vitae'
55. Seneca the Younger. 'Letters'
56. Tacitus. 'Annals'
57. Balsdon. 'Life and Leisure in Ancient Rome'
58. Robert Knapp. 'Invisible Romans'
59. Mary Beard. 'S.P.Q.R.'
60. The tombstone of the four-year-old worker is from a mining community in Spain.

61. Mary Beard. 'S.P.Q.R.'
62. Ibid
63. Ibid. The Inscription was written as a poem, probably intended to be ironic, but nevertheless full of despair and unfulfilled hopes.

Chapter Six

1. The Penguin Dictionary of English Synonyms
2. Imperium was the authority invested in a curule magistrate or promagistrate. It meant that man could not be gainsaid within the parameters of his office. It was conferred by a Lex Curiata and lasted for one year unless specifically given for longer. The number of lictors attending indicated Imperium and was also shown by the scarlet ribbon tied around a general's breastplate, which had small loops to hold it in place. Statues of commanders in armour always show this ribbon, tied at the front.
3. Fortuna Huiusce Dei is best known for her Temple in the ancient Area Sacra, at the Largo di Torre Argentina in the Campus Martius.
4. The expression 'infra-dig' was once widely used to describe a person socially inferior. It comes from the Latin 'infra dignitatum' or beneath one's dignity.
5. Claire Tomalin. 'The Invisible Woman – the story of Nelly Ternan and Charles Dickens'
6. Lynda Telford. 'Sulla'
7. Ibid
8. Suetonius. 'The Twelve Caesars – Caius Caligula'
9. Ibid
10. Suetonius. 'The Twelve Caesars – Nero'
11. Ibid
12. Soprintendenza Archaeologica di Roma 'Domus Aurea'
13. Suetonius. 'The Twelve Caesars – Nero'
14. Ibid
15. Livy 'History of Rome'
16. Suetonius 'Tiberias'
17. Suetonius 'Augustus'
18. Tacitus 'Annals of Imperial Rome'
19. Ibid
20. Pliny the Elder 'Natural History'
21. Carlo Maria Franzero. 'The Life and Times of Theodora'
22. Procopius of Caesarea. 'The Secret History'
23. Ibid
24. T.E. Gregory. 'A History of Byzantium'
25. 'Virtus' embodies manliness, valour, excellence, courage, character and worth, all the necessary qualities of the male. It derives from the Latin 'vir' for man.

26. Lynda Telford. 'Sulla'
27. Tacitus. 'Annals of Imperial Rome'
28. L. Jacobelli. 'Gladiators at Pompeii'
29. Ibid
30. Joanne Berry. 'The Complete Pompeii'
31. J. Dobbins and P. Foss (Editors) 'The World of Pompeii'
32. Claude Moatti. 'The Search for Ancient Rome'
33. Ibid
34. C.I.L. 4.3884
35. Martial. 'Liber de Spectaculis'
36. Martial. 'On the Amphitheatre' from 'Liber de Spectaculis'
37. Terracotts figurine showing the execution of a bound woman, sitting on a bull, being attacked by a large cat. From the Louvre Museum.
38. Mosaics from the Domus Sollertana at El Djem, in Tunisia, show the executions of condemned prisoners by means of leopards.
39. Mosaics from Zliten show an opening procession, gladiator fights and the executions of prisoners. One man is wheeled into the arena on a small chariot, bound and helpless, to be attacked by leopards.
40. Martial. 'Liber de Spectaculis'
41. Tertullian. (Quintus Septimus Florens Tertullian 155-240 AD) 'Apologeticus'
42. Garum was a salty, strong-smelling fish sauce. Made from fermented fish innards, used as a flavouring in many types of food. Liquamen was similar, but slightly better quality. The fermented and pungent residue was often used as a paste by poorer people.
43. Fik Meijer. 'The Gladiators'
44. Driffield Road York. Gladiator cemetery excavation by York Archaeological Trusts, 2010.
45. Fik Meijer. 'The Gladiators'
46. Juvenal. 'Satires'
47. Seneca. 'Moral Epistles – VII'
48. Fik Meijer. 'The Gladiators'
49. Cassius Dio. 'Roman History'
50. Tacitus. 'Annals'
51. Suetonius. 'Caligula'
52. Fik Meijer. 'The Gladiators'
53. Joshua T. Mark. Ancient History Encyclopaedia. April 2018.
54. Propertius. 'Elegies'
55. Richard Bauman. 'Crime and Punishment in Ancient Rome'
56. J.A. Crook. 'Law and life in Ancient Rome'
57. Ibid
58. Richard Bauman. 'Crime and Punishment in Ancient Rome'

59. Livy. 'History of the Foundation of the City of Rome'
60. 'The Digest of Justinian' Vol. II. Also known as The Pandects. A compendium of the remains of Roman laws gathered by the Emperor Justinian 530-533 AD.
61. Richard Bauman. 'Crime and Punishment in Ancient Rome'
62. Cicero. 'De Natura Deorum' – On the Nature of the Gods.
63. Nick Squires. Report in The Telegraph 17 December 2017 regarding the exile of Ovid finally being revoked.
64. G. Miglio. Amicus (inimicus) hostis: 'Le Radici concettuali della conflittualita "privata" e della conflittualita "politica" in Arcana Imperii.'
65. Philip de Souza. 'Piracy in the Graeco-Roman World'
66. Brian Campbell. 'Marriage of soldiers under the Empire' J.R.S. Volume Number 68. (1978)

Chapter Seven

1. Barry Strauss. 'The Spartacus War'
2. Lawrence Keppie. 'The Making of the Roman Army'
3. Ibid
4. Barry Strauss. 'The Spartacus War'
5. P.A.L. Greenhalgh. 'Pompey, the Roman Alexander'
6. Philip Matyszak. 'Cataclysm 90 BC – the Forgotten War that Almost Destroyed Rome'
7. Philip Matyszak. 'Sertorius and the Struggle for Spain'
8. Cicero. 'On Government'
9. Barry Strauss. 'The Spartacus War'
10. Plutarch. 'Lives – Crassus'
11. Lynda Telford. 'Sulla'
12. Sidonius Apollinaris (Gaius Modestus Apollinaris Sidonius 430-489 AD) in his poem 'Carmina' said that Spartacus used a 'sica', a curved sword, rather than the Roman gladius.
13. Latifundia estates were large tracts of public land, leased by one person and run as a single unit. Usually pastoral, rather than agricultural, they were staffed by slaves who were housed in barracks known as 'ergustula'. Running these vast estates tended to be a senatorial pastime, with the slaves often poorly treated and considered expendable. An area with several of these estates forced small farmers off the land, causing poverty and resentment.
14. Philip Matyszak. 'Cataclysm 90 BC'
15. Barry Strauss. 'The Spartacus War'
16. King Mithradates of Pontus had by this time been fighting Rome, on and off, for around fifteen years.
17. J.L. Brunaux and B. Lambot. 'Guerre et Armament chez les Gaulois – 450-52'. The huge mass grave is at Ribemont-sur-Ancre.

18. Sallust. 'Histories' (fragment)
19. Florus. 'Epitome of Roman History'
20. Sallust. 'Histories' (fragment).
21. Appian. 'The Civil Wars'
22. Cicero. 'On the response of Soothsayers'
23. Appian. 'The Civil Wars'
24. Ibid
25. Ibid
26. Lynda Telford. 'Sulla'
27. Barry Strauss. 'The Spartacus War'
28. The officers of Crassus were Quintus Marcius Rufus, Gaius Pomptinus, Lucius Quinctius, Gnaeus Tremellius Scrofa, and one Mummius, probably of the family of Lucius Mummius Achaicus.
29. Sicily was also Rome's first province. It was vitally important due to its fertility and provided much of Rome's grain, as well as cattle.
30. Cicero hated Verres. He claimed that Verres had left Sicily defenceless while blackmailing the residents with threats of slave revolts. He may not have been quite as bad as Cicero believed, but he did loot public and private works of art and fleece wealthy landowners.
31. Plutarch. 'Crassus'
32. Robert Strassler (editor) 'The Landmark Thucydides – Guide to the Peloponnesian War'
33. Sallust. 'Histories' (fragment)
34. Florus. 'Epitome'
35. Cicero. 'Orations – against Verres'
36. Aspromonte is the modern name, meaning 'harsh' or even white, referring to either bare rock or occasional snow. A very hostile terrain.
37. Appian. 'The civil wars'
38. Barry Strauss. 'The Spartacus War'
39. Ibid
40. Arthur Keaveney. 'Sulla – the last Republican'
41. Sallust. 'Histories'
42. Plutarch. 'Crassus'
43. Ibid
44. Ibid
45. Appian. 'The civil wars'
46. Plutarch. 'Crassus'
47. Paulus Orosius. 'Seven books of Histories against the Pagans'
48. Plutarch. 'Crassus'
49. Ibid
50. Ibid
51. Appian. 'The civil wars'

52. Sallust. 'Histories'
53. Florus. 'Epitome'
54. Ibid
55. Appian. 'The civil wars'
56. Florus. 'Epitome'
57. Appian. 'The civil wars'
58. Plutarch. 'Crassus'
59. The Triumphator, as well as painting his face with minim, carried a sceptre and wore a laurel wreath. He rode in a four-horse chariot with a slave behind him reminding him that he was only a mortal man. An Ovation was a toned-down version of the celebration, with a victory parade, but the general had to walk, or in Crassus's time rode a horse. He did not carry a sceptre and his wreath was made of myrtle, not laurel. Then followed the usual sacrifice and feast.
60. Suetonius. 'Deified Augustus'
61. Sextus Pompeius Magnus Pius (67-35 BC) was made Admiral of the Fleet by the Senate in 43 BC to conduct war against Marc Antony. He was later declared outlaw, seized Sicily and was able to control the grain supply and blockade Italy. In 40 BC he made an alliance with Antony against Octavianus. In 36 BC Agrippa defeated him at Mylae but he beat Octavianus at Tauromenium. He later fled to Asia and was killed there in 35 BC by Titius.
62. Maria Capozza. 'Spartaco e il sacrificio del' cavallo' in Critica Storia II (1963)
63. Florentinus. 'Institutes'. Florentinus lived during the reign of Alexander Severus and wrote twelve books of laws, collected with others into Justinian's Pandectae, or Digest.
64. Cicero. 'Letters to Atticus'
65. Cassius Dio. 'History of Rome'
66. J.E. Packer. 'Housing and population in Imperial Ostia and Rome' J.R.S. (1967)
67. 'Scriptores Historiae Augustae' 3 vols.
68. Balsdon. 'Life and Leisure in Ancient Rome'
69. Ibid
70. Lex Fufia Caninia – 'The Institutes of Gaius'
71. Lex Aelia Sentia – 'The Institutes of Gaius'
72. Petronius. 'Satyricon'
73. The Senatus Consultum Claudianum.
74. 'The Institutes of Gaius'
75. Sarah B. Pomeroy. 'Goddesses, Whores, Wives and Slaves'
76. Ibid
77. J.A. Crook. 'Law and Life in Ancient Rome'
78. Thomas A. McGinn. 'Prostitution, Sexuality and the Law in Ancient Rome'

79. Robert Knapp. 'Invisible Romans'
80. Suetonius. 'Lives of Famous Prostitutes'
81. Suetonius. 'Life of Gaius'
82. Pliny. 'Natural History'
83. Maureen Waller. 'London 1945'
84. Tacitus. 'Annals'
85. Ibid
86. The Julian Marriage Laws – 18 BC.
87. Ibid
88. Lex Julia di Adulteriis of 18 BC.
89. Andrew Borkowski. 'Textbook on Roman Law'
90. Susan Treggiari. 'Roman Marriage – Iusti Coniuges from the Time of Cicero to the Time of Ulpian'
91. Joanne Berry. 'The Complete Pompeii'
92. Robert Knapp. 'Invisible Romans'
93. Suetonius. 'Life of Gaius'
94. C.A. Nelson. 'Receipt for tax on prostitutes', Bulletin of the American Society of Papyrologists. No. 32 (1995)
95. Ulpian. 'On the Edict' from the Digest of Justinian.
96. C.I.L. 9.2029 and I.L.S. 8287 – Benevento.
97. 'The Carmina Priapeia' No. 40.
98. C.I.L. 4.4592
99. C.I.L. 4.8259
100. Ammianus Marcellinus 'The Roman History During the Reign of the Emperors Constantius, Julian, Jovianus, Valentinian and Valens.'
101. Tertullian. 'De Spectaculis' (The Shows)
102. L'Année Epigraphique 1980–2016
103. Plautus. 'The Comedies – The Weevil'
104. Robert Knapp. 'Invisible Romans'
105. Cicero. 'In Defence of Plancius'
106. Ulpian. 'Digest'

Chapter Eight

1. Catherine Edwards. 'Death in Ancient Rome'
2. Marc Hyden. 'Gaius Marius'
3. Karen Cockayne. 'Experiencing old Age in Ancient Rome'
4. Ibid
5. Proverbs. 23.22
6. Tim G. Parkin. 'Old Age in the Roman World'
7. Ulpian. 'Digest'
8. Tim G. Parkin. 'Old age in the Roman World'
9. Pliny 'Natural History'

10. Ibid
11. Cicero. 'Cato Maior de Senectute'
12. Tim. G. Parkin. 'Old Age in the Roman World'
13. Galen. 'On the preservation of health'
14. Seneca the Younger. 'The Epistles'
15. Strabo. 'Geographica'
16. Richard Holland. 'Augustus, Godfather of Europe'
17. Geographical review vol 24. 'Reclamation of the Pontine Marshes'
18. Robert Hughes. 'Rome'
19. Ibid
20. Ibid
21. Galen 'On human nature'
22. Pliny the Younger. 'Letters'
23. To be found at Regio I, Insula 6 and at Regio III, Insula 2, respectively.
24. Martial. 'Epigrams'
25. Ibid
26. Seneca. 'Epistulae Morales'
27. Pliny. 'Natural History'
28. Martial. 'Epigrams'
29. 'The Hippocratic Corpus – Kaplan Classics of Medicine'
30. Ibid
31. Seneca. 'On Benefits' from The Complete Works.
32. Joanne Berry. 'The Complete Pompeii'
33. Ralph Jackson. 'Doctors and Diseases in the Roman Empire'
34. Pliny. 'Natural History'
35. Suetonius. 'Augustus'
36. Pliny. 'Natural History'
37. T.W. Potter. 'A Republican Healing Sanctuary at Ponte di Nona near Rome and the Classical Tradition of Votive Medicine'
38. L.Vagnetti. 'Il deposito votivo de competti a Veio'
39. Ingrid D. Rowland and Thomas Noble Howe (editors) 'M. Vitruvius Pollio – Ten Books on Architecture'
40. Marcus Aurelius. 'Meditations'
41. Ralph Jackson. 'Doctors and Diseases in the Roman Empire'
42. D. Govrevitch.'Suicide among the sick in classical Antiquity.' B.H.M. 43 (1969)
43. Pliny the Younger. 'Letters'
44. Galen. 'On human nature'
45. Livy. 'History of Rome'
46. Seneca. 'Epistles'
47. Ibid
48. Pliny the Younger. 'Letters'

49. Balsdon. 'Life and Leisure in Ancient Rome'
50. Macrobius (Ambrosius Aurelius Theodosius Macrobius. 'Saturnalia'
51. Scriptores Historae Augustae. 'Hadrian'
52. S. Riccobono. 'Fontes Iuris Romani Anteiustiniani'
53. C.I.L. 2891 cf. 3001 – I.L.S. 2034 cf. 2649 and I.L.S. 2653, respectively.
54. I.L.S. 2020 cf. 2923
55. Livy. 'History of Rome'
56. The Plebs wanted political equality with the Patricians and blamed them for abuse of privilege. The Plebs seceded and departed for the Mons Sacer, in one of a number of secessions which were part of a broader 'conflict of the orders' lasting from 495 to 287 BC.
57. Pliny the Younger. 'Letters'
58. C. Wells. 'The Human Burials in Romano-British Cemeteries at Cirencester. (1982)
59. Celsus. 'De re Medica'
60. Ralph Jackson. 'Doctors and Diseases in the Roman Empire'
61. Pliny the Younger. 'Letters'
62. C. Wells. 'Bones, Bodies and Disease'
63. Ralph Jackson. 'Doctors and Diseases in the Roman Empire'
64. Celsus. 'De re medica'
65. Ibid
66. Ralph Jackson. 'Doctors and Diseases in the Roman Empire'
67. Tacitus. 'Annals'
68. The 'Praefectus Fabrum' was an important man in the Roman army. He was a civilian appointed by the general, and his title meant 'he who supervises the making' as he was responsible for equipment and supplies. His authority covered the men, the pack animals, their food and all equipment. He could assign contracts to businessmen and was very powerful and in a position to become wealthy.
69. Joanne Berry. 'The Complete Pompeii'
70. C.I.L. X 998
71. Tomb Number 100, Isola Sacra Necropolis, Ostia.
72. C.I.L. 810 and 811.
73. C.I.L. X 813
74. Joanne Berry. 'The Complete Pompeii'
75. C.I.L. X 1030
76. Suetonius. 'Tiberius'
77. I.L.S. 5065
78. Balsdon. 'Roman Women'
79. Pliny the Younger. 'Natural History'
80. Plutarch. 'Roman Questions'
81. Livy. 'History of Rome'

82. Ibid
83. Balsdon. 'Roman Women'
84. P.E. Corbett. 'The Roman Law of Marriage'
85. Pliny the Younger. 'Letters'
86. Balsdon. 'Roman Women'
87. Andrew Borkowski. 'Textbook on Roman Law'
88. S.C. refers to Senatus Consultum. Under Augustus the Senatus Consulta began to replace the laws (leges) which carried the name of the proposer. Later Senatus Consulta were designated by the name of the Consuls, or that of Caesar.
89. F.Schultz. 'Classical Roman Law'
90. Cassius Dio. 'Roman History – the reign of Augustus'

Bibliography

Primary Sources

AULUS GELLIUS – 'Noctes Atticae' Schoning im Westermann. (1977)

AMMIANUS MARCELLINUS – 'Roman History during the Reigns of the Emperors Constantius, Julian, Jovinus, Valentinian and Valens' Forgotten Books. (2012)

APPIAN – 'The Civil Wars' Penguin Classics. (1996)

AUGUSTINE OF HIPPO – 'Confessions in Thirteen Books' Penguin, (2002)

AUGUSTUS, Emperor – 'Res Gestae Divi Augustae' Editors P.A.Brunt and J.M. Moore. O.U.P. (1969)

CASSIUS DIO – 'History of Rome' 6 vols. Echo Library. (2008)

CARMINA PRIAPEIA – Mitchell S. Buck. (1937)

CELSUS – 'On the True Doctrine' C.U.P. (2008)

CELSUS – 'De re medica' eight books. Filiquarian Legacy Publishing. (2012)

CICERO – 'Selected Letters' Penguin. (1986)

CICERO – 'Orations' Nabu Press. (2010)

CICERO – 'On Divination' O.U.P. (2007)

CICERO – 'On the Commonwealth' C.U.P. (2002)

CICERO – 'On the Nature of the Gods' University of Chicago Press. (2018)

CICERO – 'De finitas et bonorum et malorum' C.U.P. (2010)

C.I.L. – 'Corpus Inscriptionum Latinarum' De Gruyer (1963)

DIONYSIUS OF HALICARNASSUS – 'Roman Antiquities' Gale, Echo Print. (2018)

FLORENTINUS – 'Institutes' (Part of Justinian's Pandectae) O.U.P. (2014)

FLORUS – 'Epitome of Roman History' Create Space Independent Publishing Platform. (2015)

GAIUS – 'The Institutes' Bloomsbury. (1997)

GALEN – 'De anatomicis administrationibus' (On anatomical procedures) O.U.P. (1956)

GALEN – 'De Sanitatis Tuenola' (Hygiene) in 'On the preservation of health' Loeb Classical Library. Harvard University Press. (2017)

GALEN – 'De Temperamentis' (On human nature). C.U.P. (2019)

HIPPOCRATIC CORPUS – Kaplan Classics of Medicine. Kaplan Trade. (2008)

HOMER – 'The Odyssey' Penguin. (2003)
HORACE – 'Odes' Princeton University Press. (2005)
HORACE – 'Satires' Penguin. (2005)
HORACE – 'Epistles' Farrow, Strauss and Giroux. (2002)
I.L.S. – 'Inscriptiones Latinae Selectae' De Gruyer. (1996)
JUSTINIAN – 'Digesta sev Pandectae' University of Pennsylvania Press. (1998)
JUVENAL – 'Satires' C.U.P. (2016)
KAHUN PAPYRUS – (Kahun Gynaecological Papyrus – 1850 BC) Trans. F. Griffith. Petrie Museum of Egyptian Archaeology. University College. London.
LIVY – 'History of Rome' Loeb Classical Library. (1989)
LUCAN – 'On the Civil Wars' Penguin/Random House. (2012)
LUCIEN OF SAMOSATA – 'Amores' Loeb Classical Library. (1967)
LUCIEN OF SAMOSATA – 'Works' Forgotten Books. (2007)
LUCIEN OF SAMOSATA – 'The Parasite' Classic Reprints. Vol 3 of 8.
MACROBIUS – 'Saturnalia' O.U.P. (2011)
MARCUS AURELIUS – 'Meditations – the Golden Book. XII.' J.M. Dent. (1904)
MARTIAL – 'Epigrams' Loeb Classical Library. Harvard University Press. (1919)
MARTIAL – 'Liber di Spectaculis' Trans by Roger Pearse. Ipswich. (2008)
ORATORUM ROMANORUM FRAGMENTA – 'Liberae rei Republica' vol. 2. Edited by Enrica Malcovati. (1955). Reprint University of Michigan. (2008)
OVID – 'Ars Amatoria' O.U.P. (1989)
OVID – 'Fasti' Penguin Classics. (2000)
OVID – 'Tristia' Penguin Classics. (1998)
PLATO – 'The Republic' Penguin Classics. (2007)
PAULUS OROSIUS – 'Seven Books of History against the Pagans' Liverpool University Press. (2010)
PATRONIUS – 'Satyricon' Penguin Classics. (2011)
PLAUTIUS – 'The Comedies' Palala Press. (2015)
PLINY THE ELDER – 'Natural History' Penguin Classics. (1991)
PLINY THE YOUNGER – 'Epistulae' Penguin Classics. (2003)
PLUTARCH – 'Lives' J.J. Chidley. (1843)
PLUTARCH – 'Roman Questions' Loeb Classical Library. (1938)
PLUTARCH – 'Moralia' Harvard University Press. (1936)
PLUTARCH – 'De Fraterno Amore' Loeb Classical Library. (1939)
PLUTARCH – 'De Amore Prolis' Loeb Classical Library. (1971)
PLUTARCH – 'On Isis and Osiris' Create Space Independent Publishing Platform. (2014)
PROCOPIUS OF CAESAREA – 'The Secret History' University of Chicago Press. (1935)
PROPERTIUS – 'The Love Elegies' Liber Publications. (2001)
RUFUS GAIUS MUSONIUS – 'Reliquae' Kessinger Legacy Reprints. (2010)
RUFUS GAIUS MUSONIUS – 'Lectures and Fragments' Create Space Independent Publishing Platform. (2015)
SALLUST – 'The war with Jugurtha and the Conspiracy of Catiline' Penguin. (2002)
SALLUST – 'Histories –fragment in 'Histories and Trimviral Historiography' Routledge. (2019)
SCRIPTORES HISTORIAE AUGUSTAE – Loeb Classical Library. (1989)

SENECA THE YOUNGER – 'Epistulae Morales ad Lucilium' Penguin Classics. (2004)
SENECA THE YOUNGER – 'De Brevitate Vitae' C.U.P. (2008)
SENECA THE YOUNGER – 'The Complete Works' Chicago University Press. (2010)
SIDONIUS APPOLINARIS – 'Poems and Letters' Harvard University Press. (1936)
SORANUS OF EPHESUS – 'Gynaecology' John Hopkins University Press. (1991)
STRABO – 'Geographica' Marix Verlag. (2005)
SUETONIUS – 'The Twelve Caesars' Penguin Classics. (1957)
TACITUS – 'The Annals of Imperial Rome' Penguin Classics. (1989)
TERTULLIAN – 'Apologeticus' Forgotten Books. (2019)
TERTULLIAN – 'De Anima' Brill Publishing. (2010)
TERTULLIAN – 'De Spectaculis' Kessinger Publishing. (2004)
VALERIUS MAXIMUS – 'Memorable Deeds and Sayings' Clarendon Press. (1998)
VITRUVIUS – 'Ten Books on Architecture' C.U.P. (2001)

Secondary Sources

ALBERTO – Angela. 'A day in the life of Ancient Rome' Europa Editions. (2009)
ADCOCK – Sir Frank Ezra. 'Marcus Crassus – Millionaire' Cambridge. (1966)
BALSDON – J.P.V.D. 'Roman Women' Bodley Head. (1962)
BALSDON – J.P.V.D. 'Life and Leisure in Ancient Rome' Phoenix. (2002)
BEARD – Mary. 'Pompeii' Profile Books. (2009)
BEARD – Mary. 'S.P.Q.R.' Profile Books. (2016)
BEDOYERE – Guy de la. 'Gods with Thunderbolts' Tempus. (2002)
BEDOYERE – Guy de la. 'Domina, the women who made Imperial Rome' Yale University Press. (2018)
BEESLEY – A.H. 'The Gracchi, Marius and Sulla' Aeterna Publishing. (2010)
BERRY – Joanne. 'The Complete Pompeii' Thames and Hudson. (2013)
BOARDMAN – John. 'The Roman World' O.U.P. (1998)
BOATWRIGHT – Mary T. 'The Romans from Village to Empire' O.U.P. (2004)
BORKOWSKI – Andrew. 'Textbook on Roman Law' O.U.P. (1997)
BRUNS – G.G. 'Fontes Iuris Romani Antiqui' Tubingen. (1909)
BRUNT – P.A. 'Social conflicts in the Roman Republic' Norton. New York. (1971)
CAMPBELL – Brian. 'Marriage of Soldiers under the Empire' J.R.S. Vol. 68 (1978)
CARTWRIGHT – Mark. 'Wine in the Ancient Mediterranean' Ancient History Encyclopaedia. (2016)
CAPOZZA – Maria. 'Spartaco e il sacrificio del cavallo' Critica Storica II. (1963)
CARCOPINO – Jerome. 'Daily Life in Ancient Rome' Yale University Press. (1968)
CARY – M and SCULLARD H.H. 'A History of Rome' Palgrave. (1975)
CAVEN – Brian. 'The Punic Wars' Weidenfeld and Nicolson. (1980)
COCKAYNE – Karen. 'Experiencing old Age in Ancient Rome' Routledge. (2011)
COLLINS – J.H. 'Tullia's Engagement and Marriage to Dolabella' Classical Journal. (1952)

CORBETT – P.E. 'The Roman Law of Marriage' Oxford. (1930)
COWAN – Ross H. 'Roman conquests – Italy' Pen and Sword. (2009)
CRAWFORD – Michael. 'The Roman Republic' Fontana. (1992)
CROOK – J.A. 'Law and life in Ancient Rome. (90 BC–212 AD) Cornell University Press. (1967)
DAL MASO – Leonardo B. 'Rome of the Caesars' Italia Artistica. (1979)
DONATI – Angela. 'Sull' inscrizione Lanuvina della Curia Mulierum' in Revista Storica dell' Antichita. (1971)
DOBSON – J. and P. Foss. 'The World of Pompeii' Routledge. (2007)
DUDLEY – Donald. 'Roman Society' Penguin. (1970)
DUPONT – Florence. 'Daily life in Ancient Rome' Blackwells. (1994)
EDWARDS – Katherine. 'Death in Ancient Rome' Yale University Press. (2007)
EYBEN – E. 'Roman notes on the course of Life' Ancient History Society No 4. (1973)
FRANZERO – Carlo Maria. 'The Life and Times of Theodora' Alvin Redman. (1961)
FINLEY – M.I. 'The Elderly in Classical Antiquity' C.U.P. (1981)
FOWLER – W. Warde. 'Social Life at Rome in the time of Cicero' London. (1908)
FRIEDLANDER – L. 'Roman Life and Manners under the Early Empire' Gough. (1913)
FRISCH – Hartvig. 'Cicero's Last Fight for the Republic' Glydendal, Copenhagen. (1946)
FROST – Ruth Sterling. 'The Reclamation of the Pontine Marshes' Geographical Review. Vol. 24 (1934)
GABBA – E. 'Republican Rome, the Army and the Allies' Oxford. (1976)
GARDNER – Jane F. 'Women in Roman Law and Society' Indiana University Press. (1991)
GARDNER – Jane F. and Thomas Wiedemann. 'The Roman Household – a Sourcebook' Routledge. (1991)
GOODENOUGH – Simon. 'Citizens of Rome' Hamlyn. (1979)
GOUREVITCH – D. 'Suicide among the Sick in Classical Antiquity' History of Medicine. No.43. (1969)
GRANT – Michael. 'History of Rome' Weidenfeld and Nicolson. (1978)
GREENHALGH – P.A.L. 'Pompey, the Roman Alexander' Weidenfeld and Nicolson. (1980)
GREGORY - T.E. 'A History of Byzantium' Wiley-Blackwell. (2010)
GRIMAL – Pierre. 'The Civilisation of Rome' Allen and Unwin. (1960)
GRUEN – E.S. 'Roman Politics and the Criminal Courts 149-78 BC' Harvard. (1968)
GRUEN – E.S. 'The Last Generation of the Roman Republic' University of California Press. (1974)
HAVELL – H.L. 'Republican Rome' Oracle. (1996)
HAZEL – John. 'Who's Who in the Roman World' Routledge. (2001)
HOLLAND – Richard. 'Augustus, Godfather of Europe' Sutton. (2004)
HUGHES – Robert. 'Rome' Weidenfeld and Nicolson. (2011)
HOPE – Valerie M. 'Roman death – the Dying and the Dead in Ancient Rome' Hambledon Continuum. (2009)
HUTCHINSON – G.O. 'Cicero's Correspondence – a Literary Study' Clarendon. (1998)

HYDEN – Mark. 'Gaius Marius' Pen and Sword. (2017)
JACKSON – Ralph. 'Doctors and Diseases in the Roman Empire' British Museum Publications. (1988)
JACOBELLI – L. 'Gladiators at Pompeii' J. Paul Getty Museum. (2003)
JACOBS – Paul W. and Diane Atnally Conlin. 'Campus Martius – the Field of Mars in the Life of Ancient Rome' C.U.P. (2014)
KEAVENEY – Arthur. 'Sulla, the last Republican' Routledge. (1982)
KEPPIE – Lawrence. 'The Making of the Roman Army, from Republic to Empire' Batsford. (1984)
KNAPP – Robert. 'Invisible Romans' Profile. (2013)
LACEY – W.K. 'Cicero and the End of the Roman Republic' Hodder and Stoughton. (1978)
LOMAS – Kathryn. 'Roman Italy, 338 BC-200 AD' U.C.L. Press. (1996)
MACQUITTY – William. 'Island of Isis' MacDonald. (1976)
MALCOVATI – Enrica. 'Oratorum Romanorum Fragmenta Liberae rei Republica' University of Michigan (2008)
MASSON – Georgina. 'Concise History of Republican Rome' Thames and Hudson. (1973)
MATYSZAK – Philip. 'Sertoriuis and the Struggle for Spain' Pen and Sword. (2013)
MATYSZAK – Philip. 'Cataclysm 90 BC – the Forgotten War that almost Destroyed Rome' Pen and Sword. (2014)
MCGINN – Thomas A. 'Prostitution, Sexuality and the Law in Ancient Rome' O.U.P. (1998)
MEIJER – Fik. 'The Gladiators – History's most Deadly Sport' Souvenir Press. (2004)
MIGLIO – G. 'Amicus (inimicus) hostis: La radici concettuali della conflittualita 'privata' e della conflittualita 'politica' (Arcana Imperii)' Giuffre. (1992)
MOATTI – Claude. 'The Search for Ancient Rome' Thames and Hudson. (2001)
MOMIGLIANO – A. 'Journal of Roman Studies' No. 112. (1957)
OGILVIE – R.M. 'The Romans and their Gods' Pimlico. (2000)
PACKER – J.E. 'Housing and Population in Imperial Ostia and Rome' J.R.S. (1967)
PARKIN – Tim. 'Old Age in the Roman World' John Hopkins University Press. (2003)
POMEROY – Sarah B. 'Goddesses, Whores, Wives and Slaves' Pimlico. (1994)
POTTER – David. 'Emperors of Rome' Quercus. (2008)
POTTER – T.W. 'A Republican Healing Sanctuary at Ponte di Nona near Rome and the Classical Tradition of Votive Medicine' Journal of British Archaeological Association. No.138. (1985)
POTTER – T.W. 'Roman Italy' Guild Publishing. (1987)
POWELL – J.G.F. 'Cicero, Cato Marior de Senectute' C.U.P. (1998)
RANCE – Caroline. 'The History of Medicine in 100 Facts' Amberley. (2015)
RICHARDSON – Keith. 'Daggers in the Forum' Cassell. (1976)
RODGERS – Nigel. 'The History and Conquests of Ancient Rome' Anness. (2003)
ROLLER – Lynn E. 'In search of God the Mother – the Cult of the Anatolian Cybele' University of California Press. (1999)
ROTONDI – G. 'Leges Publicae Populi Romani' American Philosophical Society. (1968)

ROWLANDSON – Jane. (Ed.) 'Women and Society in Greek and Roman Egypt' C.U.P. (1998)
SANDERS – H.A. 'A Latin Marriage Contract' Transactions of the American Philological Association. (1938)
SCHIFF – Stacy. 'Cleopatra – a Life' Little, Brown. (2010)
SCHULTZ – F. 'Classical Roman Law' Clarendon Press. (1951)
SCULLARD – H.H. 'Roman Politics' Oxford. (1951)
SCULLARD – H.H. 'From the Gracchi to Nero' Routledge. (1982)
SHERWIN-WHITE – A.N. 'The Lex Repetundarum and its Consequences' J.R.S. (1972)
SHORTER – Edward. 'A History of Women's Bodies' Penguin. (1984)
SNYDER – W.F. 'Journal of Roman Studies' No. 17. (1936)
SOUZA – Philip de. 'Piracy in the Graeco-Roman World' C.U.P. (2002)
SOPRINTENDENZA. 'Archaeologica di Roma, The Palatine' Electra. (1998)
STRASSLER – Robert. 'The Landmark Thucydides – The Comprehensive Guide to the Peloponnesian War' Simon and Schuster. (1998)
STRAUSS – Barry. 'The Spartacus War' Phoenix. (2010)
STOCKTON – David L. 'The Gracchi' O.U.P. (1971)
SQUIRES – Nick. Article in The Daily Telegraph, 17 December 2017, revocation of the exile of Ovid.
TATUM – W. Jeffrey. 'The Patrician Tribune, Publius Clodius Pulcher' University of North Carolina Press. (2010)
TAYLOR – L.R. American Journal of Philology (1942)
TELFORD – Lynda. 'Sulla, a Dictator Reconsidered' Pen and Sword. (2014)
TEMPEST – Kathryn. 'Cicero, Politics and Persuasion in Ancient Rome' Continuum. (2007)
TOMALIN – Claire. 'The Invisible Woman, the Story of Nelly Ternan and Charles Dickens' Viking. (1990)
TOTELIN – Laurence. 'The Story of Medicine' History Magazine, Collectors Edition. (2018)
TOYNBEE – Jocelyn. 'Death and Burial in the Roman World' John Hopkins University Press. (1996)
TREGGIARI – Susan. 'Roman Marriage, Iusti Coniuges from the Time of Cicero to the Time of Ulpian' O.U.P. (1993)
VAGNETTI – L. 'Il deposito votivo de Campetti a Veio' Rome. (1971)
WALLER – Maureen. 'London 1945' John Murray. (2020)
WATKIN – David. 'The Roman Forum' Profile (2011)
WATSON – A. 'The Law of Persons in the Later Roman Republic' Oxford. (1967)
WEINSTOCK – J.R.S. No. 36 (1946)
WELLS – C. 'The human burials' in 'Romano-British Cemeteries at Cirencester' (1982)
WILDFANG – Robin Lorsch. 'Rome's Vestal Virgins' Routledge. (2006)
WISEMAN – T.P. (Ed.) 'Roman Political Life, 90 BC-69 AD' University of Exeter. (1985)
WILSON – L.M. 'The Clothing of the Ancient Romans' Baltimore. (1938)
WOOLF – Greg. 'Rome – An Empire's Story' O.U.P. (2013)

Index

abortion 86–7, 101
Acca Laurentia 7
actors (histriones) 84, 175–85, 241, 248
adoption and fostering 87–8
adultery 12, 15, 41, 43, 65, 73, 75, 96, 98, 100, 108, 209, 235, 239–41
Aemilia Paulla 19
Aemilia Scaura 44, 74
Aesquillia Polla 274
Aetius 86
Agrippa, Marcus 66
Agrippina 170, 180–1
Agrippinus, Gaius Fabius 167
Alba 12, 13
Alba Longa, King of 7
Amulius 7
ancestor masks (imagines) 64, 146, 273–4, 276
Antistia (wife of Gnaeus Pompeius Magnus) 44
Antoninus, Aurelius 88
Antonius, Marcus 42, 45, 62, 74, 76, 89, 96, 97, 128, 183, 209, 266
Aquilia Severa 122
Area Sacra 107–8
army 147–9, 213–30, 249, 268–9
Aufidia (wife of Marcus Livius Drusus Claudianus) 62
Augustus, Emperor (Gaius Octavius also Octavianus) 9, 16, 37, 45, 52, 62–63, 66, 74, 77, 83, 94, 95, 100, 128, 139, 148, 166, 179, 183, 208, 209, 210, 230 232, 234, 240, 242, 247, 250, 255, 275, 278, 282
Aulus Gellius 90
Aurelia Cotta (mother of Gaius Julius Caesar) 125–7
Aurelius, Emperor Marcus 50, 76, 142, 265
Aventine Hill 33, 34, 124, 140

Balearic Islands 41
Basilica of St Peter 9
bathing 59–61, 123, 139, 172, 207, 244–5, 255, 258, 263, 264, 266, 268
Biria Onomastia 134
Boni, Giacomo 8
Book of Colonies 30
Bottini, Professor Angelo 231
breast-feeding 93, 102
Brennus the Gaul 15
brothels 87, 237–9, 243–5, 247–8
Brutus, Lucius Junius 12
Brutus, Marcus Junius 156

Caelia Macrina 167
caesarean section 96
calendar 51, 53, 58, 132, 138–42
Caligula, Emperor Gaius 177–8
Calpurnia 45, 239
Calpurnius Bibulus, Marcus 132–3
Calpurnius Piso, Lucius 45, 88

Campo di Fiori 50
Campus Martius 28, 107
Cannae 15, 31, 119
Capitoline Hill (Asylum Hill) 8, 11, 12, 23–4, 33, 89, 106–8, 112, 132, 203
Capitoline Museum 50, 103, 108
Caracalla, Emperor 122
Carthage 19, 30, 31, 32, 158
Catalina 120
Cato Uticenses, Marcus Porcius 17
Cato, Marcus Porcius 'the Elder' 17–18
Cato, Marcus Porcius 'the Younger' 38, 66–7, 68, 76, 84–5, 250
Cato, Marcus Porcius the Censor 66, 73
Catulus, Quintus 94
Celsus 256, 259, 266, 273
Celts 213–26
Centrale Montemartini Museum 107
Charon 194
childbirth 90–3, 101–3
children 13, 42, 45, 58, 61, 71, 74–7, 80, 82–90, 94–8, 100, 103–4, 122, 131, 148, 151, 157, 163, 166–7, 171, 172, 174, 177, 197–8, 211, 218, 220, 229, 231, 233, 235–8, 242, 245, 270, 281, 282
Christianity 106, 109, 110, 129, 160, 174, 192, 193, 207, 263, 281
Cicero, Marcus Tullius 18, 25, 29, 35, 38, 53, 56–8, 66, 81–2, 98–100, 120, 126–8, 134, 135, 140, 145, 155, 169, 183, 204, 206, 207, 214, 220–3, 231, 232–3, 248, 253, 255, 267, 279
Cicero, Quintus 58, 134, 233
Cilicia 53
Circus Maximus 11, 111, 137, 139, 141, 191
Claudia 19
Claudia (wife of Tiberius Sempronius Gracchus) 24–5
Claudia Quinta 16
Claudius Glaber, Gaius 217
Claudius Pulcher, Appius 18, 22
Claudius, Appius 14, 134
Claudius, Emperor 76, 77, 173, 177–9, 209
Claudius, Marcus 14
Cleopatra VII, Queen of Egypt 10, 45, 74, 76, 96, 97, 128, 239, 266
Cloaca Maxima 11, 256
Clodius Pulcher, Publius 18, 41–2, 89, 125–8, 135, 164–5, 280
clothing 46–8, 62, 70, 80, 83, 91, 116, 117, 119–20, 157, 158, 180, 194, 198–9, 216, 244, 246–7, 279
Colline Gate, Battle of the 44, 57, 221, 225
Colosseum 111, 190–1, 194, 196
Constantine, Emperor 196
Consualia 12
contraception 86, 101
Cornelia Scipionis Africana 'Mother of the Gracchi' 19–21, 24–6, 28, 32–3, 35–7, 43, 75, 88, 279
Crassus, Lucius Licinius 34
Crassus, Marcus Licinius 'Dives' 81, 90, 120, 156, 210, 213, 221–30, 249
Crassus, Publius Licinius 25, 221, 277
criminal system 14–15, 35, 67–8, 86, 100, 119–20, 125–8, 150, 187, 191, 192, 197, 202–210, 214, 229
Crispinius Hilarius, Gaius 89
Crixtus 218–21, 222
Cumae 15, 133
Curiatii 12–13
cursus honorum 88, 149
Cybele cult 18

Dalmatia 41
Daphnis, Lutatius 94
De Materia Medica 262
death 14, 26, 42, 75, 89, 91, 108, 118, 128, 130, 140, 162, 164, 197, 200, 215, 226–30, 232, 234, 249–51, 265, 266, 270, 272–80
death penalty 73, 76, 113, 119, 121, 122, 171, 197, 199–200, 203, 205–7, 229–30, 241

decimation 222
Dictator 11, 35, 38, 53, 67–8, 118, 133, 165
disease 69, 136, 231, 248, 251, 255–73
divination 131–5
divorce (diffareatio) 12, 16, 43, 44, 45, 64, 72–5, 82–5, 89, 95–6, 100, 103, 167, 239, 240, 242
doctors 68–9, 91–2, 102, 159, 187, 248, 255, 259–62, 265–6, 272
Dolabella, Publius Cornelius 81, 99, 120
Domitian, Emperor 86, 198
Domus Aurea 181
Domus Vestae 111
dowry 22, 43, 44, 75, 77, 81–2, 88, 98, 100, 115, 120, 155, 156–7, 241
Drusus Claudianus, Marcus Livius 62
Drusus, Gaius Livius 31
Drusus, Marcus Livius 31
Drusus, Nero Claudius 63, 64

education 9, 18, 19, 35, 36, 43, 56, 57, 61, 82, 85, 94–5, 165–6, 183, 231, 233–4, 236, 262, 267, 281
Egypt 10, 20, 58, 74, 76, 80, 102, 103, 109, 112, 128–31, 133, 151, 157, 158, 159, 160, 243, 245, 273
Elegabalus, Emperor 122
Equites (knights) 26–7, 29, 37, 40
Equitius, Lucius 37
Eumachia, daughter of Lucius 275
Eurapius 101
exile 28, 128, 135, 175, 183, 186, 204, 207–9, 210, 211, 232
exposure (infanticide) 13, 87, 131, 174, 237, 248

Fabia 120
Fabrateria Nova 27
Fannius, Gaius 30
Faustina the Younger 76
Faustulus 7
festivals 50, 53, 56–8, 61, 78, 115, 116, 117, 123, 125–7, 129, 136, 138–42, 159, 180–1, 243
Field of Mars 10
Flaccus, Fulvius 27, 28, 30–2, 33–4
Flaccus, Verrius 9
Flamines 72, 112–3, 123
Flaminia 123
Fonteius, Publius 127
Fortini, Dr Patrizia 7, 9
Frazer, Sir James 17
Fregellae 27
Fulvia (wife of Marcus Antonius) 18, 89, 96, 97, 279–80
funerals 35, 46, 64, 138–9, 160, 188, 190, 201, 203, 220, 227, 229, 269, 273–8
furnishings 63–4

Galba 88
Galenus, Claudius (Galen) 69, 91, 92, 255, 259, 262, 265, 266, 271
games (ludi) 16, 46, 56–8, 119, 127, 138–41, 160, 174, 180, 185–202, 220, 227, 275, 276–7
Gellius, Lucius 219–20
gens 13, 40–2, 146
Glabrio, Manius Acilius 44
gladiators 32, 79, 127, 138, 140, 185–202, 207, 212–13, 214–17, 220, 229, 230, 276–7
  female (ludia) 191, 197–9, 202, 211
gods and goddesses 7, 32, 35, 52, 55, 57, 78–9, 195, 105–9, 111–114, 128–31, 133, 135–42, 173–4, 183, 225, 261, 262, 276–7, 282
  Aesculapius 262–4
  Bona Dea 123–6, 131
  Castor and Pollux 110
  Fortuna 8, 61, 107–8, 111, 133, 139, 140, 157, 175–6
  Isis 109, 112, 128–31, 189
  Janus 109, 110
  Juno 107, 108, 123, 136, 141, 202
  Jupiter 8–12 24, 52, 54, 56, 107, 110, 112, 132, 136, 141–2, 181, 202

Magna Mater 16, 111, 112, 131, 139
Mars 7, 52, 54, 57, 78, 109, 114, 117–18, 123, 136, 139, 192
Mater Matuta 111
Minerva 58, 129, 140, 141, 256
Ops 8, 106–7, 114
Priapus 245
Serapis 129
Venus 7, 15, 52, 54, 108, 110, 111, 130, 186, 192, 246, 277
Vesta 44, 78, 107, 110–11, 113–14, 120, 122
Gracchus, Gaius Sempronius 19, 24, 25, 26–35, 37, 96, 144, 169
Gracchus, Tiberius Sempronius 19, 75
Gracchus, Tiberius Sempronius (son of Cornelia) 19, 21–26, 28, 31, 37–8

Hadrian, Emperor 59–60, 77, 88, 95, 129, 154, 235
hair 15, 41, 48–9, 50, 79, 91, 123, 159, 181, 258
Hannibal 15, 16, 20, 30, 190, 212
Herculaneum 51, 172
homosexuality 83, 84, 238
Horatii 12–13
Hortensius, Quintus 45, 67, 84–5
Hunter-Mann, Kurt 195

illegitimacy 37–8, 76, 87, 94, 167, 236, 269
incest 18, 76, 121, 125, 207, 241
infant mortality 90, 251
inheritance 22, 64, 75, 77, 89, 96–7, 114, 203, 206, 231, 242, 275, 278–81

jewellery 15, 46, 47, 48, 64, 70, 80, 104, 151–2, 159, 172, 178, 190–1, 217
Julia (daughter of Titus) 86
Julia Augusta see Livia Drusilla
Julia Caesaris (wife of Gaius Marius) 45, 89–90, 150–1, 156–7, 276–7
Julia Domna 110, 196
Julia Felix 43
Julia Pacata 97
Julia the Elder (daughter of Augustus) 63, 66, 100, 240
Julius Caesar, Gaius 7, 13, 16, 35, 38, 40–2, 45, 52, 53, 57, 60, 65–8, 74, 76, 81, 89–90, 94, 96, 102, 108, 113, 117, 125, 132–4, 138, 151, 156–7, 165, 185, 191, 192, 209, 214, 239, 249, 250, 256, 274, 276–7
Julius Classicianus 97
Junia Torquata 115
Junius Silanu, Lucius 77
jus liberorum 72
Justinian 184–5, 237, 240, 281
Juvenal 86, 137, 141, 172, 198–9, 211, 234, 257, 258, 269

Laelius 21
Laetorius 34
Lapis Niger 8, 9
Lares 81, 105–6, 107, 108, 111, 114, 139
latifundia 20–1
Lemuria 55
Lentulus Clodianus, Gnaeus Cornelius 42, 219–21
Lepidus, Marcus Aemilius 62, 201, 209
Lex Julia de Adulteriis Coercendis 100, 240–2
Lex Julia de Maritandis Ordinibus 96, 100
Lex Voconia de Mulierum Hereditatibus 279–80
Licinia (wife of Gaius Gracchus) 33, 34
lictor 118, 219, 227
Livia Drusilla (Julia Augusta) 16, 62–3, 66, 74, 251
Livius Andronicus 183
Livy 15–17, 66, 119, 133, 183, 206, 266, 270, 277
Lucian 58, 133
Lucretius 86
Lucrezia (wife of Collatinus) 14
Lucullus, Marcus Terentius Varro 225, 227

Maelius, Spurius 144–5
make up 49–50, 258–9
manumission 171, 231–7
Marcellus Minor, Gaius Claudius 74
Marcia (wife of Cato the Younger) 45, 67, 84–5
Marcius, Ancus 11
Marius, Gaius 16, 37, 100, 113, 132–3, 147–8, 149–50, 215, 221, 250, 251
marriage 12–16, 30, 43, 46, 55, 61, 66, 68, 71–89, 95–8, 100–3, 105, 112, 120, 149, 155, 157–9, 167, 203, 215, 236–7, 239–40, 254, 269, 278–81
  coemptio 71
  confarreation 12, 72, 79, 96, 112–13, 123
  manus 73, 280–1
  usus 71–2
Martial 69, 101, 162, 170, 192, 193, 258, 259, 260
Materfamilias 96
Maximus Scaevola 34
Medicae 68–9, 91, 101
Megalensia 16, 18
Messalina 76, 178–9, 239
Metella Dalmatica, Caecilia 13, 41, 44–6
Metellus Dalmaticus, Lucius 13, 41
Metellus Macedonius, Quintus 89
Metrobius 84, 177
Micipsa 27
midwives 68–9, 90–1, 101, 102, 131, 158, 249, 274
Milo, Titus Annius 127–8
miscarriage 87, 89–90, 103
Misenum 32, 33, 35, 36, 209
mistresses 45, 65, 72, 83–6, 151, 178, 235, 237, 239, 278
Mithradates 213, 217, 222, 251
Mnester 177–9
Montgomery, Dr Janet 195
mos maiorum 10, 35, 84, 143
Mundus 55, 78, 277–8
Mussolini 8, 107, 190

Naevoleia Tyche 275
naming conventions 13, 40–3, 62, 79, 93, 171, 234
Nero, Emperor (born Domitius Ahenobarbus) 180–2, 186, 198, 205, 207, 209, 243, 269
Nero, Tiberius Claudius 62, 74, 99
Nuceria 186–7

Octavia (daughter of Emperor Claudius) 77
Octavia the Younger 45, 74, 96
Octavianus see Augustus
Octavius, Marcus 22–3, 28, 31
old age 236, 249–5, 266–8
Opimius, Lucius 31–5
Ostia 11, 61, 91, 101, 153–4, 167, 199, 209–10, 231, 274–5
Ovid 48–9, 65, 116, 136, 208–9

Palatine Hill 8, 55, 111, 114, 139, 211, 233
Pantheon 106, 117, 129, 130
Papira (wife of Aemillius Paullus) 98
Papirius Carbo, Gaius 25
Parentalia 55, 78, 139, 277–8
parricide 205–6
Paterfamilias 13, 25, 42–5, 61, 63, 73, 87, 96, 114, 206, 241, 253, 270, 278, 280
patronage 87, 168–71, 236
Paullus, Lucius Aemilius (father of Publius Cornelius Scipio) 36, 88, 98
Paullus, Lucius Aemilius 31
Pergamum 23, 260
Pessinus 16
Philocrates 34
piracy 209–10, 213, 217, 222–3, 230
Pius Balearicus, Quintus Caecilius Metellus 41
Pius Scipio Nasica, Quintus Caecilius Metellus 41
Pius VI, Pope 190
Pius, Emperor Antoninus 154, 167
Plato 90, 221
Plautus 82

Pliny the Elder 61, 64, 87, 89, 142, 160, 167, 231, 254, 262, 267–8, 271
Pliny the Younger 60, 86, 90, 97, 122, 232, 257, 261, 264, 265, 267–8, 270, 273, 279
Plutarch 25, 26, 33–4, 97, 98, 121, 226–8
poisoning 14–15, 26, 102, 180, 248, 257, 259, 261
political system 9, 18–20, 25, 26–7, 40, 143–7, 149–50
Pompeia (daughter of Gnaeus Pompeius Magnus) 45
Pompeia Sulla (wife of Gaius Julius Casesar) 125
Pompeii 43, 50, 51, 54, 59, 60, 61, 103, 106, 124, 130–1, 134, 151, 152, 155, 159, 162, 165–6, 169, 173, 185–7, 188, 190, 191, 193, 216, 218, 232, 242, 245–6, 247, 254, 258, 261–2, 274–5
Pompeius Magnus, Gnaeus 38, 40–1, 44–5, 66, 74, 81, 89–90, 107, 108, 127, 133–4, 156–7, 210, 213–14, 225–30, 250
Pompeius Strabo, Gnaeus 40
Pompeius, Sextus 38, 63, 209, 230
Pompilius, Numa 11
Pomponius 34
Poppaea Sabina 178–9
poverty 26–8, 32, 59–60, 63, 87, 90, 130, 143, 144, 146–8, 152–5, 158–68, 171–4, 184, 194, 204, 206, 231, 238, 253–5, 264–5, 272, 274
Priscianus, Imperial Physician Theodorus 69
prostitution 7, 48, 86, 87, 108, 148, 158, 160, 176, 184–5, 237–9, 242–8
Ptolemy VIII, King of Egypt 20
Publilia (wife of Cicero) 100
puellae Faustinianae 167
Punic War, Second 15, 19, 41, 53, 66
Punic Wars 19, 20, 29
Quintilian 94
Quintus (son of Fulvius Flaccus) 34

Rape of the Sabine Women 10, 12, 80, 202
Remus 7–8, 11, 131
retirement 266–70
Romulus 7–8, 9, 11, 12, 131, 202
Rostra 9, 221, 274

sacrifice 8, 32–3, 50, 61, 78, 79, 81, 89, 111–13, 116, 117, 119, 131, 133–41, 181, 220, 225–6, 246, 263, 273, 274, 277
Saintes, Aquitaine (Mediolanum Santonum) 197
Salassi 18
Sardinia 20, 44
Satureius 24
Scaurus, Marcus Aemilius 13, 44
Scipio Africanus, Publius Cornelius 19, 24, 36, 37, 41, 75, 81, 279
Scipio Barbatus, Lucius Cornelius 190
Scipio Nasica, Publius Cornelius 22, 24–6, 41
Scipio, Publius Cornelius 'Aemilianus Africanus' 25–6, 31, 36, 37, 89
Scribonia (wife of Octavianus/ Augustus) 63, 74
Scribonia Attica Obstetrix 91, 101
Scribonia Callityche 101
Scrofa, Gnaeus Tremelius 224, 227
Sempronia (daughter of Cornelia) 19, 24–5, 26, 36–8, 89, 279
Sempronian Hall 33, 36
Sempronius, Publius 277
Seneca 142, 170, 193, 199, 209, 255, 258, 261
Septimius Severus, Emperor 86, 110, 196, 199, 211, 237, 268
Septimuleius 34
Sertorius, Quintus 213–14, 219, 222, 225
Servile War, Third 212–30
Servile Wars 212–13

Servilia Caepionis (mistress of Gaius Julius Caesar) 45, 74, 151, 156
Servilius Caepio 45, 208
Severus Pertinax, Lucius Septimius 196, 199
sewers 11, 207, 255, 256–7, 258
Sibyl 12, 15–16
Sicily 20, 63, 209, 212, 222–3, 230
Silius, Gaius 179
slavery 11, 14, 19, 20, 22, 26, 40, 51, 59, 60, 63, 68, 76, 87, 90, 94, 101, 121, 124, 128, 132, 140, 141, 148, 152, 155, 159, 160–1, 163, 165, 171, 178, 180, 183, 191, 197–200, 203–7, 211, 212, 214–30, 231–7
Social War 18, 40, 213, 216, 251
Soranus of Ephesus 69, 90, 91–3, 101–2
Soranus, Barea 171
Spain 22, 25, 30, 36, 152, 172, 195, 213–14, 219, 221, 225, 251, 269
Spartacus 198, 212–30, 249
Suetonius 142, 177–8, 181, 197, 238, 239, 243
Sulla, Faustus 45
Sulla, Lucius Cornelius 8, 9, 10, 13, 27, 37, 41, 44–6, 57, 68, 74, 84, 108, 111, 133, 149–50, 156, 176–7, 185, 209, 213, 215, 221, 225

Tarentia (wife of Cicero) 98–9, 120, 126
Tarpeia 202–3
Tarpeius, Spurius 202
Tarquinia 11
Tarquinius Priscus, Lucius 11
Tarquinius, Sextus 13–14
Tarquinius, Lucius Collatinus 13–14
Tarquinius, Lucius Superbus 12, 13, 14, 15–16
Telethusa 245
temples 8, 47, 56, 65, 106–12, 129–30, 135–7, 142, 246
  Aesculapius 262–3
  Bellona 109–10
  Bona Dea 124
  Castor 33, 34
  Diana 34
  Fides 24, 107
  Fortuna Primigenia 133
  Honus et Virtus 8, 107
  Isis 129–30, 189
  Jupiter Optimus Maximus 8, 9, 11, 12, 24, 107, 110, 141, 142
  Lares Prestites 114
  Magna Mater 16
  Minerva 129, 140, 256
  Pietas 254
  Portunus 141
  Venus 130, 246
  Victory 16, 50
Tertullian 194, 246
Tertullianum 281
Thapsus, Battle of 38
theatre 108, 119, 149, 154, 175–86, 245–6, 248
Theodora 184–5
Tiber 7, 11, 24, 34–5, 116, 120, 231, 256
Tiberius, Emperor 62, 275, 276
time 51–58, 77–9, 132, 138
Tiridates, King of Parthia 198
Tiro 231–2
Titinius, Gaius 100
travel 57, 65, 118
tribes 13, 23, 146–7, 183
Tullia (daughter of Cicero) 81, 98–100, 120
Tullianum 12, 203
Tullius Hostilius 11
Tullius, King Servius 11–12, 146, 206, 210
Twelve Tablets 203

Ulpius Amerimnus, Marcus 91, 101
Ummidia Quadratilla 64
univarae 81–2, 97–8

Val d'Aosta 18
Valeria Messala 46, 98
Valeriuis Maximus 25
Varinius, Publius 217–19
Varro 98, 214

Vatia, Lanista Gnaeus Cornelius Lentulus 214
Vatican Museum 129
Veres, Emperor Lucius 266
Verginia 14
Verginius 14
Verres, Gaius 222–3, 279
Vestal Virgins 19, 43–4, 65, 69, 98, 110–22, 123–7, 139, 140–1, 181, 202, 221, 267, 274
Via Latina 27
Vibia Chresta 244
Victoria (Medica) 69
Vulcanal 8

water supply 257
weaving 14, 58, 62, 158, 234, 245
wedding customs 13, 77–82, 115
wet-nurses 93, 159
widows 11, 34, 43, 75, 77, 82, 97–8, 100, 169, 242, 247, 267, 268, 278–9
wills 41, 43, 114–15, 118, 170, 234, 242, 257, 268, 276, 279, 280
work 157–64

York, England (Eboracum) 194, 195–7